Globalization

Globalization
A Basic Text

George Ritzer

This balanced introduction draws on academic and popular sources to examine the major issues and events in the history of globalization.

Globalization: A Basic Text is a substantial introductory textbook, designed to work either on its own or alongside *Readings in Globalization*. The books are cross-referenced and are both structured around the core concepts of globalization.

2009 • 608 pages • 978-1-4051-3271-8 • paperback
www.wiley.com/go/globalization

Readings in Globalization
Key Readings and Major Debates

Edited by George Ritzer and Zeynep Atalay

This unique and engaging anthology introduces students to the major concepts of globalization within the context of the key debates and disputes.

Readings in Globalization illustrates that major debates in the field are not only useful to examine for their own merit but can extend our knowledge of globalization. The volume explores both the *political economy* of globalization and the relationship of *culture* to globalization.

The volume is designed so it may be used independently, or alongside George Ritzer's *Globalization: A Basic Text* for a complete student resource.

2010 • 560 pages • 978-1-4051-3273-2 • paperback

Order together and save! Quote
ISBN 978-1-4443-2371-9

GLOBALIZATION : THE ESSENTIALS

GEORGE RITZER

A John Wiley & Sons, Ltd., Publication

This edition first published 2011
© 2011 John Wiley & Sons Ltd

Edition history: portions of this text appeared in *Globalization: A Basic Text*
(Wiley-Blackwell, 2010)

Wiley-Blackwell is an imprint of John Wiley & Sons, formed by the merger of Wiley's global
Scientific, Technical and Medical business with Blackwell Publishing.

Registered Office
John Wiley & Sons Ltd, The Atrium, Southern Gate, Chichester, West Sussex, PO19 8SQ,
United Kingdom

Editorial Offices
350 Main Street, Malden, MA 02148-5020, USA
9600 Garsington Road, Oxford, OX4 2DQ, UK
The Atrium, Southern Gate, Chichester, West Sussex, PO19 8SQ, UK

For details of our global editorial offices, for customer services, and for information about how
to apply for permission to reuse the copyright material in this book please see our website at
www.wiley.com/wiley-blackwell.

The right of George Ritzer to be identified as the author of this work has been asserted in
accordance with the UK Copyright, Designs and Patents Act 1988.

Library of Congress Cataloging-in-Publication Data
Ritzer, George.
    Globalization : the essentials / George Ritzer.
       p. cm.
    Includes bibliographical references and index.
    ISBN 978-0-470-65560-3 (hardcover : alk. paper) – ISBN 978-0-470-65561-0
(pbk. : alk. paper)   1. Globalization.   I. Title.
    JZ1318.R5835 2011
    303.48'2–dc22
                                                                    2010042203

A catalogue record for this book is available from the British Library.

This book is published in the following electronic formats: ePDFs 978-1-4443-9356-9;
ePub 978-1-4443-9357-6

Set in 10.5/13pt Minion by Toppan Best-set Premedia Limited
Printed in Singapore by Ho Printing Singapore Pte Ltd

1   2011

CONTENTS

6 High-Tech Global Flows and Structures 133
Technology, Media, and the Internet

7 Global Culture and Cultural Flows 153

PREFACE

Globalization: The Essentials is an abbreviated version of *Globalization: A Basic Text* (2010). While the latter is designed as a full-scale textbook for a course on globalization, this volume is considerably shorter. It can still be used as a text in such a course, but its comparative brevity enables the instructor to assign other books, as well. In addition, it can be used as a supplementary book in a variety of other courses in sociology and the social sciences. As the title suggests, this volume retains the essential elements of the original text. Four chapters, the Appendix and various other portions of the text have been deleted from *Globalization: A Basic Text* to create this volume. That material is, of course, important, but hard decisions had to be made about what to cut and not to cut. It is my belief that this shorter text continues to deliver what is most important to a fundamental understanding of this most important process of our day and in the foreseeable future.

Globalization

Conceptualization, Origins, and History

Globalization: The Essentials, by George Ritzer
© 2011 John Wiley & Sons Ltd

Globalization is increasingly omnipresent. We are living in *a* – or even *the* – "global age" (Albrow 1996). Globalization is clearly a very important change; it can even be argued (Bauman 2003) that it is *the most important change in human history*. This is reflected in many domains, but particularly in social relationships and social structures, especially those that are widely dispersed geographically. "In the era of globalization … shared humanity face[s] *the most fateful of the many fateful steps*" it has made in its long history (Bauman 2003: 156, italics added).

The following is the definition of globalization to be used in this book (note that all of the italicized terms will be discussed in this chapter and will inform the remainder of this book):

Globalization: Transplanetary process(es) involving increasing liquidity and growing multi-directional flows as well as the structures they encounter and create.

globalization is a transplanetary process or set of processes involving increasing *liquidity* and the growing multi-directional *flows* of people, objects, places and information as well as the *structures* they encounter and create that are *barriers* to, or *expedite*, those flows …

In contrast to many other definitions of globalization, this one does *not* assume that greater integration is an inevitable component of globalization. That is, globalization can bring with it greater integration (especially when things flow easily), but it can also serve to reduce the level of integration (when structures are erected that successfully block flows).

Transnationalism: Processes that interconnect individuals and social groups across specific geo-political borders.

Transnationality: Rise of new communities and formation of new social identities and relations that cannot be defined as nation-states.

A term that is closely related to globalization is **transnationalism** (Morawska 2007), or "processes that interconnect individuals and social groups across specific geo-political borders" (Giulianotti and Robertson 2007: 62). A related concept is **transnationality**, or "the rise of new communities and formation of new social identities and relations that cannot be defined through the traditional reference point of nation-states" (Robinson 2007: 1199–201).

Globalization and transnationalism are often used interchangeably, but transnationalism is clearly a more delimited process than globalization. Transnationalism is limited to interconnections that cross geo-political borders, especially those associated with two, or more, nation-states. An example is Mexican immigrants in the US sending remittances home to family members in Mexico. Globalization includes such connections, but is not restricted to them and encompasses a far wider range of transplanetary processes (e.g. direct relationships between people in many places in the world networking via the Internet). Further, geo-political borders are only one of the barriers encountered, and often overcome, by globalization. Some phenomena, labor unions for example, are better thought of as transnational than as global. That is, the relationship between labor unions in, for example, the US and Sweden is more important than are moves toward a global labor movement.

Transnationalism is most often used in thinking about, and research on, immigrants who move from one country to another, but who continue to be involved in various ways with the country from which they came (Portes 2001).

The case of baseball is useful in clarifying the distinction between globalization and transnationalism (Kelly 2007: 79–93). Baseball is a transnational sport because many of its fundamentals – techniques, strategies, etc. – and players have circulated across the borders of a small number of nations, especially Japan, Taiwan, Cuba, the Dominican Republic and, of course, the US. However, it is *not* global because it has not flowed on a transplanetary basis to a large portion of the world.

In contrast, soccer would be much more clearly a global sport because it exists in virtually every area of the world. For example, over 200 of the world's nations are members of a global organization, the Fédération Internationale de Football Association (FIFA). Another example of globalization in the realm of sports is the summer (and winter) Olympics, sponsored by the International Olympic Committee (IOC), in which about the same number of nations participate.

CONCEPTUALIZING GLOBALIZATION

In spite of the focus in this book on globalization, there are many scholars who do not accept the idea. Nevertheless, this book embraces, and operates from, a "globalist" perspective (Hirst and Thompson 1999) – globalization *is* a reality. Debates about globalization are one of the reasons that there is undoubtedly no topic today more difficult to get one's head around, let alone to master, than globalization. However, of far greater importance is the sheer magnitude, diversity, and complexity of the process of globalization which involves almost everyone, everything, and every place, in innumerable ways. (The concept of **globality** refers to the condition [in this case omnipresence] resulting from the process of globalization [Scholte 2004: 102–10].)

Before proceeding to the next section, a note is needed on the use of **metaphors** (Brown 1989), which will occupy a prominent place in the ensuing discussion. A metaphor involves the use of one term to help us better understand another term. Thus, in the next section, we will use the metaphor of a "solid" to describe epochs before the era of globalization. Similarly, the global world will be described as being "liquid." The use of such metaphors is designed to give the reader a better and a more vivid sense of the global age and how it differs from prior epochs.

> **Globality**: Omnipresence of the process of globalization.

> **Metaphors**: Use of one term to help us better understand another.

From "Solids" to "Liquids"

Prior to the current epoch of globalization (as we will see in the second part of this chapter, most observers believe that there *was* a previous epoch, if not many previous epochs, of globalization), it could be argued that one of the things that characterized people, things, information, places, and much else was their greater **solidity**. That is, all of them tended to be hard or to harden (metaphorically, figuratively, not literally, of course) over time and therefore, among other things, to remain largely in place. As a result, people either did not go anywhere or they did not venture very far from where they were born and raised; their social relationships were restricted to those who were nearby. Much the same could be said of most objects (tools, food, and so on), which tended to be used where they were produced. The solidity of most material manifestations of information – stone tablets, newspapers, magazines, books, and so on – also made them at least somewhat difficult to move very far. Furthermore, since people didn't move very far, neither did information. Places were not only quite solid and immoveable, but they tended to confront solid natural (mountains, rivers, oceans) and humanly constructed (walls, gates) barriers that made it difficult for people and things to exit or to enter.

> **Solidity**: People, things, information, and places "harden" over time and therefore have limited mobility.

Above all, solidity describes a world in which barriers exist and are erected to prevent the free movement of all sorts of things. It was the nation-state that was most likely to create these "solid" barriers (for example, walls [e.g. the Great Wall of China; the wall between Israel and the West Bank], border gates and guards), and the state itself grew increasingly solid as it resisted change. For much of the twentieth century this was epitomized by the Soviet Union and its satellite states which sought to erect any number of barriers in order to keep all sorts of things out *and* in (especially a disaffected population). With the passage of time, the Soviet Union grew increasingly sclerotic. The best example of this solidity was the erection (beginning in 1961), and maintenance, of the Berlin Wall in order to keep East Berliners in and Western influences out. There was a more fluid relationship between East and West Berlin prior to the erection of the Wall, but that fluidity was seen in the East as being disadvantageous, even dangerous. Once the Wall was erected, relations between West and East Berlin were virtually frozen in place – they solidified – and there was comparatively little movement of anything between them.

The Wall, together with East Germany and the Soviet Union, is long gone and with it many of the most extreme forms of solidity brought into existence by the Cold War. Nonetheless, solid structures remain – e.g. the nation-state and its border and customs controls – and there are ever-present calls for the creation of new, and new types of, solid structures. Thus, in many parts of Europe there are demands for more barriers to legal and illegal immigration. This has reached an extreme in the US with concern over illegal Mexican (and other Latin American) immigration leading to the erection of an enormous fence between the two countries. Thus, solidity is far from dead in the contemporary world. It is very often the case that demands for new forms of solidity are the result of increased fluidity. However, a strong case can, and will, be made that it is fluidity that is more characteristic of today's world, especially in terms of globalization.

Of course, people were *never* so solid that they were totally immobile or stuck completely in a given place (a few people were able to escape East Berlin in spite of the Wall and many will be able to enter the US illegally even when the fence on the Mexican border is completed), and this was especially true of the elite members of any society. Elites were (and are) better able to move about and that ability increased with advances in transportation technology. Commodities, especially those created for elites, also could almost always be moved and they, too, grew more moveable as technologies advanced. Information (because it was not solid, although it could be solidified in the form of, for example, a book) could always travel more easily than goods or people (it could be spread by word of mouth over great distances even if the originator of the information could not move very far; it moved even faster as more advanced communication technologies emerged [telegraph, telephone, the Internet]). And as other technologies developed (ships, automobiles, airplanes), people, especially those with the resources, were better able to leave places and get to others. They could even literally move places (or at least parts of them), as, for example, when in the early 1800s Lord Elgin dismantled parts of the Parthenon in Greece and transported them to London, where to this day they can be found in the British Museum.

However, at an increasing rate over the last few centuries, and especially in the last several decades, that which once seemed so solid has tended to "melt" and become increasingly *liquid*. Instead of thinking of people, objects, information, and places as being like solid blocks of ice, they need to be seen as tending, in recent years, to melt and as becoming increasingly liquid. It is, needless to say, far more difficult to move blocks of ice than the water that is produced when those blocks melt. Of course, to extend the metaphor, there continue to exist blocks of ice, even glaciers (although even these are now literally melting), in the contemporary world that have not melted, at least not completely. Solid material realities (people, cargo, newspapers) continue to exist, but because of a wide range of technological developments (in transportation, communication, the Internet, and so on) they can move across the globe far more readily. Everywhere we turn, more things, including ourselves, are becoming increasingly liquefied.

Karl Marx opened the door to this kind of analysis (and to the use of such metaphors) when he famously argued that because of the nature of capitalism as an economic system "everything solid melts into air." That is, many of the solid, material realities that preceded capitalism (e.g. the structures of feudalism) were "melted" by it and were transformed into liquids. However, while Marx was describing a largely destructive process, the point here is that the new liquids that are being created are inherent parts of the new world and are radically transforming it. In the process, they are having *both* constructive and destructive effects (Schumpeter 1976).

Marx's insight of over a century-and-a-half ago was not only highly prescient, but is far truer today than in Marx's day. In fact, it is far truer than he could ever have imagined. Furthermore, that melting, much like one of the great problems in the global world today – the melting of the ice on and near the North and South poles as a result of global warming (see Chapter 9) – is not only likely to continue in the coming years, but to increase at an exponential rate. Indeed, the melting of the polar icecaps can be seen as another metaphor for the increasing fluidity associated with globalization, especially its problematic aspects. And, make no mistake, the increasing fluidity associated with globalization presents *both* great opportunities *and* great dangers.

Thus, the perspective on globalization presented here, following the work of Zygmunt Bauman (2000, 2003, 2005, 2006), is that it involves, above all else, increasing **liquidity** (Lakoff 2008: 277–300). Several of Bauman's ideas on liquidity are highly relevant to the perspective on globalization employed here.

Liquidity: Increasing ease of movement of people, things, information, and places in the global age.

For example, liquid phenomena do not easily, or for long, hold their shape. Thus, the myriad liquid phenomena associated with globalization are hard-pressed to maintain any particular form and, even if they acquire a form, it is likely to change quite quickly.

Liquid phenomena fix neither space nor time. That which is liquid is, by definition, opposed to any kind of fixity, be it spatial or temporal. This means that the spatial and temporal aspects of globalization are in continuous flux. That which is liquid is forever ready to change whatever shape (space) it might take on momentarily. Time (however short) in a liquid world is more important than space. Perhaps the best example of this is global finance, where little or nothing (dollars, gold) actually changes its place (at least immediately), but time is of the essence in that the symbolic representations of money move instantaneously and great profits can be made or lost in split-second decisions on financial transactions.

Liquid phenomena not only move easily, but once they are on the move they are difficult to stop. This is exemplified in many areas, such as foreign trade, investment, and global financial transactions (Polillo and Guillen 2005: 1764–802), the globality of transactions and interactions (e.g. on Facebook, Twitter [Clive Thompson 2008: 42ff.]) on the Internet, and the difficulty in halting the global flow of drugs, pornography, the activities of organized crime, and illegal immigrants.

Finally, and perhaps most importantly, that which is liquid tends to melt whatever stands it its path (especially solids). This is clearest in the case of the much discussed death, or at least decline, of the nation-state and its borders in the era of increasing global flows (see Chapter 5). According to Cartier (2001: 269), the "forces of globalization have rendered many political boundaries more porous to flows of people, money, and things."

It is clear that if one wanted to use a single term to think about globalization today, liquidity (as well as the closely related idea of flows) would be at or near the top of the list. That is not to say that there are no solid structures in the world – after all, we still live in a modern world, even if it is late modernity, and modernity has long been associated with solidity. And it does not mean that there is not a constant interplay between liquidity and solidity, with increases in that which is liquid (e.g. terrorist attacks launched against Israel from the West Bank during the

Intifada) leading to counter-reactions involving the erection of new solid forms (e.g. that fence between Israel and the West Bank), but at the moment and for the foreseeable future, the momentum lies with increasing and proliferating global liquidity.

"Flows"

Closely related to the idea of liquidity, and integral to it, is another key concept in thinking about globalization, the idea of **flows** (Appadurai 1996; Rey and Ritzer 2010); after all liquids flow easily, far more easily than solids. In fact, it is the concept of flows that is widely used in the literature on globalization and it is the concept that will inform a good deal of the body of this book.

> **Flows:** Movement of people, things, information, and places due, in part, to the increasing porosity of global barriers.

Because so much of the world has "melted," or is in the process of "melting," and has become liquefied, globalization is increasingly characterized by great *flows* of increasingly liquid phenomena of all types, including people, objects, information, decisions, places, and so on. For example, foods of all sorts increasingly flow around the world, including sushi globalized from its roots in Japan (Bestor 2005: 13–20), Chilean produce now ubiquitous in the US market (and elsewhere) (Goldfrank 2005: 42–53), Indian food in San Francisco (and throughout much of the world) (Mankekar 2005: 197–214), and so on. In many cases, the flows have become raging floods that are increasingly less likely to be impeded by, among others, place-based barriers of any kind, including the oceans, mountains, and especially the borders of nation-states. This was demonstrated once again in late 2008 in the spread of the American credit and financial crisis to Europe (and elsewhere): "In a global financial system, national borders are porous" (Landler 2008: C1).

Looking at a very different kind of flow, many people in many parts of the world believe that they are being swamped by migrants, especially poor illegal migrants (Moses 2006). Whether or not these are actually floods, they have come to be seen in that way by many people, often aided by politicians and media personalities in many countries who have established their reputations by portraying them in that way.

Undoubtedly because of their immateriality, ideas, images, and information, both legal (blogs) and illegal (e.g. child pornography), flow (virtually) everywhere through interpersonal contact and the media, especially now via the Internet.

Decisions of all sorts flow around the world, as well as over time: "The effect of the [economic] decisions flowed, and would continue to flow, through every possible conduit. Some decisions would be reflected in products rolling off assembly lines, others in prices of securities, and still others in personal interactions. Each decision would cascade around the world and then forward through time" (Altman 2007: 255).

Even places can be said to be flowing around the world as, for example, immigrants re-create the places from which they came in new locales (e.g. Indian and

Pakistani enclaves in London). Furthermore, places (e.g. airports, shopping malls) themselves have become increasingly like flows (for more on this and the transition from "spaces of places" to "spaces of flows" see Castells 1996).

Even with all of this increasing fluidity, much of what would have been considered the height of global liquidity only a few decades, or even years, ago now seems increasingly sludge-like. This is especially the case when we focus on the impact of the computer and the Internet on the global flow of all sorts of things. Thus, not long ago we might have been amazed by our ability to order a book from Amazon. com and receive it via an express package delivery system in as little as a day. That method, however, now seems to operate at a snail's pace compared to the ability to download that book in minutes on Amazon's Kindle system (a wireless reading device to which books and other reading matter can be downloaded).

"Heavy" and "Light"

There is another set of conceptual distinctions, or metaphors, that are useful in thinking about globalization. In addition to the change from solids to liquids, we can also think in terms of change that involves movement from that which is *heavy* to that which is *light* (this is another distinction traceable to the work of Zygmunt Bauman).

The original Gutenberg bible (in mid-fifteenth-century Germany) was usually published in two volumes, ran to close to 1,400 pages, and was printed on very heavy paper or vellum. It was in every sense of the term a heavy tome (almost like the one you are now reading), difficult, because of its sheer weight and bulk, to transport. Fast forward to 2006 and a much lighter bound copy of the bible could easily be purchased from Amazon.com and transported in days via express mail virtually anywhere in the world. By 2007 that bible had become weightless since it could be downloaded using the Kindle system.

More generally, it could be argued that both pre-industrial and industrial societies were quite "heavy," that is, characterized by that which is difficult to move. This applies to those who labored in them (e.g. peasants, farmers, factory workers), where they labored (plots of land, farms, factories), and what they produced (crops, machines, books, automobiles). Because of their heaviness, workers tended to stay put, and what they produced (and what was not consumed locally) could be moved, especially great distances, only with great effort and at great expense. Later advances, especially in technology, made goods, people, and places "lighter," easier to move. These included advances in both transportation and technology that made all sorts of industrial products smaller, lighter, and easier to transport (compare the netbook computer of today to the room-size computer of the mid-twentieth century).

Karin Knorr Cetina (2005: 215) has written about what she calls "complex global microstructures," or "structures of connectivity and integration that are global in scope but microsociological in character." She has described financial markets (Knorr Cetina and Bruegger 2002: 905–50) in these terms and, more recently, global terrorist organizations such as al-Qaeda. We will have more to say about these global microstructures (see Chapter 10), but the key point here is that while Knorr Cetina sees these global microstructures as having several characteristics, of primary importance is their "lightness" in comparison to "heavy" bureaucratic systems. Thus, unlike the armed forces of the United States, al-Qaeda is not a heavy bureaucratic structure, but rather a light "global microstructure." It is al-Qaeda's (as well as the Taliban's in Afghanistan) lightness that gives it many advantages over the extremely cumbersome US military, and the huge bureaucracy of which it is part, and this helps account, at least so far, for the latter's inability to suppress al-Qaeda or to catch Osama bin Laden.

It could be argued that we moved from the heavy to the light era in the past century or two. However, by about 1980, we can be said to have moved beyond both of those epochs. We are now in an era that is increasingly defined not just by lightness, but by something approaching weightlessness. That which is weightless, or nearly so, clearly moves far more easily (even globally) than that which is either heavy or light. The big changes here involved the arrival and expansion of cable and satellite television, satellite radio, cell phones, PDAs, and, most importantly, the personal computer and the advent of the Internet (and networking sites such as Twitter). It is with the personal computer and the Internet that globalization reaches new heights in terms of the flow of things and of social relationships, in large part because they, and everything else, have approached weightlessness.

An excellent example of this can be found in the world of music. Vinyl records were quite heavy and the shift to cassettes and later CDs did not make music much lighter. However, the creation of advanced technologies such as iPods and cell phones allows us to carry around thousands of once very heavy albums in our pockets. We can carry that music with us anywhere in the world and we can exchange music over the Internet with people around the globe.

Of course, there are still many heavy things in our increasingly weightless world. Factories, offices, buildings, large and cumbersome machines (including MRI machines), newspapers, hardback books, and even some people (made "heavy" by, for example, minority status, poverty, a lack of education) continue to exist. All, of course, are nevertheless being globalized to some degree in one way or another, but their weightiness makes that process more cumbersome and difficult for them. For example, the global parcel delivery systems (e.g. FedEx) have become very efficient, but they still need to transport a physical product over great distances. Clearly, that process is still quite weighty, in comparison to, say, the downloading of weightless movies from Netflix (a website that began by allowing members to receive heavier DVDs via snail-mail). In fact, of course, it is increasingly the case that that which is weightless (e.g. iTunes and downloadable music in general, downloadable movies, blogs) is destroying that which is comparatively heavy (e.g. the CD, the DVD, newspapers).

The ideas of increasing liquidity and weightlessness being employed here do not require that the world be "flat" or be considered as such (Friedman 2005). Fluids can seep through all sorts of tall and wide structures and, in the case of a flood, those structures can even be washed away (as was the Berlin Wall, for example, and more metaphorically, the Iron Curtain), at least temporarily. Further, that which is weightless can waft over and between the tallest and widest structures. Thus, the world today is increasingly characterized by liquidity and weightlessness, but it is *not* necessarily any flatter than it ever was. Those tall, wide structures continue to be important, especially in impeding (or attempting to impede) the movement of that which is solid and heavy. It is less clear how successful these structures will be in impeding that which is liquid, light, or weightless.

The most obvious of such structures are the borders (Crack 2007: 341–54; Rumford 2007: 327–39) between nation-states and the fact that in recent years we have witnessed the strengthening (heightening, lengthening, etc.) of many of those borders. Similarly, the Chinese government has sought to restrict the access of its citizens to at least some aspects of the Internet that the government feels are dangerous to its continued rule. The electronic barrier that the government has constructed is known as the "Great Firewall" (French 2008: A1, A6). (A firewall is a barrier on the Internet; the idea of the "Great Firewall" plays off China's Great Wall.)

The huge "digital divide" in the world today (Drori and Jang 2003: 144–61), especially between North and South, is another example of a barrier. The relative absence in the South of computers and the supporting infrastructure (telephone and broadband connections) needed for a computerized world creates an enormous barrier between the North and the South. In terms of computerization, the world may be increasingly flat (although certainly not totally flat) among and between the countries in the North, but it has many hills in the South and huge and seemingly insurmountable mountain ranges continue to separate the North from the South.

The history of the social world and social thought and research leads us to the conclusion that people, as well as their representatives in the areas in which they live, have always sought to erect structural barriers to protect and advance themselves, and to adversely affect others, and it seems highly likely that they will continue to do so. Thus, we may live in a more liquefied, more weightless, world, but we do *not* live in a flat world and are not likely to live in one any time soon, if ever. Even a successful capitalist, George Soros, acknowledges this, using yet another metaphor, in his analysis of **economic globalization** when he argues: "The global capitalist system has produced a very *uneven* playing field" (Soros 2000: xix, italics added).

Economic globalization: Growing economic linkages at the global level.

"Heavy" Structures that Expedite "Flows"

The liquefaction of the social world, as well as its increasing weightlessness, is only part of the story of globalization. As pointed out already, another major part is the fact that many heavy, material, objective structures continue to exist and to be created in the globalized world. Some are holdovers from the pre-global world, but others are actually produced, intentionally or unintentionally, by global forces. In studying globalization we must look at *both* all of that which flows (or "wafts") with increasing ease, as well as all of the structures that impede or block those flows (see below for more on these) as well as serve to expedite and channel those flows. To put it another way, we must look at *both* that which is light and weightless *and* that which is solid and heavy and that greatly affects their flow in both a positive and a negative sense (Inda and Rosaldo 2008: 29).

For example, there are various "routes" or "paths" that can be seen as structures that serve both to expedite flows along their length, as well as to limit flows that occur outside their confines.

• Intercontinental airlines generally fly a limited number of well-defined routes (say between New Delhi and London) rather than flying whatever route the pilots wish and thereby greatly increasing the possibility of mid-air collisions.
• Illegal immigrants from Mexico have, at least until recently, generally followed a relatively small number of well-worn paths into the US. Indeed, they often need to pay smugglers large sums of money and the smugglers generally follow the routes that have worked for them (and others) in the past.
• Goods of all sorts are generally involved in rather well-defined "supply chains" (see Chapter 4 for a discussion of this concept) as they are exported from some countries and imported into others.
• Illegal products – e.g. counterfeit drugs – follow oft-trod paths en route from their point of manufacture (often China), through loosely controlled free-trade zones (e.g. in Dubai), through several intermediate countries, to their ultimate destination, often the US, where they are frequently obtained over the Internet (Bogdanich 2007: A1, A6).

Then there are an increasing number of formal and informal "bridges" (Anner and Evans 2004: 34–47) created throughout the globe that expedite the flow of all sorts of things. This idea applies perhaps best to the passage of people across borders legally through the process of migration (Sassen 2007: 788–95). It is clear that in the not-too-distant past there were many structural barriers to the flow of people. There are even a few places in the world today where this remains true – e.g. between the US and Cuba. However, with the end of the Cold War, there are now many bridges for people (and products) to cross openly not only between the countries of the old East and West, but also among and between virtually every country and region of the world. However, illegal migrants are likely to need to be more covert in their movements. All sorts of illegal products are also less likely to move openly across such "bridges" where they would be highly visible to the authorities. Thus, there are also more hidden structures that permit movement of illegal people and products.

It is also the case that an increasing number of people, perhaps nearly everyone, are involved in, and affected by, global relations and flows and personally partici-pate in global networks (Singh Grewal 2008) of one kind or another (networks of communication and information technology, interpersonal networks involving individuals and groups). While global networks span the globe (e.g. cables under the oceans that permit transoceanic communication [Yuan 2006: A1]), or at least much of it, there are other types of networks including transnational (those that pass through the boundaries of nation-states [Portes 2001: 181–93]), international (those that involve two or more nation-states), national (those that are bounded by the nation-state), and local (those that exist at the sub-national level) (Mann 2007: 472–96). Networks can expedite the flow of innumerable things, but they are perhaps best-suited to the flow of information (Connell and Crawford 2005: 5–26). People involved in networks can communicate all sorts of information to one another in various ways – telephone calls, snail-mail, e-mail, blogs, social networking websites, and so on. These networks have revolutionized and greatly expanded the global flow of information. As with all other structures, such networks can be blocked in various ways (e.g. the "Great Firewall").

All sorts of networks have been made possible by the Internet. The Internet can be seen as being of enormous importance in allowing information of various sorts to flow in innumerable directions. One important example involves the formation of the networks that became and constitute the alter-globalization movement (see Chapter 12). This movement (as well as its various political actions, most notably the anti-WTO [World Trade Organization] protests in Seattle in 1999 [Smith 2001: 1–20]), like much else in the world today (e.g. Barack Obama's successful 2008 presidential campaign), was made possible by the Internet (Juris 2008: 353–4).

Finally, it is not only individuals who are increasingly involved in networks. An increasing number of social structures (e.g. states, cities, law) and social institutions (the family, religion, sport) are interconnected on a global basis and these, too, enable and enhance global flows. For example, the international banking system has an infrastructure that facilitates the global movement of funds among a network of banks. Included in that infrastructure are IBANs (International Bank Account Numbers), rules, norms, and procedures on how such money transfers are to occur, and a highly sophisticated technical language that allows those in the business to communicate with one another wherever they are in the world. Another example involves global (Sassen 1991) and world cities (Marcuse and van Kempen 2000) that are increasingly interconnected with one another directly rather than through the nation-states in which they happen to exist (see Chapter 11). The financial markets of the global cities of New York, London, and Tokyo are tightly linked, with the result that all sorts of financial products flow among them and at lightning speed. More generally, in this context, we can talk in terms of the "global economy's connectedness" (Altman 2007: 255).

"Heavy" Structures as Barriers to "Flows"

While there is no question that the world is increasingly characterized by greater liquidity and increased flows, as well as various structures that expedite those flows, we also need to recognize that there are limits and barriers to those flows. The world is not just in process, there are also many material structures (trade agreements, regulatory agencies, borders, customs barriers, standards, and so on) in existence. As Inda and Rosaldo (2008: 31) argue: "Material infrastructures do not only promote mobility. … They also hinder and block it." Any thoroughgoing account of globalization needs to look at *both* flows and structures and, in terms of the latter, the ways in which they *both* produce and enhance flows as well as alter and even block them. In other words, there is interplay between flows and structures, especially between flows and the structures that are created in an attempt to inhibit or stop them. As Shamir (2005: 197–217) puts it, globalization is an epoch of increased openness *and* "simultaneously an era of growing restrictions on movement." Borders, of course, are major points at which movement is blocked. There are many examples of this including the toughening of border controls in France (and elsewhere in Europe) because of growing hostility to refugees (Fassin 2008: 212–34).

There are challenges to the idea that all there is to globalization is flows and fluidity (Tsing 2000: 327–60). In examining global flows (some of which have been anticipated above), we also need to consider those agents who "carve" the channels through which things flow, those who alter those channels over time, national and regional units that create and battle over flows, and coalitions of claimants for control over channels.

A focus on the above kinds of agents and structures, rather than flows, promises a more critical orientation to globalization in terms of the structures themselves, as well as in terms of who creates the structures through which things flow and who does and does not control and profit from them.

The idea of flows is criticized for other reasons, as well. For example, there is a kind of timelessness to the idea of flows and, as a result, it implies that they are likely to continue well into the future and there is little or nothing that can be done to stop them. This implies that everyone – scientists and businesspeople who profit from flows, as well as those at the margins of those flows and perhaps even those hurt by them – is swept up in the same processes. The focus on flows tends to communicate a kind of enthusiasm for them and the erroneous idea that virtually everyone benefits from flows of all types.

Also important in this context is what has been called "awkward connections" (Inda and Rosaldo 2008: 31). While the idea of global flows and fluids communicates a sense of total and uniform connectedness, we know that this is simply not the case and that in many places in the world, especially those that are less developed, there are awkward connections (e.g. being restricted to slow and unreliable dial up connections to the Internet), as well as no connections at all (no Internet service of any kind).

A similar idea is "frictions," or the "awkward, unequal, unstable … interconnection across difference" (Lowenhaupt Tsing 2005: 4). The key point is that the global flows that create interconnections do *not* move about smoothly; they do not move about without creating friction. Friction gets in the way of the smooth operation of global flows. However, friction not only slows flows down, it can also serve to keep them moving and even speed them up. Highways can have this double-edged quality by both limiting where people and vehicles can go while at the same time making movement "easier and more efficient" (Lowenhaupt Tsing 2005: 6). More generally, "global connections [are] made, and muddied, in friction" (Lowenhaupt Tsing 2005: 272). The key point in this context is that flows themselves produce friction that can slow or even stop global flows: "without even trying friction gets in the way of the smooth operation of global power. Difference can disrupt, causing everyday malfunctions as well as unexpected cataclysms. Friction refuses the lie that global power operates as a well-oiled machine. Furthermore, difference sometimes inspires insurrection. Friction can be the fly in the elephant's nose" (Lowenhaupt Tsing 2005: 6). A prime example of this today is the many frictions being produced in many parts of the world by large numbers of legal and illegal immigrants (e.g. the millions of migrants from Zimbabwe who have fled to South Africa eliciting violent reactions from South Africans who feel threatened by, and resent, them) (*Economist* 2008: May 22).

As has already been mentioned, the most important and most obvious barriers to global flows are those constructed by nation-states. There are borders, gates, guards, passport controls, customs agents, health inspectors, and so on, in most countries in the world. (The great exception is the countries that are part of the European Union [EU] where barriers to movement among and between member countries have been greatly reduced, if not eliminated. The EU is a kind of structure that allows people and products to move much more freely and much more quickly. At the same time, it serves to reduce the need to use hidden channels since there is far less need to conceal what is moving among and between EU countries.) Although many people (illegal immigrants) and things (contraband goods) do get through those barriers, some of them are successfully blocked or impeded by them. However, it is far more difficult to erect barriers against many newer phenomena, especially the non-material phenomena associated with cell phones and the Internet.

Specific examples of barriers created by the nation-state involve blocking economic transactions that it regards as not in the national interest. For example, in 2006 the US government blocked a deal in which a Dubai company was to purchase an American company involved in the business of running America's ports (*Economist* 2006: March 10). The government felt that such ownership would be a threat to national security since foreign nationals, perhaps enemies, could acquire information that would allow terrorists easy entrée to the ports. In another example, in early 2008 the US government blocked an effort by a Chinese company to purchase (in conjunction with an American private equity firm) an American company (3Com) that, among other things, manufactured software that prevented hacking into military computers (Weisman 2008: C1–C4).

However, many of the barriers created by nation-states that we assume are, or can be, successful do not in fact deal with the flows they are supposed to stem. It remains to be seen whether the new fence between Mexico and the US can reduce the flow of illegal immigrants to the US. Similarly, it is not clear that the wall between Israel and the West Bank will stop the flow of terrorists into Israel if (when?) hostilities in the Middle East flare up yet again.

There are many different kinds of organizations that, while they may expedite flows for some, create all sorts of barriers for others. Nation-states are, in fact, one such organization and they (generally) work to the advantage of their own citizens (and their flows as well as the flows of things important to them) in many different ways while creating many roadblocks for those from other countries. For example, nation-states create protectionist (Reuveny and Thompson 2001: 229–49) tariff systems that help their own farms, corporations, and so on to succeed by making the products of their foreign competitors more expensive. That is, the tariffs help the flow of products from a nation-state's own farms and manufacturers while inhibiting the flow into the country from its foreign competition.

Corporate organizations, say a multinational corporation like Toyota, are devoted to optimizing the flow of their automobiles to all possible markets throughout the world. They also seek to compete with and out-perform other multinational corporations in the automobile business. If they are successful, the flow of automobiles from those corporations is greatly reduced, further advantaging Toyota.

Labor unions are also organizations devoted to the flow of some things while working against the flow of others (Bronfenbrenner 2007). Unions often oppose, for example, the flow of illegal immigrants because they are likely to work for lower pay and fewer (if any) benefits (e.g. health insurance) than indigenous, unionized workers. Similarly, they oppose the flow of goods produced in non-union shops in other countries (and their own) since the success of the latter would adversely affect the shops that are unionized and that, in turn, would hurt the union and its members.

While organizations of many types, including nation-states, corporations, and labor unions, serve as structures that can operate against global flows, the fact is that there are signs that many organizations are changing and are themselves becoming more fluid and increasingly open.

One of the roots of this change is open-sourcing and the Internet. The best-known example of open-sourcing is Linux, a free computer-operating system. Anyone in the world with the needed skills can make changes in, and contributions to, it. (The best-known operating systems are produced by Microsoft [Windows and now Windows 7]. They cost a great deal and are closed in that only those who work for the company can, at least legally, work on and modify them.) In recent years a traditional closed organization – IBM – has not only embraced the Linux system, but opened up more and more of its own operations to outside inputs. The Internet has a number of open systems associated with what is known as Web 2.0 (Beer and Burrows 2007). One example is the free online encyclopedia Wikipedia (or wikis more generally) where again (virtually) anyone, anywhere in the world, can contribute to the definition of terms in it. The contrast here is the traditional (and costly) dictionary (e.g. *Merriam-Webster's Dictionary*) and encyclopedias written by selected experts (*Encyclopedia Britannica)* and closed to contributions from anyone else.

However, in spite of this new openness, most organizations and systems remain closed to various flows. This usually benefits (often economically) those in the system and disadvantages those outside the organization. Even with the new open systems, there are structural realities that help some and hinder others. For example, to contribute to Linux or Wikipedia one must have a computer, computer expertise, and access to the Internet (especially high-speed access). Clearly, those without economic advantages – in the lower classes in developed countries or who live in the less developed countries of the South (i.e. those on the other side of the "digital divide") – do not have any, many, or all, of those things. As a result, they are unable to contribute to them or to gain from them to the same degree as those in more privileged positions or areas.

Subtler Structural Barriers

This brings us to a series of other structural barriers that also serve to contradict the idea of total global fluidity. These structures are less blatant, more subtle, than the kinds of structures discussed above, but in many ways more powerful and more important from a social point of view. Included here are a variety of structures that serve to differentiate and to subordinate on the basis of *social class*, *race*, *ethnicity*, *gender*, and *region of the world* (North–South). In fact, these phenomena tend to be interrelated. Thus in the disadvantaged South, one is more likely to find large numbers of poor people in the lower social classes, disadvantaged racial and ethnic minorities, and women who are discriminated against on the basis of gender (Moghadam 2007: 135–51). As a result, various efforts by the North to subordinate the South serve to further disadvantage people there in all of those categories. Furthermore, these categories overlap – a black female who is a member of the Ibo tribe in Africa is likely to be in a lower social class. (And there is a similar overlap among those who are advantaged – for example, white, upper-class, male Anglo-Saxons in Europe and North America.) Thus, the combination of these disadvantaged statuses ("intersectionality" [Hill Collins 2000]) has a disastrous effect on those with these disesteemed characteristics.

Those who occupy superordinate positions in these hierarchies tend to erect structures that halt or slow various flows. These restrictions are designed to work to their advantage and to the disadvantage of others. Good examples involve the operations of the International Monetary Fund (IMF), World Trade Organization (WTO), and World Bank, which, for example, can serve to restrict flows of badly needed funds into Southern nations unless, for example, those nations engage in restructuring and austerity programs that are designed to slow down their economies (at least in the short run). Such programs often involve insistence that welfare programs be cut back or eliminated and the result is that the most disadvantaged members of Southern countries – racial and ethnic minorities, women, those in the lower classes – are hurt the most by these programs.

Those in superordinate positions also encourage certain kinds of flows that work to their advantage (and to the disadvantage of subordinates). For example, the so-called "brain drain" (Landler 2007: A10) is a global phenomenon and it most often takes the form of highly trained people leaving the South and moving to the North. Those in the North actively seek out skilled people in the South and expedite their movement to the North. At the other end of the spectrum, also encouraged, although less these days, is the movement of unskilled workers to the North to occupy poorly paid menial positions – for example, as farm, or household, workers.

It is also the case that the prototypical Northern male upper-class white Anglo-Saxon Protestant has, in the contemporary world, acquired a great deal of fluidity and "lightness" in the form of mobility, and thus is able to move about the globe quite readily and easily. In contrast, the Southern female, lower-class, black, Ibo is far less fluid, much "heavier," and therefore has far less capacity to move about the globe.

While the advantages of those in the North over those in the South remain, the South has been increasingly successful, at least in some instances, at gaining advantages by better controlling flows into and out of that part of the world. For example, Middle Eastern oil used to be largely controlled by Northern corporations (e.g. Shell) which kept the price low and made sure that the more developed North was adequately supplied with comparatively inexpensive oil. This adversely affected oil-producing countries, which did not get the price they deserved and furthermore a large proportion of the profits went to the Northern corporations and *not* the Middle Eastern countries from which the oil came. Now, of course, those countries (through OPEC) control the flow of oil and are profiting enormously from it.

In the end, then, globalization involves *flows* and a wide range of structures that not only expedite, but also impede, and even halt, those flows.

Having given a sense in this introductory discussion of the way globalization today – the global age – is conceptualized in this book, we turn now to some background on its origins and history.

ORIGINS AND HISTORY OF GLOBALIZATION

Telling the story of the origins and history of globalization is no easy matter since there are a number of different perspectives on these issues. In this section we will offer five different ways of thinking about what turn out to be very complex issues.

Hardwired

Nayan Chanda (2007: xiv) argues that "globalization stems, among other things, from a basic human urge to seek a better and more fulfilling life" (2007: xiii). This leads him to trace "the initial globalization of the human species, [to] when in the late Ice Age, a tiny group of our ancestors walked out of Africa in search of better food and security. In fifty thousand years of wandering along ocean coasts and chasing game across Central Asia, they finally settled on all the continents."

Chanda focuses on four specific aspects of globalization that relate to a basic "urge" for a better life – trade (or commerce), missionary work (religion), adventures and conquest (politics and warfare). All of these are key aspects of globalization, all can be traced to early human history, and all, as well as much else, will be dealt with in this volume. However, Chanda's view that globalization is hardwired into humans is not the one accepted here since we argue that we are now living in a distinctive global age.

Cycles

The second perspective is that globalization is a long-term cyclical process. It is not only difficult in this view to find a single point of origin, but the effort is largely irrelevant since there have long been cycles of globalization and it is those cycles that are of utmost importance, not any particular phase or point of origin (Scholte 2005). This view, like Chanda's, tends to contradict the idea that we live today in a new "global age." Rather, this suggests that there have been *other* global ages in the past and that what now appears to be a new global age, or the high point of such an age, is destined to contract and disappear in the future. Eventually, it, too, will be replaced by a new cycle in the globalization process.

Epochs

In an example of the third approach to the beginnings (and history) of globalization, Therborn (2000: 151–79) sees six great epochs, or "waves," of globalization, that have occurred sequentially, each with its own point of origin:

1. The fourth to the seventh centuries which witnessed the globalization of religions (e.g. Christianity, Islam).
2. The late fifteenth century highlighted by European colonial conquests.
3. The late eighteenth and early nineteenth centuries during which various intra-European wars led to globalization.
4. The mid-nineteenth century to 1918; the heyday of European imperialism.
5. The post-World War II period.
6. The post-Cold War period.

From this, Therborn concludes that globalization today is *not* unique. However, his historical or epochal view also rejects the cyclical view of globalization. Past epochs are not returning, at least in their earlier form, at some point in the future.

Events

A fourth view is that instead of cycles or great epochs, one can point to much more specific events that can be seen as the origin of globalization and give us a good sense of its history. In fact, there are *many* such possible points of origin of globalization, some of which are:

- The Romans and their far-ranging conquests in the centuries before Christ (Gibbon 1998).
- The rise and spread of Christianity in the centuries after the fall of the Roman Empire.
- The spread of Islam in the seventh century and beyond.
- The travels of the Vikings from Europe to Iceland, Greenland, and briefly to North America in the ninth through the eleventh centuries as examples of, and landmarks in, globalization.
- Trade in the Middle Ages throughout the Mediterranean.
- The activities of the banks of the twelfth-century Italian city-states.
- The rampage of the armies of Ghengis Khan into Eastern Europe in the thirteenth century (*Economist* 2006: January 12).
- European traders like Marco Polo and his travels later in the thirteenth century along the Silk Road to China. (Interestingly, there is now discussion of the development of an "iron silk road" involving a linked railroad network through a variety of Asian countries that at least evokes the image of the lure of Marco Polo's Silk Road.)
- The "discovery of America" by Christopher Columbus in 1492. Other important voyages of discovery during this time involved Vasco Da Gama rounding the Cape of Good Hope in 1498 and the circumnavigation of the globe completed in 1522 by one of Ferdinand Magellan's ships (Rosenthal 2007: 1237–41).
- European colonialism, especially in the nineteenth century.
- The early twentieth-century global Spanish flu pandemic.
- The two World Wars in the first half of the twentieth century.

It is also possible to get even more specific about the origins of globalization, especially in recent years. A few rather eclectic recent examples include:

- 1956 – The first transatlantic telephone cable.
- 1958 – While it was possible to fly across the Atlantic in the 1930s on seaplanes that made several stops along the way, the big revolution in this area was the arrival of transatlantic passenger jet travel, with the first flight being Pan Am's flight from New York to London (with a stopover for refueling required in Newfoundland).
- 1962 – The launch of the satellite Telstar and soon thereafter the first transatlantic television broadcasts.
- 1966 – The transmission from a satellite of the picture of the earth as a single location, not only leading to a greater sense of the world as one place (increased global consciousness [Robertson and Inglis 2004: 38–49]), but also of great importance to the development of the global environmental movement.

- 1970 – The creation of the Clearing House Interbank Payment System (CHIPS), making global electronic (wire) transfers of funds (now $2 trillion a day) possible among financial institutions.
- 1977 – The Society for Worldwide Interbank Financial Telecommunications (SWIFT) came into being, making more global transfers of funds possible by individuals.
- 1988 – The founding of the modern Internet based on Arpanet (which was created in 1969). While it took the Internet several years to take off, this was a turning point in global interconnection for billions of people.
- 2001 – The terrorist attacks on the Twin Towers in New York and on the Pentagon in Washington, as well as later terrorist attacks on trains in Madrid (March 11, 2004) and London (July 7, 2005), among others. The following is a specific example in support of the idea that 9/11 can be taken as a point of origin for globalization (at least of higher education): "Since the terrorist attacks of September 11, 2001, internationalization has moved high on the agenda at most universities, to prepare students for a globalized world, and to help faculty members stay up-to-date in their disciplines" (Lewin 2008: 8).

This, of course, brings us very close to the present day and it is possible that other specific events (especially the Great Recession which began in late 2007) will almost certainly come to be associated by future observers with the birth, or further development, of globalization.

Broader, More Recent Changes

The fifth view focuses on broader, but still recent, changes. There is a sense in this view that a sea change occurred in the last half of the twentieth century. Three of these momentous changes have been identified by scholars as the point of origin of globalization as it exists today:

- The emergence of the United States as *the* global power in the years following WW II.

The US not only projected its military power throughout the world (Korea in the early 1950s; disastrously in Vietnam in the 1960s and early 1970s), it extended its reach in the economic realm as it became the dominant industrial power when WW II decimated most of its competitors militarily (Germany, Japan) and/or economically (the Axis powers as well as Allies such as France and Great Britain). Many other aspects of America's global reach either accompanied these changes or soon followed. Among them were the diplomatic clout of the US government, the reach of the US media, the power of Hollywood, and so on. Such a view closely aligns globalization with the idea of Americanization (see Chapter 2).

- The emergence of multinational corporations (MNCs).

While the world's great corporations can be traced back to the eighteenth and early nineteenth centuries in, for example, Germany, Great Britain, and the United

States, they were initially largely associated with their nations of origin and did the vast majority of their business within those countries. However, over time, those corporations did more and more business internationally. In so doing, they were following Marx and Engels' (1848/2000: 248–9) dictum that because of stagnant or declining profits capitalism had to expand into international markets or die.

For example, the once great American automobile companies – Ford and General Motors – not only originated in the US, but focused, at least initially, on selling into the American market and most, if not all, of the component parts were produced by them or sub-contractors in the US. Of course, they did import raw materials of various kinds (and they did sell their automobiles overseas, especially in Europe), but in the main, the bulk of their business was done in the US. Furthermore, the vast majority of top executives, employees, and investors was American. However, that began to change over the course of the twentieth century as these corporations exported more of their automobiles to other parts of the world, opened factories in other countries to sell cars under their brand names (or others), targeted their products to the distinctive needs (e.g. for smaller, more fuel-efficient cars) of those countries, and more recently began to move more of their automobile production aimed at the US market to other countries, either in factories of their own or in the factories of sub-contractors in those countries.

In these and other ways, Ford and General Motors have become multinational corporations and MNCs are, because of their very nature, inherently part of globalization. Indeed, MNCS are not only involved in globalization but this process is internalized into the organization as all sorts of global flows (parts, people, money) occur *within* the corporation.

The case of the other of the one-time "Big Three" American automobile companies – Chrysler – is even more striking in this regard. Initially, Chrysler followed the same course as Ford and GM and became increasingly multi-national. However, Chrysler has long been the most marginal of the Big Three and, famously, had to be bailed out in 1979 by a controversial loan from the US government. However, that was only of short-term help and in 1998 Chrysler was taken over by the German manufacturer of Mercedes-Benz automobiles which changed Chrysler's name to DaimlerChrysler AG. This clearly represented the formation of an MNC, although Daimler-Benz itself (as well as Chrysler) was a multinational corporation before that, since, among other things, it actively sold its automobiles in the US as well as in many other parts of the world. However this marriage was short-lived and Daimler sold off its interest in Chrysler in 2007. In order to survive, Chrysler has been forced into a multinational merger with Fiat, the Italian automobile manufacturer.

Of course, American and German automobile companies are no longer the world leaders in that industry. Rather, the leaders are Japanese companies, especially Toyota (although it has been diminished by recent problems with quality, resulting, at times, in fatal accidents), Nissan, and Honda (with Korean companies [e.g. Hyundai-Kia] showing global strength, as well). However, these companies are today themselves MNCs as they not only sell cars in the US (and in many other nations), but also produce in factories built in various parts of North America. The case of today's automobile manufacturers is just one example of national corporations that have become MNCs and therefore much more clearly and importantly integral parts of globalization.

- The demise of the Soviet Union and the end of the Cold War.

It could be argued that globalization is even more recent and did not truly begin until the fall of the "Iron Curtain" and the Soviet Union in 1991. With those events, the division of the world into mainly "capitalist" and "communist" spheres rapidly eroded as did all sorts of barriers that existed between them. Major parts of the world were opened for the first time since the early twentieth century to all sorts of global flows – immigration, tourism, media, diplomacy, and especially the capitalistic economic transactions of MNCs and other businesses. The global processes that had spread throughout most of the "free" world before 1991 flooded into the now independent states of the old Soviet Union, especially Russia, and most of its allies.

Vestiges of communism exist as of this writing, especially in Cuba, North Korea, and, at least nominally, in China. Cuba remains, in the main, outside of global capitalism, largely because of the US embargo against trading with Cuba, in force since 1962 and expanded and codified several times since then. However, the embargo itself is a manifestation of globalization – the US setting up barriers in order to limit or halt the flow of trade with Cuba and to inhibit or prevent other nations from around the world from trading with Cuba. China, of course, is becoming a, if not soon *the*, major force in global capitalism even though the government remains communist, at least in name (Fishman 2006). In any case, China is actively involved in globalization not only economically, but in many other realms as well (the 2008 Olympics in Beijing is a good example).

The perspective adopted in this book on the current global age is most in accord with this focus on broader changes that began in the last half of the twentieth century. While all of the other perspectives deal with global processes, they were far more limited in geographic scope and far less extensive and intensive than the global processes that took off in the late twentieth century. Thus the perspective adopted here is that globalization is a relatively recent development with its major points of origin occurring after the close of WW II.

CHAPTER SUMMARY

Globalization is a transplanetary process or set of processes involving increasing liquidity and the growing multi-directional flows of people, objects, places, and information, as well as the structures they encounter and create that are barriers to, or expedite, those flows.

The sheer magnitude, diversity, and complexity of the process of globalization today leads to the conceptualization of the current era as the "global age."

Globalization can be analyzed through conceptual metaphors such as solids, liquids, flows, structures, heavy, light, and weightless.

Prior to the "global age," people, things, information, places, and objects tended to harden over time. Thus their common attribute was "solidity," the characteristic of being limited to one place. Solidity also refers to the persistence of barriers that prevented free movement of people, information, and objects in that era. Although solidity persists, it is "fluidity" that is more characteristic of the "global age."

Over the last few decades, that which once seemed solid has tended to "melt" and become increasingly mobile or "liquid." A range of technological developments in transportation and communication have enabled far greater global movement of what was previously solid.

A closely related concept is the idea of "flows." Globalization is increasingly characterized by flows of liquid phenomena including people, objects, decisions, information, and places.

In spite of greater liquidity and ever-more flows of various types, the world is still characterized by great inequality. While globalization flows more easily through the developed world, it bypasses many locales in the less developed world.

Globalization can also be analyzed through metaphors of heavy, light, and weightless. Historically, there has been movement from that which is heavy to that which is light and most recently to that which approaches weightlessness. Pre-industrial and industrial societies were "heavy," characterized by that which is difficult to move. Advances in transportation and technology made goods, people, and places lighter. We are currently in an era defined not only by lightness but also increasingly by weightlessness.

Some structures (e.g. borders) continue to be important in impeding the movement of that which is liquid, light, or weightless. Other heavy structures ("routes" or "paths") expedite flows.

There also exist subtler structural barriers which are in many ways more powerful than the material structures such as national borders. These structures serve to differentiate and subordinate on the basis of social class, race, ethnicity, gender, age, sexual orientation, and region of the world. These phenomena often tend to be interrelated. Those who occupy superordinate positions in these hierarchies tend to erect structures in order to impede flows that are not beneficial to them. They also encourage flows that work to their advantage.

The origin and history of globalization can be analyzed through five perspectives. First, globalization can be seen as being hardwired into humans, in the form of a basic urge for a better life. This instinct results in the spread of globalization through commerce, religion, politics, and warfare. Second, globalization may be perceived as a long-term cyclical process. In this view, there have been other global ages prior to the present one, and each age is destined to contract and disappear, after attaining a peak. Third, globalization can be viewed as a series of historical epochs or waves, each with its own point of origin. A fourth perspective argues that the multiple points of origin of globalization are located in seminal historical events. A fifth view focuses on broader, more recent changes in the twentieth century. It argues that the global processes in motion prior to WW II were more limited in geographic scope and less intensive than the global processes of the late twentieth and early twenty-first centuries.

DISCUSSION QUESTIONS

1. Examine the dual role of structures as barriers to, and facilitators of, global flows. Are subtler structural barriers more effective than material barriers?

2. What is the significance of networks in the current age of globalization? Is it possible for networks to act as deterrents or barriers to flows?

3. Do liquids dissolve structures blocking their path, or do they merely circumnavigate them?

4. Discuss the impact of increased liquidity on hierarchical social structures.

5. Compare the current "global age" to previous periods which have been said to be associated with globalization.

FURTHER READING

Zygmunt Bauman. *Liquid Modernity*. Cambridge: Polity, 2000.
Arjun Appadurai. *Modernity at Large: Cultural Dimensions of Globalization*. Minneapolis: University of Minnesota Press, 1996.
Jonathan Xavier Inda and Renato Rosaldo. "Tracking Global Flows." In Jonathan Xavier Inda and Renato Rosaldo, eds., *The Anthropology of Globalization: A Reader*, 2nd edn. Malden, MA: Blackwell, 2008.
Manuel Castells. *The Rise of the Network Society*. Malden, MA: Blackwell, 1996.
Anna Lowenhaupt Tsing. *Friction: An Ethnography of Global Connection*. Princeton: Princeton University Press, 2005.
Jan Aart Scholte and Roland Robertson, eds. *Encyclopedia of Globalization*. New York: MTM Publishing, 2007.
George Ritzer, ed. *The Blackwell Companion to Globalization*. Malden, MA: Blackwell, 2007.
George Ritzer. *Globalization: A Basic Text*. Malden, MA: Wiley-Blackwell, 2010.
George Ritzer and Zeynep Atalay. *Readings in Globalization: Key Concepts and Major Debates*. Malden, MA: Wiley-Blackwell, 2010.

REFERENCES

Albrow, Martin. 1996. *The Global Age*. Cambridge: Polity.
Altman, Daniel. 2007. *Connected: 24 Hours in the Global Economy*. New York: Farrar, Straus and Giroux.
Anner, Mark, and Peter Evans. 2004. "Building Bridges Across a Double-Divide: Alliances between US and Latin American Labor and NGOs." *Development in Practice* 14, 1–2.

Appadurai, Arjun. 1996. *Modernity at Large: Cultural Dimensions of Globalization*. Minneapolis: University of Minnesota Press.

Bauman, Zygmunt. 2000. *Liquid Modernity*. Cambridge: Polity.

Bauman, Zygmunt. 2003. *Liquid Love*. Cambridge: Polity.

Bauman, Zygmunt. 2005. *Liquid Life*. Cambridge: Polity.

Bauman, Zygmunt. 2006. *Liquid Fear*. Cambridge: Polity.

Beer, David, and Roger Burrows. 2007. "Sociology and, of and in Web 2.0: Some Initial Considerations." *Sociological Research Online*, 12, 5, www.socresonline.org.uk/12/5/17.html.

Bestor, Theodore C. 2005. "How Sushi Went Global." In James L. Watson and Melissa L. Caldwell, eds., *The Cultural Politics of Food and Eating: A Reader*. Malden, MA: Blackwell.

Bogdanich, Walt. 2007. "Free Trade Zones Ease Passage of Counterfeit Drugs to US." *New York Times*. December 17.

Bronfenbrenner, Kate, ed. 2007. *Global Unions: Challenging Transnational Capital Through Cross-Border Campaigns*. Ithaca, NY: ILR Press.

Brown, Richard Harvey. 1989. *A Poetic for Sociology: Toward a Logic of Discovery for the Human Sciences*. Chicago: University of Chicago Press.

Cartier, Carolyn. 2001. *Globalizing South China*. Oxford: Blackwell.

Castells, Manuel. 1996. *The Rise of the Network Society*. Malden, MA: Blackwell.

Chanda, Nayan. 2007. *Bound Together: How Traders, Preachers, Adventurers, and Warriors Shaped Globalization*. New Haven: Yale University Press.

Connell, R. W., and June Crawford. 2005. "The Global Connections of Intellectual Workers." *International Sociology* 20 (March).

Crack, Angela M. 2007. "Transcending Borders? Reassessing Public Spheres in a Networked World." *Globalizations* 4, 3.

Drori, Gili S., and Yong Suk Jang. 2003. "The Global Digital Divide: A Sociological Assessment of Trends and Causes." *Social Science Computer Review* 21, 2.

Economist. 2006. January 12. "Genghis the Globalizer."

Economist. 2006. March 10. "DP World Agree to Divest Its American Ports."

Economist. 2008. May 22. "Give Them a Better Life."

Fassin, Didier. 2008. "Compassion and Repression: The Moral Economy of Immigration Policies in France." In Jonathan Xavier Inda and Renato Rosaldo, eds., *The Anthropology of Globalization: A Reader*, 2nd edn. Malden, MA: Blackwell.

Fishman, Ted. 2006. *China Inc.: How the Rise of the Next Superpower Challenges America and the World*. New York: Scribner.

French, Howard W. 2008. "Great Firewall of China Faces Online Rebels." *New York Times*. February 4.

Friedman, Thomas. 2005. *The World is Flat: A Brief History of the Twenty-first Century*. New York: Farrar, Straus, Giroux.

Gibbon, Edward. 1998. *The History of the Decline and Fall of the Roman Empire*. London: Wordsworth.

Giulianotti, Richard, and Roland Robertson. 2007. "Recovering the Social: Globalization, Football and Transnationalism." In Richard Giulianotti and Roland Robertson, eds., *Globalization and Sport*. Malden, MA: Blackwell.

Goldfrank, Walter. 2005. "Fresh Demand: The Consumption of Chilean Produce in the United States." In James L. Watson and Melissa L. Caldwell, eds., *The Cultural Politics of Food and Eating: A Reader*. Malden, MA: Blackwell.

Hill Collins, Patricia. 2000. *Black Feminist Thought: Knowledge, Consciousness and the Politics of Empowerment*. New York: Routledge.

Hirst, Paul, and Grahame Thompson. 1999. *Globalization in Question*. Cambridge: Polity.

Inda, Jonathan Xavier, and Renato Rosaldo. 2008. "Tracking Global Flows." In Jonathan Xavier Inda and Renato Rosaldo, eds., *The Anthropology of Globalization: A Reader*, 2nd edn. Malden, MA: Blackwell.

Juris, Jeffrey S. 2008. "The New Digital Media and Activist Networking within Anti-Corporate Globalization Movements." In Jonathan Xavier Inda and Renato Rosaldo, eds., *The Anthropology of Globalization: A Reader*, 2nd edn. Malden, MA: Blackwell.

Kelly, William W. 2007. "Is Baseball a Global Sport? America's 'National Pastime' as a Global Field and International Sport." In Richard Giulianotti and Roland Robertson, eds., *Globalization and Sport*. Malden, MA: Blackwell.

Knorr Cetina, Karin. 2005. "Complex Global Microstructures: The New Terrorist Societies." *Theory, Culture & Society* 22.

Knorr Cetina, Karin, and U. Bruegger. 2002. "Global Microstructures: The Virtual Societies of Financial Markets." *American Journal of Sociology* 17.

Lakoff, Andrew. 2008. "Diagnostic Liquidity: Mental Illness and the Global Trade in DNA." In Jonathan Xavier Inda and Renato Rosaldo, eds., *The Anthropology of Globalization: A Reader*, 2nd edn. Malden, MA: Blackwell.

Landler, Mark. 2007. "Germany Agonizes Over Brain Drain." *New York Times*. February 6.

Landler, Mark. 2008. "At a Tipping Point." *New York Times*. October 1.

Lewin, Tamar. 2008. "Universities Rush to Set Up Outposts Abroad." *New York Times*. February 10.

Lowenhaupt Tsing, Anna. 2005. *Friction: An Ethnography of Global Connection*. Princeton: Princeton University Press.

Mankekar, Purnima. 2005. "'India Shopping': Indian Grocery Stores and Transnational Configurations of Belonging." In James L. Watson and Melissa L. Caldwell, eds., *The Cultural Politics of Food and Eating: A Reader*. Malden, MA: Blackwell.

Mann, Michael. 2007. "Has Globalization Ended the Rise and the Rise of the Nation-state?" *Review of International Political Economy* 4, 3.

Marcuse, Peter, and Ronald van Kempen, eds. 2000. *Globalizing Cities: A New Spatial Order?* Malden, MA: Blackwell.

Marx, Karl, and Friedrich Engels. 1848/2000. "The Communist Manifesto." In David McLellan, ed., *Karl Marx: Selected Writings*. 2nd edn. Oxford: Oxford University Press, 2000.

Moghadam, Valentine. 2007. "Gender and the Global Economy." In J. Timmons Roberts and Amy Bellone Hite, eds., *The Globalization and Development Reader*. Malden, MA: Blackwell.

Morawska, Eva. 2007. "Transnationalism." In Mary C. Waters and Reed Ueda, eds., *The New Americans: A Guide to Immigration Since 1965*. Cambridge, MA: Harvard University Press.

Moses, Jonathon W. 2006. *International Migration: Globalization's Last Frontier*. London: Zed Books.

Polillo, Simone, and Mauro F. Guillen. 2005. "Globalization Pressures and the State: The Worldwide Spread of Central Bank Independence." *American Journal of Sociology* 110, 6 (May).

Portes, Alejandro, ed. 2001. "New Research and Theory on Immigrant Transnationalism." *Global Networks* 1, 3.

Reuveny, Rafael, and William R. Thompson. 2001. "Explaining Protectionism: 17 Perspectives and One Common Denominator." *Global Society* 15, 3.

Rey, P. J., and George Ritzer. 2010. "Conceptualizing Globalization in Terms of Flows." *Current Perspectives in Social Theory* 27.

Robertson, Roland, and David Inglis. 2004. "The Global Animus: In the Tracks of World Consciousness." *Globalizations* 1, 1.

Robinson, William I. 2007. "Transnationality." In Jan Aart Scholte and Roland Robertson, eds., *Encyclopedia of Globalization*. New York: MTM Publishing.

Rosenthal, Joel T. 2007. "Voyages of Discovery." In Jan Aart Scholte and Roland Robertson, eds., *Encyclopedia of Globalization*. New York: MTM Publishing.

Rumford, Chris. 2007. "Does Europe Have Cosmopolitan Borders?" *Globalizations* 4, 3.

Sassen, Saskia. 1991. *The Global City: New York, London, and Tokyo*. Princeton: Princeton University Press.

Sassen, Saskia. 2007. "Migration." In Jan Aart Scholte and Roland Robertson, eds., *Encyclopedia of Globalization*. New York: MTM Publishing.

Scholte, Jan Aart. 2004. "Globalization Studies: Past and Future: A Dialogue of Diversity." *Globalizations* 1, 1.

Scholte, Jan Aart. 2005. *Globalization: A Critical Introduction*, 2nd edn. New York: Palgrave.

Schumpeter, Joseph A. 1976. *Capitalism, Socialism and Democracy*. 5th edn. London: George Allen and Unwin.

Shamir, Ronen. 2005. "Without Borders? Notes on Globalization as a Mobility Regime." *Sociological Theory* 23, 2 (June).

Singh Grewal, David. 2008. *Network Power: The Social Dynamics of Globalization*. New Haven: Yale University Press.

Smith, Jackie. 2001. "Globalizing Resistance: The Battle of Seattle and the Future of Social Movements." *Mobilization* 6.

Soros, George. 2000. *Open Society: Reforming Global Capitalism*. New York: Public Affairs.

Therborn, Goran. 2000. "Globalizations: Dimensions, Historical Waves, Regional Effects, Normative Governance." *International Sociology* 15.

Thompson, Clive. 2008. "I'm So Totally, Digitally Close To You." *New York Times Magazine*. September 7.

Tsing, Anna. 2000. "The Global Situation." *Cultural Anthropology* 15, 3.

Weisman, Steven R. 2008. "Foreign Buyer Beware: US Security Concerns Block China's 3Com Deal." *New York Times*. February 21.

Yuan, Li. 2006. "Big Phone Firms Delve Undersea for Asian Growth." *Wall Street Journal*. December 18.

Theorizing Globalization

Globalization: The Essentials, by George Ritzer
© 2011 John Wiley & Sons Ltd

Chapter 1 offered an approach to, as well as various tools for looking at and thinking about, globalization. It also offered a variety of perspectives on the origins and the historical background of the contemporary process of globalization. This chapter deals with a set of ideas and theories that will prove helpful in thinking about globalization. (It should be noted that a whole other set of theories that relate specifically to the globalization of culture will be discussed in Chapter 7.) While some of these theories relate more to epochs prior to the current global age, they not only help in understanding those eras, but are also helpful in better understanding globalization today.

IMPERIALISM

Imperialism is a broad concept that describes various methods employed by one country to gain control (sometimes through territorial conquest) of another country (or geographic area) and then to exercise control, especially political,

> **Imperialism**: Methods employed by one nation-state to gain power over an area(s) and then to exercise control over it.

economic, and territorial, over that country (or geographic area), and perhaps many other countries. The term comes from the Roman *imperium* (Markoff 2007: 609–14) and was first associated with domination and political control over one or more neighboring nations. The term "empire" is derived from *imperium* and it was used to describe political forms that had characteristics of Roman rule, especially the great power of the leader (the Roman *imperator* or emperor) and the huge chasm between the power of the ruler and the ruled (Gibbon 1998). Over time, the notion of empire, and of the process of imperialism, came to be associated with rulership over vast geographic spaces and the people who lived there. It is this characteristic that leads to the association between imperialism and globalization. In fact, many of the processes discussed in this book under the heading of globalization – trade, migration, communication, and so on – existed between the imperial power and the geographic areas that it controlled.

The term imperialism came into widespread use in the late nineteenth century as a number of nations (Germany, Italy, Belgium, Great Britain, France, the United States) competed for control over previously undeveloped geographic areas, especially in Africa. (Before that, Spain, Portugal and the Netherlands had been other leading imperialist nations.) While used mainly descriptively at first, imperialism came to have a negative connotation, beginning, perhaps, with the Boer War (1899–1902). Questions were being raised about the need for political (and cultural) control by the imperial powers.

Vladimir Lenin (1917/1939), the first leader of the Soviet Union, was an important early theorist of imperialism, especially in his book, *Imperialism: The Highest Stage of Capitalism* (see also J. A. Hobson's [1902/1905/1938] *Imperialism*). The title of Lenin's work well expresses his view (and Hobson's) that the economic nature of capitalism leads capitalistic economies, and the nation-states that are dominated by such an economic system, to seek out and control distant geographic areas. Control over foreign markets and foreign investments was needed to provide resources for capitalist industries and also to create new markets for those industries. In other words, a capitalist economic system tended to expand imperialistically throughout the world.

The (mainly European) capitalist nations and firms are seen as having expanded throughout the world and carved up that world among themselves. From a revolutionary point of view, Lenin sees imperialism as a parasitic system and one that was part, and reflected the decay, of capitalism.

There are several arguments against the view that imperialism is a purely economic phenomenon. For one thing, in its early years the flow of profits to the dominant countries was not as great as many assumed. For another, imperialism had much more to do with European politics and competition among European nation-states. Perhaps of greatest importance was the European sense of superior culture and the belief that it gave Europeans the right to exploit, and in the process civilize, the rest of the "less developed" world (Ashcroft, Griffiths, and Tiffin 1998: 126).

The continuing importance of the idea of imperialism has been challenged in one of the most important books in the study of globalization, Michael Hardt and Antonio Negri's *Empire* (2000). In their view, the often heavy-handed, nation-based forms of imperialism described above have been replaced by a far more subtle and complex network of global political/economic/cultural processes that are exercising a new form of control that is better captured in their view by the idea of *empire* rather than imperialism. We will examine their work in detail later in this chapter, but the key point is that while the process may have changed, efforts at gaining hegemonic control continue unabated.

Related to Hardt and Negri's argument is the idea that the decline of the importance of the nation-state makes it difficult to continue to talk in terms of imperialism which, at its base, is a view that a given nation exercises control over other nations (or geographic areas) around the world. It is this decline that leads to Hardt and Negri's more "decentered" view of globalization. That is, imperialism was a modern process and perspective that was "centered" on the nation-state (Great Britain, the Soviet Union, the US), but the declining importance of the nation-state requires a very different view of control exercised on a global scale. To Hardt and Negri it is the power exercised by a decentered empire that has replaced that exercised by imperialism and practiced by nation-states.

David Harvey (2003) has more recently articulated the idea that a "new imperialism" has arisen, with the United States as its prime (if not only) representative. He calls this "capitalist imperialism" and sees it as a contradictory fusion of economics and politics. Thus, Harvey offers a more integrated view of imperialism than did Lenin (or Hobson). More specifically, it involves a fusion of the *political* – "imperialism as a distinctively political project on the part of actors whose power is based in command of a territory and a capacity to mobilize its human and natural resources towards political, economic, and military ends" – and the *economic* –

"imperialism as a diffuse political-economic process in space and time in which command over and use of capital takes primacy" (Harvey 2003: 26). There are fundamental differences between the two (political interest in territory and capitalist interest in command, and use, of capital), but the "two logics intertwine in complex and sometimes contradictory ways" (2003: 29). For example, to the American government the Vietnam War made sense from a political point of view, but it hardly made sense from an economic perspective and may even have adversely affected the American economy. More generally, Harvey wonders whether we are now seeing an increase in US political imperialism (e.g. Iraq and Afghanistan), while the US is declining in importance from the perspective of economic imperialism (e.g. the rise in economic power of China, the EU, India, etc.).

COLONIALISM

Colonialism is clearly related to imperialism (Williams and Chrisman 1994), and the terms are sometimes used interchangeably, but colonialism has a more specific meaning. At the most extreme, imperialism involves a control *without* the creation of colonies (Harvey 2006: 21). **Colonialism** generally involves settlers as well as much more formal mechanisms of political control than those of imperialism. Thus, colonialism often entails the creation by the colonial power in the country (or geographic area) that has been colonized of an administrative apparatus to run its internal affairs, including its settlements. According to Edward Said, "imperialism means the practice, the theory, and the attitudes of a dominating metropolitan centre ruling a distant territory; 'colonialism', which is almost always a consequence of imperialism, is the implanting of settlements on distant territory" (cited in Ashcroft, Griffiths, and Tiffin 1998: 45). While both imperialism and colonialism involve economic and political (as well as cultural) control, imperialism is (following Lenin) more defined by economic control (and exploitation), while colonialism is more about political control.

> **Colonialism:** Creation by the colonial power of an administration in the area that has been colonized to run its internal affairs.

Although colonialism has an ancient history, it can be said to have had two great and more recent ages. The first, beginning in the fifteenth century, was led by European powers, especially Spain and Portugal, and involved creating colonies in Africa, Asia, and the Americas. The second, or modern, phase lasted roughly between 1820 and the end of WW I. It involved other European powers (most importantly Great Britain, France, and Germany), as well as the US and Japan.

Some colonies (e.g. India as a colony of the British) persisted well into the twentieth century. However, during that period the momentum shifted in the direction of *decolonization*, or "the process of revealing and dismantling colonialist power in all its forms. This includes dismantling the hidden aspects of those institutional and cultural forces that had maintained the colonialist power and that remain even after political independence is achieved" (Ashcroft, Griffiths, and Tiffin 1998: 63).

Decolonization movements began to succeed with greater frequency as the twentieth century unfolded. They were followed by decolonization and the achievement of political independence (Grimal 1878). Decolonization was particularly important after the close of WW II. That was followed by a period of neo-colonialism (Nkrumah 1965), where efforts at control over the former colonies, and other nation-states, grew much more indirect, subtle (e.g. through cultural and educational institutions), and focused on economic control and exploitation. The subtlety of neo-colonialism made it more insidious and harder to detect and therefore more difficult to resist and combat.

> **Post-colonialism**: Developments that take place in a former colony after the colonizing power departs.

Today, few, if any, colonies remain, with the result that we can now think in terms of **post-colonialism** (Bhambrah 2007: 871–84). Clearly, this implies the era in once-colonized areas *after* the colonizing power has departed (although post-colonial thinking and work could already be well under way before the colonizing power departs). However, in recent years it has come to take on more specific meanings that relate to various developments that take place in a former colony after the colonizing power departs. For example, it relates to a critical issue in globalization studies today, that of national identity, especially the difficulty of gaining identity (as an Indian, for example) after a colonial power (the British in the case of India) has departed. The most notable work on this is Edward Said's *Orientalism* (1979/1994: 93) which deals with this problem in the context of both overt and more subtle negative stereotypes developed in the West about those who live in the East. The issue raised is the difficulty experienced by "Orientals" in developing a positive identity in light of all the negativity about them in the West which, of course, dominated the East in various ways (imperialism, colonialism, etc.), until very recently. This negativity is especially clear in the history of Western literature (and film) about the East.

DEVELOPMENT

Development can be seen as a historical stage (roughly the 1940s to the 1970s) that preceded the global age (McMichael 2008: 21). Specifically, development can be viewed as a "project" that predated the project of globalization. As a project, it was primarily concerned with the economic development of specific nations, usually those that were not regarded as sufficiently advanced economically.

> **Development**: A "project" primarily concerned with the economic development of specific nation-states not regarded as sufficiently developed.

A key aspect of development projects was **import-substitution**. That is, in order to undergo development, Southern countries had to develop their own industries instead of focusing on producing for export and relying on imports from

> **Import-substitution**: Countries (usually in the South) "encouraged" to develop their industries: instead of producing for export, rely on imports.

other countries, especially the North. Thus, for example, developing countries were urged to develop an automobile industry. Such an industry was important not only in itself, but because it would lead to other kinds of development such as parts manufacturing and road building (McMichael 2008: 42). Such independence would not seem to be in the interest of the developed nations of the North. For example, wouldn't the US prefer to sell its automobiles to Brazil rather than having Brazil produce its own automobiles? While it might, the fact is that the US and other developed nations of the North benefited from import-substitution development by increasing foreign direct investment (FDI) in the industries that emerged in less developed countries, and they reaped great profits from these investments. (**Foreign direct investment** is investment by a firm in one nation-state in a firm in another nation-state in order to gain control over it.)

> **Foreign direct investment (FDI)**: Investment by a firm in one nation-state in a firm in another nation-state with the intention of controlling it.

Also to be included under the heading of the development project was foreign aid offered by developed countries to those that were less developed. This encompassed financial assistance, as well as aid in terms of food (for example, the US shipping its excess wheat to developing countries). While such aid was certainly helpful in the short run, in the longer run it often adversely affected the ability of some countries to grow and produce their own food (e.g. wheat) and therefore led to greater food dependency in some less developed countries.

Many are critical of development theory on a variety of grounds. For example, Paul Collier (2007) critiques those interested in development for focusing on those nations that have a good chance of succeeding while ignoring the poorest nations (and failed nation-states) that are at the bottom of the global hierarchy on various dimensions (life expectancy, infant mortality, long-term malnutrition, etc.).

There is also a body of work critical of development theory known as **dependency theory** (Cardoso and Faletto 1979). It emphasizes the fact that the kinds of programs discussed above led not so much to the development of the nation-states of the South, but more to a decline

> **Dependency theory**: Development of the nation-states of the South contributed to a decline in their independence; to an increase in their dependence on the North.

in their independence and to an increase in their dependence on the countries of the North, especially the US. Underdevelopment is not an aberrant condition, or one caused by the less developed nations themselves, but it is built into the development project (as well as into global capitalism). It also involves the idea that instead of bringing economic improvement, development brings with it greater impoverishment.

Andre Gunder Frank (1969) argues that behind the whole idea of development is the notion that the present of less developed countries resembles the past of the developed countries. Thus, if the less developed countries simply follow the same path taken by developed countries, they too will become developed. However, the developed countries were never in the same position as less developed countries today; the developed countries were *un*developed while the less developed countries were (and are) *under*developed. The result is that the path followed by the former is not necessarily the best one for the latter.

Frank also rejects the idea that the underdevelopment of a country is traceable to sources internal to that country. Rather, he argues that it is a product of the capitalist system and of the relationship between developed and underdeveloped countries within that system. Further, he rejects the idea that the solution to under-development lies in the diffusion of capital, institutions, values, and so on from the developed world. He contends that the less developed countries can only develop if they are independent of most of these capitalist relationships which, after all, are really the cause of their lack of development. It is capitalism that is the cause of development in the developed nations and of underdevelopment in the less developed nations.

> **World system theory**: Sees the world divided mainly between the *core* and the *periphery* with the latter dependent on, and exploited by, the core nation-states.

Dependency theory has tended to wane, but it has been replaced by, and to some degree incorporated in, a broader theory known as **world system theory** (Wallerstein 1974). This theory envisions a world divided mainly between the *core* and the *periphery* with the nation-states associated with the latter being dependent on, and exploited by, the core nation-states.

The development project was basically a failure since the world clearly remained, and remains, characterized by great inequalities, especially economic inequalities, between the North and the South. More pointedly, most nations associated with the South did not develop to any appreciable degree. Indeed, it could be argued that they fell further behind, rather than gaining on, the developed countries. Furthermore, the whole development project came to be seen as offensive since it tended to elevate the North, and everything about it, especially its economic system, while demeaning everything associated with the South. In its place, the globalization project at least sounded more equitable since it was inherently multilateral and multi-directional while development was unilateral and unidirectional, with money and other assistance flowing from the North to the South. There is much evidence that the globalization project has not worked out very differently from the development project in terms of differences between the North and South. Furthermore, many of the institutions created during the period of dependency (those associated with the UN) continue to function and play a central role in globalization. This raises the question of whether globalization is simply development with another, less offensive, label. This would be the view taken by those who are critics of neo-liberalism, which undergirds much of contemporary economic globalization (see below).

AMERICANIZATION

Americanization is another process that, like those discussed above, is related to globalization, but is not identical, or reducible, to it. However, there are certainly those who think it is. For example, former US Secretary of State Henry Kissinger (1999) says that "globalisation is really another name for the dominant role of the United States." This view

> **Americanization**: Imports by non-Americans of that which is closely associated with America/Americans.

has probably never been fully accurate and, in any case, US power and influence around the world are clearly in decline in the early twenty-first century. Nevertheless, Americanization has been a central part of globalization. Richard Kuisel (1993: 96) defines Americanization as "the import by non-Americans of products, images, technologies, practices and behaviour that are closely associated with America/Americans."

Long before globalization became a central academic and lay concern, there were many works over a long period of time that dealt with America's global influence, especially on Europe. While the continuation of this work to this day indicates that there has been no diminution of interest in Americanization, there was a particularly heavy concentration on this topic in the 1960s, at or near the summit of America's global power (especially its industrial power given the decades it took Europe [and Japan] to recover economically from the devastation of WW II), and no work epitomizes this better than the Frenchman J.-J. Servan-Schreiber's *The American Challenge* (1968).

Echoing Georges Duhamel's (1931) notion of an American "menace," Servan-Schreiber saw America as a business, industrial, and economic threat to Europe. His view, and the fear of the day, is reflected in the opening line of his book (which seems laughable in the light of subsequent developments such as the rise of European [e.g. BMW] and the decline of American [e.g. GM] industry): "Fifteen years from now it is quite possible that the world's third greatest industrial power, just after the US and Russia, will not be Europe, but *American industry in Europe*" (Servan-Schreiber 1968: 3). Whatever the errors in this view in light of today's realities (in addition to those mentioned above, the rise of the EU, Japan, and China), it is reflective of the sense of the day of the power, especially industrially, of Americanization.

In the ensuing years, fears of Americanization, or at least of US industries, declined and were replaced by other ideas and fears, most of which were seen as threatening to the US, as well. One such idea, reflective of the remarkable post-war development of Japanese industry, was "Japanization" (Elger and Smith 1994), and that was later supplemented, and to some degree replaced, by fears of the "Asian Tigers" (e.g. Singapore), the European Union, and, most recently, and likely more enduringly, China (Huntington 1996).

However, other nations' fears of Americanization and its economic power have certainly not disappeared. Concern about the expansion of American industry was replaced (at least until the Great Recession) to a large degree by a growing fear, reflective of a sea change in the American economy, of American dominance globally in the realm of consumption (Goodman 2007: 330–51). The fear was no longer of industrial giants, many of which are declining (and disappearing), like US Steel and GM, but rather of the impact of behemoths in the realm of consumption such as Wal-Mart, Coca-Cola, McDonald's, and Visa (Ritzer 1995, 1999/2005).

Nothing reflected this change better than the fact that the largest corporation in the world was no longer the production-oriented General Motors, but rather the consumption-oriented retailer, Wal-Mart (Soderquist 2005). This fear of the giants in the realm of consumption, which was and is also found within the US, is reflected in concerns over processes that have been labeled "Coca-Colonization" (Kuisel 1993), "McDonaldization" (Ritzer 2008), "Disneyization" (Bryman 2004), and "Wal-Martization." As new leaders in the field of consumption, almost always US in origin, came to the fore, they led to new labels and new fears. For example, the growth of Starbucks (at least until recently [Simon 2009]) led to concern over "Starbuckization" (Ritzer 2008). Judging by the proliferation of its coffee shops in many countries in the world (at least 40 as of this writing), there was clear reason for such concern (Stone 2008: C1, C2) (although Starbucks ran into a roadblock in mid-2008 due to the looming recession, and it cut 600 shops and reduced its future expansion plans). Thus, if Servan-Schreiber had revised his book in, say, 2007, he would undoubtedly have focused on the threats posed by the exportation of America's consumer products and its "means (or cathedrals) of consumption" (Ritzer 1999/2005) – fast-food restaurants, superstores, shopping malls, and so on – in Europe. (see Chapter 7).

Anti-Americanism as a Global Process

Americanization has long been accompanied by a counter-reaction, in various places in the world, that can be thought of as anti-Americanism. Just as Americanization has proliferated as a process closely linked to globalization, so, too, has anti-Americanism. Not only is it an increasingly global phenomenon, but it is also one that seems to flow far more readily than Americanization to the far reaches of the globe. It also seems more intense than in the past and there is certainly far more attention and publicity devoted to it. But what, exactly, is anti-Americanism?

Anti-Americanism is not a homogeneous phenomenon, even if the word itself conveys a sense of a kind of general criticism that is expressed similarly in much of the world. There are distinct forms, causes, and expressions of anti-Americanism; in other words there are anti-Americanism*s* rather than an overarching anti-Americanism (Singh 2006). It is such an amorphous concept that both opposition to US cultural, economic, and political policies, as well as more sweeping negative generalizations about the US, are included under the heading of anti-Americanism. It can encompass everything from casual and superficial criticism of the US to a deep-seated and widely shared animosity (O'Connor 2007: 1–21).

One well-known definition of *anti-Americanism* is:

a predisposition to hostility toward the United States and American society, a relentless critical impulse toward American social, economic, and political institutions, traditions, and values; it entails an aversion to American culture in particular and its influence abroad, often also contempt for the American national character (or what is presumed to be such a character) and dislike of American people, manners, behavior, dress, and so on; rejection of American foreign policy and a firm belief in the malignity of American influence and presence anywhere in the world. (Hollander 1992: 339, emphasis in the original)

This is a rather breath-taking definition of anti-Americanism encompassing a wide range of specific phenomena. Its attraction is its sweep, but the diversity of phenomena encompassed by that sweep makes it clear that our sense of anti-Americanism needs greater refinement.

O'Connor (2007) argues that anti-Americanism can be seen as prejudice because it prejudges America, Americans, and American action, it offers a one-sided view of things American, and its view of America is undifferentiated. To overcome such a prejudice, and to develop a far better critique of America, that critique must be "based on details and evidence, rather than broad prejudices and stereotypes; from analysis, not knee-jerk rejection" (O'Connor 2007: 19). More generally, O'Connor argues that this prejudice, like all others, (1) needs to be challenged and confronted; (2) needs to be seen as making clear the need for a more differentiated view of the US; and (3) needs to be viewed as being in opposition to intelligent thought. Thus, "the challenge is how to engage with America without letting anti-American prejudices overwhelm critique" (O'Connor 2007: 21). Overall, O'Connor argues that to take anti-Americanism seriously, it must be based on intelligent critique well grounded in facts rather than based on prejudice against the US.

NEO-LIBERALISM

The term **neo-liberalism** involves, in David Harvey's (2005) view, a combination of classical liberalism's commitment to individual liberty with *neo*classical economics devoted to the free market and opposed to state intervention in that

> **Neo-liberalism**: Liberal commitment to individual liberty, a belief in the free market and opposition to state intervention in it.

market. Liberalism came to be called neo-liberalism (Fourcade-Gourinchas and Babb 2002: 533–79) as a result of developments in the 1930s. Liberal ideas were revitalized and transformed because of the need to counter the interventionism and the collectivism that dominated much thinking (especially Keynesian, as well as Marxian, theories) and many political systems (especially the New Deal in the US and the rise of the Soviet Union) in the early twentieth century (Turner and Gamble 2007: 865–7). Neo-liberalism's intellectual leaders were economists, especially Friedrich von Hayek and Ludwig von Mises. An organization devoted to liberal ideas – the Mont Pelerin Society (MPS) – was created in 1947. Its members were alarmed by the expansion of collectivist socialism (especially in, and sponsored by, the Soviet Union) and the aggressive intervention by liberal governments in the market (e.g. Franklin Roosevelt's "New Deal"). Those associated with MPS, especially the famous and highly influential Chicago economist, Milton Friedman, played a key role in the efforts to protect traditional liberal ideas, to develop neo-liberal theory, and to sponsor its utilization by countries throughout the world (Goodman 2008: 3).

Friedman taught economics at the University of Chicago beginning in 1946, and Hayek ("patron saint of the Chicago School" [Klein 2007: 131]) was a colleague there for a time in the 1950s. The Chicago economics department became the center of the neo-liberal approach and it produced a number of students who became known as the "Chicago Boys." After they finished their advanced degrees, they either went back to their home countries or served as consultants in various places throughout the world. In either case, they spread the neo-liberal doctrine taught at Chicago by Friedman and played a central role in it becoming policy in a number of nations.

A key development in the history of neo-liberalism was the election of Salvador Allende as President of Chile in 1970. Allende was a Marxist and the US, especially through the CIA, sponsored a coup engineered by the Chilean military (with CIA assistance) in September, 1973 (Dallek 2007). Allende was killed in the coup and he was replaced by the general who led it, Augusto Pinochet, who soon became President of Chile.

Many of the Chicago Boys had returned to Chile[1] after their training at the University of Chicago and with Pinochet's ascension to power they were given an opportunity to implement Friedman's neo-liberal ideas which, in a highly critical account, Naomi Klein calls the "shock doctrine" (Klein 2007). This involved the view that a total overhaul of an economy required a shock (like the Chilean coup); and the economic policies put in place were designed to change the economy dramatically and, at least in theory, to breathe life into it. The basic free market premises of this economic doctrine were derived from Friedman's teachings and writings (especially *Capitalism and Freedom* [2002]). They involved the privatization of industry, the deregulation of the economy, and reductions in a nation's spending on social welfare programs. In the political arena, laws and regulations were dismantled, leaving people to deal with the shock of the resulting lawlessness. Actions associated with each of these profoundly shook the economy, as well as the larger society. The nation's capitalists were the main beneficiaries of this shock therapy, especially privatization, which put them in an ownership position and in control of the newly privatized industries. They also benefited from the deregulation of the economy which left them free to operate – and profit – almost at will. The main victims of this shock therapy were the nation's poor whose economic situation was made worse by the shredding of the social safety net that served to protect them, at least to some degree.

Of far greater global importance was the influence of these ideas, and the shock doctrine, in the 1980s under the conservative political administrations of Margaret Thatcher in Great Britain and Ronald Reagan in the US. Early in their administrations both leaders undertook shock therapy by, for example, taking on, and defeating, powerful labor unions. Such shocks were then used as a basis for radically overhauling their economies by applying the neo-liberal ideas of the Chicago School. A decade later, the collapse of the Soviet Union seemingly left few alternatives to neo-liberalism. Indeed, shortly after the collapse of communism, Russia and other countries once in its orbit (e.g. Poland) came in for shock therapy and the institution, at least in part, of a free market economy.

Much of the world came to accept, or was coerced into accepting, neo-liberalism. Major forces in this were the IMF and the World Bank (see Chapter 3), both of which were heavily staffed by products of the Chicago economics department ("there was a virtual conveyor belt delivering Chicago Boys to the two institutions" [Klein 2007: 280]), and which practiced a form of shock therapy known as **structural adjustment**. That is, in order to receive aid from these organizations, receiving nations had to restructure their economies and societies in line with neo-liberal theory. That theory came to be most associated with the US and the Washington-based global organizations it exerted great control over (again the IMF and the World Bank [Plehwe 2007: 514–28] are prime examples). In fact, neo-liberalism (Campbell and Pederson 2001; Harvey 2005) is often referred to as the "Washington Consensus" (Serra and Stiglitz 2008) because of its linkage to the political and economic position of the US and the physical location of such organizations in that nation's capital. The term "Washington Consensus" was coined by, and is associated with the work of, John Williamson (1990a, 1990b, 1993; Cavanagh and Broad 2007: 1243–5). Most generally, in the Washington Consensus "unimpeded private market forces were seen as the driving engines of growth" (Cavanagh and Broad 2007: 1243). Absent was any concern for equity, redistribution, social issues, and the environment.[2]

> **Structural adjustment**: Conditions of economic "restructuring" imposed by organizations such as the World Bank and the IMF on borrowing nation-states.

The Washington Consensus had its heyday in the 1980s and early 1990s (as reflected in the creation of the North American Free Trade Association [NAFTA] in 1994), but began to collapse soon after as a result of an avalanche of developments (financial shocks in Mexico in 1994 and 1998; the Asian financial crisis of 1997–8; the collapse of Argentina's economy in 2001; the scandals associated with Enron and WorldCom during this period, which were linked to excessive application of such neo-liberal ideas as deregulation and privatization; and so on). A variety of groups – workers, environmentalists, farmers, and peasants, those in poor and less developed nations, and so on – came together in opposition to the Washington Consensus. Then there were the actions of the alter-globalization movements (especially the anti-WTO protests in Seattle) (see Chapter 12).

Neo-liberalism has recently been called into question in the developed world because of the meltdown in the global economy in late 2007. The US government was led to intervene in the market in various ways, including engineering a 2008 takeover of the investment firm Bear Stearns by J.P. Morgan. Later the US was forced to nationalize, or nearly so, the giant mortgage companies Fannie Mae and Freddie Mac, as well as the huge insurance conglomerate AIG, which were driven to near-insolvency by the same economic crisis. The US government was forced to invest many billions of dollars in the largest American banks (e.g. Citibank) in order to keep them afloat. Huge sums were also invested in the American automobile companies. As I write, there is movement toward giving the US government greater oversight over the markets involved in the crisis and a greater role in developing regulations that better control these markets and prevent the excesses of various banks and investment houses that were a root cause of the crisis. Such intervention would be anathema to Milton Friedman who long argued for the need to allow the markets to work out such difficulties on their own. The only role he saw for the government was the management of the money supply ("monetarism"), but otherwise the market was to be left to its own devices. From this perspective, Bear Stearns, Fannie Mae and Freddie Mac, AIG, and Citibank should all have been allowed to fail (as happened in the case of the one-time financial giant, Lehman Brothers).

In Latin America, Friedman's ideas have come under attack for failing to take poverty and inequality into consideration. According to a well-known Peruvian economist: "The problem with Milton Friedman and his fellow libertarians is they never took into consideration the importance of class. … They ignored the way elites were able to distort the policies they prescribed for their own benefit" (Goodman 2008: 3).

Neo-Liberalism: Basic Ideas

William Easterly is opposed to any form of collectivism and state planning because it inhibits, if not destroys, freedom. To Easterly, freedom, especially economic freedom, is highly correlated with economic success. This is the case because economic freedom "permits the decentralized search for success that is the hallmark of free markets" (Easterly 2006: 35).

Easterly offers several reasons why economic freedom is related to economic success and why central planning has been an economic failure. First, it is extremely difficult to know in advance what will succeed and what will fail. Economic freedom permits a multitude of attempts and the failures are weeded out. Over time, what remains, in the main, is the successes and they serve to facilitate a high standard of living. Central planners can never have nearly as much knowledge as myriad individuals seeking success and learning from their failures and those of others. Second, markets offer continuous feedback on what is succeeding and failing; central planners lack such feedback. Third, economic freedom leads to the ruthless reallocation of resources to that which is succeeding; central planners often have vested interests that prevent such a reallocation. Fourth, economic freedom permits large and rapid increases in scale by financial markets and corporate organizations; central planners lack the flexibility to make large-scale changes rapidly. Finally, because of sophisticated contractual protections, individuals and corporations are willing to take great risks; central planners are risk-averse because of their personal vulnerability if things go wrong.

More generally, neo-liberalism as a theory comes in various forms, but all are undergirded by some or all of the following ideas (Antonio 2007: 67–83). Great faith is placed in the **free market** and its rationality. The market needs to be allowed to operate free of any impediments, especially those imposed by the nation-state and other political entities. The free operation of the market will in the "long run" advantage just about everyone and bring about both improved economic welfare and greater individual freedom (and a democratic political system).

> **Free market**: A market free of any impediments.

Related to the belief in the free market is a parallel belief in *free trade*. Where there are restraints on the free market and free trade, there is a commitment to **deregulation** to limit or eliminate such restraints.

> **Deregulation**: Commitment by nation-states to limit or eliminate restraints on the free market and free trade.

There is great belief in the need for the *global capitalist system to continue to expand*. It is presumed that such expansion would bring with it increased prosperity and decreased poverty.

The principles of the free market are not restricted to the economy (and the polity) but can be applied to *every* sphere of society, including culture, politics, and the social world (Norberg 2003: 17). Some go even further and argue that transactions in every sphere of life *should* be like those in the economy. The key to all those transactions is the *individual*; neo-liberalism is radically individualistic.

The Neo-Liberal State

Many of the ideas associated with the neo-liberal economy apply to the closely linked concept of the neo-liberal state (Harvey 2006: 25). The state in general is to be subordinated to the economy. In the neo-liberal state the focus is on those who gain from capital accumulation (the capitalists). In contrast, in a social democratic state the emphasis is on the well-being of all, especially through maintaining something approximating full employment.

Free markets and free trade are linked to a *democratic political system*. Thus the political system, especially the freedom of democracy, is associated with economic well-being and with the freedom of individuals to amass great individual wealth (Norberg 2003: 61).

There is a commitment to *low taxes* and to *tax cuts* (especially for the wealthy) where taxes are deemed too high and too burdensome. Low taxes and tax cuts are believed to stimulate the economy by encouraging people to earn more and ultimately to invest and to spend more.

Tax cuts for business and industry are also encouraged, with the idea that businesses would use the tax savings to invest more in their operations and infrastructure, thereby generating more business, income, and profits. This is seen as benefiting not only them, but society as a whole. Higher profits would "trickle down" and benefit most people in society.

Spending on *welfare* should be *minimized* and the *safety net* for the poor should be *minimized*. Such spending and such a welfare system are seen as hurting economic growth and even as harming the poor (Norberg 2003: 97). Cuts in welfare are designed to reduce government expenditures and thereby to allow the government to cut taxes and/or to invest in more "productive" undertakings. It is also presumed that without the safety net more poor people would be forced to find work, often at the minimum wage or with low pay. More such workers presumably allow companies to increase productivity and profits. Reduction of the safety net also creates a larger "reserve army" that business can draw on in good economic times in order to expand its workforce.

Limited government: No government can do things as well as the market and a government should not intervene in it.

There is a strong and generalized belief in **limited government**. The theory is that no government or government agency can do things as well as the market (the failure of the Soviet Union is seen as proof of that). Among other things, this leaves a government that is, at least theoretically, less able, or unable, to intervene in the market. It also presumably means a less expensive government, one that would need to collect less in taxes. This, in turn, would put more money in the hands of the public, especially the wealthier members of society who, in recent years, have benefited most from tax cuts. Wolf (2005: xvii) argues that the state must not only be limited, but its job is to cooperate with open global markets.

The neo-liberal state is very interested in privatizing various sectors (e.g. "transportation, telecommunications, oil and other natural resources, utilities, social housing, education" [Harvey 2006: 25]) in order to open up these areas for business and profit-making. It seeks to be sure that those sectors that cannot be privatized are "cost effective" and "accountable."

It works to allow the free movement of capital among and between economic sectors and geographic regions within the borders of a given nation-state. The neo-liberal state also works hard to reduce barriers to the free movement of capital across national borders and to the creation of new global markets.

The neo-liberal state extols the virtues of free competition. And it is opposed to, and works against, groups (e.g. unions, social movements) that operate to restrain business interests and their efforts to accumulate capital.

In sum, contrary to many observers, Harvey (2006: 28) argues that "neo-liberalism has not made the state or particular institutions of the state (such as the courts) irrelevant." Rather, the institutions and practices of the state have been transformed to better attune them to the needs and interests of the neo-liberal market and economy.

Critiquing Neo-Liberalism: Karl Polanyi

Much of the contemporary critique of neo-liberalism, especially as it relates to economics, is traceable to the work of Karl Polanyi, especially his 1944 book, *The*

Great Transformation: The Political and Economic Origins of Our Time. He is the great critic of a limited focus on the economy, especially the focus of economic liberalism on the self-regulating, or unregulated, market, as well as on basing all on self-interest. In his view, these are not universal principles, but rather were unprecedented developments associated with the advent of capitalism.

Polanyi (1944) shows that the laissez-faire system came into existence with the help of the state and it was able to continue to function as a result of state actions. Furthermore, if the laissez-faire system was left to itself, it threatened to destroy society. Indeed, it was such threats, as well as real dangers, that led to counter-reactions by society and the state (e.g. socialism, communism, the New Deal) to protect themselves from the problems of a free market, especially protection of the products of that market, and those who labored in it (Munck 2002: 10–21). The expansion of the laissez-faire market and the reaction against it is called the **double movement** (Hall 2007: 338–40).

> **Double movement**: Coexistence of the expansion of the laissez-faire market and the reaction against it.

While economic liberalism saw such counter-reactions (including any form of protectionism) as "mistakes" that disrupted the operation of the economic markets, Polanyi saw them as necessary and desirable reactions to the evils of the free market. Presciently, Polanyi (1944: 145) pointed to "the inherent absurdity of the idea of a self-regulating market." He also described as mythical the liberal idea that socialists, communists, New Dealers, and so on were involved in a conspiracy against liberalism and the free market. Rather than being a conspiracy, what took place was a natural, a "spontaneous," collective reaction by society and its various elements that were threatened by the free market.

In his time, Polanyi (1944: 251) sees a reversal of the tendency for the economic system to dominate society: "Within the nations we are witnessing a development under which the economic system ceases to lay down the law to society and the primacy of society over that system is secured." This promised to end the evils produced by the dominance of the free-market system, and also to produce *more*, rather than less, freedom. That is, Polanyi believed that collective planning and control would produce more freedom, more freedom for all, than was then available in the liberal economic system.

It is interesting to look back on Polanyi's ideas with the passage of more than 60 years and especially with the rise of a global economy dominated by the kind of free market system he so feared and despised. Polanyi's hope lay with society and the nation-state, but they have been rendered far less powerful with the rise of globalization, especially the global economy. Very telling here is Margaret Thatcher's (in)famous statement: "there is no such thing as society." Without powerful social and political influences, one wonders where collective planning and social control over the market are to come from. Clearly, such planning and control are more inadequate than ever in the global age. Beyond that, one wonders whether the creation of truly global planning and control is either possible or desirable. Nevertheless, it is likely that were he alive today, the logic of Polanyi's position would lead him to favor global planning and control because of his great fears of a free-market economy, now far more powerful and dangerous because it exists on a global scale.

Contemporary Criticisms of Neo-Liberalism

Among the problems with neo-liberalism as a theory is the fact that it assumes that everyone in the world wants very narrow and specific types of economic well-being (to be well-off economically, if not rich) and political freedom (democracy). There are great cultural differences in the ways in which well-being (to not have to work very hard) and freedom (to be unfettered by the state even if it is not democratically chosen) are defined. Neo-liberalism very often comes down to the North, the US, and/or global organizations (e.g. the IMF) seeking to impose *their* definitions of well-being and freedom on other parts of the world. Furthermore, there is great variation on this among individuals in each of these societies, with the result that these definitions are different from at least some of theirs, but are nonetheless imposed on them.

Another problem lies in the fact that the theory conceals or obscures the social and material interests of those who push such an economic system with its associated technological, legal, and institutional systems. These are *not* being pursued because everyone in the world wants them or will benefit from them, but because *some*, usually in the North, are greatly advantaged by them and therefore push them.

Harvey offers a number of other criticisms of neo-liberalism including the fact that it produced financial crises in various countries throughout the world (e.g. Mexico, Argentina), its economic record was dismal since it redistributed wealth (from poor to rich) rather than generating new wealth, it helped to commodify virtually *everything*, it contributed to the degradation of the environment, and so on.

Naomi Klein is highly critical of the reforms associated with shock therapy including the "dismal reality of inequality, corruption and environmental degradation" (2007: 280). She touches on Joseph Schumpeter's (1976: 81–6) famous theory of creative destruction (see Chapter 4), which argues that the essence of capitalism is the need to destroy in order to create. However, she argues that in the case of neo-liberalism and the shock doctrine, this has "resulted in scarce creation and spiraling destruction" (Klein 2007: 224). She is especially critical of the central role played in all of this by the US, as well as by the global institutions over which it exercises great control.

Structural adjustment in particular has come under attack from many quarters. For example, James Ferguson (2006) has criticized its impact on Africa. Economically, he argues that it has led to inequality, marginalization, and the lowest economic growth rates ever recorded and, in some cases, even negative growth. Politically, it has led to the decline of the state, "whose presence barely extends beyond the boundaries of their capital cities. Vast areas of the continent have been effectively abandoned by their national states" (2006: 13). Corruption is widespread and, in many cases, functions that were once state-based have been privatized.

However, neo-liberalism is now open to much more general and severe criticism in the wake of the Great Recession. It is clear that neo-liberalism played a major role in spawning that recession, especially in its opposition to the regulation of financial transactions and the economy in general. The lack of restraint allowed the economy to expand without limits and then to collapse in disastrous fashion.

Finally, in relationship to the topic of this book, Harvey (2005) relates neo-liberalism to globalization in various ways. First, the scope of neo-liberalism is global in the sense that it has become an economic and political system that characterizes a wide range of societies throughout the world. However, nations have both common paths to neo-liberalism as well as basic differences that relate to their different histories and character. Second, neo-liberalism is an idea system that has flowed around the world. Third, Harvey sees various international organizations, especially the IMF, WTO, and World Bank, as dominated by neo-liberal ideas and as imposing them, in the form of various demands for restructuring, on a number of societies throughout the world. These organizations are, of course, dominated by the US which is indirectly, as well as directly and overtly (e.g. in Iraq, Afghanistan), exporting neo-liberalism throughout the globe. We can add to this the fact that opposition to neo-liberalism is also global and the reach of that opposition has grown during the Great Recession.

NEO-MARXIAN THEORIES

Neo-Marxists have done more than critique neo-liberalism, they have developed their own perspectives on, and theories of, capitalism. While neo-liberalism is supportive of capitalism, the neo-Marxists are, needless to say, critical of it. In this section we offer two examples of a neo-Marxian approach that are explicitly and implicitly critical of the neo-liberal theory outlined in this chapter.

Transnational Capitalism

Leslie Sklair distinguishes between two systems of globalization (Sklair 2002). The first – the neo-liberal capitalist system of globalization – is the one that, as we have seen, is now predominant. The other is the socialist system that is not yet in existence, but is foreshadowed by current alter-globalization movements, especially those oriented toward greater human rights throughout the world. The alter-globalization movements, and the possibility of socialism, are made possible by the problems in the current system of neo-liberal globalization, especially class polarization and the increasing ecologically unsustainable capitalist globalization.

While the nation-state remains important in his view, Sklair focuses on transnational practices that are able to cut across boundaries – including those created by nation-states – with the implication that territorial boundaries are of declining

importance in capitalist globalization. As a Marxist, Sklair accords priority to economic transnational practices and it is in this context that one of the central aspects
of his analysis – *transnational corporations* – predominates. Underlying this is the
idea that capitalism has moved away from being an inter-national system to being
a globalizing system that is decoupled from any specific geographic territory or
nation-state.

The second transnational practice of great importance is political and here the
transnational capitalist class predominates (Carroll and Carson 2003: 29–58).
However, it is not made up of capitalists in the traditional Marxian sense of the
term. That is, they (e.g. corporate executives) do not necessarily own the means of
production.

The transnational capitalist class may not be capitalist in a traditional sense,
but it is transnational in various ways. First, its "members" tend to share global
(as well as local) interests. Second, they seek to exert various types of control
across nations. That is, they exert economic control in the workplace, political
control in both domestic and international politics, and culture-ideological control
in everyday life across international borders. Third, they tend to share a global
rather than a local perspective on a wide range of issues. Fourth, they come from
many different countries, but increasingly they see themselves as citizens of the
world and not just of their place of birth. Finally, wherever they may be at any
given time, they share similar lifestyles, especially in terms of the goods and services
they consume.

The third transnational practice is culture-ideology and here Sklair accords great
importance to the *culture-ideology of consumerism* in capitalist globalization. While
the focus is on culture and ideology, this ultimately involves the economy by adding
an interest in consumption to the traditional concern with production (and the
transnational corporations) in economic approaches in general, and Marxian theories in particular. It is in this realm that the ability to exert ideological control over
people scattered widely throughout the globe increased dramatically, primarily
through the greater reach and sophistication of advertising, the media, and the
bewildering array of consumer goods that are marketed by and through them.
Ultimately, they all served to create a global desire to consume what benefits transnational corporations, as well as the advertising and media corporations that are
both examples of such corporations and that profit from them.

Ultimately, Sklair is interested in the relationship among the transnational social
practices and the institutions that dominate each by arguing that transnational
corporations utilize the transnational capitalist class to develop and solidify the
consumerist culture and ideology that grew increasingly necessary to feed the
demands of the capitalist system of production. As a Marxist, Sklair is not only
interested in critically analyzing capitalist globalization, but in articulating an alternative to it and its abuses. He is particularly interested in various human rights
movements in which, he believes, can be found the seeds of the alternative to
neo-liberal capitalist globalization, i.e., socialist globalization. He predicts that these
and other movements will gain momentum in the twenty-first century as they

increasingly resist the ways in which globalization has been appropriated by transnational corporations.

Empire

The most important and widely discussed and debated Marxian approach to globalization is Michael Hardt and Antonio Negri's *Empire* (2000) (as well as the closely associated *Multitude* [2004]). Hardt and Negri associate modernity with *imperialism* (see above), the defining characteristic of which is a nation(s) at the center that controls and exploits, especially economically, a number of areas throughout the world. They *decenter* this process thereby defining **Empire** as a postmodern reality in which such dominance exists, but *without* any single nation (or any other entity) at its center. The reality of Empire is everywhere; it is omnipresent.

> **Empire** involves global dominance without a nation-state at its center; decentered global dominance.

Empire does not yet exist fully; it is in formation at the moment, but we can already get a sense of its parameters. Empire governs the world with a single logic of rule, but there is no single power at the heart of Empire. Instead of a single source of command, power is dispersed throughout society and the globe. The sovereignty of the US is an important precursor to Empire and the US continues to occupy a privileged position in the world today. However, it is in the process of being supplanted by Empire.

Empire is lacking in (or will lack) geographic or territorial boundaries. It can also be seen as lacking temporal boundaries in the sense that it seeks (albeit unsuccessfully) to suspend history and to exist for all eternity. It also can be seen as lacking a lower boundary in that it seeks to expand downward into the depths of the social world. This means that it seeks control of the basics of the social world (thought, action, interaction, groups), and goes even further in an effort to control people's brains and their bodies. In a way, Empire is far more ambitious than imperialism in that it seeks to control the entirety of life down to its most basic level.

The key to the global power of Empire lies in the fact that it is (or seeks to be) a new juridical power. That is, it is based on the constitution of order, norms, ethical truths, a common notion of what is right, and so on. This juridical formation is the source of the power of Empire. Thus, it can, in the name of what is "right," intervene anywhere in the world in order to deal with what it considers humanitarian problems, to guarantee accords, and to impose peace on those who may not want it or even see it as peace. More specifically, it can engage in "just wars" in the name of this juridical formation; the latter legitimates the former. Such wars become a kind of sacred undertaking. The enemy is anyone or anything that the juridical formation sees as a threat to the ethical order, as it defines such an order, in the world. Thus the right to engage in just war is seen as boundless, encompassing the entire space of civilization. The right to engage in just war is also seen as boundless in time; it is permanent, eternal. In a just war, ethically grounded military action is legitimate and its goal is to achieve the desired order and peace. Thus Empire is not based on force per se, but on the ability to project force in the service of that which is right (precursors of this can be seen in the two US wars against Iraq, as well as the incursion into Afghanistan).

Empire is, then, a postmodern Marxian perspective on globalization and the exertion of power around the world. However, instead of capitalists, or capitalist nations, exerting that power, it is the much more nebulous Empire that is in control. If there are no more capitalists in Empire, what about the proletariat? To Hardt and Negri, the time of the proletariat is over. But if the proletariat no longer exists to oppose Empire, where is the opposition to it to come from? After all, operating from a Marxian perspective, Hardt and Negri must come up with an oppositional force. In fact, they do not disappoint on this score and label that oppositional group the "multitude." This is an interesting choice of term for many reasons. For one thing, it is much more general and abstract than the proletariat and also moves us away from a limited focus on the economy. Secondly, it is clear that there are lots of at least potential opponents of Empire; indeed, those in control in Empire constitute only a small minority vis-à-vis the multitude.

The *multitude* is that collection of people throughout the world that sustains Empire in various ways, including, but *not* restricted to, its labor (it is the real productive force in Empire). Among other ways, it also sustains Empire by buying into the culture-ideology of consumerism and, more importantly, in actually consuming a variety of its offerings. Like capitalism and its relationship to the proletariat, Empire is a parasite on the multitude and its creativity and productivity. Like Marx's proletariat (which all but disappears in this theory), the multitude is a force for creativity in Empire. Also like the proletariat, the multitude is capable of overthrowing Empire through the autonomous creation of a counter-Empire. The counter-Empire, like Empire, is, or would be, a global phenomenon created out of, and becoming, global flows and exchanges. Globalization leads to **deterritorialization** (and the multitude itself is a force in deterritorialization and is deterritorialized) and the latter is a prerequisite to the global liberation of the multitude. That is, with deterritorialization social revolution can, as Marx predicted, occur, perhaps for the first time, on a global level.

Deterritorialization: Declining significance of the geographic location in which culture exists.

Thus, while Hardt and Negri are certainly critics of globalization, whether it be modern neo-liberal capitalist imperialism or postmodern Empire, they also see a utopian potential in globalization. Thus, globalization per se is *not* the problem, but rather the neo-liberal form that it has taken, or takes, in imperialism and Empire. That utopian potential has always been there, but in the past it has been smothered by modern sovereign powers through ideological control or military force. Empire now occupies, or soon will, that controlling position, but its need to suppress that potential is counterbalanced by the need of the multitude to manifest and express that utopian potential. Ultimately, it is in globalization that there exists the potential for universal freedom and equality. As globalization progresses, it serves to push us more and more in the direction of the creation of counter-Empire.

While Hardt and Negri foresee counter-Empire, they, like Marx in the case of communism, offer no blueprint for how to get there or for what it might look like. Like communism to Marx, counter-Empire will arise out of actual practice (*praxis*), especially that of the multitude. Counter-Empire must be global, it must be everywhere, and it must be opposed to Empire. Counter-Empire is made increasingly likely because Empire is losing its ability to control the multitude. Thus, Empire must re-double its efforts (e.g. through police power) and this serves to mobilize the multitude and make counter-Empire more likely.

CHAPTER SUMMARY

This chapter examines several concepts and theories related to globalization – imperialism, colonialism (and post-colonialism), development (and dependency), Americanization, neo-liberalism, as well as important neo-Marxian alternatives to it.

Imperialism describes methods employed by one country to gain territorial control over another, in order to exercise political, economic, and territorial control over it. The idea of imperialism has come to be associated with rule over vast regions. This characteristic leads it to be associated with globalization. Lenin argued that economic factors are the essence of imperialism. According to this view, factors inherent in capitalism lead nations to undertake imperial ventures. Harvey makes the case for a new imperialism in the form of *capitalist imperialism* with the US as its prime representative. This form of imperialism consists of a complex and contradictory fusion of political and economic imperialism.

Colonialism involves more formal mechanisms of control over a territory, entailing the creation of an administrative apparatus to run a colony's internal affairs. The end of WW II saw a strong drive toward decolonization. Colonization was replaced by a more insidious attempt at economic control and exploitation, through *neo-colonialism*. *Post-colonialism* relates to developments in former colonies after the departure of the colonizing power.

Development as a project focused on the economic development of specific nations. The project advocated import-substitution, wherein instead of relying on imports from the North, the South was encouraged to produce its own industrial products. The North benefited greatly from this policy since this implied an increase in foreign direct investment (FDI) in the nascent industries in the South. This approach also included foreign aid and financial assistance in terms of food products.

A major critique of the development project emerged in the form of *dependency theory*. Adherents of this theory argued that instead of promoting development, in reality the development project led to the South's greater dependency on the North. Underdevelopment is not traceable to internal sources in a particular nation.

Rather, it is a product of the relationship between developed and underdeveloped countries in the capitalist system. Globalization is often criticized as a less offensive version of the development project.

Americanization is defined as the export of products, images, technologies, practices, and behavior that are closely associated with America and Americans. Discourse on the issue emerged, at least in part, as a result of concern about, and the study of, America's influence on Europe. While after WW II the US was seen as the savior (at least by some) of Europe, by the 1960s it was perceived more as a business, industrial, and economic threat to Europe. More recently, the industrial threat posed by the US was replaced by a fear of American dominance in global consumption. Apart from the economic realm, the process of Americanization is also evident in Europe, and throughout the world, in such areas as politics, law, the military, and culture. Anti-Americanism is an intense and non-homogeneous global process, comprising distinct forms, causes, and expressions.

Neo-liberalism emerged in the 1930s as a combination of the liberal commitment to individual liberty and neo-classical economics. The free operation of the market and minimal intervention by the state were the cornerstones of the theory. Under neo-liberalism, the operation of free markets is considered to be crucial. It emphasizes a commitment to deregulation of the markets. Free markets are also portrayed as being intrinsically linked to a democratic political system that facilitates individual economic well-being. Tax cuts are advocated as a mechanism to stimulate investment in the economy, which consequently demands a reduction of government expenditure, especially in terms of welfare expenditure.

Although the theory advocates "limited government," it favors state intervention to facilitate business interests and the reduction of barriers to the free movement of capital across national borders. Rather than rendering the state irrelevant, neo-liberalism has modified the functioning of the state in order to facilitate the functioning of the market.

Polanyi's critique of neo-liberalism highlights the fact that the laissez-faire system came into existence through the assistance of the state. Left to itself, that system threatens to destroy society. Free markets induce a natural collective reaction by society.

Neo-liberalism has been criticized for its narrow definition of well-being, which is equated with economic well-being. The theory also conceals the vested interests of those who push for such an economic system. Adoption of neo-liberal theory has produced severe financial crisis in various countries, and has led to increasing commodification as well as environmental degradation.

Neo-liberal theory has evoked implicit as well as explicit criticism from neo-Marxian thinkers. Sklair places emphasis on transnational practices that are able to cut across boundaries – through transnational corporations, the transnational capitalist class, and the culture-ideology of capitalism. Transnational corporations utilize the capitalist class to develop and solidify the consumerist ideology that is necessary to meet the demands of the capitalist system. Hardt and Negri critique the neo-liberal form of globalization in terms of imperialism and empire. They locate a postmodern turn in imperialism, leading to a decentering of the imperialist empire and the creation of Empire. However, they accord positive potential to the process of globalization, foreseeing a counter-Empire characterized by non-agential collective action.

DISCUSSION QUESTIONS

1. Is globalization simply another name for processes such as imperialism, colonialism, development, and Americanization? Examine the similarities and differences among these processes.

2. Trace the shifting definitions of imperialism. Is it relevant as an analytical tool for the current global age?

3. Is Americanization a relevant concept? What particular aspect of it is most relevant today?

4. What is anti-Americanism? Has it increased or declined over the years?

5. What are the positive developments that emerged from the neo-liberal perspective? Discuss the reasons for the popularity of this perspective in various academic, policy, and business spheres.

6. Examine Polanyi's critique of neo-liberalism. How does it differ from later neo-Marxist critiques implied in the work of Sklair or Hardt and Negri?

FURTHER READING

Vladimir Lenin. *Imperialism: The Highest Stage of Capitalism*. New York: International Publishers, 1917/1939.

David Harvey. *The New Imperialism*. Oxford: Oxford University Press, 2003.

Philip McMichael. *Development and Social Change: A Global Perspective*, 4th edn. Thousand Oaks, CA: Pine Forge Press, 2008.

J.-J. Servan-Schreiber. *The American Invasion*. New York: Atheneum, 1968.

Richard F. Kuisel. *Seducing the French: The Dilemma of Americanization*. Berkeley: University of California Press, 1993.

Milton Friedman. *Capitalism and Freedom*. Chicago: University of Chicago Press, 1950.

David Harvey. *A Brief History of Neoliberalism*. Oxford: Oxford University Press, 2005.

Naomi Klein. *The Shock Doctrine: The Rise of Disaster Capitalism*. New York: Metropolitan Books, 2007.

Thomas Friedman. *The World is Flat: A Brief History of the Twenty-first Century*. New York: Farrar, Straus and Giroux, 2005.

Karl Polanyi, *The Great Transformation: The Political and Economic Origins of Our Time*. Boston: Beacon Press, 1944.

Leslie Sklair. *Globalization: Capitalism and Its Alternatives*. Oxford: Oxford University Press, 2002.

Michael Hardt and Antonio Negri. *Empire*. Cambridge, MA: Harvard University Press, 2000.

NOTES

1 On the role of neo-liberalism in another Latin American country, see Babb (2001).
2 Many feel that the Washington Consensus has eroded and has long since passed its peak; see Held (2005: 95–113); Broad (2004: 129–54).

REFERENCES

Antonio, Robert J. 2007. "The Cultural Construction of Neoliberal Globalization." In George Ritzer, ed., *The Blackwell Companion to Globalization*. Malden, MA: Blackwell.

Ashcroft, Bill, Gareth Griffiths, and Helen Tiffin. 1998. *Post-Colonial Studies: The Key Concepts*. New York: Routledge.

Bhambra, Gurminder K. 2007. "Sociology and Postcolonialism: Another 'Missing' Revolution?" *Sociology* 41, 5.

Broad, Robin. 2004. "The Washington Consensus Meets the Global Backlash: Shifting Debates and Policies." *Globalizations* 1, 2.

Bryman, Alan. 2004. *The Disneyization of Society*. London: Sage.

Campbell, John L., and Ove K. Pederson, eds. 2001. *The Rise of Neoliberalism and Institutional Analysis*. Princeton: Princeton University Press.

Cardoso, F. H., and E. Faletto. 1979. *Dependency and Development in Latin America*. Berkeley, CA: University of California Press.

Carroll, W. K., and C. Carson. 2003. "The Network of Global Corporations and Elite Policy Groups: A Structure for Transnational Capitalist Class Formation?" *Global Networks* 3, 1.

Cavanagh, John, and Robin Broad. 2007. "Washington Consensus." In Jan Aart Scholte and Roland Robertson, eds., *Encyclopedia of Globalization*. New York: MTM Publishing.

Collier, Paul. 2007. *The Bottom Billion: Why the Poorest Countries Are Failing and What Can Be Done About It*. New York: Oxford University Press.

Dallek, Robert. 2007. *Nixon and Kissinger: Partners in Power*. New York: Harper Perennial.

Duhamel, Georges. 1931. *America the Menace: Scenes from the Life of the Future*. Boston: Houghton Mifflin.

Easterly, William. 2006. "Chapter 2: Freedom versus Collectivism in Foreign Aid." *Economic Freedom of the World: 2006 Annual Report*.

Elger, Tony, and Chris Smith. 1994. *Global Japanization: The Transnational Transformation of the Labor Process*. London: Routledge.

Ferguson, James. 2006. *Global Shadows: Africa in the Neoliberal World*. Durham, NC: Duke University Press.

Fourcade-Gourinchas, Marion, and Sarah Babb. 2002. "The Rebirth of the Liberal Creed: Paths to Neoliberalism in Four Countries." *American Journal of Sociology* 108, 3.

Frank, Andre Gunder. 1969. "The Development of Underdevelopment." *Monthly Review* 18, 4.

Friedman, Milton. 2002. *Capitalism and Freedom*. Chicago: University of Chicago Press.

Gibbon, Edward. 1998. *The History of the Decline and Fall of the Roman Empire*. London: Wordsworth.

Goodman, Douglas. 2007. "Globalization and Consumer Culture." In George Ritzer, ed., *The Blackwell Companion to Globalization*. Malden, MA: Blackwell.

Goodman, Peter S. 2008. "A Fresh Look at the Apostle of Free Markets." *New York Times*. April 13.

Grimal, H. 1878. *Decolonization*. London: Routledge.

Hall, Derek. 2007. "Double Movement." In Jan Aart Scholte and Roland Robertson, eds., *Encyclopedia of Globalization*. New York: MTM Publishing.

Hardt, Michael, and Antonio Negri. 2000. *Empire*. Cambridge, MA: Harvard University Press.

Hardt, Michael, and Antonio Negri. 2004. *Multitude*. New York: Penguin.

Harvey, David. 2003. *The New Imperialism*. Oxford: Oxford University Press.

Harvey, David. 2005. *A Brief History of Neoliberalism*. Oxford: Oxford University Press.

Harvey, David. 2006. *Spaces of Global Capitalism: Towards a Theory of Uneven Geographical Development*. London: Verso.

Held, David. 2005. "At the Global Crossroads: The End of the Washington Consensus and the Rise of Global Social Democracy?" *Globalizations* 2, 1.

Hobson, J. A. 1902/1905/1938. *Imperialism: An Empirical Study*. London: George Allen and Unwin Limited.

Hollander, Paul. 1992. *Anti-Americanism: Critiques at Home and Abroad, 1965–1990*. New York: Oxford University Press.

Huntington, Samuel P. 1996. *The Clash of Civilizations and the Remaking of the World Order*. New York: Simon and Schuster.

Kissinger, Henry. 1999. "Globalization and World Order." Independent Newspapers Annual Lecture. Dublin: Trinity College, October 12.

Klein, Naomi. 2007. *The Shock Doctrine: The Rise of Disaster Capitalism*. New York: Metropolitan Books.

Kuisel, Richard F. 1993. *Seducing the French: The Dilemma of Americanization*. Berkeley, CA: University of California Press.

Lenin, Vladimir. 1917/1939. *Imperialism: The Highest Stage of Capitalism*. New York: International Publishers.

Markoff, John. 2007. "Imperialism." In Jan Aart Scholte and Roland Robertson, eds., *Encyclopedia of Globalization*. New York: MTM Publishing.

McMichael, Philip. 2008. *Development and Social Change: A Global Perspective*, 4th edn. Thousand Oaks, CA: Pine Forge Press.

Munck, Ronaldo. 2002. "Globalization and Democracy: A New Great Transformation." *Annals* 581 (May).

Nkrumah, Kwame. 1965. *Neo-Colonialism: The Last Stage of Imperialism*. Atlantic Islands, NJ: Humanities Press International.

Norberg, Johan. 2003. *In Defense of Global Capitalism*. Washington, DC: Cato Institute.

O'Connor, Brendon. 2007. "What is Anti-Americanism?" In Brendon O'Connor, ed., *Anti-Americanism: History, Causes, and Themes*, Vol. 1: *Causes and Sources*. Oxford: Greenwood World Publishing.

Plehwe, Dieter. 2007. "A Global Knowledge Bank? The World Bank and Bottom-Up Efforts to Reinforce Neoliberal Development Perspectives in the Post-Washington Consensus Era." *Globalizations* 4, 4.

Polanyi, Karl. 1944. *The Great Transformation: The Political and Economic Origins of Our Time*. Boston: Beacon Press.

Ritzer, George. 1995. *Expressing America: A Critique of the Global Credit Card Society*. Thousand Oaks, CA: Pine Forge Press.

Ritzer, George. 1999/2005. *Enchanting a Disenchanted World: Revolutionizing the Means of Consumption*. Thousand Oaks, CA: Pine Forge Press.

Ritzer, George. 2008. *The McDonaldization of Society*, 5th edn. Thousand Oaks, CA: Pine Forge Press.

Said, Edward W. 1979/1994. *Orientalism*. New York: Vintage Books.

Schumpeter, Joseph A. 1976. *Capitalism, Socialism and Democracy*. 5th edn. London: George Allen and Unwin.

Serra, Narcís, and Joseph E. Stiglitz, eds. 2008. *The Washington Consensus Reconsidered: Towards a New Global Governance*. New York: Oxford University Press.

Servan-Schreiber, J.-J. 1968. *The American Challenge*. New York: Atheneum.

Simon, Bryant. 2009. *Everything but the Coffee: Learning about America from Starbucks*. Berkeley, CA: University of California Press.

Singh, Robert. 2006. "Are We All Americans Now? Explaining Anti-Americanisms." In Brendan O'Connor and Martin Griffiths, eds., *The Rise of Anti-Americanism*. New York: Routledge.

Sklair, Leslie. 2002. *Globalization: Capitalism and Its Alternatives*. Oxford: Oxford University Press.

Soderquist, Don. 2005. *The Wal-Mart Way: The Inside Story of the Success of the World's Largest Company*. Nashville, TN: Thomas Nelson.

Stone, Brad. 2008. "The Empire of Excess." *New York Times*. July 4.

Turner, Rachel S., and Andrew Gamble. 2007. "Neoliberalism." In Jan Aart Scholte and Roland Robertson, eds., *Encyclopedia of Globalization*. New York: MTM Publishing.

Wallerstein, Immanuel. 1974. *The Modern World-System: Capitalist Agriculture and the Origins of the European World-Economy in the 16th Century*. New York: Academic Press.

Williams, Patrick, and Laura Chrisman. 1994. *Colonial Discourse and Post-Colonial Theory: A Reader*. New York: Columbia University Press.

Williamson, John. 1990a. *The Progress of Policy Reform in Latin America*. Policy Analysis in International Economics, No. 28. Washington, DC: Institute of International Economics.

Williamson, John. 1990b. "What Washington Means by Policy Reform." In John Williamson, ed., *Latin American Adjustment: How Much Has Happened?* Washington, DC: Institute for Internal Economics.

Williamson, John. 1993. "Democracy and the 'Washington Consensus'." *World Development* 21.

Wolf, Martin. 2005. *Why Globalization Works*. New Haven: Yale University Press.

Structuring the Global Economy

Globalization: The Essentials, by George Ritzer
© 2011 John Wiley & Sons Ltd

Because of the importance of the economy in globalization, we devote two chapters to it. In this chapter the focus is on economic structures, while in the next the focus shifts to economic processes and flows. However, it is useful to reiterate the point that this is a largely artificial distinction since structures are composed of processes and processes can be structured.

In order to understand the major economic structures involved in globalization today one must have a sense of their place in economic history (Frieden 2006; Hirst and Thompson 1999).

BEFORE BRETTON WOODS

A Prior Epoch of Globalization

One important view is that a global economic system, specifically a global capitalist system, emerged in about 1896 and reached something of a peak throughout the world by 1914.[1] There are some interesting analogies between the growth of the global capitalist economy during that period and today:[2]

- During the earlier epoch global progress was spurred by developments in transportation such as the railroad and the steam ship, whereas in more recent years it has been the airplane that has played a central role in global development.
- The telegraph greatly enhanced global communications in the early twentieth century, while it is the Internet that plays that role nearly a century later.
- Global economic development, both then and now, depended on large-scale flows of capital.
- In addition, such development in both periods entailed large-scale immigration and even the growing importance of **remittances** to those who remained in the homeland (for a discussion of remittances today see Chapter 11).
- More generally, global economic specialization (Smith 1776/1977) among the nations of the world became the norm, then and now.
- Furthermore, this specialization operated on the basis of the "law" of

> **Remittances**: Transactions by which migrants send money back to their country of origin.

comparative advantage (Ricardo 1817/1971); that is, that nations should concentrate on what they do best. This comparison is internal – that is, a nation should concentrate on what it does best in comparison to the other things *it* does (or could do) and *not* in comparison to what other nations do.
- This is related to another similarity between today and a century ago and that is an emphasis on free trade and the elimination of trade barriers (e.g. tariffs).[3]

Not only are there structural similarities between global economic development in the two periods, but the problems created in the two epochs are also similar. First, poor nations and the peoples who inhabit them were and are subjugated by the operations of the global economy. Second, not all parts of the world (e.g. traditional economies) gain(ed) (or gain[ed] equally) from the growth of the global economy. There were/are even sub-areas within those parts of the world that did advance that did/do not share equally in the gain. Third, not only were/are there losers in this economic competition among geographic areas, but also certain industries and social classes lose out, at least in comparison to the winners. Fourth, within nations the poor tend(ed) to suffer most when those nations are forced to repay their debts to other, more developed, nations. In sum, the global economy of a century ago (and much the same could be said today) "was not equally good for everyone and was bad for many" (Frieden 2006: 26).

While a strong case can be made for a prior epoch of economic globalization, what is not recognized in this argument – and what is central to this book – is that there is far more to globalization than that which relates to the economy. For example, Jeffry Frieden mentions the global spread of the English language and of soccer/football, but he fails to accord such cultural phenomena the importance they deserve. Further, while Frieden devotes more attention to political issues, they are usually part of, or subordinated to, economics and economic globalization. Thus, he (along with many others) fails to give political and cultural globalization their proper role in his overall perspective on globalization. The cultural and the political are just two of the aspects of globalization given short shrift, or ignored, by Frieden. Thus, even if we accept his argument (shared by others) that economic globalization is not new, this argument tells us little or nothing about these other aspects of globalization. Nonetheless, the argument about a prior epoch of economic globalization is very useful in terms of the discussion to follow on the emergence of more recent global economic structures.

Economic Development during and after WW II

Frieden sees the development of economic globalization after WW II in the context of this prior epoch of economic globalization, as well as its collapse as a result of WW I, the Depression, and WW II. All of these events had negative effects on almost all major economies (the US economy was a major exception, at least in terms of the effect of the two world wars). Of particular importance in the 1930s was the movement of many countries – notably fascist Italy and Germany – in the direction of **autarky**, or the turn inward of a nation in order to create as much economic self-sufficiency as possible. Such a turn inward is, of course, anathema to globalization which requires that various entities – including nation-states – be outward-looking, rather than inward-looking, not only in the way they view the world but in their actual dealings with other parts of the world. For its part, the US in the 1930s had a strong tendency toward *isolationism*,[4] although such an orientation was not quite as antithetical to economic globalization as autarky, largely because it was more political than economic.

> **Autarky**: The turn inward of a nation-state in order to become as economically self-sufficient as possible.

However, even in the midst of WW II, the Western world, especially the US and Great Britain, began planning for a more open international economy. A great fear was the recurrence of the Depression after the end of WW II, especially because of the difficulties those societies would have in absorbing the massive manpower created by the demobilization of the military when the war ended. There was also fear of a resurrection of barriers to trade and the free flow of money that had become commonplace prior to WW II. The focus of the planners was on reducing trade barriers and on creating conditions necessary for the free flow of money and investment. Another concern was the creation of conditions needed for financial stability around the globe. This was the background for a meeting in July 1944 at the Mount Washington Hotel in Bretton Woods, New Hampshire, which led to the beginning of the "Bretton Woods System" by the end of the three-week meeting.

BRETTON WOODS AND THE BRETTON WOODS SYSTEM

A key factor in the Depression was thought to be a lack of cooperation among nation-states. That lack of cooperation was associated with high tariffs and other import restrictions and protectionist practices, as well as the propensity of governments to devalue their currencies in order to gain an edge in global trade over other countries. The latter also made exchange rate wars among the nations involved more likely.

Those concerns were the backdrop for the creation of the Bretton Woods system and its five key elements (Bordo and Eichengreen 1993; Boughton 2007: 106–7). First, each participating state would establish a "'par value' for its currency expressed in terms of gold or (equivalently) in terms of the gold value of the US dollar as of July 1944" (Boughton 2007: 106). For example, the US pegged its currency at $35 per ounce of gold, while, to take one example, the figure for Nicaragua was 175 cordobas per ounce. This meant that the exchange rate between the two currencies was five cordobas for one dollar.

"Second, the official monetary authority in each country (a central bank or its equivalent) would agree to exchange its own currency for those of other countries at the established exchange rates, plus or minus a one-percent margin" (Boughton 2007: 106–7). This made international trade possible at or near the exchange rate for the currencies of the countries involved without the need for any outside intervention.

Third, the International Monetary Fund (IMF) was created (Babb 2007: 128–64) (as was the forerunner of the World Bank – see below) to establish, stabilize, and oversee exchange rates. Forty states became IMF members in 1946 and were required to deposit some of their gold reserves with the IMF. The IMF was empowered to approve the par values of currencies and member states could not change that value by more than 10 percent. If a currency was destabilized, the IMF was prepared to lend member states the money needed to stabilize their currency.

Fourth, the member states agreed to eliminate, at least eventually, "all restrictions on the use of its currency for international trade" (Boughton 2007: 107).

Finally, the entire system was based on the US dollar (at the end of WW II the US had about three-fourths of the world's gold supply and accounted for over one-fifth of world exports). The US agreed to make the dollar convertible into other currencies or gold at the fixed par value. The dollar became, in effect, a global currency. Of course, as the Bretton Woods system came into existence and had a chance to develop, it changed dramatically over time.

Bretton Woods had its most powerful effects on global trade, the global monetary order, and global investment (Peet 2003).

In terms of *global trade*, a key was the idea of the "unconditional most-favored-nation" which "required governments to offer the same trade concessions [reductions in trade barriers, non-discrimination against a nation's products] to all" (Frieden 2006: 288). Restrictions on international trade were reduced over the years through various meetings ("rounds") under the auspices of GATT (General Agreement on Tariffs and Trade) and later the WTO (see below).

In terms of the *monetary order*, it was the IMF that took center stage. The goal was to provide security, as well as flexibility, to the monetary order. What emerged between 1958 and 1971 was a system in which the US could not change the value of its dollar, while all other countries could, but as infrequently as possible. This made exchange rates stable enough to encourage international trade and investment which otherwise would have been discouraged by dramatic fluctuations in rates.

In terms of *global investment*, a key role was envisioned for the World Bank, but massive US aid through the Marshall Plan, and rapid European post-war recovery, made its work in that period of much less significance than had been anticipated. A key development in terms of investment involved MNCs, especially American-based firms in fields like automobiles and computers, constructing their own plants and/or investing in indigenous companies in other countries. This kind of investment took center stage because the industries involved required very large, often global, organizations in order to function effectively. In addition, this kind of investment made it possible to get around trade barriers by opening plants within the countries with such barriers.

The global openness encouraged by Bretton Woods also contributed to the emergence or expansion of social welfare programs, indeed the welfare state, in many countries. Welfare states sought to deal with various problems – recession, layoffs, reductions in wages, and bankruptcies of uncompetitive firms. The creation of a social safety net within a given country served to protect it and its citizens from these problems, at least to some degree. In the process, it gave a nation and its entrepreneurs the cover they needed to be actively involved in the global marketplace.

The combination of all of these aspects and dimensions of Bretton Woods satisfied many different nations and constituencies (e.g. capital and labor) and in the process "oversaw the most rapid rates of economic growth and most enduring economic stability in modern history" (Frieden 2006: 300).

Given this brief background on Bretton Woods, let us now look in more detail at some of the economic organizations spawned by it either directly or indirectly.

General Agreement on Tariffs and Trade (GATT)

GATT was a system for the liberalization of trade that grew out of Bretton Woods and came into existence in 1947 (Hudec 1975). It operated until 1995 when it was superseded by the World Trade Organization (WTO) (see below). While GATT focused on trade in goods, the WTO also took on responsibility for the increasingly important trade in services. While GATT was simply a forum for the meeting of representatives of countries, the WTO is an independent organization.

GATT was deemed more acceptable than the International Trade Organization (ITO) by the US (and others) and in 1947 a number of initial trade agreements were negotiated by 23 nations. Since then, multinational trade agreements have been negotiated under GATT's (and later the WTO's) institutional umbrella. Over the years a number of "rounds" of negotiation were completed (e.g. the Kennedy Round ending in 1967; the Tokyo Round which concluded in 1979). It was out of the Uruguay Round (1986–93) that an agreement was reached to create the WTO. While GATT has been superseded by the WTO, many of its elements were incorporated into the WTO, although they continue to change and evolve as a result of changing global economic realities. Negotiations on trade have continued under the auspices of the WTO and as of this writing the highly disputatious Doha Round has just ended in failure. Over the years, WTO negotiations have dealt with such issues as reducing tariffs on the trading of goods, dealing with non-tariff barriers (e.g. quotas, national subsidies to industry and agriculture), and liberalizing international trade in agriculture.

More recently, attention has shifted to such issues as "international trade in services, trade-related international property rights (TRIPS), and trade-related investment measures (TRIMS)" (House 2007: 477–9).

Trade-Related Aspects of Intellectual Property Rights (TRIPS): WTO agreement to protect the interests of those that create ideas.

Trade-Related Aspects of Intellectual Property Rights (TRIPS) (Correa 2000) was negotiated through the WTO, as a result of the 1986–94 Uruguay Round of negotiations. This involves intangible ideas, knowledge, and expressions that require their use to be approved by their owner. Involved here is a wide range of intellectual property, such as movies, books, music recordings, and computer software, which exists, or whose value lies, largely in the realm of ideas. There are other, more material products, such as pharmaceuticals and advanced technologies, that are also viewed as having a significant intellectual component.

Trade-Related Investment Measures (TRIMs): WTO agreement on trade measures governments can impose on foreign firms.

Trade-Related Investment Measures (TRIMs) "are a range of operating or performance measures that host-country governments impose on foreign firms to keep them from having a distorting effect on trade in goods and services" (Grimwade 2007: 1178). There are a number of specific restrictions and constraints on foreign firms that can be included under this heading, including requirements for minimum amounts of local content or sourcing, how much of a foreign producer's output must be exported, and limits on the value of goods imported by a foreign firm in relation to the amount it exports, and so on (Grimwade 2007: 1178–80).

World Trade Organization (WTO)

The WTO is a multilateral organization headquartered in Geneva, Switzerland, with, as of 2008, 152 member nations (Krueger 2000; Trachtman 2007: 1308–15). Its focus on trade places it at the heart of economic globalization and has made it a magnet for those opposed either to the broader process of trade liberalization and promotion or to some specific aspect of WTO operations. The WTO encompasses much of what was GATT's mandate, but has moved onto other issues and areas such as services (General Agreement on Trade in Services [GATS] [Koivusalo 2007: 479–81]), intellectual property (TRIPS), and so on.

Each member state in the WTO has an equal vote. To a large extent, the WTO is the organization of these member states and not (with some exceptions) a supra-national organization. Agenda items to be voted on generally flow from a number of more informal groups.

There are stresses and strains between developed and developing nations in the WTO that are manifest in and between these groups, as well as in the WTO as a whole. One bone of contention has been meetings of the larger trading powers in the so-called "Green Room" and the exclusion of smaller powers from these meetings. Protests over such matters have led to greater transparency in the internal operations of the WTO (and elsewhere). There is also no mechanism for involvement of inter-national non-governmental organizations (INGOs) in WTO decision-making and this has led INGOs to stage regular protests and demonstrations against the WTO.

While GATT focused on tariff reduction, the WTO has come to focus more on non-tariff-related barriers to trade. One example is differences between nations in relation to regulations on such items as manufactured goods or food. A given nation can be taken to task for such regulations if they are deemed to be an unfair restraint on the trade in such items. However, the WTO has been criticized for not going far enough in countering the trade barriers retained by developed countries in such domains as agricultural products and some services.

Of course, the WTO continues to be concerned with tariff barriers, as well as restrictions on trade in services. The WTO also deals with other types of protection-ism. Overall, WTO operations are premised on the neo-liberal idea that all nations benefit from free and open trade, and it is dedicated to reducing, and ultimately eliminating, barriers to such trade. While there are winners under such a system, there are also losers.

International Monetary Fund (IMF)

The goal of the IMF is macroeconomic stability for both member nations and, more generally, the global economy (Cardim de Carvalho 2007: 658–63). More specifically, the IMF deals with exchange rates, balances of payments, international capital flows, and the monitoring of member states and their macroeconomic policies. The IMF is a lightning rod for critics who see it as supporting developed countries and their efforts to impose their policies on less developed countries. Its supporters see it as key to the emergence and further development of the global economy.

As a result of changes in the global economy, the nature and functions of the IMF have changed since its creation in 1944. In the beginning it managed the exchange rate system created at Bretton Woods. The IMF closely watched a nation's balance of payments in order to be sure it could sustain the agreed-upon exchange rate for its currency. If there were problems in the latter, the IMF concerned itself with two matters. The first was policy errors by a nation which, presumably, could be corrected. The second was more fundamental economic problems (relating, for example, to productivity). Above all, the IMF wanted to be sure that a nation did not use such problems as an excuse to lower its exchange rate and therefore improve its competitive position vis-à-vis other nations. If a fundamental disequilibrium occurred, the IMF had the power to authorize a change in the exchange rate of a nation's currency.

The IMF could also give adjustment loans to nations (initially, largely developed countries) in disequilibrium so that they were able to meet their international financial obligations. The fund was created on the basis of quotas for member nations. The quota for each nation was related to the limits on its borrowing (should it become necessary), as well as its voting power in the IMF.

When the fixed, albeit adjustable, exchange-rate system collapsed in the early 1970s, the first of the IMF's functions changed so that it was in charge of the much more amorphous goal of seeking stable exchange rates in order to prevent exchange rate wars among its member nations. By the end of the 1970s developed nations had fully recovered from WW II and ceased seeking adjustment loans; such loans were now given to developing countries with balance-of-payments problems. With a new clientele, the conditions for such loans changed and became more stringent, including the demand for structural adjustments in such nations.[5] Among such adjustments were demands for a tight monetary policy and fiscal austerity. More specifically, the IMF might demand "currency devaluation, measures to reduce government spending or (more rarely) increase taxation, deregulation of interest rates and of foreign exchange transactions, slower expansion of domestic credit creation, and measures to manage and reduce external indebtedness" (Killick 2007: 1095). This policy was traceable to a growing belief that balance-of-payments imbalances were caused by inflationary policies and processes (i.e., "loose" monetary policy, expansionist fiscal policies) in a given nation. Structural adjustments were designed to rein in such tendencies toward inflation and became conditions ("conditionalities") of help from the IMF. A nation receiving help agreed to alter its policies in order achieve a balance of payments in a short period of time (usually a year).

As the IMF became the lender of last resort for developing countries in the late 1970s and 1980s, it underwent further changes. Such countries were unlikely to be able to achieve a balance of payments in a short period of time. Thus, longer-term structural adjustment programs were required. The IMF adopted general models of the requirements for the operation of a market economy and these tended to be imposed on developing economies without regard for differences among and between their economies. These structural adjustments not only took the IMF into uncharted waters and new directions, but they also became highly controversial and ultimately a target of groups opposed to globalization, at least as it was conceived and practiced by the IMF.

Such protests were also related to the IMF governance structure which is dominated by the US (with about 17 percent of the total IMF vote and veto power over any strategic decision); developed nations control more than 50 percent of the votes. (Votes are a function of a fixed number for each nation *plus* additional voting power based on each nation's quota of contributions to the Fund.) The managing director of the IMF usually comes from Western Europe; the deputy managing director from the US. In order to cope with criticisms of this structure, the IMF has been moving in the direction of greater transparency in its dealings with member nations, dealing more with NGOs, and being more concerned with social issues (e.g. poverty) in its dealings with developing nations.

The changing nature of global economic crises in the late twentieth century led to further changes in the IMF. It shifted from an interest in balance-of-payments issues that were related to current (trade and income) accounts to capital account movements of financial assets. This led to the creation of a Capital Markets Department to monitor financial markets and to suggest ways of stabilizing them.

In the 1990s the IMF was actively involved in helping to resolve the economic crises in Latin America, Asia, and Russia. It loaned large amounts of money, but as the countries involved repaid their loans, income to the IMF declined and by 2007, with interest income declining, it found itself running a deficit (about $400 million a year). It cut 380 members of its staff (it employed about 4,000 people in 2007) and saved a considerable amount of money as a result (*Economist* 2008: February 7). There was even some talk that it would need to sell its gold bullion reserves (about $70 billion). A new managing director (Dominique Strauss-Kahn) from France took office in October, 2007. He indicated that the very existence of the IMF might be in jeopardy.

The IMF increasingly seemed marginal or irrelevant. It had about $300 billion in reserves and credit lines, but it confronted a global economy where trillions of dollars flowed throughout the world every day. In light of its increasingly marginal economic position, the IMF began to focus on other issues such as working to "prevent crises, monitoring the global economy and providing technical assistance" (Weisman 2007b: C1). Others thought it should focus on data gathering and the dissemination of financial information in order to forestall economic surprises.

The IMF faced other problems such as protests from the rest of the world over the continuing dominance of the IMF by the Western powers (in addition to the new IMF director from France, the new [in 2007] World Bank director – Robert B. Zoellick – was, as has been the tradition, from the US). Further, the countries bailed out in the 1990s had become powerful economically and increasingly resented being dictated to by the Fund. There were also lingering resentments over IMF interventions that demanded austere budgets and other fiscal tightening in exchange for loans. As the Russian IMF representative described it, the resentment was over the traditional approach of the IMF – "you need our money, we tell you what to do" (Weisman 2007b: C5).

However, the Great Recession brought about a dramatic change in the fortunes of the IMF. A number of economies were on the brink of disaster (Iceland, for example), or close to it (Hungary, Ukraine), and they gladly accepted funds from the IMF (*Economist* 2008: October 23). Even healthy economies (Brazil, South Korea) were receiving economic help from the IMF (Landler 2008). The long decline of the IMF was at an end, at least for the time being, and there were calls, even from former critics, for a massive increase in the lending capacity of the IMF to help deal with the global economic meltdown (*Economist* 2009: February 5).

World Bank

The World Bank (officially the International Bank for Reconstruction and Development [IBRD]), a specialized agency of the UN, is the most important element of the World Bank Group (WBG) (Gilbert and Vines 2000; Bradlow 2007: 1262–7). The IBRD (or the Bank) was established in 1944 at Bretton Woods and began operations in 1946. Membership is open to all member states of the IMF and as of this writing it includes 184 nations. It provides funds to government-sponsored or -guaranteed programs in so-called Part II countries (member states that are middle-income or creditworthy poorer nations). It also provides advice and analytical services to such states. Among the missions of the Bank are:

- encouraging "development of productive facilities and resources in less developed countries";
- funding for "productive purposes" when private capital cannot be obtained on reasonable terms;
- encouraging international investment in order to promote international trade and development and equilibrium in balance of payments;
- helping member countries improve their productivity, standard of living, and labor conditions (Bradlow 2007: 1264).

Over the years the Bank has expanded far beyond its original focus on projects involving physical infrastructure (e.g. transportation, telecommunication, water projects, etc.) capable of generating income. It now deals with a broad range of issues related to economic development including "population, education, health, social security, environment, culture… aspects of macroeconomic policy and structural reform … [and] poverty alleviation" (Bradlow 2007: 1265). In addition, it now makes loans to deal with a variety of governance matters such as "public-sector management, corruption, legal and judicial reform, and some aspects of human rights and broader policy reforms" (Bradlow 2007: 1265). Support is also given to help women deal with gender inequality and discrimination. The Bank continues to expand its range of concerns and activities (e.g. most recently, child labor, reconstruction after a conflict, etc.). NGOs and affected peoples have grown increasingly involved in projects financed by the Bank.

Decisions are supposed to be made on purely economic, not political, grounds and the Bank is not supposed to intervene in the political affairs of member states. However, exactly what is deemed political is not defined and it is often difficult to ascertain whether, and to what degree, political considerations have been involved in Bank decisions.

All of the member states have a say in the WBG, but a state's number of votes varies depending on its size and its importance in the world economy. Each member state appoints a governor to the Board of Governors which meets once a year. There is also a 24-member Board of Executive Directors empowered to handle the most important functions (e.g. financing operations, budget) of the larger and more unwieldy Board of Governors. The president of the Bank is chief of the Bank's operating staff. The president is officially appointed to a five-year renewable term by the Board, but by tradition the president is appointed by the President of the United States. This was much in the news in 2007 when the then-president of the Bank, Paul Wolfowitz (a prominent neo-conservative and neo-liberal; see Chapter 5), a close advisor to President George W. Bush who had nominated him to the post, was forced by the Board to resign.[6]

The resources of the Bank include both a relatively small sum paid in by member countries and a much larger amount that can be called in by the Bank if it finds it needs the money. The Bank uses its potential access to the latter to issue highly rated bonds and in this way raises about $25 billion per year. It is this money that provides the bulk of the funds that it uses to finance loans of various sorts. Countries that receive the loans benefit from the fact that the Bank offers low interest rates. Since its money is borrowed, the Bank depends on the ability of nations to which it has loaned money to pay back those loans. Its lending decisions are based on a given country's ability to repay loans.

Over the years, especially since the 1980s, the operations of the Bank have become increasingly controversial. First, the Bank is seen as dominated by rich developed nations, and less developed countries and non-states (e.g. NGOs) have little say in it. Second, there are concerns that the Bank serves certain interests (e.g. the nation-state, international capital, and wealthy nations) and thereby adversely affects those of others (especially the poor and less developed nations). Third, as a result of its expanded mandate described above, the Bank is seen as having lost focus and encroaching on the activities of other agencies (thereby weakening them).

In late 2007, a controversy arose over the Bank's annual World Development Report, this one devoted to agriculture. Given its mandate to use funds from rich nations to reduce poverty in poor ones, the report was a shocker since it showed that the Bank had long neglected agriculture in sub-Saharan Africa. This neglect occurred in spite of the fact that sub-Saharan Africa is one of the poorest regions in the world and one that is almost totally dependent on agriculture. In fact, in the 1980s and 1990s the Bank had helped push the public sector in sub-Saharan Africa – which was seen as inefficient and dominated by poor management practices – out of agriculture on the neo-liberal assumption that agriculture would improve if privatization and market forces (e.g. through the de-control of prices) were allowed to operate. However, the private sector has not filled the void and this has had disastrous consequences for agriculture in the region (e.g. farmers find it difficult to get credit). As one economist put it, "markets can't step in and won't step in when people have nothing. And if you take help away, you leave them to die" (quoted in Dugger 2007: A3). Another economist commented, "Here's your most important client, Africa, with its most important sector, agriculture, relevant to the most important goal – people feeding their families – and the bank has been caught with two decades of neglect" (quoted in Dugger 2007: A3). While some observers felt that the Bank was not given enough credit for its positive contributions, and much of the blame lay with African governments, the Bank itself acknowledged its mistakes in this domain.

With the 2007 Report, the Bank announced its intention to return to a focus on agriculture in developing nations, especially in Africa. It is late in doing so since both the Bill and Melinda Gates and the Rockefeller foundations have already been focusing on this issue in Africa. While many of the details are to be worked out and negotiated with African governments, the Bank has decided to shift back to an earlier focus on agriculture from later concerns with such issues as health (e.g. AIDs) and primary education (Dugger 2007: A6). Of course, the Bank, like the IMF, has become deeply immersed in the economic issues produced by the Great Recession and that might sidetrack it, at least for a time. (Even before the recession, the Bank was following, and concerned about, debt levels, especially of developing countries.)

In spite of a wide range of difficulties, the Bank is an important force globally. First, it is a forum for a vast number of nations to discuss development and development financing. Second, it remains a significant source of funds for developing countries. Third, it is an important source of information on development and provides valuable advice and support to the nations that are its members.

THE END OF BRETTON WOODS

While many of the economic organizations discussed above remain in place and are of great importance in the global economy, and many of those to be discussed below were at least inspired by Bretton Woods, it can be argued that Bretton Woods itself died on August 15, 1971. President Richard Nixon took the US off the gold standard, resulting in a devaluation of the dollar and the end of the standard by which the currencies of other nations operated. IMF staff circulated the following notice: "R.I.P. We regretfully announce the not unexpected passing away after a long illness of

Bretton Woods, at 9 P.M. last Sunday. Bretton was born in New Hampshire in 1944 and died a few days after his 27th birthday" (quoted in Frieden 2006: 342).

The demise of the Bretton Woods system is traceable to several factors (Frieden 2006: 339–60). For one thing, it had been based on the preeminence of the US and the dollar. However, as many of the economies of the world recovered from WW II – in part *because* of Bretton Woods – other nations and currencies grew in importance (e.g. Japan and the yen, the European Union's euro, and more recently China and the yuan). Second, international finance was restored to major importance after years of being subordinated to a focus within national economies. This led to the growth in speculation in international currencies. For example, as indications arose that the interest rates in a given country were likely to rise, speculators would buy up that currency and in the process sell off currencies that were likely to decline because of lower interest rates. With the declining importance of the US, and increasing doubt that it could sustain the exchange rate set by Bretton Woods, speculators turned their attention to the US dollar. To defend the dollar, the Federal Reserve had to raise interest rates and this led to a recession in the US because it raised the price of American products and made it more difficult for American firms to compete in the global marketplace. Eventually the Nixon administration was unwilling to accept this because of the adverse political consequences resulting from a recession caused by rising interest rates.

The agreements and understandings that undergirded international trade and investment also came under attack. There was an agreement among GATT members not to raise tariffs on nonagricultural products. However, countries began to find other ways to protect themselves from foreign competition. For one thing, they accused other countries of "dumping" their products, that is, selling products at less than the cost of production in order to dominate a given market. For another, countries sought to convince other nations to "voluntarily" restrict (through Voluntary Export Restraints – VERs) their exports to them. This indicated a move back toward protectionism and away from the openness that was the hallmark of GATT.

Another indication of this shift was a growing reaction against foreign direct investment (FDI). Epitomizing this was Servan-Schreiber's *The American Challenge* (1968). Basically, as we have seen in Chapter 2, Servan-Schreiber saw Europe as coming to be dominated by American MNCs and their direct investments in Europe. As a result of such views, developed countries such as France, as well as less developed countries, began to put limits and restrictions on such investments.

CHANGES IN, AND CRITIQUES OF, BRETTON-WOODS-ERA ORGANIZATIONS

In the twenty-first century, the organizations that were spawned by Bretton Woods – the World Bank, the International Monetary Fund, and the World Trade Organization – are undergoing dramatic changes (Weisman 2007a: C1, C8). A former US Secretary of Treasury commented: "The Bretton Woods system has become outmoded. … It has served us very well for a long time, but these institutions haven't changed with the times. They need to be rethought and restructured" (Weisman 2007a: C8).

Recent changes in the organizations are traceable to several major forces including globalization (a concept and a process not even dreamt of in 1944), major trade disputes, and the increasing power and ambition of growing economic powers, especially in Asia. In terms of the latter, the World Bank has been loaning large sums of money to countries whose economies did not need such loans (e.g. China; including $710 million in early 2009 to help rebuild areas hit by a 2008 earthquake). In fact, of the Bank's $23 billion in loans in 2006, $13 billion went to "middle-income" countries rather than to poor countries. Even in terms of the funds that do go to poor countries, the World Bank is an increasingly small player in comparison to various international and private aid organizations. As a result, one professor said: "… it's hard to see what good it [the World Bank] has done anywhere" (quoted in Weisman 2007a: C8). The Bank argues it is helping large numbers of the poverty-stricken in less developed countries, while its critics say it is the opening of markets there, and not bank loans, that has helped in poverty reduction.

Then there is the issue of the leadership of these organizations, especially the preeminent position occupied by the US. This has become increasingly controversial for various reasons including the fact that the US is not contributing as much money as it used to, at least in comparison to other nations.

The IMF is saddled with such problems as relentless criticism of past austerity programs imposed on poor countries in exchange for bailouts, and the bailouts themselves for legitimating and supporting bad policies by countries receiving them; a shift in global power away from the US and Europe and toward countries like China; and the fact that the IMF has been rendered increasingly less relevant by a growing global economy. Thus, former US Secretary of State George Schulz said, "If it [IMF] disappeared tomorrow, I don't think people would miss it very much" (quoted in Weisman 2007a: C8). On the other hand, there are those who argue that although things are relatively calm for the moment, the IMF will be needed during the next global financial crisis.

The biggest problem facing the WTO is the possibility that the failure of the Doha Round could lead to a reversal of the long trend toward more open trading systems. The fear is a new era of protectionism which, in turn, would lead to a slowdown in the global economy. This fear was exacerbated in the Great Recession as one began to hear outcries in the US to "buy American." Similar calls were being heard elsewhere in the world.

One of the most effective critics of Bretton-Woods-era organizations is the noted economist Joseph E. Stiglitz. His critique is especially powerful because he had great practical experience as a member of President Bill Clinton's Council of Economic Advisors and as Chief Economist at the World Bank. Thus, he was able to view the operations of the global economic system not only from the inside, but also from prominent positions within powerful institutions within that system. It is the fact that this is a critique from within, rather than from those who are on the periphery of the system and who feel they are being exploited by it, that gives Stiglitz's argument so much power.

For Stiglitz (2002: ix), globalization is defined as "the removal of barriers to free trade and the closer integration of national economies."[7] It should be clear, therefore, that he is falling into the familiar trap, especially common among, but not restricted to, economists, of defining globalization as economic globalization. As has been pointed out on several occasions, and as this book makes abundantly clear, there is much more to globalization than its economic aspects. It should also be clear that to Stiglitz, economic globalization *is* neo-liberal economic globalization (especially "closer integration" and the "removal of barriers"), but he takes this position at the same time that he is a critic of it.

Stiglitz argues that economic globalization *can* be a positive force and *can* enrich everyone in the world, including the poor. However, this has not been the case because of the way globalization, and especially international trade agreements, have been managed, including their imposition on less developed nations. As a result, Stiglitz sees an increase in global poverty as well as a growing gap between the global rich and the global poor. In this way globalization has *not* fulfilled its promise. Furthermore, globalization has not provided the global economic stability that many thought it promised (Stiglitz refers not only to the Asian financial crisis, but to the other crises in Russia and Latin America).

Stiglitz accepts various criticisms of the West. For example, he agrees with the argument that the West has been hypocritical in seeking the elimination of trade barriers in other parts of the world, while maintaining its own barriers to trade. He also accepts the idea that the West has been the driving force in an economic agenda that has furthered its interests while disadvantaging less developed parts of the world.

In terms of the IMF, Stiglitz sees several major changes since its creation at Bretton Woods in 1944. The IMF was created on the basis of the belief that markets often worked badly, but now it has become a strong champion of market supremacy. It was founded on the idea of the need to pressure developing countries to expand economically (e.g. increase expenditures, reduce taxes, lower interest rates – all designed to stimulate the economy), but now it will provide funds to developing countries only if they "engage in policies like cutting deficits, raising taxes, or raising interest rates that lead to a *contraction* of the economy" (Stiglitz 2002: 12–13, italics added). Stiglitz attributes this about-face in the IMF to the 1980s and the Reagan–Thatcher years. The IMF and the World Bank became missionary institutions pushing neo-liberal, "Washington Consensus" ideas (such as market liberalization [the removal of barriers], fiscal austerity, and privatization) on developing countries that were inclined to go along with them because they badly needed funds from these institutions.

Originally, the IMF was to maintain global stability by dealing with *macroeconomic* issues such as a "government's budget deficit, its monetary policy, its inflation, its trade deficit, its borrowing from abroad" (Stiglitz 2002: 14). In short, the task of the IMF was to be sure a nation was living within its means. The World

Bank was supposed to eradicate poverty by dealing with *structural issues* such as "what the country's government spent money on, the country's financial institutions, its labor markets, its trade policies" (Stiglitz 2002: 14).

However, the IMF grew increasingly imperialistic, seeing almost all structural issues as having macroeconomic implications. As a result, it saw virtually everything falling within its domain. It not only felt that it had the answers to dealing with these issues, but it tended to apply one set of answers to every country; in Stiglitz's words, "it tends to take a 'one-size-fits-all' approach" (2002: 34). It also tended to ignore the inputs from the countries it was ostensibly helping. And the countries that were ignored had little recourse because they needed the funds that the IMF was offering in exchange for structural changes and reforms.

In spite of its great ambitions, or perhaps because of them, Stiglitz sees the IMF as a failure in terms of its missions of providing funds (to create jobs etc.) to countries to weather economic downturns and more generally to create greater global economic stability. (It certainly failed in terms of the latter and it remains to be seen whether its efforts in the Great Recession to provide funds to countries in need will work.) Among the more specific failures of the IMF was the fact that its structural adjustment programs did not bring sustained growth, its imposition of economic austerity often stifled economic growth, and the opening of markets too quickly to competition led to job losses and increased poverty. In Stiglitz's view, the IMF has not only failed, but its failure (and that of the World Bank) has been magnified by the fact that it came to play a much greater global role than was originally envisioned.

Once distinct, the World Bank and the IMF became increasingly intertwined. Early on, the World Bank focused on making loans for specific projects (e.g. roads, dams), but it later moved to broader "structural adjustment loans." However, such loans required the approval of the IMF and, along with its approval, the IMF also often imposed various conditions on the receiving nations. As a result, the IMF moved from its original role in dealing with crises to becoming a perpetual part of life for developing countries.

Another set of critiques focuses on who is in charge of the IMF and the World Bank. As we saw above, the top positions at the IMF and the World Bank are held by Europeans and Americans. More generally, the nations and the largest corporations and financial institutions of the developed world dominate these organizations. This, of course, leaves the rest of the world out when it comes to leadership positions and is the source of considerable dissatisfaction. There is no overarching global system to ensure that this system functions better and more equitably. As a result, we have what Stiglitz calls "*global governance without global government*" (Stiglitz 2002: 21). The system is run by the few with the few as the main beneficiaries. Most of the people in the world have no say in these systems and are either not helped or are adversely affected by them.

Still another criticism of the IMF is the lack of transparency in its decision-making and in its operations. Those countries served by it do not know how it operates or the bases for its decisions. Further, the IMF is not accountable to those nation-states.

Stiglitz offers a long list of more specific IMF errors and blunders:

1. The privatization of state-run systems (e.g. steel mills) was often done too quickly and the new privatized businesses were often ineffective, in part because they weren't ready to operate on their own. As a result, consumers suffered, as did workers as privatization brought with it job loss. Privatization often also went hand-in-hand with corruption (see below).
2. The push to liberalize financial and capital markets, and to reduce barriers to trade, often hurt small emerging countries (e.g. through higher unemployment) and contributed to the financial crises of the 1990s. Furthermore, resentment was generated in those countries because the pressure to liberalize them came with restrictions on finance, capital, and trade.
3. The emphasis on foreign investment often adversely affected indigenous businesses in less developed countries.
4. The IMF failed in the sequencing and pacing of the changes: "forcing liberalization before safety nets were put in place, before there was adequate regulatory framework, before the countries could withstand the adverse consequences of the sudden changes in market sentiment that are part and parcel of modern capitalism; forcing policies that led to job destruction before the essentials of job creation were in place; forcing privatization before there were adequate competition and regulatory frameworks" (Stiglitz 2002: 73).
5. The IMF failed to deal with a variety of issues such as job creation, land reform, improved education and health services, and helping workers adversely affected by its policies.

Stiglitz lays much of the blame for the East Asian financial crisis of the 1990s on the IMF, especially its push to liberalize capital accounts. While this served to open East Asian countries to investment, it also served to make them vulnerable to large and irrational movements of funds, especially out of East Asia. Once the crisis began, the IMF exaggerated the economic problems in East Asia and forced excessive austerity (e.g. through higher interest rates) on the countries involved. Countries were ordered to reduce imports, but this served to exacerbate problems by extending the crisis to those countries that exported those products. The later focus of the IMF on restructuring (closing banks burdened with bad loans, closing companies with bad debts or allowing them to be taken over by their creditors) also caused more problems than it solved. Ultimately, IMF policies destabilized the area leading to riots. In the end, those East Asian countries that did *not* accept IMF intervention (e.g. Malaysia and China) tended to fare better than those that did, at least in the short run. Stiglitz concludes that the IMF failed because it reflected "the interests and ideology of the Western financial community" (Stiglitz 2002: 130), as well as because of its lack of a coherent program grounded in economic fundamentals. It, and much else, needs to be reformed in order to operate in a fairer manner and with a more "human face."

OTHER IMPORTANT ECONOMIC ORGANIZATIONS

The Organization for Economic Cooperation and Development (OECD)[8] is a broad group of, at the moment, 30 developed nations. The OECD is "the most encompassing 'club' of the world's rich countries" (Ougaard 2007: 914–17). While the OECD has little formal power, it is highly influential.

The European Union (EU) is a product of the post-WW II era, as well as the Bretton Woods era, and now encompasses 27 member states. It is the largest domestic market in the developed world (soon to be surpassed by China), with over 500 million citizens. The Euro Zone encompasses those nations in Europe that have adopted the euro as their basic currency. Most, but not all, nations using the euro are members of the EU. Some Western European nations (e.g. Great Britain, Sweden, and Denmark) have never accepted the euro, and retain their traditional currencies. There is also growing opposition to the euro in some of the nations that have accepted it (Italy, France, the Netherlands), on a variety of grounds (e.g. it is believed to have led to an increase in prices and to have depressed economic growth rates because of the policies of the European Central Bank which sets policies for Euro Zone nations). The criticisms of the euro are mounting and as I write it is being threatened by economic problems in Greece and looming difficulties in Portugal and Spain.

The North American Free Trade Agreement (NAFTA) came into effect on January 1, 1994. It was based on the idea that the US, Canada and Mexico were to eliminate most barriers to trade and investment over the ensuing 15 years (Anderson 2007: 887–91). The US, especially under former President George W. Bush, sought to expand the idea to include all 34 countries in the Western hemisphere (except Cuba) in the Free Trade Area of the Americas (FTAA). This idea has not only not caught on, but has encountered increasing opposition from Latin American leaders such as Hugo Chávez of Venezuela.

MERCOSUR, sometimes called the Southern Common Market, was created by the Treaty of Asuncion in 1991 with the goal of a common market in South America by 1995 (Roett 1999).

The Organization of Petroleum Exporting Countries (OPEC) was formed in 1960 and included the major oil exporters of the day – Iran, Iraq, Kuwait, Saudi Arabia, and Venezuela (there are now 11 members; Indonesia, Algeria, Libya, Nigeria, Qatar, and the United Arab Emirates have been added). It was motivated by the comparatively low price being paid for oil at the time and the fact that oil prices had long failed to keep up with inflation. OPEC has succeeded in greatly increasing the price of oil and its member nations have grown rich, some (e.g. Saudi Arabia) incredibly rich.

THE MULTINATIONAL CORPORATION (MNC)

By most accounts the other major player – strong actor – in economic globalization (beyond the nation-state and the organizations discussed above) is the

multinational corporation (MNC). Also of importance are transnational corporations (TNCs).[9] While TNCs involve operations in more than one country, MNCs operate in more

> **Multinational corporation (MNC):** Corporation that operates in more than two countries.

than two countries. We will generally use the term MNC in this book to encompass both MNCs and TNCs. There are many who believe that the MNC has grown more powerful, perhaps much more powerful, than the nation-state[10] *and* any of the organizations described above that are based on nation-states. For example, de la Dehesa (2006: 85) argues: "We have to get used to the fact that, thanks to the globalization process, companies rather than states will be the leading actors in the world economy."

There is no question that MNCs are increasingly important on the global scene. Adapting Dicken's (2007: 106) definition of a TNC, an MNC is "a firm that has the power to *coordinate* and *control* operations" in more than two countries "even if it does not own them." This means that they operate in an array of economic, political, social, and cultural environments. While MNCs have proliferated and grown in recent years, companies that operate, have interests, and have activities outside a home country (if one can be identified) are not new, and this was exemplified by, among others, the East India Trading Company (fifteenth century to late nineteenth century) and the Hudson's Bay Company (late seventeenth century, with vestiges to this day).

Defined in this way MNCs are hard to quantify, but if we rely on ownership data (a more restrictive criterion than those posed in the definition above), there are about 61,000 MNCs in the world today carrying out production through over 900,000 affiliates. They account for about a tenth of the world's Gross National Product (GNP) and about a third of total world exports. While there are many MNCs, the fact is that a relatively small number of "global corporations" (e.g. Toyota, IBM) predominate. And the vast majority – 96 of the top 100 – are in the developed world (Dicken 2007). However, as we will see, MNCs from developing countries are increasing in number and importance.

MNC activity is usually measured by foreign direct investment (FDI). This involves investments by one firm in another firm that exists abroad in a different nation-state, with the intention of gaining control over the latter's operations. It can also involve setting up a branch (subsidiary) operation in another country. FDI has grown substantially in recent years and this is a major indication of the growth of MNCs. More than two-thirds of the world's FDI is directed toward developed *not* less developed countries.

Another form of MNC activity is **portfolio investment**. This involves the purchase of equity in companies in other countries, but the motivation is financial gain and not to obtain control over those companies.

> **Portfolio investment:** Purchase of equities in companies in other countries for financial gain, not control.

Why do companies become multi- (or trans-) national? One set of reasons relates to market-oriented investments made necessary by the geographic unevenness of markets. A company may reach a saturation point in its domestic market;

identify new markets that require its direct presence; find that unless it becomes trans- or multinational it will have its markets restricted because of political regulations (e.g. import tariffs); find that a foreign market is so idiosyncratic that it can deal with it only by being physically present in it; or discover that there are strong cultural and political reasons for it to be present in other countries.

There are also reasons relating to market-oriented investment necessitated by the geographic unevenness of assets. A company in these circumstances may invest in another country in order to access natural and human resources. The latter can involve accessing human resources with high skill and knowledge and/or low-paid personnel with little in the way of skill or knowledge whose attraction is their low cost.

Dicken outlines various ways in which corporations become trans- or multinational. One is "**greenfield investment**" which involves the building of totally new facilities in another country. This is obviously favored by host countries, but is highly risky from the point of view of the MNC. A second is merger and acquisition (e.g. the acquisition of America's Chrysler Corporation by the German Daimler-Benz – now dissolved). A third is strategic collaborations which, while they have existed

> **Greenfield investment**: Building of totally new corporate facilities in another country.

for quite some time, have grown in number, increased in scale, and become increasingly central to a firm's transnational strategy. Strategic collaborations among companies in different countries have various objectives, such as gaining access to specific markets and technologies, sharing the risks associated with market entry, sharing other costs and uncertainties, and achieving economies associated with synergy. There are, of course, risks involved in this, such as losing control over key technologies and the great complexity involved in running strategic collaborations.

However they are created, MNCs lead to the development of far more complex networks. For a start, the firm's internal network now needs to be tied into networks in other countries. These larger, more complex networks are inherently more difficult to control. There are difficulties involved in finding a balance between centralized control and local sensitivity; economies of scale in production and responsiveness to local market conditions; core and peripheral knowledge; and global integration and local responsiveness. Then there are more specific issues such as the location of corporate headquarters (usually the home country); core research and development centers (also usually the home country); sales and marketing (usually dispersed globally); and production activities (also usually dispersed).

In terms of production activities, there are various possibilities:

- globally concentrated production in a single location – this produces economies of scale, but it maximizes transportation costs and doesn't make use of local expertise;

- production specifically for a local or national market – this limits economies of scale;
- production of a specialized product for a regional market (e.g. the EU);
- segmenting production and locating different parts in different geographic locations, producing a form of transnational vertical integration.

There is great variation in MNCs, but interestingly Dicken argues that few of them are actually truly global. They are more likely to be regional (e.g. in Europe, North America, or East Asia). However, they do vary in terms of size and shape.

There are also always tensions where MNCs are involved, including those with nation-states, local communities, labor, consumers, and civil society organizations. MNCs have also helped lead to the creation of counter-forces such as multi-scalar regulatory systems (e.g. the WTO), international institutes of technical standards (e.g. the ISO [International Organization for Standardization]), and the resurgence of the nation-state.

While most observers emphasize the power of MNCs and their increasing ascendancy over the nation-state, Dicken demurs. He sees the nation-state as of continuing importance and as having various advantages over the MNC (e.g. their control over continuous territories versus the discontinuous territories under the MNC's control). To Dicken, MNCs are not the "unstoppable juggernauts" they are to other observers and critics, especially vis-à-vis the nation-state.

Dicken's perspective also runs counter to the dominant view that the global world is increasingly placeless or defined by non-places (Auge 1995; Ritzer 2007). Dicken contends that as far as MNCs are concerned, place and geography still matter. He contends that MNCs continue to evidence various characteristics traceable to their home base, their place of origin, including their cognitive, cultural, social, political, and economic traits. As he puts it, no matter how transnational they become, MNCs continue to evince the "aroma of native land." Thus, he sees little evidence that these organizations are "converging towards a single model" (Dicken 2007: 135). He also rejects the view of various perspectives (see Chapter 10) that argue that MNCs throughout the world are becoming standardized, homogenized.

THE MYTH OF ECONOMIC GLOBALIZATION?

All of the above (as well as what is to come in the next chapter) points to the growing importance of economic globalization. While that is the predominant view, as well as the one adopted here, there are those who do not accept it. For example, Paul Hirst and Grahame Thompson famously argue that globalization, especially economic globalization, is a myth. They argue that such a highly internationalized economy, although it may not have been labeled "global," is not unprecedented. In fact, the current world economy may well be less open than the world economy during the period 1870 to 1914 (see the beginning of this chapter). Most companies continue to be based in nations in terms of assets, production facilities, and sales (this is also Dicken's view). Their multinational business stems from such a national base. And there does not appear to be much in the way of movement toward the development of multinational businesses. There is no massive shift of investment and employment from advanced to developing countries. Foreign direct investment (FDI) continues to be mainly in the advanced industrial economies and not in less developed countries. Trade continues to involve mainly Europe, Japan, and North America (to this list enumerated in 1999 would now need to be added China and perhaps India); it is not truly global. It is those nations that possess the ability to govern the global economy (Hirst and Thompson 1999: 2).

While these are solid arguments, they really come down to the point that contemporary economic globalization may not be as new or as great as many contend. However, they do not contradict the idea that today's economy is globalized. The view adopted here is that the economy is more global than Hirst and Thompson argue and that it has grown even more globalized since their argument was published a decade ago.

CHAPTER SUMMARY

This chapter examines the major global economic structures. Similarities between the current global capitalist system and a prior system which functioned between 1896 and 1914 are analyzed. Turmoil beginning with WW I ended the earlier global capitalist system and set the stage for the emergence of the current global capitalist system.

Fears of another Depression after World War II led to the Bretton Woods system in 1944. This was an attempt to create institutional structures which would foster international economic cooperation and encourage the free flow of capital around the world. The US dollar was adopted as the standard, almost a "global currency," in order to establish stable international exchange rates.

The Bretton Woods system led to the creation, either directly or indirectly, of various global economic structures. While the International Trade Organization (ITO) was unsuccessful because of a lack of US support, the General Agreement on Trade and Tariffs (GATT) sought to facilitate the liberalization of trade by the reduction of tariff barriers. GATT was eventually replaced by the World Trade Organization (WTO), which added a concern for the reduction of non-tariff barriers. This included the General Agreement on Trade in Services (GATS), protection of intellectual property through TRIPS, and TRIMS measures that allow a nation-state to control the distorting effects of foreign investment. The WTO is a forum for international negotiations on trade, with member countries participating in successive "rounds" of discussions.

Bretton Woods also led to the creation of the International Monetary Fund in order to create a stable global monetary system and to act as a "lender of the last resort." Another key institution was the World Bank, which started out (and continues) with a specific focus on developing physical infrastructure in middle-income nations. The IMF and the World Bank have come under criticism for furthering the neo-liberal agenda. The IMF (and later the World Bank in consultation with it) imposed structural adjustment programs on developing countries, extending loans only if certain "conditionalities" (reduction of government expenditure and integration with the world market) were met by the borrowers.

Joseph Stiglitz criticizes these institutions for their policy of imposing liberalization on developing countries, especially their use of a one-size-fits-all approach. Stiglitz believes that premature opening of markets under the structural adjustment programs increased the vulnerability of some countries to economic crises, as for instance in the 1997 Asian crisis. The lack of transparency and the dominance of the US and Europe in the governing structures of these organizations have also been severely criticized.

Regional coalitions also play a key role in the global economic system. While the European Union, with its common market and the establishment of the euro as a common currency, is perhaps the best known, others include NAFTA, MERCOSUR, and OPEC. While these organizations face various internal challenges, they also engage with (and provide important mechanisms for nation-states to engage with) economic globalization.

Also analyzed is another significant economic player – the multinational corporation (MNC). Many believe the MNC has grown more powerful than the nation-state. MNC activity is measured in terms of foreign direct investment and portfolio investment. MNCs employ various mechanisms such as greenfield investments, mergers and acquisitions, and strategic collaborations.

There are those who argue that economic globalization is a "myth." For example, they contend that the world economy is actually less open than in earlier epochs. The position taken here is that the world economy is much more global than is argued by such critics.

DISCUSSION QUESTIONS

1. Discuss the relevance of Bretton Woods institutions such as the IMF and the World Bank in the current global context.

2. Analyze the "global" nature of multinational corporations.

3. Make a case that economic globalization is a "myth."

4. Examine the role of regional coalitions in the global economic system.

5. Examine the role of the nation-state with respect to the changes in the world economic system.

FURTHER READING ···

Jeffry A. Frieden. *Global Capitalism: Its Fall and Rise in the Twentieth Century*. New York: W.W. Norton & Co., 2006.

Joseph E. Stiglitz. *Globalization and Its Discontents*. New York: W.W. Norton and Co., 2002.

Chris Rumford. *The European Union: A Political Sociology*. Oxford: Blackwell, 2002.

Peter Dicken. *Global Shift: Mapping the Changing Contours of the World Economy*. 5th edn. New York: Guilford Press, 2007.

Guillermo de la Dehesa. *Winners and Losers in Globalization*. Malden, MA: Blackwell, 2006.

NOTES ···

1 Typical of economic historians and economists more generally, as well as many journalists and laypeople, Frieden often seems to equate global capitalism with globalization. For example, "The opening years of the twentieth century were the closest thing the world had ever seen to a free world market for goods, capital, and labor. It would be a hundred years before the world returned to that level of *globalization*" (Frieden 2006: 16, italics added). However, it is important to bear in mind that such a view of globalization relates *only* to the economy and tells us little about globalization in general, as well as about the globalization of other realms such as political and cultural globalization.

2 However, there are certainly factors that are specific to each period. One example is the triumph of the gold standard in the earlier epoch as a result of the rejection by the American electorate of its passionate supporter – William Jennings Bryant – in the presidential election of 1896.

3 However, it would be a mistake to assume that trade was totally free and that tariffs were eliminated. Many barriers remained, again then as now, because, for example, nation-states wanted to protect their farmers as well as their most vulnerable, often their newest, industries.

4 There is great concern in the Great Recession about a return to isolationism.

5 While there are no hard-and-fast dividing lines, the World Bank also engaged in structural adjustment programs which tended to focus on such issues as "the civil service, privatizations, reforms of international trade policies, reforms at the sectoral level (such as agriculture, education, utilities), the improvement of property rights and other measures to promote the growth of the private sector, anti-corruption measures, and so on" (Killick 2007: 1095; see also Babb 2005: 199–222).

6 He was forced to resign because of improprieties involving an intimate relationship with a prominent woman associated with the Bank.

7 Stigliitz (2002: 9) also offers a more detailed definition: "the closer integration of the countries and peoples of the world which has been brought about by the enormous reductions in cost of transportation and communication, and the breaking down of artificial barriers to the flows of goods, services, capital, knowledge, and (to lesser extent) people across borders."

8 www.oecd.org.

9 Dicken (2007); Pearce (2007: 1193–8); see also the UN journal, *Transnational Corporations*.

10 One exception is Wolf (2005: 247).

REFERENCES ···

Anderson, Sarah. 2007. "North American Free Trade Agreement." In Jan Aart Scholte and Roland Robertson, eds., *Encyclopedia of Globalization*. New York: MTM Publishing.

Auge, Marc. 1995. *Non-Places: An Introduction to an Anthropology of Supermodernity*. London: Verso.

Babb, Sarah. 2005. "The Social Consequences of Structural Adjustment: Recent Evidence and Current Debates." *Annual Review of Sociology* 31.

Babb, Sarah. 2007. "Embeddedness, Inflation, and International Regimes: The IMF in the Early Postwar Period." *American Journal of Sociology* 113.

Bordo, Michael D., and Barry Eichengreen, eds. 1993. *A Retrospective on the Bretton Woods System*. Chicago: University of Chicago Press.

Boughton, James. 2007. "Bretton Woods System." In Jan Aart Scholte and Roland Robertson, eds., *Encyclopedia of Globalization*. New York: MTM Publishing.

Bradlow, Daniel D. 2007. "World Bank Group." In Jan Aart Scholte and Roland Robertson, eds., *Encyclopedia of Globalization*. New York: MTM Publishing.

Cardim de Carvalho, Fernando J. 2007. "International Monetary Fund." In Jan Aart Scholte and Roland Robertson, eds., *Encyclopedia of Globalization*. New York: MTM Publishing.

Correa, Carlos. 2000. *Intellectual Property Rights: The TRIPS Agreement and Policy Options*. London: Zed Books.

de la Dehesa, Guillermo. 2006. *Winners and Losers in Globalization*. Malden, MA: Blackwell.

Dicken, Peter. 2007. *Global Shift: Mapping the Changing Contours of the World Economy*. 5th edn. New York: Guilford Press.

Dugger, Celia W. 2007. "World Bank Neglects African Agriculture, Study Says." *New York Times*. October 15.

Economist. 2008. February 7. "It's Mostly Firing."

Economist 2008. October 23. "Who's Next?"

Economist 2009. February 5. "Supersizing the Fund."

Frieden, Jeffry A. 2006. *Global Capitalism: Its Fall and Rise in the Twentieth Century*. New York: W. W. Norton & Co.

Gilbert, Christopher L., and David Vines, eds. 2000. *The World Bank: Structure and Policies*. Cambridge: Cambridge University Press.

Grimwade, Nigel Stewart. 2007. "Trade-Related Investment Measures." In Jan Aart Scholte and Roland Robertson, eds., *Encyclopedia of Globalization*. New York: MTM Publishing.

Hirst, Paul, and Grahame Thompson. 1999. *Globalization in Question*. Cambridge: Polity.

House, Robert. 2007. "General Agreement on Tariffs and Trade." In Jan Aart Scholte and Roland Robertson, eds., *Encyclopedia of Globalization*. New York: MTM Publishing.

Hudec, Robert. 1975. *The GATT Legal System and World Trade Diplomacy*. New York: Praeger.

Killick, Tony. 2007. "Structural Adjustment Programs." In Jan Aart Scholte and Roland Robertson, eds., *Encyclopedia of Globalization*. New York: MTM Publishing.

Koivusalo, Meri. 2007. "General Agreement on Trade in Services." In Jan Aart Scholte and Roland Robertson, eds., *Encyclopedia of Globalization*. New York: MTM Publishing.

Krueger, Anne O. 2000. *The WTO as an International Organization*. Chicago: University of Chicago Press.

Landler, Mark. 2008. "Healthy Countries to Receive IMF Loans." *New York Times*. October 30.

Ougaard, Morton. 2007. "Organization for Economic Co-operation and Development." In Jan Aart Scholte and Roland Robertson, eds., *Encyclopedia of Globalization*. New York: MTM Publishing.

Pearce, Robert. 2007. "Transnational Corporation." In Jan Aart Scholte and Roland Robertson, eds., *Encyclopedia of Globalization*. New York: MTM Publishing.

Peet, Richard. 2003. *Unholy Trinity: The IMF, World Bank, and the World Trade Organization*. New York: Zed Books.

Ricardo, David. 1817/1971. *On the Principles of Political Economy and Taxation*. Harmondsworth, UK: Penguin.

Ritzer, George. 2007. *The Globalization of Nothing*, 2nd edn. Thousand Oaks, CA: Pine Forge Press.

Roett, Riordan, ed. 1999. *Mercosur: Regional Integration and World Markets*. Boulder, CO: Lynne Rienner.

Servan-Schreiber, J.-J. 1968. *The American Challenge*. New York: Atheneum.

Smith, Adam. 1776/1977. *An Inquiry into the Nature and Causes of the Wealth of Nations*. Chicago: University of Chicago Press.

Stiglitz, Joseph E. 2002. *Globalization and Its Discontents*. New York: W. W. Norton and Co.

Trachtman, Joel P. 2007. "World Trade Organization." In Jan Aart Scholte and Roland Robertson, eds., *Encyclopedia of Globalization*. New York: MTM Publishing.

Weisman, Steven R. 2007a. "Cracks in the Financial Foundation." *New York Times*. May 23.

Weisman, Steven R. 2007b. "I.M.F. Faces a Question of Identity." *New York Times*. September 28.

Wolf, Martin. 2005. *Why Globalization Works*. New Haven: Yale University Press.

Global Economic Flows

Globalization: The Essentials, by George Ritzer
© 2011 John Wiley & Sons Ltd

| n this chapter we examine the global economy in further detail, focusing on economic flows.

TRADE

A good place to get a quick snapshot of global trade (Mann and Pluck 2007: 1159–66), as well net economic flows in and out of a nation-state, is a nation's trade surpluses and deficits.

Trade Surpluses and Deficits

Of special interest and importance as far as trade surpluses and deficits are concerned are the positions of the two global economic giants – the US and China – in terms of their trade balances. On the one side is the US which by the end of November, 2007, had a trade *deficit* of $701.6 billion (it ended the year at $738.6 billion) (Peters 2007: C3). (The deficit dropped slightly in 2008 and dramatically in 2009 to about half the 2007 figure because of the Great Recession.) For its part, China announced that it had a record trade *surplus* of $177.47 billion in 2006 (Peters 2007: C3). China's surplus was 75 percent greater than it had been in the previous year (2005). Through November, 2006, the Chinese surplus with the US was almost equal to its surplus with *all* other countries in the world. The US deficit with China alone was $22.9 billion, and that was just for the month of November, 2006. The US has a larger deficit with China than with any other country in the world. The US is negotiating with China over the size of its deficit, blaming it, at least in part, on Chinese monetary policies that, in the US view, artificially undervalue the yuan, thereby making Chinese exports less expensive and therefore more affordable to Americans. Of course, there is much more to the American attraction to Chinese products than their low prices traceable to China's (perhaps) undervalued currency. The fact is that many Chinese products are attractive because they are priced low, mainly as a result of the low cost of labor there, *and* because their quality is high, at least for the price being paid.

The trade deficit with China has certainly hurt American industry, but it has greatly aided the American consumer who has access to a wide range of low-priced imports from China (and elsewhere). While only 7.5 percent of total US spending on consumer goods is on products imported from China, it is much higher for certain products such as footwear (85 percent), toys (80 percent), and clothing (40 percent) (Barboza 2008a: A1, A8).

Global Trade: Economic Chains and Networks

Trade in goods and services is clearly central to the global economy. Much of that trade takes place in interconnected circuits of one kind or another. These interconnections are clear, as are the basic liquid- and flow-oriented themes of this book (see Chapter 1), in the various chains and networks that exist in the global economy, specifically in global trade.

Gary Gereffi (2005: 160–83) has outlined several of the most important economic chains and networks involved in global trade:

- *Supply chains.* This a general label for value-adding activities in the production process. A supply chain begins with raw materials and follows the value-adding process through a variety of inputs and outputs and ultimately to a finished product. For example, the process might begin with some comparatively inexpensive raw material (say cotton) and at various steps along the way workers and technologies add value to the cotton (e.g. transforming it into thread, producing a T-shirt) so that in the end the finished product – the T-shirt in this case – has greater value than the cotton with which the process began (Rivoli 2005).
- *International production networks.* This involves the networks of producers involved in the process of producing a finished product. Multinational corporations (MNCs) are seen as playing a central role, as being the "flagships," in these networks.
- *Global commodity chains* (Gereffi and Korzeniewicz 1994). This brings together the idea of value-adding chains and the global organization of industries. It also accords a central place to the growing importance of the sellers of global products. This includes buyer-driven chains such as Wal-Mart which play an increasing role in determining what industries produce and how much they produce. Since such companies do not manufacture their own products, they are buyers of products that are then sold under their brand names. Also included here are "brand companies," or "manufacturers without factories" (the best known of these is Nike [Rothenberg-Aalami 2004: 335–54]). Buyer-driven chains are distinguished from producer-driven chains (e.g. Toyota). There is a focus on the governance structure of global commodity chains (e.g. are they governed by producers or buyers?). Also of concern is the role of lead firms (Wal-Mart, Nike) in the creation of "global production and sourcing networks" (Gereffi 2005: 168).
- *Global value chains.* Gereffi argues that this is emerging as the overarching label for all work in this area and for all such chains. Here is the way he describes global value chains:

> Emphasis on the relative value of those economic activities that are required to bring a good or service from conception to, through the different phases of production (involving a combination of physical transformation and the input of various producer services), delivery to final consumers, and final disposal after use. (Gereffi 2005: 168)

This conceptualization has several advantages. First, it "focuses on value creation and value capture across the full range of possible chain activities and end products (goods and services)" (Gereffi 2005: 168). Second, "it avoids the limiting connotations of the word *commodity*, which to some implies the production of undifferentiated goods with low barriers to entry" (Gereffi 2005: 168). Third, while it accepts a number of ideas from earlier approaches – the nature and consequences of organizational and geographic fragmentation; the role of power in the chain; "industry (re-)organization, coordination, governance" (Gereffi 2005: 168); and the ways in which firms are linked in the global economy – it goes beyond them to include the broader institutional contexts (e.g. trade policy, trade regulations, trade standards) of these chains. However, the most important advantage of the idea of global value chains is that it encompasses both production and consumption (and even post-consumption).

Global Value Chains: China and the US

To give specificity to the idea of global value chains we look at several specific examples of such chains, all of which involve trade between China (Brandt and Rawski 2008) and the US (although many other countries in the world are involved in these or similar chains).

Scrap metal
An important example of a global value chain involves scrap metal (Seabrook 2008: 47–59). This seems like a rather prosaic commodity, but it is more important than many think and its fate tells us a great deal about globalization. For one thing, about two-thirds of the steel made in the US comes from recycled steel rather than from iron ore and coke ("virgin steel"). For another, this is big business, especially since prices for scrap metals (e.g. steel, copper) have increased dramatically as a result of skyrocketing global demand for such commodities. In addition, it is not surprising that, given its high level of consumption (of cars, lawnmowers, and the like), *the* major global source of scrap metal is the US, but increasingly the work involved in extracting usable metal from scrap is done elsewhere in the world, especially China.

Scrap metal is interesting in this regard because, by definition, its origins go back to other chains involved in the use of raw materials (say, iron ore) and the production of finished products (say, automobiles). Furthermore, it also includes consumption of those products as well as their ultimate disposal as scrap or junk. For example, we would need to go back to the extraction of raw materials for an automobile (perhaps in part made from scrap), the production of the automobile, its sale to a consumer, its use by the consumer and perhaps others (in the case of used cars), and ultimately to the end of the useful life of the car. It is at this point that the junked car is transformed into various types of scrap, especially scrap metals.

Unsorted aluminum and copper scrap is shipped from scrap metal companies in the US to recycling companies in China. Why ship it all the way to China? The reason, of course, is primarily the willingness of people there to do work that most Americans would refuse *and* to do it for very low wages; those who do the recycling work in China are paid about $140 a month. Here is a description of the work:

Inside the open-walled shed, four hundred women, working in groups of twenty, surrounded fifteen-foot piles of metal. The women wore gloves and masks and white uniforms. They picked through the pieces by hand, sorting the aluminum into differ- ent grades ... and each grade had its own bucket. They also separated out small pieces of copper wire and whatever else they might find ... American coins, left in gummy car ashtrays, were not uncommon. (Seabrook 2008: 57)

The men did the smelting work turning the scrap into liquid metal which is later cooled in molds.

A few examples, among many, of the uses to which the scrap metal can be put include the use of aluminum to make "engine casings of new cars ... as well as irons, coffee pots, grills and frying pans" (Seabrook 2008: 55). As we might expect, some of the scrap metal that is sent to China is turned into various products that are shipped back to the US to be sold as new products and then, once again, eventually scrapped. More interesting is the fact that much of that which is made from the scrap is now increasingly likely to be used in China itself to create the infrastructure for that country's meteoric growth and expansion: "Most of the scrap metal that goes to China is turned into materials for the Chinese construction industry – rebar, beams and floor decking. That steel flows into the skyscrapers sprouting all around Chinese cities and into new factory towns, the copper is used to wire the millions of houses being built for China's new middle class." The great irony of this is that "China's industrial might is being constructed out of the ruins of [the US]" (Seabrook 2008: 55).

The future seems clear since the world's largest scrap yard has recently been built not far from Shanghai. A large steel mill is nearby to process the scrap metal. While American scrap yards depend on huge mechanical mega-shredders, the Chinese scrap yard relies on "hundreds of men working at tables with alligator shears, cutting every piece of scrap by hand. The result looked like metal pasta. The mega- shredder, for all its grunt, couldn't do that" (Seabrook 2008: 59). It seems likely that in the future the Chinese will no longer need American scrap metal, they will not need to engage in trade with the US for such scrap since they will be producing more than enough of their own.

Waste paper
One of the richest women in the world is Zhang Yin (estimated to be worth $1.5 billion and her family is worth billions more). The source of her wealth? Her busi- ness, Nine Dragons Paper (72 percent of which is controlled by the Zhang family) and Los Angeles-based America Chung Nam (the largest exporter to China), takes mountains of waste paper from the US, ships it to China, recycles it into corrugated boxes, the boxes are used to ship goods to various places around the world – includ- ing the US – and, once the boxes have arrived at their destination and been unpacked, they are turned into scrap and the process begins all over again.

Nine Dragons Paper is already one of the world's largest producers of paper and it could possibly soon be number one in the world, surpassing such well-known giants as Weyerhauser. It is difficult to compete with Nine Dragons Paper because the company works with less expensive paper, its factory burns comparatively inexpensive coal, and it uses the latest technologies (while competitors like Weyerhauser are saddled with less efficient technology that is three or four decades old) (Barboza 2007: C1, C8).

T-shirts

The neo-liberalism that undergirds the global market is based on the belief that markets should be free, open, and have no barriers to free and open trade. While there have been many efforts to lower or remove such barriers, the fact is that such barriers remain in many areas. One particularly interesting and instructive example is found in Pietra Rivoli's work on the global value chain for T-shirts (Rivoli 2005). The global value chain here involves, among other things, cotton grown in and shipped from the US; T-shirts manufactured in China; the shipping to, and sale in, the US of those new T-shirts; the eventual disposal of them (often very quickly); and finally the shipping and sale of those used T-shirts in Africa. Below we look at this global value chain, but this time instead of focusing on the various steps involved, we will deal primarily with the nature of the various markets involved.

We can begin with cotton production in Texas. With its high labor costs, how is it the US can lead the world (at least most of the time) in cotton production and export? While part of the answer lies in the fact that the industry is embedded in a set of other highly advanced institutions (e.g. American universities that do cutting-edge scientific research on cotton production), the fact is that a large part of the answer lies in the fact that US government subsidies ($4 billion in 2000) distort the global market and give American producers a tremendous advantage. For example, as a result of the 2002 Farm Bill, American cotton farmers got a minimum of over 72 cents per pound, while the average market price was 38 cents. This amounts to a government subsidy of about 34 cents per pound so that US cotton can compete on the global market. In fact, the WTO (heavily controlled by the US) ruled that in this the US violated global trade rules, giving it a great advantage. The irony, of course, is that the US champions free trade and often chastises other nations for doing precisely what it does in the market for cotton.

The American cotton industry is aided – unfairly – in other ways. For example, American textile manufacturers are prevented from using foreign cotton even when they can get it at a lower price. The US government pays American textile manufacturers to use American cotton. And the US government helps in other ways as well, such as its Crop Disaster Program and its Farm Loan Program. Few, if any, of America's global competitors in the cotton market have support of this type and certainly not of this magnitude.

Similarly, the global trade in T-shirts, especially those produced in China, has not been free and open, especially with respect to the sale of Chinese-made T-shirts in the US. The Multi-Fibre Agreement (1975–2005) put quotas on the number of T-shirts that could be imported into the US from various producing countries. The main purpose of the law was to prevent China from garnering all, or close to all, of that market. In fact, were this to be a free and open market, China *would* have dominated most of the market because according to many observers it produces the best quality T-shirts at the lowest price. The Multi-Fibre Agreement was a state-imposed mechanism to limit the ability of the Chinese to sell T-shirts in the American market. After it expired at the end of 2005, imports of Chinese T-shirts to the US (and the EU) were capped for three more years (Chanda 2007: 82).

In fact, the only free and open neo-liberal market found by Rivoli is that for used T-shirts shipped from the US to African countries like Tanzania. There, many small entrepreneurs battle it out on a level playing field. They compete to get the most saleable T-shirts from huge bales shipped from the US. Consumers then get to pick from the wares offered by a number of highly competitive sellers of T-shirts. Rivoli found the African T-shirt market quite refreshing in comparison to the distortions and barriers in the markets for American cotton and Chinese T-shirts. Here is where we finally encounter an example of the flat world touted by Thomas Friedman (2005), but that world is not to be found throughout the other aspects of the global market – certainly not in the case of American cotton or new Chinese T-shirts.

Based on this analysis, Rivoli comes to the conclusion that the greatest problems in this realm are not traceable to the operation of the market, but to various actions, especially by governments, to exclude sectors of the global economy from the free operation of the market. While there is merit to her neo-liberal argument, at least in this limited context, the fact is that most critics of the global market blame the market itself more than the states for such problems.

iPhones

The global value chain for the Apple iPhone is fascinating. The story starts with the mystery that while 3.7 million iPhones were sold in 2007, only 2.3 million were registered on the wireless networks that are Apple's exclusive partners in the US and Europe. The phones are only supposed to be used on these networks from which Apple earns a royalty (for example, perhaps $120 a year per phone from its American network partner, AT&T). The loss of royalty income to Apple over the three succeeding years was expected to approach $1 billion. So, where are the other phones?

The phones themselves are manufactured in China and exported to the US and Europe. However, many of them end up being bought there, and then smuggled to other nations, mainly China, where consumers love high-tech gadgets like the iPhone. In fact, within months of the introduction of the iPhone in mid-2007, "iClones" were on sale in China at a fraction of the cost of the iPhone. While the clones closely resemble the originals, many Chinese consumers prefer the cachet of the iPhone and are willing to pay the $400–$500 in additional cost for the original.

The phones are being bought in the US and Europe, sometimes in large quantities, by tourists, airline personnel, small businesspeople, and full-time smugglers, and brought back to China. They might be paid $30 or so for each phone they bring into China. The phones need to be "unlocked" and to have Chinese software added so that they will work in China and outside the official networks, but that is quick, easy, and inexpensive (perhaps costing as little as $25). In fact, stores in China that sell the iPhones also offer unlocking as an additional service. In this way, about one-third of the iPhones manufactured by Apple in China end up, contrary to the company's policies and wishes, right back in China (after a brief excursion to the US or Europe).

To deal with this, Apple has been negotiating with China Mobile. With 350 million subscribers, it is the largest mobile-phone service provider in the world. However, those negotiations have, at least until now, not succeeded. More generally, the business model developed by Apple to sell iPhones to selected carriers is being threatened and some feel that it should be abandoned, allowing owners to sign up with any carrier. This would greatly increase iPhone sales, but it would drastically cut, or eliminate, the huge royalties anticipated by Apple (Barboza 2008b: A1, A8).

INCREASING COMPETITION FOR COMMODITIES

A wide range of commodities constitute the starting point for many of the global value chains discussed above. However, one of the most striking developments in recent years has been the increasing global competition for various commodities. The best-known and most obvious example is oil (see below), but much the same thing has happened in the markets for natural gas, copper, lithium (especially for batteries for electric cars), nickel, silver, gold, as well as even more mundane commodities such as rice, wheat, corn, and soybeans (Krauss 2008: C1, C8). The increasing demand for these commodities, and many others, is no longer fueled mainly by the needs of the countries we traditionally think of as highly developed (e.g. the US, the members of the EU, Japan), but now by massive development in other parts of the world, especially India (Dossani 2008) and China. The latter, especially China, are industrializing at a rapid pace (the Chinese economy grew at 10 percent in 2007; the US economy grew at 2.5 percent in that year), and those relatively new industries place large and increasing demands on all sorts of commodities, especially the oil needed to power them (China accounted for 31 percent of the increased demand for oil between 2003 and 2007; in addition, it accounted for 64 percent of the increased demand for copper, 70 percent for aluminum, and 82 percent for zinc). In spite of these enormous gains, it is important to remember that the North, especially the US, remains the major consumer of most of the world's commodities.

However, demand for commodities goes well beyond that of specific industries needing specific commodities for their production processes. This industrial development is linked to the emergence of a similarly expanding consumer society with consumers in countries like China and India demanding the same sorts of products that consumers in the US and the EU possess. The result involves the need for everything from more airplanes to transport people who now want to see the world, to gas-guzzling and polluting trucks to deliver the things they want to consume, to the automobiles they now want to have both as consumables and as technologies that allow them to consume much else (e.g. tourism within China and Asia). All of these planes, trucks and cars require gasoline, and need to be produced in factories that consume huge amounts of energy; and in order to be produced all of them require a wide range of commodities. A global commodities specialist sums this up well: "It is absolutely a fundamental change in the global economic structure. ... Global commodities ranging from oil to base metals to grains are moving higher as billions of people in China and around the world get wealthier and are consuming more as they produce products for us, and increasingly for themselves" (quoted in Krauss 2008: C1). As an economist put it, "The world is coming alive and the lights are coming on across Asia. ... What we are dealing with is a tremendous demand for resources" (quoted in Krauss 2008: C8).

The developing countries, especially China, are devouring huge quantities of many commodities (of course the developed countries have long devoured, and continue to devour, much larger quantities of these commodities):

> The country accounts for about a fifth of the world's population, yet it gobbles up more than half of the world's pork, half of its cement, a third of its steel and over a quarter of its aluminum. It is spending 35 times as much on imports of soya beans and crude oil as it did in 1999. ... China has swallowed over four-fifths of the increase in the world's copper supply since 2000. (*Economist* 2008: March 13)

The result of all of this was massive increases in the prices of all sorts of commodities (e.g. the price of copper tripled and that of zinc doubled in a five-year period in the early twenty-first century; the cost of both wheat and soybeans increased by 70 percent in 2007). The prices of many commodities reached record highs in 2008, before dropping off quite dramatically as the Great Recession gained momentum. Interestingly, China is in the process of positioning itself for the post-recession years by investing in commodities of all sorts. In February, 2009 it invested $41 billion in oil companies in Brazil, Russia, and Venezuela and over $20 billion in aluminum and zinc companies in Australia (Barboza 2009). China has huge cash reserves from the boom that ended in late 2007 and it is using some of the money to prepare itself for what it hopes will be the next boom in the global economy. If China is right, that is when we will see a resumption in the upward trend in the commodity process.

THE ECONOMIC IMPACT OF THE FLOW OF OIL

Not only does greater demand lead to higher prices, but it becomes harder and harder to find additional resources (e.g. new oil fields) and increasingly difficult to obtain them. Thus, oil wells far out in the ocean are more expensive to build than those on land, and the oil itself is harder to get out and, as a result, more expensive. Getting oil from sand pits is more difficult and costly than from underground oil wells. All of these increasing difficulties translate into higher costs and higher prices.

And these changes have ripple effects throughout the economy. For example, the high price of oil and gasoline has led to increased efforts to create and use various biofuels, especially ethanol (see Chapter 9) from corn (among other sources including sugar cane). The result is a huge increase in demand for (the US accounted for 60 percent of that increase in 2007), and the price of, corn.

Oil Wealth

There was a huge influx of petrodollars into oil-producing countries, after 2002 and especially in 2007 and 2008, as a result of the great run-up in oil prices through mid-2008. In 2000 oil exports earned OPEC about $243 billion; by 2007 it was estimated to rise to $688 billion (Weisman 2007: A1, A16). As of 2007, the Gulf States alone were earning $5 billion a week. Since they cannot possibly spend it all, they need to invest somewhere. The chairman of an energy company commented, "The oil-producing countries simply cannot absorb the amount of wealth they are generating. ... We are seeing a transfer of wealth of historic dimensions" (quoted in Weisman 2007: A16). This huge and growing income has enormous implications, but at the minimum those nations, their leaders, and their corporations (private and state-run) have huge sums of money to invest. The decisions on where they should invest their money give them great power and influence. One of the things the beneficiaries of this boom are doing – or not doing – is investing in Northern (especially American) companies. The North is likely to benefit greatly if the money flows back in the form of new investments, but it is likely to suffer if the oil-producing nations turn inward, or elsewhere (especially China), in order to get a higher return on their investment.

On the positive side, the Abu Dhabi Investment Authority invested $7.5 billion in the American-based Citicorp and with that investment became one of the company's largest shareholders. Citicorp had found itself in economic difficulty and in need of an influx of cash because of bad investments related to the 2007 sub-prime mortgage crisis (see below).

Many other American-based companies have been the recipients of huge investments of petrodollars including Advanced Micro Devices, Carlyle Group, and Walt Disney. While such investments are a good thing from the point of view of the economic condition of these corporations, some worry about oil-producing nations "buying up America" (and other countries) and gaining control over its key corporations.

However, investments in the US are not as attractive as they once were. In part, this is because of the rise in, and increasing attractiveness of, other economies (notably China). And in part it is because the decline in the US dollar over the last several years has led to worry that it will decline further and that this will lead to an erosion in the value of foreign investments in the US. On the other hand, the declining dollar makes investments in the US cheaper and therefore more desirable to other countries.

The increase in the price of oil, and the increasing difficulty in obtaining enough of it, is both roiling and restructuring the globe and the position of many nations, corporations, and individuals (Landler 2007: A1, A17). At the national level we have become accustomed to thinking of OPEC nations such as Saudi Arabia and Abu Dhabi as profiting handsomely from the oil business, but in recent years other nations have also become wealthy and more important global players as a result of the oil boom. Russia, nearly bankrupt in the late 1990s, is awash with oil money and it is using it in various ways, including reasserting itself on the global stage (e.g. the invasion of Georgia in late 2008) in ways reminiscent of the old Soviet Union. In Venezuela, President Hugo Chávez is using oil profits to fuel a move toward socialism and to acquire a more powerful position in Latin America. He has also used them to fund massive public spending and to create subsidies designed to offer Venezuelans free health care and education and less expensive food. Angola ended a decades-long civil war in 2002; by 2007 its economy was growing by 24 percent. The government was investing in roads, airports, and railroad tracks. Hotel rooms in the capital city, Luanda, were booked months in advance.

At the individual level, great wealth and affluence are being produced at the very top. Individual Russians are traveling the world, buying expensive art, and bidding up the price of the most desirable real estate in, for example, London. In Angola most of the wealthiest people are current and former government officials. While such people are clearly skimming a large proportion of oil income off the top, the great majority of Angolans are profiting little, if at all, from the oil boom. In 2007 two out of three Angolans lived on $2 a day or less, the same as in 2002 at the end of the civil war. While Angola is an extreme case, there is little evidence in many other parts of the world that the poor are benefiting greatly from the oil boom.

The International Energy Agency has urged advanced nations to work with India and China to reduce the burgeoning use of oil. It is the increased demand, especially from China and India, which is playing a huge role in pushing up the price of oil on the world market. Increased use there, and elsewhere, is also tied, of course, to higher carbon dioxide emissions (projected to increase by 57 percent over the next quarter-century) and accompanying disastrous effects on the world's climate. It is estimated that in 2006–7, those two countries accounted for 70 percent of the growth in the demand for energy. Their use of energy is projected to double between 2005 and 2030. China is expected to overtake the US as the world leader in energy consumption in around 2010. For their part, representatives of China and India argue that they are being unduly singled out on this issue. After all, the developed countries have already developed and China and India should be given an opportunity to catch up before there is any discussion of limiting their expansion (Mouawad 2007: C3).

RACE TO THE BOTTOM AND UPGRADING

A dominant idea in thinking about less developed economies from a global perspective is the so-called "**race to the bottom**." The basic argument is that for less developed countries to compete and succeed in the

Race to the bottom: Countries involved in a downward spiral of competitiveness.

global economy, they must undercut the competition in various ways, such as offering lower wages, poorer working conditions, longer hours, ever-escalating pressure and demands, and so on. It is often the case that one nation is willing to go further than the others in order to attract the interest of MNCs. An ever-spiraling decline in wages etc. occurs in the "winning" less-developed nation, at least until it is undercut by other countries eager for work and willing to offer even lower pay, poorer working conditions, and so on. In other words, the countries that get the work are those that win the race to the bottom. These, of course, are almost always pyrrhic victories since the work is earned on the basis of creating poorly paid and horrid circumstances for the workers within the "victorious" nation.

Upgrading in the Less Developed World?

The current global economic system is based, at least in part, on a race to the bottom by less developed countries and the exploitation of them and their industries by the more developed countries. However, we must not ignore the fact that there is evidence of a process of upgrading in less developed countries and their industries (Bair and Gereffi 2003: 143–69). That is, at least some of them enter the global economic market at or near the bottom, but over time begin to move up. This, for example, is clear in China today, where the early success of Chinese industry was based on their victory in the race to the bottom, but the Chinese are now moving away from that and to the production of higher-value products, with higher pay and better working conditions for at least some Chinese workers.

Another example is to be found in Mexico, especially its *maquiladoras* (Gereffi 2005: 163). The early, first-generation *maquiladoras* were labor-intensive, employed limited technologies, and assembled finished products for export (e.g. apparel) using components imported from the US. Second-generation *maquiladoras* "are less oriented toward assembly and more toward manufacturing processes that use automated and semi-automated machines and robots in the automobile, television, and electrical appliance sectors" (Gereffi 2005: 163). In their third generation, *maquiladoras* "are oriented to research, design, and development, and rely on highly skilled labor such as specialized engineers and technicians," and they "have matured from assembly sites based on cheap labor to manufacturing centers whose competitiveness derives from a combination of high productivity, good quality, and wages far below those prevailing north of the border" (Gereffi 2005: 163). Of course, this indicates that while the *maquiladoras* may have advanced, the lot of the workers may not have kept pace with this development.

Industrial upgrading: Nation-states, firms and even workers move from low-value to relatively high-value production.

This point can be made more generally under the heading of **industrial upgrading** through which economic actors – nations, firms, and even workers – "move from low-value to relatively high-value activities in global production networks" (Gereffi 2005: 171). This can occur in four sequential stages – assembly, original equipment manufacture

(OEM), original brand name manufacturing (OBM), and original design manufacturing (ODM). Depending on the nation and industry in question (e.g. apparel, electronics, fresh vegetables), one sees varying degrees of movement up this hierarchy.

A similar point is made, albeit in far more general terms, by Rivoli in her study of the global market for T-shirts (Rivoli 2005). If one takes the long historical view, the nations, especially specific areas and the industries located there, that won the race to the bottom are now among the most successful global economies in the world. In textiles, the race to the bottom was won first by England (especially Manchester), then the US (New Hampshire and later Charlotte, North Carolina), then Japan (Osaka), and Hong Kong. Most recently it was the Chinese and their textile industry and it is clear that, having won the race to the bottom in that industry, they are moving up industrially and economically.

Rivoli generalizes from this to argue that nations and areas within them must win the race to the bottom in order ultimately to succeed. Victory in this race is, in her view, the "ignition switch" that turns the economy on and gets it rolling. Thus, she concludes that those who criticize globalization from below are misguided in their efforts to end this race. However, she does recognize that activists have, through their actions over the years, altered the nature of the race by raising the bottom. More generally she concludes that the "bottom is rising" (Rivoli 2005: 107).

However, Rivoli's view on this is hotly debated and much disputed because of its clear association with neo-liberalism. As a result, it seems to endorse the race to the bottom for all countries interested in development. This not only leads them into poverty for at least a time, but it greatly advantages the wealthy North which is guaranteed a continuing source of low-priced goods and services as one country replaces another at the bottom. Winning the race to the bottom is no guarantee of adaptive upgrading, but it is a guarantee of low wages and poverty for an unknown amount of time.

OUTSOURCING

Outsourcing is the transfer of activities once performed by an entity to a business (or businesses) in exchange for money. It is a complex phenomenon that is not restricted to the economy, not only a macro-level phenomenon, and not simply global in character. Dealing with the first issue, while outsourcing in the economic realm is of greatest importance and the issue of concern here, it also occurs in many other institutions such as health care and the military. In terms of health care, one example is the work of the radiologist, which is increasingly being outsourced. This is made possible because the material with which radiologists deal (x-rays, results of MRIs) is now usually digitized and therefore sent easily and quickly via the

> **Outsourcing**: Transfer of activities once performed by an entity to a business (or businesses) in exchange for money.

Internet to radiologists anywhere in the world. Thus, a digitized x-ray taken in London can be read quickly and easily by a lower-paid radiologist in Asia. Similarly, the military has outsourced many of its functions. For example, NATO forces from various countries serving in Afghanistan may be flown there on leased Ukrainian airplanes or by the commercial airlines of NATO nations rather than on planes from their own air forces. While both of these examples exist outside the economy, they *are* examples of outsourcing and *are* manifestations of globalization.

Secondly, we need to go beyond the macro-level of outsourcing (e.g. a British corporation outsourcing work to one in India) to deal with it at the meso- and micro-levels. Thus, we can include under the heading of outsourcing at the meso-level restaurants that outsource the cooking of their food to outside organizations (e.g. Sysco), and at the micro-level parents who outsource the care of their young children (Pyle 2006: 283–95) or aged parents to institutions, specifically day-care and assisted-living centers.

Inclusion of these levels makes for a more satisfying and more complete sense of outsourcing, although much of it may not relate directly to globalization. Nonetheless, globalization is often involved even at these levels as exemplified by the fact that the micro-level of care for children or aged parents in developed countries is often outsourced to immigrants, legal or illegal, from less developed countries. These migrants can be seen as part of a global care chain (see Chapter 11), and those who care for children, as well as the children themselves, as part of the globalization of parenthood. It is even the case that motherhood is being outsourced with, for example, Indian women serving as surrogate mothers for couples from Israel (Gentleman 2008: A9).

Offshore outsourcing: Transfer of activities to entities in other countries.

The form of outsourcing most closely and importantly associated with globalization is **offshore outsourcing** which involves sending work to companies in other countries. For example, a variety of Indian firms have become very important settings for the outsourcing of various kinds of work – the best known of which is that performed by call centers (Mirchandani 2004: 355–73) – from, especially, the US and Great Britain (although offshore outsourcing is a two-way street and such work is also finding its way into these developed countries). Indian companies are even making progress in performing outsourced call-center work for Japanese firms, necessitating, of course, the employment of those fluent in Japanese (*Economist* 2007: October 11). While blue-collar manufacturing work has long been outsourced offshore, and the offshore outsourcing of low-level service work is of more recent vintage, what is eye-catching is the increasing offshore outsourcing of high-level white-collar and service work such as IT (information technology), accounting, law, architecture, journalism, and medicine. There are many advantages of offshore outsourcing to both outsourcers (e.g. 24/7 availability of workers) and outsourcees (e.g. job and wealth creation) and that is why it has grown so dramatically and is likely to continue to grow. However, there are many costs, especially in the country doing the outsourcing and most notably in job loss and destruction. It is the array of costs that has made offshore outsourcing a hot-button issue in the US and other developed nations and has led to calls for the government to act to restrict it.

However, as we saw above in the case of health care and the military, offshore outsourcing is not restricted to the economy and is therefore globalizing in a far broader sense than is usually understood. For example, the offshore outsourcing of war has a long history (including British outsourcing of fighting much of the Revolutionary War to paid mercenaries, especially the Hessians), but it boomed, at least in the case of the US, following the end of the Cold War. A variety of for-profit private organizations have emerged to which various war functions are outsourced. So many aspects of the war in Iraq were outsourced that one wag joked that President George Bush's "coalition of the willing" might thus be more aptly described as the "coalition of the billing."

In-sourcing involves the fact that offshore outsourcing necessarily involves tasks being taken in by firms in other countries. In the case of the US (and other developed countries), the work that is outsourced to, say, India is simultaneously in-sourced by that country. It is also the case that while they are offshore outsourcing a great deal of work, the US and Great Britain, among others, are also in-sourcing some work that had been performed in other countries.

FINANCIAL GLOBALIZATION

The world's economies have become more tightly interconnected as a result of globalization. One reflection of that is the well-known phrase, "When the American economy sneezes, the rest of the world catches a cold." However, dramatic economic events in other parts of the world also have an impact on most, if not all, of the world's economies. This is clear, for example, in the global impact of the financial crises that struck Asia and Russia in the 1990s. However, it remains the case that the more powerful the economy, the greater the effect of its crises on the rest of the world. The corollary is that problems in weaker economies have less of an effect across the globe. Thus, Argentina had a serious financial crisis in the late 1990s and early 2000s, but its impact on the global economy was comparatively small.

The Great Recession

Thus, when the US suffers a financial crisis it does have a profound effect on the rest of the world's economies. This was demonstrated most recently in the sub-prime mortgage crisis (associated with the Great Recession of 2008–9) which had its roots in problems associated with a dramatic increase in the issuing of highly risky "sub-prime" mortgages by American banks. These were mortgages sold primarily to relatively low-income people (whose ability to repay those loans was not checked closely) in order to allow and induce them to buy homes. They were offered low interest rates (rates below the prime interest rate), or the possibility of paying only on the principal with no interest payments, but those highly attractive terms lasted for only a few years. After that, the interest rates were to "float," rising to the higher rate prevalent at the time. This served to raise homeowners' monthly payments, sometimes substantially. Many of those who bought homes at the sub-prime rate did not realize that such an increase would occur or how much more they would need to pay each month. They also believed that they would be able to refinance their homes at an attractive fixed interest rate when the initial low interest rate ended, but they found that the emerging crisis had left banks unable or unwilling to offer them new credit at low rates. The crisis began in earnest when large numbers of comparatively low-income home owners were unable to make their monthly payments and the banks foreclosed on their homes. Banks would ordinarily sell foreclosed homes, but the booming housing market of the early 2000s had collapsed and many banks were left with far too many valueless properties and this translated into large write-offs and huge losses. More importantly, many low-income homeowners were ruined as a result of losing their home and their investment in it. The losses experienced by American banks contributed to a global banking crisis and other financial and economic institutions were adversely affected, as well. This was a big factor in the huge bailout of the financial system by the US government in late 2008.

An underlying cause of the global crisis is the fact that American banks no longer hold many of the mortgages that they write, but rather they "securitize" (bundle) them with other mortgages and sell the bundles as "mortgage-backed securities" to other banks and financial institutions, often throughout the world (Gotham 2006: 231–75). Those who bought these bundles of debt rarely fully understood, or even cared about, the details of the securities that were in the bundles. The assumption was that mortgages were generally safe and if there were some risky investments in the bundle, they were more than compensated for by the safe ones. When the sub-prime crisis developed, financial institutions in the US and throughout the world came to realize that a large portion of the bundles of debt that they had purchased was valueless. This led financial institutions to mark down billions of dollars in assets and some nearly went bankrupt.

Not surprisingly major banks (e.g. Citicorp, Washington Mutual) and other financial institutions in the US (e.g. Fannie Mae, Freddie Mac, AIG – all eventually nationalized in whole or in part by the US) experienced severe difficulties either because they had issued sub-prime mortgages or had invested in bundles of securitized mortgages. However, the crisis was not restricted to the US. For example, the Northern Rock bank in Great Britain was saved from bankruptcy in late 2007 by an infusion of money from the Bank of England (*Economist* 2008: January 24). In early 2008 the British government reluctantly took control of (nationalized) Northern Rock, at least temporarily (Werdigier 2008: C1, C4). The crisis continued to expand in 2008 involving the global economy to an ever-increasing degree.

Throughout late 2007 there was much discussion of whether and how much the sub-prime crisis, and the related implosion of the housing market, was going to affect the overall American economy. By early 2008 it became clear that the impact was going to be profound, with indications that the US economy was facing a recession increasing later in 2008. The US Stock Market dropped dramatically to more than 15 percent below its peak in late 2007, and after a slight recovery dropped again in late 2008 (Grynbaum 2008: C1, C7). This occurred in the context of a view that because of the great strength and growth of other economies around the world (e.g. the EU, Japan, China, India), they were much less likely to catch a "cold" just because the US "sneezed" (Goodman 2008: C1, C4). Another way of putting this is that a number of the more powerful economies in the world had "decoupled" from the US economy. That is, they had become strong enough, had enough internal demand, and could do business with so many other countries, that their economies were no longer closely linked ("coupled") with that of the US (Gross 2008: 39–42). This seemed to be especially true of emerging economies which trade a great deal with each other, as well as with countries such as China (*Economist* 2008: March 6).

However, this quickly proved fallacious, at least in the short run, as many global stock markets plunged as much, or more, than the US Stock Market. Since the US is the major consumer of much of the world's products, a recession or financial crisis there was likely to have a profoundly negative effect on many global economies dominated by the production of goods exported to the US. The negative effect on other economies could, in turn, adversely affect their ability to buy American goods and services, or to invest in the US and its businesses, further worsening the crisis there. Thus, the effects of the crisis flowed easily and rapidly back and forth throughout the world in 2008 contributing to an ever-deepening global economic crisis. As one economist put it in early 2008: "The real fear is that there's a kind of total systems breakdown" (quoted in Goodman 2008: C4). This fear came dangerously close to a reality in the financial crisis later in the year.

Even the booming Chinese economy began to feel the pinch. Sales of T-shirts and knitwear declined significantly and some Chinese factories were in danger of being forced out of business (Bradsher 2008: C1, C4). The Chinese economy clearly remains closely tied to the American economy. This may be even truer of less robust economies than that of China (and India). For example, the Japanese economy seemed to feel the effects of the American decline more than these other economies. A Japanese economist remarked: "Now we see 're-coupling'. … The economy of Japan is proving disappointingly fragile to external shocks" (quoted in Bradsher 2008: C4).

In another reflection of globalization, Citicorp sought to solve its financial problems caused by the sub-prime crisis by soliciting massive investments from other parts of the world, especially the oil-producing states of the Middle East. On the one hand, this served to make Citicorp itself a more global company. On the other hand, such foreign investments in US corporations led to increasing fears in the US of other nations buying into, and coming to control, large American corporations (Goodman and Story 2008: 1, 29). In fact, foreign direct investment (FDI) in US corporations increased greatly in 2007, rising to over $400 billion (over $100 billion *more* than US FDI abroad). In 2006 foreign FDI in the US was about half that amount.

The biggest concern about foreign control involved financial investments in the US by **sovereign wealth funds** (which amounted to over $21 billion in 2007). These funds are owned by nation-states (not corporations or individual investors) and when they invest in other countries, it is in fact those nation-states that are doing the investing. Among the largest sovereign wealth funds are the Abu Dhabi Investment Authority (ADIA), the Government of Singapore Investment Corporation, and the China Investment Corporation. In a sense, the activities of these funds involve a new form of state capitalism. As of early 2008, as a result in large part of the huge increase in oil prices, sovereign wealth funds (especially in the Middle East) were estimated to have almost $3 trillion dollars that they were seeking to invest. The largest, ADIA (begun in 1976), alone may have more than $1 trillion (it is funded by Abu Dhabi's yearly surplus of about $50 billion) (Thomas 2008: C1, C4). Furthermore, the likelihood is that the resources of these funds (projected to reach $12 trillion by 2015) will continue to increase rapidly as oil prices continue to be high or, more likely, rise further. In just the first month of 2008, funds owned by Singapore, Kuwait, and South Korea invested a huge amount of money to prop up not only Citicorp, but also another giant US financial corporation, Merrill Lynch (*Economist* 2008: January 17). These and other financial corporations were teetering on the brink because of the global credit crunch caused by the Great Recession, and many, including Merrill Lynch, collapsed in late 2008.

> **Sovereign wealth funds**: Funds controlled by nation-states that often invest in other countries.

In one sense the flow of money from sovereign wealth funds to beleaguered companies in the US and elsewhere is just business as usual in a global world; it is just another global flow of one of the things that flows most readily around the globe – money. At the same time, it has led to cries for the creation of barriers to those flows. In the US the worry is that through sovereign wealth funds, other nations are gaining control over its institutions (e.g. its banks and financial institutions) and its resources. One US Senator commented: "In the short run, that they are investing here is good. … But in the long run it is unsustainable. Our power and authority is eroding because of the amounts we are sending abroad for energy and consumer goods" (quoted in Thomas 2008: C4). As a result, many American politicians were in favor of greater control over, and restrictions on, the flow of money from sovereign wealth funds to the US. Similar reactions have occurred in other countries (e.g. France, Germany).

CONSUMPTION

While aspects of globalization that relate to consumption have been mentioned above, especially in the discussion of global value chains, in this section we focus more directly on consumption itself in a global context (Sassatelli 2008).

Consumption is highly complex, involving mainly consumer objects, consumers, the consumption process, and consumption sites (Ritzer, Weidenhoft, and

Goodman 2001: 410–27). Before we get to those topics, it is important to note that there has been a tendency to closely associate consumption, as well as the globalization of consumption, with America and Americanization (see Chapter 2). This is largely traceable to the affluence of the US after the close of WW II and the economic difficulties encountered by most other societies in the world during this period. Thus, the US developed an unprecedented and unmatched consumer society for several decades after the end of the war and at the same time began exporting it – and its various elements – to much of the rest of the world. While much of American consumer society came to be adopted elsewhere, it was also modified in various ways, even in the immediate aftermath of WW II in the European nations ravaged by the war and being aided through America's Marshall Plan (Kroen 2006: 251–77).

This last point brings us to the issue of globalization and how it is implicated in all of this beyond the mere fact that consumption sites, goods, and the like have become both ubiquitous and increasingly similar throughout the world. In a world increasingly dominated by neo-liberalism, the emphasis in the economy is to greatly increase global flows of everything related to consumption and to greatly decrease any barriers to those flows. Of particular interest here is the expediting of global flows of consumer goods and services of all types *and* of the financial processes and instruments that expedite those flows. Thus, for example, the relatively small number of credit card brands with origins in the US (especially Visa and MasterCard) are increasingly accepted and used (including by locals) throughout more and more parts of the world. This serves to promote not only global consumption, but also the flow of global consumers (including tourists).

More importantly, this serves to expedite the global flow of **hyperconsumption** (buying more than one can afford) and **hyperdebt** (owing more than one will be able to pay back). The global flow of many of the same goods and services, and the increasing global use of credit cards and other credit instruments, leads more and more societies throughout the world in the direction of American-style hyperconsumption and hyperdebt. Many countries that at one time were very conservative as far as consumption and debt are concerned have plunged headlong in these directions. China and India, with their enormous populations enjoying an unprecedented economic boom, also appear to be headed in much the same direction. Thus, globalization means that hyperconsumption and hyperdebt, as well as the problems associated with them, are increasingly likely to become global phenomena and problems.

Hyperconsumption: Buying more than one can afford.

Hyperdebt: Owing more than one will be able to repay.

While there was, and continues to be, an important American component to the globalization of consumption, it is important to recognize that the heyday of the US in this area (and many others) is long past and in any case there has always been much more to the globalization of consumption (and everything else) than Americanization (Brewer and Trentmann 2006: 1–17). That is, local areas have certainly not always, or perhaps ever, been overwhelmed by American imports, but have integrated them into the local cultural and economic realities, that is they have "glocalized them" (see Chapter 7). Furthermore, other nations and regions have been significant exporters of important aspects of consumer society (e.g. Mercedes-Benz and BMW automobiles from Germany). Finally, much of consumption remains largely, if not totally, local in character (e.g. "binge" consumption in Belize [Wilk 2006: 123–43]). The growing consumption of khat, or *qat* – a mild stimulant – in Kenya (Anderson and Carrier 2006: 145–66) is not only locally defined, but there is active resistance to external definitions of it (the US defines it as a dangerous drug).

Consumption also plays itself out differently in different parts of the world. For example, both the US and Japan can be seen as consumer societies, but Japan differs from the US in many ways including the fact that it never fully embraced the idea of a consumer society and, more specifically, continues to manage to save a significant amount, in contrast to the US where the savings rate approaches zero (Garon 2006: 189–217).

Consumer Objects and Services

Much of consumption revolves around shopping for and purchasing objects of all kinds (Quarter Pounders, snowboards, automobiles, etc.), but in recent years an increasing amount of consumption relates to various services (legal, accounting, educational, etc.). While many objects and services remain highly local (e.g. the khat mentioned above; the services of street-based letter writers for illiterate Indians), an increasing number have globalized. On the one hand, there are, for example, the global objects such as automobiles from the US, Germany, and Japan. On the other hand, there are global services such as those offered by accounting firms (e.g. KPMG International), as well as package delivery services (e.g. DHL).

Of particular importance in terms of objects and services is the issue of brands and branding (Holt 2004). Brands are of great importance both within nations as well as globally. Indeed, much money and effort is invested in creating brand names that are recognized and trusted throughout the world. In fact, all of the corporate names mentioned in the previous paragraph have achieved global brand recognition. In her best-selling book *No Logo: Taking Aim at the Brand Bullies*, Naomi Klein details the importance of the brand (e.g. Nike, McDonald's) in the contemporary world and the degree to which brands are both globalized (logos are virtually an international language) and having a global impact (Klein 2000).

Consumers

Increasing numbers of people throughout the world are spending more and more time as consumers. Not long ago it was very different as most people spent most of their time as producers. Not only do more people spend more time consuming, but they are increasingly more likely to define themselves by what they consume

(Bimmers, Patek Philippe watches, and so on), than by their roles as producers and workers. Furthermore, consumers are on the move throughout the world, often as tourists. Not only is tourism a form of consumption, but much tourism is undertaken in order to consume the goods and services on offer at other locales throughout the world.

Consumption Processes

Increasing numbers of people know what is expected of them as consumers; they generally know what to do in the consumption process wherever they happen to be in the world. This includes knowing how to work their way through a shopping mall, use a credit card, or make a purchase online. Others have not yet encountered, let alone learned how to handle, these processes, but many of them certainly will in the not-too-distant future. Where these processes are known, there is a remarkable similarity throughout the world in the process of consuming in a supermarket, a shopping mall, or a fast-food restaurant.

Consumption Sites

American and Western-style consumption sites – shopping malls, fast-food restaurants, clothing chains, discounters such as Wal-Mart, Disney-like theme parks, Las Vegas-style casino hotels, Internet sites such as Amazon.com and ebay – have spread throughout much of the world.

Global Resistance

The global spread of chain stores, theme parks, and so on, has led to many concerns and to resistance in many parts of the world (one now even sees resistance, or at least increasing concern, in the US). While we discuss resistance to consumption sites here, there is far broader global opposition to all aspects of consumption, especially hyperconsumption (e.g. Slow Food, the Voluntary Simplicity Movement, etc.).

For example, in Paris there is much concern about the Champs-Elysées, "'the most beautiful avenue on earth,'" and the way it is increasingly dominated by large outlets, often megastores, associated with global chains such as McDonald's, Adidas, Gap, Benetton, Disney, Nike, Zara, Virgin, Cartier, Louis Vuitton, and Sephora, as well as huge auto showrooms for Toyota, Renault, and Peugeot. A major reason is that burgeoning rental costs on the Champs-Elysées increasingly mean that it is only the large chains that can afford them. As a result, local institutions such as clubs and movie theatres are disappearing from the Champs-Elysées. A movement has emerged to stop the "'banalization'" of the most famous avenue in Paris, if not the world; to stop what has already occurred in other major areas such as Times Square in New York and Oxford Street in London. A first step was the banning of the opening of an H&M megastore (a Swedish chain with about 1,500 shops in nearly 30 countries) on the Champs-Elysées. A study commissioned by the city of

Paris concluded that, "the avenue progressively is losing its exceptional and symbolic character, thus its attractiveness." An alternative view, however, is that these changes represent a democratization of the Champs-Elysées. They offer an escape for the less affluent, especially multi-ethnic young people, some of whom have been expressing their general dissatisfaction with French life.

It must be noted in closing that a very large proportion of the world's population is excluded from many of the kinds of consumption and consumption sites discussed in the last several pages.

CHAPTER SUMMARY

This chapter focuses on global economic flows. Global trade operates through various economic networks such as supply chains, international production networks, global commodity chains and, most importantly, global value chains. Global value chains follow the creation of value through different stages, from the creation of a product, to its disposal after use.

Commodities are often the first link in this chain. The demand for commodities is sky-rocketing, fueled primarily by enormous demand in the developed countries and increased consumption in developing countries (especially China). Oil is a case in point. Not only are prices escalating because of increased demand, but it is also becoming increasingly difficult to procure oil. These problems will be exacerbated in the future by a decrease in the global supply of oil, as well as by the fact that some of the current oil-exporting countries will start to import (rather than to export) oil to meet their domestic needs.

Some countries stimulate trade and investment through low prices and low wages. This often leads to a "race to the bottom" among countries vying for increased investment and export business. However, some theorize that after a point, there is a move toward industrial "upgrading." Countries that entered the world market at the bottom, such as China and Mexico, move on to produce higher-value products at higher wages. However, as some countries upgrade, others enter at the bottom, guaranteeing a supply of low-priced, low-wage products to the North.

Outsourcing is also an important global flow. Offshore outsourcing involves contracting work to companies located in other countries. Apart from the economic domain, this process is also prevalent in the health care and military domains. Not only does the process operate at a macro-level, but increasingly, it can also be observed at micro- and meso-levels.

National economies across the globe are highly interconnected through financial markets; cyclical fluctuations in one country will have an impact on many others. The more powerful the economy, the greater the likelihood that its crises will spread around the world. One very recent example is the US sub-prime mortgage crisis and resulting Great Recession that spread throughout much of the world.

Global economic flows also include the movement of corporations, people, and ideas, across both geographic and virtual boundaries. The flow of consumer goods and services is also being expedited. Hyperconsumption (buying more than one can afford) and hyperdebt (owing more money than one can afford to repay) are important concepts in this analysis. Not only do people spend more time in consumption, they are also increasingly defining themselves through their consumption practices.

Consumption sites are increasingly becoming global. Resistance to these sites of consumption, as well as to hyperconsumption and hyperdebt, is also global.

DISCUSSION QUESTIONS

1. Locate the major barriers to global economic flows. Are they effective? Are they necessary?

2. Examine the linkages between the process of "race to the bottom" and "upgrading."

3. Examine the linkages between the process of outsourcing and the "race to the bottom."

4. Examine globalization in the sphere of consumption as well as production.

5. Does the ongoing global economic crisis signal the end of hyperconsumption and hyperdebt?

FURTHER READING

Giovanni Arrighi. *Adam Smith in Beijing: Lineages of the Twenty-First Century*. London: Verso, 2007.

Pietra Rivoli. *Travels of a T-Shirt in a Global Economy: An Economist Examines the Markets, Power, and Politics of World Trade*. Chichester: John Wiley, 2005.

Gary Gereffi and Miguel Korzeniewicz, eds. *Commodity Chains and Global Capitalism*. Westport, CT: Praeger, 1994.

Joseph Schumpeter. *Capitalism, Socialism and Democracy*. London: Routledge, 2006.

Roberta Sassatelli. *Consumer Culture: History, Theory and Politics*. London: Sage, 2007.

Douglas Holt. *How Brands Become Icons: Principles of Cultural Branding*. Cambridge, MA: Harvard Business School, 2004.

Adam Arvidsson. *Brands: Meaning and Value in Media Culture*. London: Routledge, 2006.

Naomi Klein. *No Logo: Taking Aim at the Brand Bullies*. Toronto: Vintage, Canada, 2000.

Alan Bryman. *The Disneyization of Society*. London: Sage, 2004.

REFERENCES

Anderson, David M., and Neil Carrier. 2006. "'Flowers of Paradise' or 'Polluting the Nation': Contested Narratives of Khat Consumption." In John Brewer and Frank Trentmann, eds., *Consuming Cultures, Global Perspectives: Historical Trajectories, Transnational Exchanges*. Oxford: Berg.

Bair, Jennifer, and Gary Gereffi. 2003. "Upgrading, Uneven Development, and Jobs in the North American Apparel Industry." *Global Networks* 3, 2.

Barboza, David. 2007. "Blazing a Paper Trail in China." *New York Times*. January 16.

Barboza, David. 2008a. "China Inflation Exacting a Toll Across the US." *New York Times*. February 1.

Barboza, David. 2008b. "Through Friends and Smugglers, China's Consumers See iPhones." *New York Times*. February 18.

Barboza, David. 2009. "In a Global Spree, China Buys Up Commodities." *New York Times*. February 21.

Bradsher, Keith. 2008. "Throughout Asia, Exporters Brace for Tremors from a US Pullback." *New York Times*. January 25.

Brandt, Loren, and Thomas G. Rawski, eds. 2008. *China's Great Economic Transformation*. Cambridge: Cambridge University Press.

Brewer, John, and Frank Trentmann. 2006. "Introduction: Space, Time and Value in Consuming Cultures." In John Brewer and Frank Trentmann, eds., *Consuming Cultures, Global Perspectives: Historical Trajectories, Transnational Exchanges*. Oxford: Berg.

Chanda, Nayan. 2007. *Bound Together: How Traders, Preachers, Adventurers, and Warriors Shaped Globalization*. New Haven: Yale University Press.

Dossani, Rafiq. 2008. *India Arriving: How this Economic Powerhouse is Redefining Global Business*. New York: AMACOM/American Management Association.

Economist. 2007. October 11. "Adding Sugar."

Economist. 2008. January 17. "The Invasion of the Sovereign Wealth Funds."

Economist. 2008. January 24. "Hocking the Rock."

Economist. 2008. March 6. "The Decoupling Debate."

Economist. 2008. March 13. "The New Colonialists."

Friedman, Thomas. 2005. *The World is Flat: A Brief History of the Twenty-first Century*. New York: Farrar, Straus, Giroux.

Garon, Sheldon. 2006. "Japan's Post-war 'Consumer Revolution', or Striking a 'Balance' between Consumption and Saving." In John Brewer and Frank Trentmann, eds., *Consuming Cultures, Global Perspectives: Historical Trajectories, Transnational Exchanges*. Oxford: Berg.

Gentleman, Amelia. 2008. "India Nurtures Business of Surrogate Motherhood." *New York Times*. March 10.

Gereffi, Gary. 2005. "The Global Economy: Organization, Governance, and Development." In Neil Smelser and Richard Swedberg, eds., *Handbook of Economic Sociology*. Princeton: Princeton University Press.

Gereffi, Gary, and Miguel Korzeniewicz, eds. 1994. *Commodity Chains and Global Capitalism*. Westport, CT: Praeger.

Goodman, Peter S. 2008. "Trading Partners Fear U.S. Consumers Won't Continue Free-Spending Ways." *New York Times*. January 25.

Goodman, Peter S., and Louise Story. 2008. "Foreigners Buy Stakes in the US at a Record Pace." *New York Times*. January 20.

Gotham, Kevin. 2006. "The Secondary Circuit of Capital Reconsidered: Globalization and the US Real Estate Sector." *American Journal of Sociology* 112 (July).

Gross, Daniel. 2008. "The US Economy Faces the Guillotine." *Newsweek*. February 4.

Grynbaum, Michael M. 2008. "Investors See Recession, and Market Drops." *New York Times*. January 18.

Holt, Douglas. 2004. *How Brands Become Icons: Principles of Cultural Branding*. Cambridge, MA: Harvard Business School.

Klein, Naomi. 2000. *No Logo: Taking Aim at the Brand Bullies*. Toronto: Vintage, Canada.

Krauss, Clifford. 2008. "Commodities' Relentless Surge." *New York Times*. January 15.

Kroen, Sheryl. 2006. "Negotiations with the American Way: The Consumer and the Social Contract in Post-war Europe." In John Brewer and Frank Trentmann, eds., *Consuming Cultures, Global Perspectives: Historical Trajectories, Transnational Exchanges*. Oxford: Berg.

Landler, Mark. 2007. "High-Priced Oil Adds Volatility to Global Scramble for Power." *New York Times*. November 7.

Mann, Catherine L., and Katharine Pluck. 2007. "Trade." In Jan Aart Scholte and Roland Robertson, eds., *Encyclopedia of Globalization*. New York: MTM Publishing.

Mirchandani, Kiran. 2004. "Practices of Global Capital: Gaps, Cracks and Ironies in Transnational Call Centres in India." *Global Networks* 4, 4.

Mouawad, Jad. 2007. "Cuts Urged in China's and India's Energy Growth." *New York Times*. November 7.

Peters, Jeremy W. 2007. "Trade Deficit Drops for Third Consecutive Month." *New York Times*. January 11.

Pyle, Jean. 2006. "Globalization, Transnational Migration, and Gendered Care Work: Introduction." *Globalizations* 3, 3.

Ritzer, George, Wendy Weidenhoft, and Douglas Goodman. 2001. "Theories of Consumption." In George Ritzer and Barry Smart, eds., *Handbook of Social Theory*. London: Sage.

Rivoli, Pietra. 2005. *Travels of a T-Shirt in a Global Economy: An Economist Examines the Markets, Power, and Politics of World Trade*. Hoboken, NJ: John Wiley.

Rothenberg-Aalami, Jessica. 2004. "Coming Full Circle? Forging Missing Links Along Nike's Integrated Production Networks." *Global Networks* 4, 4.

Sassatelli, Roberta. 2008. "Consumer Society." In George Ritzer, ed., *The Blackwell Encyclopedia of Sociology Online*. Submitted February. Oxford: Blackwell.

Seabrook, John. 2008. "American Scrap: An Old-School Industry Globalizes." *New Yorker*. January 14.

Thomas, Jr., Landon. 2008. "Cash-Rich, Publicity-Shy." *New York Times*. February 28.

Weisman, Steven R. 2007. "Oil Producers See the World and Buy It Up." *New York Times*. November 28.

Werdigier, Julia. 2008. "Government to Control Struggling British Bank." *New York Times*. February 18.

Wilk, Richard. 2006. "Consumer Culture and Extractive Industry on the Margins of the World System." In John Brewer and Frank Trentmann, eds., *Consuming Cultures, Global Perspectives: Historical Trajectories, Transnational Exchanges*. Oxford: Berg.

Global Political Structures and Processes

Globalization: The Essentials, by George Ritzer
© 2011 John Wiley & Sons Ltd

The focal concern in this chapter is the political structures involved in globalization. However, these structures, like all structures, are often better seen as flows or as encompassing sets of flows. For example, a nation-state or a bureaucracy is often thought of as a structure, but in the main it is the sum of the processes (communication, decision-making, etc.) that take place within it. To put this another way, structures can be seen as "congealed flows." In that sense, the bulk of this chapter also deals with political processes (and flows). However, before we get to our focus on political structures, we need to be more explicit about the political flows themselves.

ON POLITICAL FLOWS

While the focus in this chapter will be on the development and nature of a wide range of political structures relevant to globalization, there certainly are a number of separable political flows of various sorts that are relevant to an understanding of contemporary globalization. In fact, it could be argued that virtually all of the flows discussed throughout this book are political and of great relevance to political structures of all sorts. Some, of course, are of more direct political relevance than others.

- The global flow of people (Chapter 8), especially refugees and illegal immigrants, poses a direct threat to the nation-state and its ability to control its borders.
- The looming crises associated with dwindling oil and water supplies (Chapter 9) threaten to lead to riots and perhaps insurrections that could lead to the downfall of extant governments.
- The inability of the nation-state to control economic flows dominated by MNCs, as well as the current economic and financial crisis that is sweeping the world (Chapter 4), is also posing a profound threat to the nation-state (e.g. in Eastern Europe).
- Environmental problems of all sorts (Chapter 9), especially those related to global warming, are very likely to be destabilizing politically.
- Borderless diseases (Chapter 10), especially malaria, TB, and AIDs in Africa, pose a danger to political structures.
- War (Chapter 10) is the most obvious global flow threatening the nation-states involved, especially those on the losing side.
- Global inequalities (Chapter 11), especially the profound and growing North–South split, threaten to pit poor nations against rich nations.
- Terrorism (Chapter 10) is clearly regarded as a threat by those nations against which it is waged (hence the so-called "war on terrorism" in the US).

Thus, a significant portion of this book deals with political processes, or with many processes that are directly or indirectly related to politics. In addition, there is a discussion (especially in Chapter 12) of various efforts to deal with global problems, many of which (e.g. trade protection and liberalization; efforts to increase political transparency and accountability) are political in nature. Finally, political structures (e.g. nation-states, the UN) initiate a wide range of global flows (e.g. the violence sponsored by Robert Mugabe's government in Zimbabwe that led to the mass migration of millions of people from the country).

THE NATION-STATE

The Treaty of Westphalia (1648) ended the Thirty (and Eighty) Years' War(s) in Europe and instituted an international system which recognized sovereign states at its core. Thus, it is not sovereign states that were new (absolutist states, for example, had long existed), but rather the recognition accorded them at Westphalia. The treaty was widely interpreted as giving states the right to political self-determination, to be considered equal from a legal point of view, and as prohibiting them from intervening in the affairs of other sovereign states. Critics of the traditional interpretation of Westphalia contend that none of these things were inherent in the original treaty, but were read into it later by those who wanted to buttress the state system. Furthermore, it is argued that this interpretation set in motion an anarchic and conflictive relationship between states and perhaps set the stage for inter-state wars, especially WW I and WW II. Nevertheless, nation-states remained preeminent until the current era of globalization when global flows began, at least in the eyes of many observers (including mine), to undermine the nation-state (Hayman and Williams 2006: 521–41).

The nation-state, of course, has two basic components – "nation" and "state." **Nation** "refers to a social group that is linked th[r]ough common descent, culture, language, or territorial contiguity" (Cerny 2007: 854). Also important in this context is **national identity**, the "fluid and dynamic form of collective identity, founded upon a community's subjective belief that the members of the community share a set of characteristics that make them different from other groups" (Guibernau 2007: 849–53). While the notion of a nation was highly circumscribed (e.g. regionally) in the Middle Ages, from the seventeenth century on the idea of nation was broadened and enlarged by a number of forces (political leaders, bureaucrats, the bourgeoisie, the proletariat, intellectuals, etc.) that pushed for "**nationalism**," a doctrine and/or political movement that seeks to make the nation the basis of a political structure, especially a state. The

Nation: Social group linked through common descent, culture, language, or territorial contiguity.

National identity: A fluid and dynamic form of collective identity; members of the community believe that they are different from other groups.

Nationalism is a doctrine and (or) political movement that seek to make the nation the basis of a political structure, especially a state.

state emerged as a new institutional form in the wake of the demise of the feudal system. The state offered a more centralized form of control (in comparison to, say, city-states) and evolved an organizational structure with "relatively autonomous office-holders outside other socioeconomic hierarchies, with its own rules and resources increasingly coming from taxes rather than from feudal, personal or religious obligations" (Cerny 2007: 855). Also coming to define the state was its claim to sovereignty. This involved the ability to engage in collective action both internally (e.g. to collect taxes) and externally (e.g. to deal with other states, to engage in warfare, etc.). The **nation-state** can therefore be seen as an integration of the subgroups that define themselves as a nation with the organizational structure that constitutes the state.

> **State**: Organizational structure outside other socioeconomic hierarchies with relatively autonomous office-holders.

> **Nation-state**: Integrates sub-groups that define themselves as a nation with the organizational structure of the state.

Threats to the Nation-State

As a result of the heritage of Westphalia, we came to think of the nation-state as an autonomous, rather self-contained, entity, but in fact many of the global flows that slice through the state (see below, as well as throughout this book) indicate that the nation-state is not, and undoubtedly never has been, such a "container." As a result, one observer (and this author would agree) concludes that the "state is today highly contingent and in flux" (Cerny 2007: 854).

Global flows
The nation-state is especially threatened by the global economy and global economic flows. An extreme argument is made by Ohmae who contends that, "The uncomfortable truth is that, in terms of the global economy, nation-states have become little more than bit actors" (1996: 12). He talks in terms of a borderless global economy that nation-states are unable to control.

A similar argument is made by Strange who contends that the decline of the nation-state is linked to technological and financial changes, as well as to "the accelerated integration of national economies into one single global market economy" (Strange 1996: 13–14). While nation-states once controlled markets, it is now the markets that often control the nation-states. In this context, Strange takes on the Westphalia system and dubs it a "Westfailure." She does so because the state has failed to control the financial system (she cites the Asian financial crisis, but the Great Recession is an even better example), to protect the environment, and to deal with social inequality (Strange 1999: 345–54).

There are a variety of other factors threatening the autonomy of the nation-state including flows of information, illegal immigrants, new social movements, terrorists, criminals, drugs, money (including laundered money, and other financial instruments), sex-trafficking, and much else. Many of these flows have been made possible by the development and continual refinement of technologies of all sorts.

The nation-state has also been weakened by the growing power of global and transnational organizations (e.g. the EU) that operate largely free of the control of nation-states. Another factor is the growth of global problems (AIDs, global warming, terrorism; see Chapters 9 and 10) that cannot be handled, or handled very well, by a nation-state operating on its own. A more specific historical factor is the end of the Cold War, which had been a powerful force in unifying, or at least holding together, some nation-states. One example is Yugoslavia and its dissolution with the end of the Cold War, but the main one, of course, is the dissolution of the Soviet Union into a number of independent nation-states (Russia, Ukraine, Georgia, etc.). Then there are "failed states" (Boas and Jennings 2007: 475–85) (e.g. Somalia), where there is, in effect, no functioning national government, as well as states that are in the process of breaking down (Li 2002: 1–20). Clearly, failed states, and states that are disintegrating, are in no position to maintain their borders adequately.

One way of summarizing much of this is to say that the nation-state has become increasingly *porous*. While this seems to be supported by a great deal of evidence, the fact is that no nation-state has *ever* been able to control its borders completely (Bauman 1992: 57). Thus, it is not the porosity of the nation-state that is new, but rather what is new is a dramatic *increase* in that porosity and the kinds of flows that are capable of passing through national borders.

International human rights

Another threat to the autonomy of the nation-state is the growing interest in international human rights (Elliott 2007: 343–63; Chatterjee 2008; Fredman 2008). Indeed, the issue of human rights, defined as the "entitlement of individuals to life, security, and well-being" (Turner 1993: 489–512; 2007: 591), has emerged as a major global political issue. It is argued that because these rights are universal, the nation-state cannot abrogate them. As a result, global human rights groups have claimed the right to be able to have a say about what is done to people within (for example, torture of terror suspects) and between (for example, illegal trafficking in humans [Farr 2005]) sovereign states. Thus, in such a view, human rights are a global matter and not exclusively a concern of the state (Levy and Sznaider 2006: 657–76). Furthermore, the implication is that the international community can and should intervene when a state violates human rights or when a violation occurs within a state border and the state does not take adequate action to deal with the violation.

A concern for human rights on a global scale emerged in reaction to the Holocaust (Bauman 1989) and other twentieth-century atrocities. On December 10, 1948, the UN General Assembly approved a Universal Declaration of Human Rights. For example, according to Article 13: (1) Everyone has the right to freedom of movement and residence within the borders of each State. (2) Everyone has the right to leave any country, including his own, and to return to his country. What is clear in this Declaration and its Articles is that human rights take precedence over the nation-state and that the UN is seeking to exert control over the state, at least on these issues.

As a result, at least in part, of growing interest in human rights in recent years, more people throughout the world have come to define themselves as global citizens and have agitated against human rights abuses throughout the world. The creation of the International Criminal Court (ICC) in 2002 created a venue in which those accused of human rights abuses could be tried and found guilty. However, such an international system is seen by some as a threat to the sovereignty of the nation-state (Sorensen 2007: 1075–8). As a result, the US, for one, has refused to recognize the ICC.

"Shadows of war"

Carolyn Nordstrom sees a different kind of threat to nation-states in what she calls the "shadows of war." Shadows of war are defined as "the complex sets of cross-state economic and political linkages that move outside *formally* recognized state-based channels" (Nordstrom 2004: 106). These "shadows of war" are *not* restricted by or to the nation-state; it is these "extra-state" processes (those that exist outside formal state channels; e.g. flows of black market goods) that are of central importance, especially in less developed countries. The myriad flows (e.g. of pharmaceuticals) that occur in this way help in the development of those countries and link them to transnational and cosmopolitan consumption sites. Nordstrom concludes:

> The sheer power carried in extra-state systems – the power to shape global economic and political realities – demonstrates the partial nature of state authority. And this demonstrates that the state's power is not preeminent, but a carefully crafted illusion that exists only because a population chooses to grant it believability. No single system of power reigns supreme, no ultimate hegemony prevails in the world. (2004: 235)

Nordstrom accords great importance to the "extra-state." On the one hand, when a nation-state collapses, in order to survive the people who live in such locales rely on extra-state networks that link people and countries globally. These are very flexible systems that are capable of adapting to the most extreme circumstances. On the other hand, it is often the case that extra-states (such as al-Qaeda) pose a greater threat to nation-states, including those that achieve superpower status (these days only the US), than do other nation-states. "Looking at the history of extra-state groups defeating the colonial world, people have learned that the extra-state is the most powerful way of challenging the state and combating a superpower" (Nordstrom 2004: 249).

IN DEFENSE OF THE NATION-STATE

There are at least some who contest the position taken above. A variety of arguments are made including that the nation-state continues to be *the* major player on the global stage (Gilpin 2001), that it retains at least some power in the face of globalization (Conley 2002: 378–99), that nation-states vary greatly in their efficacy in the face of globalization (Mann 2007: 472–96), and that the rumors of the demise of the nation-state are greatly exaggerated.

Daniel Beland argues that "the role of the state is enduring – and even increasing – in advanced industrial societies" (Beland 2008: 48). He sees greater demands being placed on the state because of four major sources of collective insecurity: terrorism (see Chapter 10); economic globalization, leading to problems such as outsourcing and pressures toward downsizing, as well as the current economic crisis (see Chapter 3); threats to national identity due to immigration (see Chapter 8); and the spread of global diseases such as AIDs (see Chapter 10). Further, the state does not merely respond to these threats, it may actually find it in its interest to exaggerate or even create dangers and thereby make its citizens more insecure (Glassner 2000). A good example is the US and British governments' arguments prior to the 2003 war with Iraq that Saddam Hussein had Weapons of Mass Destruction (WMDs) that posed a direct threat to the US and Great Britain. The US even claimed that Iraq could kill millions by using offshore ships to lob canisters containing lethal chemical or biological material into American cities (Isikoff and Corn 2006). The collective insecurity created by such outrageous claims helped foster public opinion in favor of invading Iraq and overthrowing Saddam Hussein.

The other side of this argument in support of the nation-state is that global processes of various kinds are just not as powerful as many believe. For example, global business pales in comparison to business *within* many countries, including the US. For another, some question the porosity of the nation-state by pointing, for example, to the fact that migration to the US and other countries has *declined* substantially since its heights in the late nineteenth and early twentieth centuries (Gilpin 2001).

A related point is that it would be a mistake simply to see globalization as a threat to, a constraint on, the nation-state; it can also be an *opportunity* for the nation-state (Conley 2002: 378–99). For example, the demands of globalization were used as a basis to make needed changes (at least from a neo-liberal point of view) in Australian society, specifically allowing it to move away from protectionism and in the direction of (neo-)liberalization, to transform state enterprises into private enterprises, and to streamline social welfare. In this, the rhetoric of globalization, especially an exaggeration of it and its effects, was useful to those politicians who were desirous of such changes. In other words, Australian politicians used globalization as an ideology in order to reform Australian society.

"IMAGINED COMMUNITY"

Whether or not it is being superseded by globalization, the nation-state remains important. In thinking about the nation-state, especially in the era of globalization, we need to understand that it is not a "natural" phenomenon, but is rather a social and political construction. This means that the nation-state had to be literally created, as, for example, the early leaders of the United States did in fusing the original independent states into a unified nation-state. It also means that the nation-state has to be defined by those within it, as well as those without, as such an entity. This can occur in various ways, but one of the key ideas in thinking about the unification of the nation-state is Benedict Anderson's (2006) notion of "imagined communities."

Anderson (2006: 6) *defines* the nation as "an imagined political community." Clearly, this means that for Anderson a nation exists primarily within the realm of ideas, subjectively within people's minds as an image. Anderson attributes four characteristics to an imagined nation. First, it is *imagined* because it is impossible in all but the smallest communities to have face-to-face contact with more than a few of one's peers. Because there are at least some, and likely many, not available for personal contact, one must imagine who they are, what they believe, what holds them together, and so on. Second, it is imagined to be *limited*, "because even the largest of them, encompassing perhaps a billion living human beings, has finite, if elastic, boundaries, beyond which lie other nations. No nation imagines itself as coterminous with mankind" (Anderson 2006: 7). Third, the nation-state is imagined to be *sovereign*, that is as being free. Finally, it is imagined to be a community, "because, regardless of the actual inequality and exploitation that may prevail in each, the nation is always conceived as a deep, horizontal comradeship" (Anderson 2006: 7).

Anderson sees the eighteenth century as the beginning of the dawn of the nation (in the sense that he defines it) and nationalism, and he links it to two key developments – the modern novel and the modern newspaper – which he includes under the heading of "print capitalism." Key to the modern novel was the idea of an actor moving calendrically through "homogenous, empty time." He sees this as "a precise analogue of the idea of the nation, which also is conceived as a solid community moving steadily down (or up) history" (Anderson 2006: 26). The novels tended to have a national imagination as well as an imagination of the characters moving through the sociological landscape presented in them.

In the case of the newspaper, the reader also has a sense that what appears in its pages operates calendrically. This is the case when one reads about a community – say the refugees in Darfur – for several days in a row. However, it is also the case when the story disappears from the newspaper for a time. The reader assumes that the Darfur community continues to move along and thus has little trouble picking up the "story" (note the similarity to a novel and its story line) when articles once again are published on Darfur. In addition, large numbers of people buy and read the newspaper on a given day and a given reader imagines that she is part of the larger community that is reading the same stories.

It was the mass sale and distribution of novels and newspapers that was critical to the rise of the imagined nation. It was also important that they were produced not in the language of the elites (e.g. Latin), or in many different vernaculars, but in a limited number of print languages. It was through this that people who previously could not understand one another "gradually became aware of hundreds of thousands, even millions, of people in their particular language-field, and at the same time that *only those* hundreds of thousands, or millions, so belonged. These fellow-readers, to whom they were connected through print, formed, in their secular, particular, visible invisibility, the embryo of the nationally imagined community" (Anderson 2006: 44).

Print capitalism also gave a new fixity to language that helped give solidity and long-term continuity to the notion of the nation. However, while a national print language was important historically, that does not mean that today nations (as well as nation-states) and print languages are coterminous. Clearly, various languages exist within a given nation-state (India encompasses many different languages) and languages stretch far beyond the borders of given nation-states (people in many countries speak French).

The imagined community is clearly a much greater reality than ever before because of developments far beyond print capitalism and not dealt with by Anderson. I am thinking here of the new digital media – especially cell phones, e-mail, the Internet, blogs, etc. – that allow widely dispersed populations to maintain, create, and disseminate a continuing sense of an imagined community. Globalization has not only meant the dispersal of many people but it has also provided them with newer technologies that allow them to be part of truly (global) imagined communities. Thus, although the nation-state itself may be of declining importance, it may be as important, and in fact more important, today in the age of globalization as an imagined reality.

CHANGES IN GLOBAL NATION-STATE RELATIONS

Beyond the nation-state there has been a wide range of formal and informal political relations among and between nation-states that have served to structure international and, more recently, global relations. Thus, during WW II the major divide was between those nation-states associated with the Allies (mainly the US, Great Britain, France, Russia) and those linked to the Axis (primarily Germany, Japan, Italy). During the Cold War, the major split was between Soviet bloc countries and those allied with the West. In the nearly two decades since the collapse of the Soviet Union the global political situation has been more fluid and various efforts have been made to offer a picture of the new global political world.

Parag Khanna (2008a, 2008b: 34ff.) offers one interesting perspective on this emerging new world. He bases his analysis on a distinction between globalization and geopolitics. Basically, globalization involves free flows, especially of an economic nature. In contrast, geopolitics involves largely political and military efforts aimed at gaining control over, but frequently disrupting, those flows (and much else). While the US was hegemonic in the era of geopolitics, it is greatly weakened as globalization competes with, and gains ascendancy over, geopolitics. However, based on the fact that the widely acknowledged prior epoch of globalization was brought to an end by the geopolitics associated with the onset of WW I, Khanna (2008a: 341) worries that geopolitics may once again undermine globalization.

Khanna argues that with the demise of the Soviet Union in 1991, US geopolitical hegemony was expected to last well into the future, but it failed to get past the end of the century. Instead, he sees the emergence in the twenty-first century of a new Big Three in the world – the EU, China, and the US. As Khanna (2008b: 64) puts it, the "web of globalization now has three spiders." However, in his view, the US is the one of the Big Three that is declining while the other two are likely to continue their recent ascent. (However, he does not foresee the US being replaced by the other two; they will coexist and compete actively and aggressively with one another.) He dismisses the other possibilities for world power status – Russia (Blum 2008) is being depopulated and is reduced to being run by "Gazprom.gov"; Islam is sharply divided (especially, Sunnis vs. Shias) and wars rage within Islam; India is far behind China and does not seem to have the same kind of global ambitions and appetite.

There is a lengthy set of points to be made about the strength of the EU and the likelihood that it will continue to grow in global importance:

- The EU is, at the moment, adding a nation-state a year and there is a fairly lengthy list of nation-states eager to enter.
- New pipelines bring the flow of oil to EU countries from Libya, Algeria, and Azerbaijan.
- The EU is already the largest market in the world having surpassed the US.
- The euro has been growing stronger and is stronger than the dollar; there is pressure in various quarters to move away from the dollar (e.g. oil is priced by OPEC in dollars per barrel) and to the euro as the global currency (although the value of the euro diminished early in the Great Recession).
- Europe is a leader in technological developments.
- London is replacing New York as the global financial capital (this trend is likely to accelerate as a result of the financial crisis and the demise of major American financial firms) and as a reflection of that China plans to locate the Western offices of its state investment fund in London, not New York.
- Europe (and the EU) is more of a political model for those in Africa or the Middle East than the US.
- Foreign students find it increasingly difficult to study in the US because of all sorts of barriers and impediments and, in any case, many find European educational institutions more attractive.

However, a recent financial crisis in Greece and looming financial crises in Spain and Portugal are causing some observers to question the strength of the EU.

China is expanding as a global power in a variety of ways:

- It is making all sorts of deals with, and sending a wide range of personnel (engineers, military personnel, etc.) to, a number of locales in the world – Africa, Latin America, etc.

- Its trade with the world is massive and has been growing (although, like much else, it has been hit hard by the recession).
- It maintains relations with, and even supplies arms to, all of the countries that the US shuns as "rogue states" (e.g. Iran, North Korea).
- Of course, China's greatest power is in East Asia where it is aided by the fact that about 35 million ethnic Chinese live throughout the other countries of East Asia and are well positioned within their economies.
- China is drawing more and more nations in the region into its political orbit and there is a possibility that it could eventually stand at the center of an Eastern version of NATO.

When the US is also taken into account, what is being produced, then, is "three hemispheric pan-regions, longitudinal zones dominated by America, Europe and China … because a vertically organized region contains all climatic zones year-round, each pan-region can be self-sufficient and build a power base from which to intrude in others' terrain" (Khanna 2008b: 37). This ability to intrude into each other's world is exacerbated by globalization and made easier in a "shrinking world."

The main battleground among the Big Three will be what Khanna calls the "second world," which is distinct from the core first-world countries and the peripheral third-world countries (Wallerstein 1974). These are the "swing states" over which the Big Three will compete and the outcome of that battle will determine who will win out in the geopolitics of the future. The most important of these swing states are in "Eastern Europe, Central Asia, South America, the Middle East and Southeast Asia" (Khanna 2008b: 39).

The most controversial of the second-world countries is Russia, but its shrinking population (if current trends continue, it will decline to almost the size of Turkey by 2025), the depopulation of, especially, eastern Russia (increasingly occupied by Chinese), and the concentration of development in the western part of the country (especially in and around Moscow) indicate it is better thought of as a second-world country than as a serious competitor to the Big Three. Europe is investing heavily in Russia and Europe is a major market for its oil and natural gas (although it has alternatives for these commodities). Thus, Khanna (2008b: 39) sees Russia as increasingly becoming almost an annex of Europe, although another alternative open to Russia would be to turn east away from the EU which, in his view, would lead Russia to become a "petro-vassal of China." Informal annexation by Europe seems more attractive and a more likely option. In fact, according to Khanna, some EU officials talk openly of the annexation of Russia.

Khanna lists many other nations as central to this second world including Turkey, Kazakhstan, Venezuela, Brazil, Saudi Arabia, Iran, Malaysia, Thailand, and so on. These countries and others are continually up for grabs and none of the Big Three will be able to include them permanently in its orbit. These countries may ally themselves with one of the Big Three for a time over a given issue, but then with another of the Big Three over another issue. The second-world countries will also form alliances among and between themselves.

Khanna puts these changes in the context of the decline of Americanization and the rise of globalization: "What I have seen in these and dozens of other [second-world] countries is that *globalization* is not synonymous with *Americanization*; in fact, nothing has brought about the erosion of American primacy faster than globalization" (2008b: 62, italics added). What he means is that globalization has eroded the geopolitical position of the US.

UNITED NATIONS (UN)

The United Nations (UN), in spite of its myriad problems, is the premier global organization in the realm of politics. The UN began operations on October 24, 1945. It is organized on the basis of the nation-states that are its members (there were 192 member states in 2007). As a "state-centric" organization (Weiss, Forsythe, and Coate 2004; Weiss and Zach 2007: 1217–23), the UN stands in opposition, at least in general, to those who argue that globalization has brought about, or is bringing about, the demise of the (nation-)state. The UN is a global setting in which nation-states meet and deliberate. However, the UN is not merely a setting in which nation-states meet; it is also an independent actor.

The two best-known state-based organs in the UN are the Security Council and the General Assembly. The latter is the UN's main deliberative body, while the former is responsible for the maintenance of international peace and security. The day-to-day operations of the UN are handled by the Secretariat, employing about 9,000 people in New York and approximately another 40,000 people throughout the world. The ability of the UN to function adequately is greatly and chronically hampered by severe budget limitations.

The UN can be seen as concerned primarily with four broad areas. The first involves *military* issues. The UN was envisioned as a major force in managing peace and security, especially in inter-state relations. However, it was marginalized during the Cold War[1] largely because in the Security Council both the US and the Soviet Union could veto proposed interventions. A turning point in the military role of the UN was the 1991 authorization by the Security Council of the use of force to deal with Iraq's invasion of Kuwait. Throughout the 1990s the UN engaged in a wide variety of actions that were not anticipated by its founders and which had been regarded previously as the province of states. These included interventions in civil wars in less developed countries, "election and human rights monitoring, disarmament, and even the assumption of state functions (in Cambodia and East Timor, for example)" (Weiss and Zach 2007: 1219). However, the expansionism of the UN in these areas was tempered by failures in the 1990s in Somalia and Yugoslavia. In the military realm it is also important to mention the fact that the UN has been actively involved in arms control and disarmament. The second area involves *economic* issues. In this realm, the main focus of the UN has been to promote actions that would lead to reductions in global inequality. Third are *environmental* issues (e.g. pollution, hazardous wastes) which are dealt with primarily through the United Nations Environment Programme.[2] Finally, there are matters of *human protection*.

A variety of UN-sponsored human rights treaties and agreements have protected human rights (see above) around the world.

The UN is both a creation and a creature of the United States. Its name was suggested by President Franklin Delano Roosevelt, the UN charter was adopted in San Francisco, and it has been housed in New York City since the 1950s. The US has also been the largest single contributor to the UN. However, the UN is minuscule in comparison to the US – its budget is about 0.07 percent of the budget of the US government. It is for this reason that the UN continues to be relatively weak and that the US has felt free to go it alone whenever it has serious disagreements with the UN (Ferguson 2004).

United Nations Conference on Trade and Development (UNCTAD)[3]

UNCTAD was created in 1964 by the UN General Assembly primarily to improve the economic situation of less developed nations, as well as to improve the nature of their relationship to the developed nations. It sought markets for the manufactured goods of less developed countries and stable prices for their commodities. It was opposed by the developed nations because it opposed the (neo-)liberalism that predominated at the time of its formation. However, in 1992 it changed course, accepted the predominant neo-liberal economic system, ceased to seek systemic change, and sought instead the integration of less developed countries into the global economy (Williams 2007: 1211–13). UNCTAD continues to focus on trade and development, but its goal is to improve the position of less developed nations in these areas by finding ways of allowing them to benefit more from, and function better in, the global economy.

United Nations Educational, Scientific, and Cultural Organization (UNESCO)

With headquarters in Paris, UNESCO has been in existence since 1946. Its primary focus is in the areas of "education, the natural and social sciences, and culture" (Kazancigil 2007: 1213–15). It had a number of successes in its first four decades of existence, but it was hampered by the Cold War and more recently by the neo-liberalism of economic globalization. It has sought the free movement of knowledge and information, but neo-liberals favor turning these into goods which can be bought and sold on the market. The triumph of neo-liberalism has meant that both the budget and the activities of UNESCO have been in decline.

International Atomic Energy Agency (IAEA)

The IAEA became well known in early 2003 when its current head, Mohammed ElBaradei, led a team to look into the status of nuclear weapons in Iran. (It had earlier shown that, contrary to US assertions, Saddam Hussein's Iraq had no nuclear weapons.) Its subsequent report indicated that Iran failed to meet safeguard obligations relative to nuclear development and weaponry.

The IAEA is an autonomous organization, established on July 29, 1957. It is not controlled by the UN, but it does report to both the General Assembly and the Security Council. The vast majority of the nations involved in the IAEA are members of the UN. The Iran case illustrates one of the IAEA's best-known roles as the world's "watchdog" on nuclear issues. As such, it inspects nuclear facilities to ensure that they are for peaceful use, disseminates information and standards designed to help make sure that nuclear facilities do not become dangerous, and serves as a center for scientific information on the peaceful use of nuclear technology.

GLOBAL GOVERNANCE

The decline of the nation-state, along with at least some of its governance function, has given rise to three new forms of governance (Whitman 2003: 253–72). The first is *governance without government* (Rosenau and Czempiel 1992), governance without government management. For example, various matters are managed within the nation-state without the involvement of state government. Thus, locales and regions within the nation-state may manage themselves. The second is *governance through various public policy networks*. At the global level, this involves government by various international institutions as well as INGOS (International Non-Governmental Organizations; see below) and private sector organizations of various sorts. Finally, *governance at the global level can be normatively mediated and moderated*. Included here are efforts driven by values including the Commission on Global Governance as well as the "Global Compact" created by former UN Secretary-General, Kofi Annan. (The Global Compact encompasses ten basic principles by which businesses around the world should voluntarily conduct their affairs [Soederberg 2007: 500–13].) It is the latter two forms that directly speak to globalization and governance, but all three of the forms relate to the decline of the nation-state even in the realm of governance.

There is some evidence of, and some increasing pressure toward, the emergence of various forms of global governance. James Rosenau (Rosenau and Czempiel 1992; Rosenau 2002) links this to the increasing "fragmegration" of the global order. This reflects increasing global diversity as well as the array of contradictory forces that have been unleashed as a result. Among those contradictory forces are globalization and localization, centralization and decentralization, and integration and fragmentation (*fragmegration*).

There is a series of more specific factors behind the growth in demand for more global governance. At the top of the list must be the declining power of nation-states. If states themselves are less able to handle various responsibilities, this leaves open the possibility of the emergence of some form of global governance to fill the void. A second factor is the vast flows of all sorts of things that run into and often right through the borders of nation-states. This could involve the flow of digital information of all sorts through the Internet. It is difficult, if not impossible, for a nation-state to stop such flows and in any case it is likely that such action would be politically unpopular and bring much negative reaction to the nation-state involved in such an effort. For example, China's periodic efforts to interfere with the Internet have brought great condemnation both internally and externally. Then there is the mass migration of people and their entry, often illegally, into various nation-states. If states are unable to control this flow, then there is a need for some sort of global governance to help deal with the problem. The flow of criminal elements, as well as their products (drugs, laundered money, those bought and sold in sex trafficking, etc.), is a strong factor in the call for global governance. In these cases and others, there is a need for some degree of order, some sort of effective authority, and at least some potential for the improvement of human life. These are but a few of the things that can be delivered by some form of global governance.

Another set of issues that has led to calls for global governance involves horrendous events within nation-states that the states themselves either foment and carry out, or are unable to control. For example, in Darfur, Sudan, perhaps hundreds of thousands have been killed and millions of people displaced and the lives of many more disrupted in a conflict that dates back to early 2003. The government of Sudan and its military have been implicated in the conflict between ethnic and tribal groups and the Sudanese government has been resistant to outside interference in its internal affairs. Of course, this is far from the only event of its kind. Other prominent examples in recent history include death and disruption in Rwanda (in 1994 militant Hutus killed hundreds of thousands of Tutsis and more moderate Hutus), and Kosovo (a semi-independent province in Serbia and the site of conflict in the 1990s between ethnic Albanians and Serbs and the mass murder of Albanians). One could even go back to WW II and argue that the Holocaust could have been prevented, or at least mitigated, had there been a viable form of global governance to put pressure on Nazi Germany and ultimately to intervene in a more material way, perhaps militarily.

Then there are global problems that single nation-states cannot hope to tackle on their own. One, of course, is the global financial crises and panics (including the current one) that sweep the world periodically and which nations are often unable to deal with on their own. Indeed, some nations (e.g. the nations of Southeast Asia) have often been, and are being, victimized by such crises. Unable to help themselves, such nations are in need of assistance from some type of global governance.

Nation-states have long struggled to deal with problems like these through various inter-state systems (e.g. alliances such as NATO [North Atlantic Treaty Organization]), but the more recent trend is toward the development of more truly global structures and methods of dealing with various sorts of issues and problems.

CIVIL SOCIETY

While civility and civil society have ancient roots and examples (e.g. in Aristotle), John Keane (2003) traces what we now consider civil society to the appearance of the West on the global stage beginning around 1500 (see also Eberly 2008). Until the nineteenth century (Lipschutz 2007: 304–8), civil society was not distinguished from a state dominated by laws. The philosopher G. W. F. Hegel played a key role in re-defining civil society as that which exists between the family and the state; a realm that is not only separated from them, but one where an individual can participate directly in various social institutions. To Hegel, like Marx and Engels (and Keane), the economy was considered part of civil society.

The major figure in social theory associated with the idea of civil society is Alexis de Tocqueville. Tocqueville lauded the early American propensity to form a wide range of associations (e.g. religious, moral) that were not political in nature and orientation. Such civil associations allowed people to interact with one another and to develop, renew, and enlarge feelings, ideas, emotions, and understandings. Such civil associations also allowed people to band together and to act. Without such associations they would be isolated and weak in large-scale contemporary societies (Tocqueville 1825–40/1969: 513, 515).

The distinction between the market (and state, and family) and civil society is a twentieth-century innovation usually associated with the Italian Marxist thinker Antonio Gramsci (1992). In his view, to challenge the hegemony of the state (controlled by the market which, in turn, dominated the family), the opposition had to gain positions in civil society (e.g. universities, the media) in order to generate their own ideas to counter the hegemonic ideas emanating from the capitalist economic system.

While the West often conquered the world through uncivilized, even violent means, it "gave birth as well to modern struggles for liberty of the press, written constitutions, religious toleration, new codes of 'civil manners' (often connected with sport), non-violent power-sharing, and talk of democracy and human rights, whose combined 'ethos' gradually spawned the growth of civil society institutions" (Keane 2003: 44). A robust civil society was already in existence by the nineteenth and early twentieth centuries (e.g. peace societies, cooperatives, workers' movements), but it was soon set back dramatically by the two world wars. It was largely in the aftermath of WW II that the modern civil society movement took shape and expanded dramatically.

Mary Kaldor (2003, 2007: 153–7) accords central importance to the 1970s and 1980s, especially in Latin America and Eastern Europe. In both regions, there was opposition to military dictatorship and efforts to find an autonomous and self-organizing base outside of the state in order to oppose the military. It was also during this period that civil society became increasingly global as improved travel and communication made linkages among various civil society groups throughout the world increasingly possible. These groups mounted appeals to international authorities and were able to create a global political space for themselves where they argued for, and helped bring about, international agreements on such issues as human rights. Of great importance in the 1990s "was the emergence of transnational networks of activists who came together on particular issues, including landmines, human rights, climate change, dams, HIV/AIDS, or corporate responsibility" (Kaldor 2007: 155). Much of the contemporary globalization from below, or "alter-globalization," movement (see Chapter 12) is now an integral part of global civil society.

Following Kaldor (2007: 154), **civil society** is defined (we will soon offer a definition of global civil society) as: "the process through which individuals negotiate, argue, struggle against, or agree with each other and with the centers of political and economic authority." It is a realm in which people can engage each other more or less directly and in which they can, among other things, analyze and criticize their political and economic institutions. People can do this, and thereby act publicly, by acting through "voluntary associations, movements, parties, and unions" (Kaldor 2007: 154). Thus, civil society involves *both* settings and actions that take place within those settings. It also represents an ideal toward which many people and groups aspire – an active, vital, and powerful civil society that can influence, and act as a counterbalance to, potent forces in the realm of the polity and the economy (Seckinelgin 2002: 357–76). It is particularly the case that civil society stands as a counterbalance and an alternative to *both* the nation-state and the economic market, especially the capitalist market.

> **Civil society**: Process through which individuals negotiate, argue, struggle against, or agree with each other and with those in authority.

While historically civil society was nation-state-centered, that is, linked to groups and actions within states, in more recent years it has been associated with more global actions and therefore with a somewhat different set of organizations including "social movements, nongovernmental organizations (NGOs), transnational networks, religious organizations, and community groups" (Kaldor 2007: 153). In other words, we have moved increasingly toward the notion of a global civil society (Alexander 2006), although civil society remains a force within states and societies, as well (Smith and West 2005: 621–52).

John Keane (2003: 8, italics in original) offers a definition of **global civil society** as:

> **Global civil society**: Global, non-governmental, pluralistic form of society composed of interlinked social processes oriented to civility.

a dynamic non-governmental system of interconnected socio-economic institutions that straddle the whole earth, and that have complex effects that are felt in its four corners. Global civil society is neither a static object nor a fait accompli. *It is an unfinished project that consists of sometimes thick, sometimes thinly stretched networks, pyramids and hub-and-spoke clusters of socio-economic institutions and actors who organize themselves across borders, with the deliberate aim of drawing the world together in new ways. These non-governmental institutions and actors tend to pluralise power and to problematise violence; consequently, their peaceful or "civil" effects are felt everywhere, here and there, far and wide, to and from local areas, through wide regions, to the planetary level itself.*

This definition emphasizes five tightly linked characteristics of global civil society; it is *non-governmental, a form of society composed of interlinked social processes, oriented to civility (non-violence), pluralistic (including the strong potential to reduce conflict),* and *global.*

Keane gives us a good feel for *global* civil society, as well as both its unfinished and varied character. However, one of the things that sets Keane's view on civil society apart is his argument that the economic market is deeply implicated in civil society. While many see civil society as distinct from *both* the nation-state and the market, Keane (2003: 76) puts forth the "'no market, no civil society' rule." Civil society could not survive without the market, money, and the money economy. Indeed, there is no clear dividing line between civil society and the market; the market is embedded in civil society and vice versa. For example, those who work in the market draw upon the civil society's norms of sociability such as "punctuality, trust, honesty, reliability, group commitment and non-violence" (Keane 2003: 77).

Keane (2003: 78) draws three basic conclusions from this relationship: "markets are an intrinsic *empirical* feature, a functionally intertwined prerequisite, of the social relations of actually existing global civil society"; "global civil society as we know and now experience it could not survive for more than a few days without the market forces unleashed by turbocapitalism"; and "the market forces of turbocapitalism could themselves not survive for a day without *other* civil society institutions, like households, charities, community associations and linguistically shared social norms like friendship, trust and cooperation."

To buttress his point, Keane argues that labor is not restricted to the market economy, but is a kind of social activity also found in non-market settings like households and charities, arts and entertainment, recreation, intimate relationships, communications media, and sacred settings and institutions. Further, markets and capitalist firms even have a civilizing effect on civil societies through, for example, their forms of face-to-face negotiations and by nurturing social codes such as those associated with charity (e.g. the Gates Foundation).

However, Keane also recognizes that the capitalist market can disturb, even disrupt, global civil society through, for example, the great social inequality it produces or by choosing where to invest and, especially, where not to invest, and where it chooses to withdraw investments. Of perhaps greatest importance from a negative point of view is the tendency for the capitalist market to strengthen "the hand of market domination over the non-profit institutions of society, which tend to be pushed and pulled, twisted and torn into bodies that obey the rules of accumulation and profit maximization" (Keane 2003: 90). Indeed, it is for this reason that many argue for the need to distinguish between market-based organizations and civil society.

Civil society is not a reality that is ever, or could ever be, completed. Rather it is an ongoing and ever-present project. This is especially the case in the era of globalization where civil societies that were created in nation-states now must be extended to the global level. In fact, it could be argued that without a global civil society the promises of national civil society may die. The challenges and the dangers of today's world have become global with the result that civil society must itself become global if it is to have any chance of countering them and, more generally, of creating a true civil society.

In practice, civil society has been dominated for decades by critical agents and agencies, but more recently neo-liberalism and neo-liberal organizations (e.g. the World Bank) have picked up on the idea to create organizations (NGOs), often funded by government and international agencies, oriented to reforming the market and government. Some see these NGOs as compromising the very notion of civil society and argue that they should not be thought of as part of it. However, as both Keane and Kaldor point out, civil society is a broad and internally contradictory category that includes a wide range of groups.

How do we account for the recent rise of civil society in general, and NGOs in particular? A number of factors are involved. Perhaps the most important are the various flows that we have already mentioned many times, including flows of both resources (money, information, popular culture, etc.) and threats (e.g. pollution, drugs, sex trafficking, etc.) (Mathews 1997: 50–66). As the power of the nation-state to deal with these flows, and in the case of negative flows (see Chapter 10) to mitigate or prevent them, has declined, the role of civil society in general, and of myriad NGOS in particular, has grown.

A variety of movements and organizations have come together since the 1990s to become significant components of the global civil society. One type involves various groups of transnational activists participating in efforts to deal with global warming, AIDs, landmines, and so forth. Then there is the global alter-globalization movement as well as the anti-war movement, especially its most recent iteration spurred by the invasion of Iraq. Of growing significance in the realm of global civil society is the wide range of organizations dealing primarily with issues that relate to the environment, human rights, and economic development. Among the most notable of these are INGOS (see below), CARE, Worldwide Fund for Nature, Greenpeace, Amnesty International, Friends of the Earth, Médecins Sans Frontières, Oxfam, and so on. Perhaps of greatest importance today in thinking about civil society are groups that represent the poor, especially those in less developed countries, and their efforts to improve the position of the poor within the global economy.

International Non-Governmental Organizations (INGOS)

International non-governmental organizations (INGOs): International not-for-profit organizations performing public functions but not established or run by nation-states.

INGOs are international not-for-profit organizations that perform public functions but are not established or run by nation-states (examples in addition to those mentioned above include Transparency International, Global Witness, Center for Public Integrity, Clean Clothes Campaign, International Organization for Standardization [ISO], International Electrotechnical Commission [IEC], and various professional associations). They are private, voluntary, and non-profit and most are oriented to bringing about some sort of social and/or political change. INGOs are advocates for any number of things, but they also "routinely influence the domestic policies of states, participate in multilateral forums and institutions, promote interstate cooperation, and facilitate political participation on the part of governments and the public" (Warkentin 2007: 883–7).

The first modern INGOs are traceable to the nineteenth century (the International Red Cross was founded in Switzerland in 1865), but they have boomed in recent years. As their number, influence, and power have grown, they have become highly controversial. Some see them as the harbingers of a future democratic civil society. Others are highly critical of them (see below).

While many INGOs have grown highly influential, their power does not involve rational-legal authority (Weber 1921/1968) (such as having their leadership elected), but rather comes from rational-moral authority (Thomas 2007: 84–102). This stems from the fact that they claim (often successfully) that they represent and express universal human interests, are democratic both as organizations and in terms of their goals, and are committed to global progress and the creation of a more rational world. Their great moral power also comes from their neutrality; their disinterestedness. At the most general level, they serve to frame global policy issues in areas such as women's rights, population, education, and the environment.

As moral powers, they exist less as actors on the world stage, and more to advise states, firms, and individuals on how they ought to act on various issues and under an array of circumstances.

INGOs have several characteristics that make them invaluable in the global arena. First, they are often grassroots organizations and therefore are much more in touch with the needs and interests of their membership than larger, more formal, and more bureaucratized organizations associated with nation-states or the international community. Second, they are often more effective in achieving their goals than other types of organizations (for example, they are often able to get relief faster to people in poor countries or to victims of disasters). Third, they are very good at garnering media attention in efforts to force more formal organizations (e.g. states) into action.

A turning point in the history of INGOs occurred in 1992 when a treaty to control the emission of greenhouse gases was signed as a result of the actions of a variety of groups that not only exerted external pressure, but were actually involved in the decision-making process. A number of other successes followed including creation by the UN of a high commissioner for human rights, prevention of the approval of the Multilateral Agreement on Investment (which would have liberalized foreign investment and limited the role of nation-states in such actions), and protests at World Trade Organization meetings, especially the Seattle action of 1999.

One of the most notable successes of INGOs was an international treaty spearheaded by the International Campaign to Ban Landmines (ICBL). The treaty was signed in 1997 by 122 nations which agreed to stop selling and using landmines. On the surface the fact that so many nation-states were involved in signing the treaty would seem to indicate that this was an accomplishment linked to the old state-centered system. In fact, however, much of the credit went to the approximately one thousand NGOs that had been involved in lobbying in about 60 countries for such a treaty (Bond 2000).

However, there are negative sides to the growth of INGOS (and civil society).

- Fundamentally INGOs are special interest groups and therefore they may not take into consideration wider sets of concerns and issues.
- In addition, they are not democratic, often keep their agendas secret, and are not accountable to anyone other than their members.
- They are elitist (many involve better-off and well-educated people from the North) – that is, undemocratic – organizations that seek to impose inappropriate universal plans on local organizations and settings.
- Thus, they have the potential to be "loose cannons" on the global stage.
- They are seen as annoying busybodies that are forever putting their noses in the business of others (Thomas 2007: 84–102).
- They often pander to public opinion and posture for the media both to attract attention to their issues and to maintain or expand their power and membership.
- As a result, they may distort the magnitude of certain problems (e.g. overestimating the effects, and misjudging the causes, of an oil spill) in order to advance their cause and interests.
- Their focus on one issue may adversely affect the interest in, and ability to deal with, many other important issues.
- The nature of the focus, and indeed the very creation, of an INGO may be a function of its ability to attract attention and to raise funds. As a result, other worthy, if not more worthy, issues (e.g. soil erosion, especially in Africa) may fail to attract much, if any, attention and interest.
- In some cases, well-meaning INGOs conflict with one another, such as those wishing to end certain practices (e.g. logging) versus those that see those practices as solutions (e.g. logging producing wood as a sustainable resource that is preferable to fossil fuels).
- The North's control over INGOs has actually increased, leading to questions about their relevance to the concerns of the South.
- However, perhaps the strongest criticism of INGOs is that they "seem to have helped accelerate further state withdrawal from social provision" (Harvey 2006: 52). In that sense they can be seen as neo-liberalism's "Trojan horses," furthering its agenda while seeming to operate against some of its worst abuses.

Thus, global civil society is extremely broad and includes organizations and parties that may well be in conflict with one another (e.g. the Western neo-liberals who dominate the major INGOs and the often non-Western critics of neo-liberalism, including radical religious fundamentalists, who dominate less well organized groups). What they all have in common is that they exist more-or-less outside the confines of the nation-state and offer at least the possibility that people can be a part of ongoing debates in the world and perhaps even involved in movements toward greater democracy and emancipation (Munck 2002: 10–21; Teune 2002: 22–34).

Beyond their moral power, some INGOs (see below) have become formally involved in **international governmental organizations** (IGOs), especially the UN (Martens 2001: 388–404). INGOs stand to gain from such formal associa-

> **Intergovernmental Organizations (IGOs)** are organizations such as the UN that are international in scope.

tions in various ways. There are *symbolic* gains such as greater legitimacy associated with being involved with such an internationally visible organization. There are also the more *material* gains since such an organization might provide badly needed funding to various INGOs; work may even be sub-contracted to INGOs and they can earn income for performing the required tasks.

Of course, there are dangers to INGOs involved in this course of action. They can easily become co-opted by the IGO involved. Less extremely, INGOs may need to become more rationalized, bureaucratized, and professionalized in order to deal with the needs and demands of the IGO. This, in turn, can lead to a more subtle change of orientation, and a decline in radicalism, in an INGO. Other possible changes in INGOs include a loss of flexibility (as they must satisfy the demands of the IGO which, after all, may well be the source of badly needed funds), a decline in capacity to act quickly, and, perhaps most troubling, a loss of autonomy and perhaps even identity.

For their part, IGOs are affected by the involvement of INGOs. They, too, can gain symbolically and increase their legitimacy through the involvement of high-minded INGOs. Further, they can gain in a material sense because of the fact that less bureaucratized INGOs can perform tasks that would be much more costly, and done much more slowly and inefficiently, were they performed by IGOs.

The mutual involvement of INGOs and IGOs is perhaps clearest in the case of UNESCO since INGOS were involved in it from its inception in 1945. In fact, in order to handle its large and diverse responsibilities, UNESCO created a variety of INGOs, such as the International Council of Museums (ICOM). In other cases, UNESCO funded extant INGOs (e.g. the International Council of Scientific Unions [ICSU] in existence since 1931) in order to handle tasks (in the case of ICSU the promotion of scientific research and its application to the betterment of humankind) that UNESCO otherwise might be required to handle. Finally, UNESCO helped INGOs by either not getting involved in domains already well handled by INGOs or by withdrawing from areas when a viable INGO emerged. Thus, with the emergence of the World Wildlife Fund (WWF) in 1961, UNESCO effectively ceded to it environmental issues with which it had, up to that time, been concerned.

CHAPTER SUMMARY

This chapter opens with a discussion of various political flows, but the main focus is on the development and functioning of global political structures. Starting with more traditional structures such as the nation-state, the discussion moves on to the development of regional and global political structures and processes.

The origin of the modern nation-state is traced to the Treaty of Westphalia which led to the notion that nation-states are autonomous. Later developments led to the fusion of the cultural concept of a nation and the structure of the state; to the idea of the nation-state. With globalization, the nation-state faces innumerable challenges, leading to a significant loss of control over economic flows and transnational organizations. A debate has emerged over whether the "nation-state is dead." Although the role of the nation-state has declined, it is still an important political structure. However, in the global age, the "porosity" of the nation-state, the increasing global flows through it, should be a focal concern.

Benedict Anderson's "imagined community" is an important idea in thinking about the nation-state. As a result of the development of "print capitalism," it came to be conceived of as being actively constructed, socially and politically, by people who identify with the community that is represented by the nation-state. This concept is extended further by examining how the nation-state transcends its geographic boundaries in the face of rapidly developing technology and increasing immigration flows. Emphasis is placed on the "re-imagining" of the nation-state in the light of such global flows.

In terms of the changing geo-political scenario, the world can be seen as evolving through three stages – bipolar (during the Cold War), unipolar (ascendancy of the US), and finally to a tri-polar future with the US, EU, and China as the three centers of power.

Also examined is the emergence of the United Nations, as well more specific organizations such as UNCTAD, UNESCO, and IAEA.

The concept of global governance is explicated. This has emerged as an alternative to the inter-state system in addressing various global problems. Global governance has developed in response to the decline of the nation-state, as well as to global crises that the nation-state cannot control.

Also of great political importance is civil society. Although it has ancient origins, the modern concept of civil society was fleshed out by thinkers such as Hegel and Gramsci. Civil society came to be conceived of as clearly separated from the state on the one hand and the market and family on the other. However, there are contemporary debates over whether civil society is truly separate from the market, in light of the disruptive influence that the latter might have on the former. This can be traced, in part, to the tension that is internal to civil society which is comprised of a number of highly disparate organizations. Local civil society now coexists with "global civil society." Non-Governmental Organizations (NGOs) coexist with International Non-Governmental Organizations (INGOs).

There is a perception that global civil society could be a "replacement" for the nation-state. In many areas it is seen as already filling the vacuum created by the decline of the nation-state. While civil society has its strengths (greater efficiency, closer to the people), it also faces challenges in terms of a narrowness of focus, and charges of elitism and control by the North. INGOs may also share a symbiotic relationship with inter-governmental organizations (IGOs), which, while being beneficial in symbolic and material terms, creates challenges for the INGOs in terms of loss of radicalism and autonomy.

DISCUSSION QUESTIONS

1. Examine the interaction between the nation-state and civil society, differentiating between local and global civil society.

2. Make the case *for* the "death of the nation-state" focusing especially on the role played by global flows in the "demise" of the nation-state.

3. Make the case *against* the "death of the nation-state" focusing especially on the role played by barriers (especially those erected by the nation-state) to global flows.

4. Analyze the concept of global governance and discuss the adequacy of such a government as a political tool in the "real world."

5. Discuss the advantages of, and challenges to, the nation-state, in the context of "imagined communities."

6. Examine the relevance of global political structures such as the UN in light of global flows and processes.

FURTHER READING

Robert J. Holton. *Globalization and the Nation-State*. New York: St. Martin's Press, 1998.

E. Ohmae. *The End of the Nation-State: The Rise of Regional Economies*. New York: Free Press, 1996.

Susan Strange. *The Retreat of the State: The Diffusion of Power in the World Economy*. Cambridge: Cambridge University Press, 1996.

Carolyn Nordstrom. *Shadows of War: Violence, Power, and International Profiteering in the Twenty-First Century*. Berkeley: University of California Press, 2004.

Daniel Beland. *States of Global Insecurity: Policy, Politics and Society*. New York: Worth, 2008.

Benedict Anderson. *Imagined Communities*. Revised edn. London: Verso, 2006.

Parag Khanna. *The Second World: Empires and Influence in the New Global Order*. New York: Random House, 2008.

John Keane. *Global Civil Society*. Cambridge: Cambridge University Press, 2003.

Mary Kaldor. *Global Civil Society: An Answer to War*. London: Polity, 2003.

NOTES

1 The Cold War is a term used to define the conflicting relationship between the Soviet Union and its allies and the West, especially the United States, between the end of WW II and the fall of the Soviet Union in 1991. It was a "cold" war because it never became a "hot," a shooting, war involving the protagonists, at least directly.

2 www.unep.org.

3 www.unctad.org; Taylor (2003: 409–18).

REFERENCES

Alexander, Jeffrey. 2006. "Global Civil Society." *Theory, Culture & Society* 23.

Anderson, Benedict. 2006. *Imagined Communities: Reflections on the Origin and Spread of Nationalism*. New edn. London: Verso.

Bauman, Zygmunt. 1989. *Modernity and the Holocaust*. Ithaca, NY: Cornell University Press.

Bauman, Zygmunt. 1992. *Intimations of Postmodernity*. London: Routledge.

Beland, Daniel. 2008. *States of Global Insecurity: Policy, Politics and Society*. New York: Worth.

Blum, Douglas W., ed. 2008. *Russia and Globalization: Identity, Security, and Society in an Era of Change*. Washington, DC: Johns Hopkins University Press.

Boas, Morten, and Kathleen M. Jennings. 2007. " 'Failed States' and 'State Failure': Threats or Opportunities?" *Globalizations* 4, 4.

Bond, Michael. 2000. "The Backlash Against NGOs." *Prospect* (April). www.prospectmagazine.co.uk.

Cerny, Philip G. 2007. "Nation-State." In Jan Aart Scholte and Roland Robertson, eds., *Encyclopedia of Globalization*. New York: MTM Publishing.

Chatterjee, Deen K., ed. 2008. *Democracy in a Global World: Human Rights and Political Participation in the 21st Century*. Lanham, MD: Rowman & Littlefield.

Conley, Tom. 2002. "Globalisation as Constraint and Opportunity: Reconceptualising Policy Capacity in Australia." *Global Society* 16, 4.

Eberly, Don. 2008. *The Rise of Global Civil Society: Building Communities and Nations from the Bottom Up*. New York: Encounter Books.

Elliott, Michael A. 2007. "Human Rights and the Triumph of the Individual in World Culture." *Cultural Sociology* 1, 3.

Farr, Kathryn. 2005. *Sex Trafficking: The Global Market in Women and Children*. New York: Worth.

Ferguson, Niall. 2004. *Colossus: The Rise and Fall of the American Empire*. New York: Penguin.

Fredman, Sandra. 2008. *Human Rights Transformed: Positive Rights and Positive Duties*. New York: Oxford University Press.

Gilpin, Robert. 2001. *Global Political Economy*. Princeton: Princeton University Press.

Glassner, Barry. 2000. *Culture of Fear: Why Americans Are Afraid of the Wrong Things*. New York: Basic Books.

Gramsci, Antonio. 1992. *Prison Notebooks*. New York: Columbia University Press.

Guibernau, Montserrat. 2007. "National Identity." In Jan Aart Scholte and Roland Robertson, eds., *Encyclopedia of Globalization*. New York: MTM Publishing.

Harvey, David. 2006. *Spaces of Global Capitalism: Towards a Theory of Uneven Geographical Development*. London: Verso.

Hayman, P. A., and John Williams. 2006. "Westphalian Sovereignty: Rights, Intervention, Meaning and Context." *Global Society* 20, 4 (October).

Isikoff, Michael, and David Corn. 2006. *Hubris: The Inside Story of Spin, Scandal and the Selling of the Iraq War*. New York: Crown.

Kaldor, Mary. 2003. *Global Civil Society: An Answer to War*. London: Polity.

Kaldor, Mary. 2007. "Civil Society." In Jan Aart Scholte and Roland Robertson, eds., *Encyclopedia of Globalization*. New York: MTM Publishing.

Kazancigil, Ali. 2007. "United Nations Educational, Scientific and Cultural Organization." In Jan Aart Scholte and Roland Robertson, eds., *Encyclopedia of Globalization*. New York: MTM Publishing.

Keane, John. 2003. *Global Civil Society*. Cambridge: Cambridge University Press.

Khanna, Parag. 2008a. *The Second World: Empires and Influence in the New Global Order*. New York: Random House.

Khanna, Parag. 2008b. "Waving Goodbye to Hegemony." *New York Times Magazine*. January 27.

Levy, Daniel, and Natan Sznaider. 2006. "Sovereignty Transformed: A Sociology of Human Rights." *British Journal of Sociology* 57, 4.

Li, Rebecca S. K. 2002. "Alternative Routes to State Breakdown: Toward an Integrated Model of Territorial Disintegration." *Sociological Theory* 20, 1 (March).

Lipschutz, Ronnie D. 2007. "The Historical and Structural Origins of Global Civil Society." *Globalizations* 4, 2.

Mann, Michael. 2007. "Has Globalization Ended the Rise and the Rise of the Nation-state?" *Review of International Political Economy* 4, 3.

Martens, Kerstin. 2001. "Non-Governmental Organisations as Corporatist Mediator: An Analysis of NGOs in the UNESCO System." *Global Society* 15, 4.

Mathews, Jessica. 1997. "Power Shift." *Foreign Affairs* 76, 1.

Munck, Ronaldo. 2002. "Globalization and Democracy: A New Great Transformation." *Annals* 581 (May).

Nordstrom, Carolyn. 2004. *Shadows of War: Violence, Power, and International Profiteering in the Twenty-First Century*. Berkeley, CA: University of California Press.

Ohmae, E. 1996. *The End of the Nation-State: The Rise of Regional Economies*. New York: Free Press.

Rosenau, James. 2002. "Governance in a New Global Order." In David Held and Anthony McGrew, eds., *Governing Globalization: Power, Authority and Global Governance*. London: Polity.

Rosenau, James N., and Ernst-Otto Czempiel, eds. 1992. *Governance without Government: Order and Change in World Politics*. Cambridge: Cambridge University Press.

Seckinelgin, Hakan. 2002. "Civil Society as a Metaphor for Western Liberalism." *Global Society* 16, 4.

Smith, Jackie, and Dawn West. 2005. "The Uneven Geography of Global Civil Society." *Social Forces* 84 (December).

Soederberg, Susanne. 2007. "Taming Corporations or Buttressing Market-Led Development?: A Critical Assessment of the Global Compact." *Globalizations* 4, 4.

Sorensen, Georg. 2007. "Sovereignty." In Jan Aart Scholte and Roland Robertson, eds., *Encyclopedia of Globalization*. New York: MTM Publishing.

Strange, Susan. 1996. *The Retreat of the State: The Diffusion of Power in the World Economy*. Cambridge: Cambridge University Press.

Strange, Susan. 1999. "The Westfailure System." *Review of International Studies* 25.

Taylor, Ian. 2003. "The United Nations Conference on Trade and Development." *New Political Economy* 8, 3.

Teune, Henry. 2002. "Global Democracy." *Annals* 581 (May).

Thomas, George M. 2007. "Globalization: The Major Players." In George Ritzer, ed., *Blackwell Companion to Globalization*. Malden, MA: Blackwell.

Tocqueville, Alexis de. 1825–40/1969. *Democracy in America*. Garden City, NY: Doubleday.

Turner, Bryan S. 1993. "Outline of a General Theory of Human Rights." *Sociology* 27, 3.

Turner, Bryan S. 2007. "Human Rights." In Jan Aart Scholte and Roland Robertson, eds., *Encyclopedia of Globalization*. New York: MTM Publishing.

Wallerstein, Immanuel. 1974. *The Modern World-System: Capitalist Agriculture and the Origins of the European World-Economy in the 16th Century*. New York: Academic Press.

Warkentin, Craig. 2007. "Nongovernmental Organizations." In Jan Aart Scholte and Roland Robertson, eds., *Encyclopedia of Globalization*. New York: MTM Publishing.

Weber, Max. 1921/1968. *Economy and Society*, 3 vols. Totowa, NJ: Bedminster Press.

Weiss, Thomas G., David P. Forsythe, and Roger A. Coate. 2004. *The United Nations and Changing World Politics*, 4th edn. Boulder, CO: Westview Press.

Weiss, Thomas G., and Danielle Zach. 2007. "United Nations Organization." In Jan Aart Scholte and Roland Robertson, eds., *Encyclopedia of Globalization*. New York: MTM Publishing.

Whitman, Jim. 2003. "Global Dynamics and the Limits of Global Governance." *Global Society* 17, 3 (July).

Williams, Marc. 2007. "United Nations Conference on Trade and Development." In Jan Aart Scholte and Roland Robertson, eds., *Encyclopedia of Globalization*. New York: MTM Publishing.

High-Tech Global Flows and Structures

Technology, Media, and the Internet

Globalization: The Essentials, by George Ritzer
© 2011 John Wiley & Sons Ltd

This chapter deals with three of the most cutting-edge aspects of the social world in general, and globalization in particular. Grouped under the heading of high-tech global flows and structures are technology, the media, and the Internet. While for discussion purposes many technologies (e.g. containerized shipping, universal product codes [UPCs]) are treated separately in this chapter, the media and the Internet are themselves technologies. Further, the Internet encompasses many crucially important new technologies, and the media are being transformed by a variety of new technologies (including the Internet – for example blogs are increasingly supplanting newspapers). All, of course, are, or can be, globe-straddling.

TECHNOLOGY

Technological changes of all sorts (many of which have been touched on in previous chapters) have played a huge role in globalization. Such changes have affected global processes for a century, or more, depending on how one conceives of the history of globalization, but they have accelerated in recent years (especially in the global age), creating, or at least expediting, global processes.

One example of such a more recent technological development in the realm of commerce was the creation of the world's first container ship in 1956. Instead of loading and unloading goods of various sorts, containers already filled with products were loaded on, and unloaded from, ships. A new era of shipping was born that allowed much more rapid loading and unloading of ships, and the seamless transfer of containers between ships and from ships to trucks or trains. That new technology cut the cost of the transportation of goods by almost 100 percent. Of course, container technology has improved further over the years, with the result that the costs of shipping have been reduced much further. For example, we now have so-called "monster ships" that can carry containers that are equal to the carrying capacity of roughly 20 miles of trucks. As a result of modern containerization: "It often costs more to send a container by road one hundred miles from port to its final destination than it does to ship the container by sea from Shanghai to Rotterdam" (Chanda 2007: 57).

Similarly, the development and expansion of air freight greatly speeded up the transportation of goods and in some cases even reduced costs (although it is still cheaper to transport many things – automobiles, for example – by ship). A key technological development here was the introduction of the Boeing 747 in 1970, with its wide body, and the arrival soon afterward of a cargo version of the plane.

Another important advance also occurred in 1970 with the founding of Federal Express (FedEx). While FedEx was, and is, an innovative organization, the key technological advance associated with it involved the use of computer technology to track deliveries of packages by jet planes and other conveyances. The rest is history as FedEx has become a household name and a visible presence throughout the world. "On its first night, [FedEx] delivered just 186 packages. The company now operates all over the world, delivering an average of three million packages a day" (Chanda 2007: 64).

Then there is the seemingly modest creation of the Universal Product Code (UPC) which began in grocery stores in the US in June, 1974. "Today, more than five million bar-coded products are scanned and sold all over the world. Sensors housed in store shelves can now read the bar codes on boxes of shoes, shirts, or shampoo, and automatically alert suppliers when stocks run low, allowing replenishments to arrive quickly without the need for costly inventories" (Chanda 2007: 65). This has greatly expedited the movement of products from all over the world to warehouses and ultimately retail outlets across the globe.

From the point of view of globalization, in fact perhaps from any point of view, all of these developments pale in comparison to the creation of the first personal computers in the mid-1970s and then the Internet in the 1990s. Personal computers and the Internet are now deeply implicated in, and essential to, all of the technological developments mentioned above, as well as most others. Personal computers and the Internet paved the way for global Internet transactions and interpersonal relationships of all sorts (e.g. Facebook).

The preceding are just a few of the technological advances that have contributed greatly to the globalization of commerce and of interpersonal relations. Not only are there innumerable other technological advances in these areas that could be mentioned here, but the globalization of every other realm covered in this volume has been affected, and greatly expedited, by technological change.

Medical Technologies

New health-care technologies (e.g. MRIs, CAT scans, PET scans, DaVinci robotics) have not only been created at a rapid rate, but because of global improvements in transport, they flow around the world much more rapidly than ever before. These are extraordinarily expensive technologies largely created in the North. The developed countries are able to afford these technologies and they spread throughout the North. This is especially the case for the world leaders, Japan and the United States, which possess an extraordinary number of these technologies relative to the size of their populations. The machines are not only more likely to exist in developed countries, but they are more likely to be used intensively because patients, either on their own or because of health insurance, are able to afford the very expensive scans, tests, and surgeries (e.g. of the prostate with the DaVinci robotic system) associated with them. Furthermore, the wide-scale existence of such expensive machines leads to pressure to use them; it is costly to purchase such machines and they cannot be allowed to remain idle for long periods of time. Also concentrated in developed countries are the highly trained personnel needed to run and maintain the machines, administer the tests, and interpret the results of, say, an MRI. In contrast, few of these technologies flow to less developed, Southern countries, they are used there less intensively, and there are relatively few trained people there capable of conducting the tests and interpreting the results.

Space-Based Technologies

The space that surrounds the globe is, by its very nature, global and already involves, and will increasingly involve, globalization. Although the US has dominated this domain, especially through the launching of satellites, other nations are involved in, and more generally affected by, activities in space. In the military realm, space continues to be largely an American realm. For example, the US uses its satellites for surveillance of enemies and potential enemies throughout the world (*Economist* 2008: January 17). However, that dominance is being, and will be, contested by others, especially China, and the ultimate fear here on many levels, including from the perspective of globalization, is a war in and over space that could truly devastate every part of the globe.

However, space-based technology is not restricted to military uses. Satellites are used to transmit TV and other images around the world. Of growing importance are the global positioning systems (GPS) that rely on satellites to allow those flying civilian airplanes, as well as millions of automobile drivers, to use global navigational systems (GNS) in order to locate where they are and how they should get to where they intend to go (Bovet 2007: 1046–50). There are now many varieties of inexpensive and portable GNS devices that can be moved in and out of automobiles and can be used for other purposes such as providing guidance for those who wish to go off trekking or mountain-climbing.

Among other non-military examples of the use of space-based technology are space tourism, which Virgin Atlantic plans to develop, and Google Moon which is sponsoring a competition among private companies to put a rover on the moon.

Leapfrogging

The popular image of technological change, as it relates to globalization, is that such advances flow around the world gradually and systematically. While this does occur in many cases and in many places (especially in the North), it is also the case that global technological changes can occur erratically and irregularly; the flows can be sporadic. And, of course, one of the reasons for that is the fact that barriers to such flows exist in many parts of the world, especially in the South. For example, the lack of electricity in many parts of the world serves to exclude many new technologies.

Instead of flowing smoothly around the world, technological advances (e.g. the medical technologies discussed above) often "hop" over some areas while "landing" in others. Similarly, some geographic areas are able to skip over some technological advances and go straight to later developments. This is known as *leapfrogging*.

Leapfrogging: Developing nations bypassing earlier technologies and adopting more advanced technologies.

Leapfrogging mainly involves developing nations bypassing earlier technologies, enabling them to adopt more advanced technologies. For example, some developing countries have gone straight to solar energy or energy from biomass rather than building huge, centralized systems (e.g. enormous and very expensive power plants operating on the basis of coal, oil, or nuclear energy) for the transmission of power.

Others have skipped the twentieth-century fixed-line phone systems and gone directly to the twenty-first-century mobile phone technology (*Economist* 2008: February 7 ["The Limits of Leapfrogging"]). For example, in Bangladesh there are only one million land-line phone connections in a nation of 150 million people. However, there are already 16 million cell-phone users (Horst 2006: 143–59), and 2 million more are being added every month (Sullivan 2006: A12–A13). Globally, there are over 3.3 billion mobile phone subscriptions, but about 3 billion people – mostly in Africa and Asia – do not yet have access to cell phones (Corbett 2008: 34ff.). Bringing more cell phones (and many other technologies) to these areas would have an enormous impact on people's lives. It would also have a significant global impact, especially on the world economy and global social relationships. And many of those without cell phones understand this since as soon as they have a modest increase in income, they invest in telecommunications technologies, especially the cell phone. This technology can increase their well-being (e.g. by being able to get help in case of emergency) and their productivity.

In terms of the latter, one example is "setting up farm cooperatives in Nepal, where farmers would bring their vegetables to a local person with a mobile phone, who then acted as a commissioned sales agent, using the phone to check market prices and arranging for the most profitable sale" (Corbett 2008: 38). In another example, "fishermen off the coast of Kerala in southern India … invested in cell phones and started using them to call around to prospective buyers before they'd even gotten their catch to shore, their profits went up an average of 8 percent while consumer prices in the local market went down by 4 percent" (Corbett 2008: 38). More generally, one study showed that when a country added 10 cell phones for every 100 people, its GDP rose 0.5 percent (Corbett 2008: 38).

The use of cell phones to transfer funds is particularly important:

> Ugandans are using prepaid airtime as a way of transferring money from place to place, something that's especially important to those who do not use banks. Someone working in Kampala, for instance, who wishes to send the equivalent of $5 back to his mother in a village will buy a $5 prepaid airtime card, but rather than entering the code into his own phone, he will call the village phone operator [see below] and read the code to her. She then uses the airtime for her phone and completes the transaction by giving the man's mother the money, minus a small commission. (Corbett 2008: 39)

This is a forerunner to formalized mobile banking; in fact, such formal systems already exist in South Africa, Kenya (Vodafone's M-Pesa), and the Philippines. One estimate is that a billion people will be using such systems within a few years.

The cell phone is a major development in itself, but its impact is greatly magnified by the arrival of computers and the Internet and connections to it via cell phones. Using Voice over Internet Protocol (VoIP – Skype and Vonage are the best-known companies in this area) people can make inexpensive (or even free) phone calls to other computers and phones throughout the world. Even those people who live in remote areas (of, for example, Bangladesh, with an average annual income of $440), and who lack computers, can access the Internet at centers with electricity. This allows them to access services (medical, weather reports, e-mail) considered basic in the North, but only recently within their reach. In addition, "People now download job applications and music, see school exam results, check news and crop prices, make inexpensive Internet phone calls or use Web cameras to see relatives. Students from villages with few books now have access to online dictionaries and encyclopedias" (Sullivan 2006: A12).

A key player in this development in Bangladesh is the cell-phone provider GrameenPhone Ltd., created in 1996, and owned, in part, by Grameen Bank, which won the 2006 Nobel Peace Prize (along with its founder Muhammad Yunus). There are now 250,000 "phone ladies" in Bangladesh who have used micro-credit from the Grameen Bank to purchase $150 cell-phone kits and then used the phone to become village phone operators. They earn an income by charging a small fee for allowing residents to make or receive calls. This has not only helped the operators and their villages, but GrameenPhone, with revenues of about $1 billion, is now Bangladesh's largest telecom company.

However, as promising as leapfrogging may be to developing countries, a World Bank study showed that most technologies that spread in this way do *not* find their way to very many people, or do not spread very widely throughout developing countries. This is the case because of a lack of basic twentieth-century infrastructure in these countries such as roads, railroads, schools, electrical grids, water pipelines, and sewerage systems (*Economist* 2008: February 7 ["Of Internet Cafes and Power Cuts"]). While leapfrogging may be useful to some in developing countries, more fundamental changes in infrastructure are needed in order to make most new technologies truly available to the bulk of the population.

In addition to a lack of infrastructure, other barriers to the spread of advanced technology in less developed countries are widespread illiteracy, a lack of research and development capacity, a lack of strong systems to finance development, and the absence of strong and stable governments. In terms of the last of these, twenty-first-century rioting and warfare in Kenya, Chad, Somalia, and elsewhere created all sorts of problems, including not only serving as barriers to technological development, but perhaps setting such development back years, if not decades. Not only does warfare prevent new developments, but it also serves to adversely affect existing infrastructure such as roads, railroads, shipping facilities, and airports. All of these tend to deteriorate as a direct result of hostilities or more indirectly because of neglect. Money and attention are devoted to conflict rather than to the care and maintenance, let alone advancement, of infrastructure.

India's "One Lakh Car" (or NANO)

A potentially dramatic new technological development in early 2008 was the unveiling, by the Indian corporation, Tata, of the world's least expensive car, priced at one lakh, that is 100,000 rupees, or about $2,500 (*Economist* 2008: January 10). From a technological point of view, the NANO is unimpressive and offers primitive and inexpensive automobile technology (it will be no threat to, say, the Lexus, but it sells for perhaps one-thirtieth the price of a Lexus). For example, it offers only manual transmission and will generate a maximum of 33 horsepower. What is important about this car is the delivery of a low-priced automobile to Indians who are now in a position to afford it, but for whom a Lexus, or even a Hyundai, would be completely out of their price range.

Thus, large numbers of Indians will soon be driving their own automobiles, many for the first time. This will be a highly liberating experience for them, but it also means that the exhaust from many more automobiles will be polluting the atmosphere in India and that will contribute enormously to the growth in carbon dioxide emissions and ultimately to worsening global warming. While road accidents and deaths will undoubtedly increase with the proliferation of NANOs, in the short run it will involve an increase in safety for many Indians who currently travel precariously by motorcycle, often with a child nestled at the front, between the father and the handlebars, and with the mother sitting side-saddle in the rear.

Problematic Technological Flows

While all of the above are, in the main, positive developments, there are many technological flows that have largely, if not totally, negative consequences. The flow of military technology of all sorts comes immediately to mind (although the sellers of such hardware obviously benefit from this). Later in this chapter we will discuss some other problematic flows (computer viruses and Spam), but of a more everyday character.

MEDIA

Media Imperialism

Media imperialism is a sub-category under the broader heading of cultural imperialism (see Chapter 7). The conventional view for quite some time was that it was the Western (especially US) media, and the technologies associated with those media, that were imperialistic and that dominated less developed nations and their cultures. Thus, it was television programs created in the US, movies from Hollywood (Cowen 2002), books by American authors and published originally in the US, US media conglomerates such as Fox and Time Warner, and so on, that were seen as imposing themselves on less developed nations and playing a key role not only in their media, but in shaping their culture. For example, the idea that American movies have dominated not only less developed nations, but much of the world as a whole, is supported in *Global Hollywood 2*: "Los Angeles–New York culture and commerce dominate screen entertainment around the globe, either directly or as an implied other, and the dramatic success of US film since the First World War has been a model for its export of music, television, advertising, the Internet and sport" (Miller et al. 2005: 9).

While still a powerful perspective, other views have emerged on this issue that indicate that Western, especially American, media are not as powerful as they once were or had been thought to be (Sparks 2007). First, alternative global media giants have arisen to compete with those emanating from the West. One example is the Arabic Al Jazeera which began operations in 1996 and is based in Qatar. It is a global source of news (Bielsa 2008: 347–66), designed to compete with CNN and the BBC. Another example is Bollywood, India's answer to Hollywood and the source of large numbers of movies that are distributed throughout much of the world (Tyrell 1999: 265–81; Larkin 2003: 170–92).

Then there are the local and regional media, which have always been important, and, in many ways, their power has grown in recent years. Another factor is the expansion of the Internet as a source of highly diverse media of all sorts. Finally, the global distribution of, say, an American movie or television program does not mean that it is going to be viewed and understood everywhere in the same way that its creators intend, or interpreted in the same way as it is by an American audience.

The idea that media products are interpreted differently by different audiences throughout the world is in line with the widely accepted contemporary view, most associated with postmodern social theorists, that media products are simply "texts" and what is of greatest importance is not what authors "intend," but rather the interpretations of the "readers" and "viewers." People are not passive recipients of the media, but actively construct their products. Thus, the emphasis on the power of the person/reader/viewer serves to undermine the whole idea of media imperialism.

Much has been written about this in the past, in terms, for example, of the way in which non-American viewers interpreted popular TV programs such as *Dallas* (Ang 1985). However, we need to think about this more in terms of contemporary TV offerings such as the popular *24*. To most viewers in the US this is seen as an inspiring vision of how the nation can respond, often quite ruthlessly, to new global threats that emerged after 9/11. Some American viewers are concerned about the negative images offered of their supposed adversaries, especially Muslims, but such a reaction is likely to be much more extreme among Muslim viewers in the US, as well as in other parts of the world. Less extremely, many viewers in Europe are likely to read this program as a celebration of American individualism, aggressiveness, and over-willingness to take dangerous and reckless actions that further endanger, rather than improve, the chances of world peace. The meaning of *24*, like that of every other cultural product, is in the eyes of the beholder, and the culture in which the beholder exists profoundly shapes that interpretation.

"Media Were American"

In 1977 Jeremy Tunstall authored a book entitled *The Media Are American*. Over two decades later he published *The Media Were American: U.S. Mass Media in*

Decline (2008). The timing of the publications, and the nature of their titles, tell us much of what we need to know about the role of American mass media in an increasingly globalized world. Tunstall's basic point in the most recent book is that the global influence of the American media peaked in the mid-twentieth century and has been in decline ever since. It is not American media, nor media from any other country, that dominate the world. Rather, national media have not only survived, but are increasingly important (they are dominant in those countries that include the overwhelming majority of the world's population). The largest countries in the world are now either media self-sufficient, or have a rough balance of imports and indigenous media. That leaves a large number of countries (about 150), with a relatively small total population, that are largely dependent on media imports. Overall, outside the US about 10 percent of world media time is devoted to US media, about 10 percent to other media imports (largely from the immediate region, continent, subcontinent or language area), and about 80 percent to domestic and national media.

A variety of other findings point to the fact that no media dominate the world. While Euro-American media are the world leaders, people in fact spend more time with their national media than with any such imports. CNN is indeed global but it is largely watched by Americans abroad; few locals anywhere in the world watch CNN, at least on a regular basis. In Brazil (and elsewhere) it is telenovelas that are predominant and they are produced by a large Brazilian company, Globo. There are regional media pecking orders with, for example, Mexico the leader in Latin America. China is a growing media power in East Asia in general, especially in Taiwan, Hong Kong, Singapore, and Malaysia (Yang 1996: 287–319).

New Global Media

In spite of the arguments against media imperialism, the fact is that we have witnessed the rise of the "new" global media (e.g. Apple's iTunes, Facebook, Twitter, Google, Microsoft), with great power to impose their systems on large portions of the world (McChesney 1999: 11–15). While the major players change over time, especially through mergers of various types, the global media (this applies to traditional media such as newspapers, TV, and movies, as well as to the newly emerging media on, or related to, the Internet) are increasingly dominated by a relatively small number of huge corporations. In virtually all sectors the goal is to produce a relatively noncompetitive global environment in order to maximize profits. This process is fairly well advanced in the "old media" and it is ongoing in the case of the "new media." There, competition continues, but largely because the process is so new and the dust has yet to settle. Thus, for example, Facebook and MySpace succeeded in vanquishing a number of early competitors (e.g. Friendster) for the position of dominant social-networking site, but they continue to compete with each other, with the possibility of new competitors arising in this relatively new arena. Furthermore, giants in the industry such as Newscorp, Microsoft, Google, and Yahoo are either seeking to create their own versions of successful new media, especially on the Internet, or they are seeking to buy into, or gain control over, already successful websites (Microsoft purchased a small share of Facebook in late 2007 and has been seeking, unsuccessfully so far, to gain control of Yahoo), as well as those that show signs of being successful. In terms of the former, in late 2007 Google announced plans to compete more effectively with Facebook by forming an alliance with various other companies to advance its own social network, Orkut, as well as others such as LinkedIn, hi5, Friendster, Plaxo, and Ning (Helft and Stone 2007: C1–C8). While control over the new Internet media is far from clear or resolved, it seems clear that in the long run they, too, will succumb and the world of Internet media will become increasingly less competitive.

Indymedia

However, the movement in the direction of global media giants is countered, at least to some degree, by the rise of independent media ("Indymedia") as another source of media diversity that serves to counter media imperialism. Indymedia have come to be associated with globalization, especially the globalization-from-below, or alter-globalization, movement (see Chapter 12). The first independent media center associated with the alter-globalization movement was created at the first big protest against globalization at the Seattle meetings of the WTO in late 1999: "Indymedia journalists reported directly from the streets, while activists uploaded their own text, audio, video, and image files" (Juris 2005: 189–208). Such centers soon sprang up throughout the US and later throughout the world. Indymedia play a particularly important role during protests, actions, and gatherings, through, for example, e-mails, formal updates, and the virtually immediate upload and dissemination of videos and images, including live video and audio streaming. Expertise on such matters is now widespread and Indymedia is not dependent on professionals in the media. It is highly reflexive, leading to a situation where those involved are often filming one another in the streets. Indymedia is also involved in disseminating information and technologies so that activists throughout the world can become involved.

However, in recent years the Indymedia have declined somewhat in importance as a result of the rise of blogs that perform many of the same functions.

Also worth mentioning here as a threat to the aspirations of the global media are "hacktivists" – those who hack into computer programs in order to further various causes, in this case the alter-globalization movement.

All of this can be seen as related to the movement toward open-sourcing (e.g. Linux) and Web 2.0. Those involved in Indymedia are not only involved in, and producing, the protests in their roles as media personnel, but they are consuming them as well (they are prosumers; see below). In the process, the authority and power structures of the traditional mass media are countered and made far less consequential.

Thinking about the Global Media

Much of current thinking on the media in general, and especially on the relationship between globalization and the media, has its roots in Marshall McLuhan's prescient ideas on the "global village" (McLuhan and Fiore 2005). McLuhan focuses on the medium itself (although Herbert Marcuse argued that the problem was not technologies such as the media, but rather the way they were employed in capitalism [Marcuse 2006]). In the new media age, McLuhan famously argued, the "medium is the message." That is, it is the medium (e.g. television) that is most important, not necessarily the content (e.g. a particular television program) presented on and via the medium. This led to a new sense of the power of the media to shape individual subjectivity and culture, not only locally but globally. As important as his insights were, McLuhan failed to link the global proliferation of the media to their origins in large-scale social structures and social institutions.

Guy DeBord (1967/1994) is a French social theorist known for his work on spectacle, media spectacle, the globalization of such a spectacle, and the ability of spectacle to produce and reproduce capitalism and consumer culture on a global scale. Over the years, media spectacles have grown ever-grander and they can be flashed around the world with blinding speed. The increasing sophistication and ubiquity of media spectacles makes it increasingly difficult to distinguish what the spectacle is referring to from the spectacle itself. Of course, as the media have grown more powerful, their role in the globalization of spectacle has increased dramatically.

This is perhaps best exemplified by the emergence of TV news as entertainment. The focus is on the spectacular visual rather than on what are the most important news events of the day. If an event has no significant visual associated with it, it is likely to get little or no TV time. On the other hand, news with little or no importance to most people (e.g. a crane collapse in New York City; an out-of-control hot-air balloon supposedly with a child on board) gets lots of TV attention because effective, even powerful, visuals are associated with it. Of course, the most important spectacles are those associated with events that are *both* very significant and offer powerful visuals. Perhaps the ultimate example of this is the terrorist attacks of 9/11 and the sight, shown endlessly on television, of the collapse of the twin towers. Similar visuals and spectacle were associated with the bombing of the London Underground (7/7/05), and the subway in Madrid (3/11/04), as well as the Bali bombings (10/1/05).

This focus on media spectacles tends to emphasize the global power of the media, but other perspectives (Rojek 2003) have focused on the importance of marginal voices and counter-hegemonic narratives rather than the global media. From a global point of view, this means that it is not just the hegemonic messages from the media giants that circulate throughout the world, but so do counter-hegemonic messages from the margins. For example, through the use of cell phones in the less developed world, such messages can be transmitted rapidly to large numbers of people. From this perspective, a world of differences can now circulate globally and serve as a counterweight to the global power of the media. Since the mass media tend to produce and/or to disseminate hegemonic discourses, it is those on the margin who are the major source of counter-hegemonic discourse throughout the world.

While this is an optimistic perspective, a more pessimistic view is presented in various circles, including in a variety of neo-Marxian theories, especially those associated with what is known as the Frankfurt School (Wiggershaus 1994). The theorists associated with that school of thought tended to shift the traditional focus of Marxian analysis away from the economy, and to the culture, of which the media are a significant component. To the Frankfurt theorists, the media were of economic significance as a new source of capital realization, but of far greater importance was their role in the social control of people and their unprecedented ability to influence and shape the larger culture. Instead of leading to counter-hegemonic discourses, the Frankfurt thinkers tended to see the media, and other components of what they called the "culture industry," as foreclosing the possibility of emancipatory discourse and action.

The view of the Frankfurt School has tended to win out over the more optimistic view. As a result, the emphasis tends to be on the effect of the global media rather than the counter-reactions of people to it and its messages. Global media culture is seen as overwhelmingly linked to both MNCs and to **globalization from above** rather than **globalization from below** (Kellner and Pierce 2007: 383–95; see Chapter 12). Not only are the global media heavily influenced by MNCs, but they often are MNCs themselves. As a form of globalization from above, that which emanates from the global media is largely controlled by the MNCs. These global media giants are, in the main, largely unregulated and they tend to produce largely homogeneous products (e.g. newscasts, entertainment programming). Since they are global in nature, they are usually beyond the control of any single nation-state. In fact, the nation-state is often reduced to the role of distributing cultural forms and commodities for the media conglomerates. While there are globally known examples of powerful media conglomerates (CNN, Fox) based in the US, there are many others including Brazil's Globo and Mexico's Televisa. They are all examples of globalization from above in that they extend media and consumer culture into diverse communities, serve to blur national boundaries, and have at least the potential not only to supplement, but also to replace, local culture.

Despite the global reach and power of media conglomerates, one finds the global-local (or better grobal-glocal; see Chapter 7) struggle in this realm as indigenous viewers struggle to counter, or at least redefine, global messages. There is even the

Globalization from above is a process that is created and disseminated by largescale forces (such as the nation-state and the MNC), especially those associated with the North, and imposed on the South (especially their nation-states and businesses).

Globalization from below takes the form of individual actors, and groups of actors, opposing and acting to oppose globalization in both developed and less developed countries.

(remote) possibility that the indigenous – especially when a number of indigenous movements, perhaps across the globe, band together – can triumph over the global (globalization from below). In fact, new media, especially those associated with the Internet (e.g. blogs), make such opposition more likely and powerful. Also in this realm mention must be made of alter-globalization movement websites (e.g. McSpotlight), locally produced and community-based Indymedia with hundreds of centers in many different countries (it gives voice to local issues and community concerns), blogs, and the Live 8 concerts and other activities involving U2's Bono. In the more traditional media there is EZLN's Radio Insurgente associated with Mexico's Zapatista Movement.

However, some of these media activities from below are themselves spectacles and this raises the point that they may well serve more to further than to counter the development of the society of the spectacle discussed by DeBord. Clearly, a far more radical step would be a restructuring of the media and using it in other less – or even non- – spectacular ways.

Mentioned above are media spectacles associated with various terrorist attacks, but others include those associated with the invasion of Iraq in 2003, the subsequent toppling of the statue of Saddam Hussein in Baghdad, and George W. Bush's appearance on an aircraft carrier announcing (prematurely) the end of hostilities in Iraq ("mission accomplished"). However, these spectacles can cut both ways. They can serve not only to control people (e.g. leading them to believe that the war in Iraq was over), but also to energize them (e.g. Al Jazeera's use of many of the same spectacles to help create opposition to the Iraq war and to the US more generally), and to make the contradictions that exist within them abundantly clear (as was the case when the televising of accelerating hostilities in Iraq made it clear that Bush's pronouncements about the end of the war were simply untrue). Similarly, the contradiction between the American claim to the moral high ground and reality was made clear when photos taken by American soldiers of the abuses at the Abu Ghraib prison escaped the filters of the mainstream media and made their way via the Internet directly into people's homes throughout the world. Overall, some see the development of such alternate media sources as a positive development. Indeed, they argue that these represent signs that a shift away from the control of the media conglomerates, a democratization of the global media, is underway (Kellner and Pierce 2007: 383–95).

THE INTERNET

The Internet is one of several digital technologies that have all had a profound effect on many things, including globalization. Digital technologies store and transmit data based on the binary (or dichotomous) coding of data. (This is in contrast to analog which involves the continuous coding of data.) Other digital technologies include the computer, chips, and semiconductor processors, as well as CDs and DVDs.

Since its birth in the 1990s, the Internet has profoundly affected almost every aspect of life, especially in the developed world. In the case of globalization, the Internet has expedited the globalization of many different things and is, itself, a profound form and aspect of globalization. The Internet is global in several senses, but the most important is that while its users are not equally divided between the North and South, rich and poor, etc., they do exist virtually everywhere in the world (Drori 2006). It is also global in the sense that it was produced and is maintained by a number of global and transnational corporations and organizations including multinational corporations (e.g. Intel), and IGOs and INGOs (e.g. World Intellectual Property Organization [WIPO] which regulates intellectual property rights, Internet Corporation for Assigned Names and Numbers [ICANN] which coordinates domain names, and United Nations Education, Science, and Culture Organization [UNESCO] which promotes computer and Internet use in schools) throughout the world.

Online Social Networking

Involved here are social-networking sites (SNSs) such as Facebook, Twitter, and MySpace that involve communication, networking, and the creation of friendship networks among those involved. They are part of Web 2.0 which also includes Wikipedia, the blogosphere, podcasts, and much else. What defines Web 2.0 is the fact that the material on it is generated by the users (consumers) rather than the producers of the system. Thus, those who operate on Web 2.0 can be called **prosumers** because they simultaneously produce what they consume, such as the interaction on Facebook and the entries on Wikipedia (Ritzer and Jurgenson 2010).

Prosumers: Those who simultaneously produce what they consume.

Given the character of the Internet, all of these sites are global in nature. That is, assuming one is on the "right side" of the "digital divide" (see Chapter 11), wherever one is in the world, one will be able to "prosume" on these sites. Further, while Facebook and MySpace are the most popular SNSs in the US, Canada, and Australia, there are many other such sites throughout the world (about 120 in total):

Orkut, with 67 million users, was most used in Brazil and India; Friendster (65 million users), available in traditional and simplified Chinese, Indonesian, Japanese, Korean, Spanish, was most used in Asia; hi5 (70 million users) was popular in Central and South America and parts of Asia; sites with smaller user numbers were dominant in particular countries (Cyworld in South Korea – 2.1 million, LiveJournal in Russia – 15 million, Mixi in Japan – 17 million, LunarStorm in Sweden – 1.2 million, Skyrock_ Blog in France – 22 million, Arto in Denmark). (Gorman 2010)

It is the global nature of these sites, and the ability of people throughout (much of) the world to participate in SNSs, that make them a truly global phenomenon.

Further, they are likely to become increasingly important in the future, if for no other reason than the fact that it is young people who are the ones who are primarily involved in them. In addition, we are not only in the early history of these sites as part of Web 2.0, but there is already talk of a Web 3.0 which promises even greater advances, including in the ability to communicate globally.

Spam

It is argued, quite ironically, that "Spam is one of globalization's true success stories" (Spector 2007: 41). The main form of Spam is, of course, unsolicited bulk e-mail, often of a commercial nature (e.g. offers of products to enhance sexual performance), and while it is a bane to the World Wide Web, it is a global "success" in the sense that it stems from virtually everywhere on the globe (especially Eastern Europe, Russia, China, and Nigeria), goes everywhere, and is almost impossible to contain, let alone stop. It is one of the *flows* that are a defining feature of globalization. Virtually as soon as methods are devised to stop the influx of Spam, spammers find ways to get around those defenses. Programs are widely available on the Internet that allow anyone from anywhere to get into the Spam "business." One needs virtually no computer expertise in order to become a contributor to the increasing avalanche of Spam around the world. Since Spam may now represent as much as 90 percent of all e-mails – more than 100 billion of them – it represents a real threat to the World Wide Web. The faith of at least some in the entire system is being shaken because of the mass of useless and sometimes offensive messages that one must wade through in order to get to legitimate messages.

Computer Viruses

The idea of a computer virus made its first appearance in science fiction in the late 1960s and early 1970s. Over a decade later a graduate student wrote the first program that was able to replicate and propagate itself. His professor, seeing its similarity to a biological phenomenon, suggested it be called a "computer virus." The first global computer virus was likely created in Pakistan in 1986. Since then, of course, many different viruses (and worms), some benign, some malicious ("malware"), have been created, circled the globe, and in some cases caused great damage to computers and computer systems. Some of these viruses (e.g. CodeRed, MyDoom), unknown to their owners and/or users, "infect" computers and can be used to access personal information illegally. For example, they can be used to gain access to credit card numbers and then those numbers can be used to charge all sorts of goods and services illegally. At the same time, global organizations, including law enforcement agencies, have emerged to try to warn people about new viruses and to develop counter-measures to protect against them (Chanda 2007: 236–41). To the degree that they are successful, the latter are barriers to the largely free flow of computer viruses around the globe.

The Internet in China

As of the end of 2007 there were 210 million Internet users in China, an increase of more than 50 percent over the previous year and more than three times the number of users in India, which is usually thought of as a high-tech nation (*Economist* 2008: January 31). China overtook the US in 2008 in the number of Internet users. Since only a small percentage of China's population currently uses the Internet, China will become the world leader in Internet use by an increasingly wide margin. Furthermore, Chinese Internet users are young (70 percent are under 30), and this also augers well for future Chinese involvement in the Internet.

What is most interesting about the Internet in China today from the perspective of this book is how well it illustrates the basic argument about the relationship between global flows and structural barriers to those flows. Among the major flows through the Internet in China are pirated films, music, and TV shows that can be watched free of charge; the delivery to mobile phones of mobile-Internet content (e.g. ringtones); online multiplayer games; online communities with social networking and instant messaging; gossip, photos, videos of American and European sports, etc.

On the surface it seems that Internet flows in China are not much different from the flows elsewhere in the world. However, what *is* different is the active efforts by the Chinese government to erect barriers to those flows. In fact, that barrier – the "Great Firewall" – exists, although the majority of Chinese Internet users are completely oblivious to its existence (French 2008: A1, A6). (Cuba also seeks to block at least some Internet traffic, although cyber-activists there are increasingly rebelling against such restrictions and finding ways around them [McKinley 2008: A1, A6].) This is part of a larger effort by the Chinese government to block various flows including the censoring of news, control over television, and limits on bookshops and movie theaters. Barriers on the Internet include restricted access to a large number of foreign websites (e.g. Wikipedia, Flickr, YouTube, and sometimes MySpace). There are filters on Google in China designed to keep out material regarded by the government as politically sensitive. An awkward payment system controlled by the government restricts online shopping. In early 2008 new rules came into effect limiting online video. Hard news regarded by the government as undesirable is blocked.

Overall, there are many flows into and through China on the Internet, but much else is limited or blocked altogether. The result, at least at the moment, is a fairly unique Internet world in China (for example it has its own online communities). However, the long-run question here, and in much else that relates to China in an increasingly global world, is how long these differences will remain. That is, how long can China buck the tide of global flows and erect barriers that few if any other countries in the world erect?

In fact, there are already early signs of rebellion against the Great Firewall, although of course the history of China, especially in the crushing of the Tiananmen Square revolt, shows that the government could destroy that rebellion in its infancy.

The resistance is currently taking many forms, from lawsuits by Internet users against government-owned service providers claiming that blocking sites is illegal, to a growing network of software writers who develop code aimed at overcoming government restrictions. An Internet-based word-of-mouth campaign has taken shape, in which bloggers and web-page owners post articles to spread awareness of the Great Firewall, or share links to programs that will help Internet users evade it (French 2008: A6).

Perhaps no change has done more to further the process of globalization than the Internet. It occupies pride of place in many analyses of globalization, especially in Friedman's (2005) analysis of globalization as involving a "flat world." The Internet is flat in the sense that virtually anyone anywhere can become involved in it. However, there are reservations about the flat world argument. That is, the whole of social history indicates that there are *always* strong pressures to erect barriers that serve to impede movement of all types. Both the flat world thesis, and the weaknesses in the argument, are nicely illustrated in the case of the Internet in China today and the continuing efforts by the state to erect barriers to it.

CHAPTER SUMMARY

High-tech flows and structures such as technology, media, and the Internet are closely interconnected. Technology plays an important role in expediting global processes. Significant cornerstones have been the development of containerized ships, air freight, the personal computer, and the Internet.

The global flow of technology does not go to all parts of the world, and it might "skip" areas due to the presence of barriers such as lack of electricity. There are instances of countries "leapfrogging" in the process of technological advancement; they skip certain technologies and move on directly to more advanced developments. Barriers to technology include lack of basic infrastructure (such as electricity), illiteracy, lack of strong systems of finance, and unstable political conditions.

The global flow of media is often characterized as media imperialism. TV, music, books, and movies are perceived as being imposed on developing countries by the West. Media imperialism undermines the existence of alternative global media originating from developing countries themselves, such as Al Jazeera and Bollywood, as well as the influence of the local and regional media. The Internet can be seen as an arena for alternative media. Cultural imperialism denies the agency of viewers, but people around the world often interpret the same medium (e.g. a movie) in significantly different ways.

Global media are dominated by a small number of large corporations. This is being extended from old media to new media. As a result, in the long run, the Internet could end up being less diverse and competitive. Indymedia, associated with the alter-globalization movement, helps to counter this trend. It disseminates information to facilitate global participation of activists. Hacktivists extend activism to the Internet by hacking into computer programs to promote a particular cause.

Global media have been seen as tending toward homogenization, both through McLuhan's concept of the "global village" as well as through the more pessimistic approach of the Frankfurt School, which theorizes the creation of a "culture industry" under capitalism. However, the sector is witnessing a grobal-glocal struggle and the potential for democratization of global media is largely dependent on the further development of alternative media sources.

The Internet is a truly global phenomenon since it is used in all parts of the world. It is produced and maintained by global corporations, IGOs, and INGOs, thus reducing the influence of the nation-state. Web 2.0 (e.g. Wikipedia, Facebook) involves the creation of content by the users themselves; they are prosumers who simultaneously produce and consume content. The Internet has prompted a flat world thesis; anyone can be involved in it, at least theoretically. However, there are efforts to create barriers to impede such involvement, for instance the "Great Firewall" erected by the Chinese government in an effort to control Internet access and use.

DISCUSSION QUESTIONS

1. What is media imperialism? How do global flows of technology affect media imperialism?

2. Discuss the idea that "the world is flat" in the context of global flows of technology.

3. Discuss the potential of the Internet to be a global "democratic" space.

4. Examine the role of Indymedia in the alter-globalization movement.

5. Discuss the impact of global technological flows on the nation-state.

FURTHER READING

Nayan Chanda. *Bound Together: How Traders, Preachers, Adventurers, and Warriors Shaped Globalization*. New Haven: Yale University Press, 2007

Marshall McLuhan and Quention Fiore. *The Medium is the Massage*. Berkeley: Gingko Press, 2005.

Colin Sparks. *Globalization, Development and the Mass Media*. London: Sage, 2007.

Ien Ang. *Watching Dallas: Soap Opera and the Melodramatic Imagination*. London: Routledge, 1985.

Jeremy Tunstall. *The Media Were American: US Mass Media in Decline*. Oxford: Oxford University Press, 2008.

Toby Miller, et al. *Global Hollywood 2*. London: British Film Institute, 2005.

Gili S. Drori. *Global E-Litism: Digital Technology, Social Inequality, and Transnationality*. New York: Worth, 2006.

REFERENCES ···

Ang, Ien. 1985. *Watching Dallas: Soap Opera and the Melodramatic Imagination*. London: Routledge.

Bielsa, Esperanca. 2008. "The Pivotal Role of News Agencies in the Context of Globalization: A Historical Approach." *Global Networks* 8, 3.

Bovet, Christian. 2007. "Satellites." In Jan Aart Scholte and Roland Robertson, eds., *Encyclopedia of Globalization*. New York: MTM Publishing.

Chanda, Nayan. 2007. *Bound Together: How Traders, Preachers, Adventurers, and Warriors Shaped Globalization*. New Haven: Yale University Press.

Corbett, Sara. 2008. "Can the Cellphone Help End Global Poverty?" *New York Times Magazine*. April 13.

Cowen, Tyler. 2002. *Creative Destruction*. Princeton: Princeton University Press.

DeBord, Guy. 1967/1994. *The Society of the Spectacle*. New York: Zone Books.

Drori, Gili S. 2006. *Global E-Litism: Digital Technology, Social Inequality, and Transnationality*. New York: Worth.

Economist. 2008. January 10. "No Lakh of Daring."

Economist. 2008. January 17. "The Militarisation of Space: Disharmony in the Spheres."

Economist. 2008. January 31. "The Internet in China: Alternative Reality."

Economist. 2008. February 7. "Of Internet Cafes and Power Cuts."

Economist. 2008. February 7. "The Limits of Leapfrogging."

French, Howard W. 2008. "Great Firewall of China Faces Online Rebels." *New York Times*. February 4.

Friedman, Thomas. 2005. *The World is Flat: A Brief History of the Twenty-first Century*. New York: Farrar, Straus, Giroux.

Gorman, Lyn. 2010 "Online Social Networking." In George Ritzer, ed., *Blackwell Encyclopedia of Sociology Online*. June 7. Malden, MA: Wiley-Blackwell. www.blackwellreference.com/subscriber/tocnode?id=g9781405124331_yr2010_chunk_g978140512433121_ss1-37

Helft, Miguel, and Brad Stone. 2007. "For Google, A New Shot at Facebook." *New York Times*. October 31.

Horst, Heather. 2006. "The Blessings and Burdens of Communication: Cell Phones in Jamaican Transnational Social Fields." *Global Networks* 6, 2.

Juris, Jeffrey. 2005. "The New Digital Media and Activist Networking within Anti-Corporate Globalization Movements." *Annals* 597 (January).

Kellner, Douglas, and Clayton Pierce. 2007. "Media and Globalization." In George Ritzer, ed., *The Blackwell Companion to Globalization*. Malden, MA: Blackwell.

Larkin, Brian. 2003. "Itineraries of Indian Cinema: African Videos, Bollywood, and Global Media." In Ellen Shohat and Robert Stam, eds., *Multiculturalism, Postcoloniality, and Transnational Media*. New Brunswick, NJ: Rutgers University Press.

Marcuse, Herbert. 2006. *One-Dimensional Man: Studies in the Ideology of Advanced Industrial Society*. London: Routledge.

McChesney, Robert. 1999. "The New Global Media." *The Nation*. November 29.

McKinley, Jr., James C. 2008. "Cyber-Rebels in Cuba Defy State's Limits." *New York Times*. March 6.

McLuhan, Marshall, and Quentin Fiore. 2005. *The Medium is the Massage*. Corte Madera, CA: Gingko Press.

Miller, Toby, Nitin Govil, John McMurria, Ting Wang, and Richard Maxwell. 2005. *Global Hollywood 2*. London: British Film Institute.

Ritzer, George, and Nathan Jurgenson. 2010. "Production, Consumption, Prosumption: The Nature of Capitalism in the Age of the Digital 'Prosumer.'" *Journal of Consumer Culture* 10, 1: 13–36.

Rojek, Chris. 2003. *Stuart Hall*. Cambridge: Polity.

Sparks, Colin. 2007. *Globalization, Development and the Mass Media*. London: Sage.

Spector, Michael. 2007. "Damn Spam: The Losing War on Junk E-mail." *The New Yorker*. August 6.

Sullivan, Kevin. 2006. "Internet Extends Reach of Bangladeshi Villagers." *New York Times*. November 22.

Tunstall, Jeremy. 1977. *The Media Are American: Anglo-American Media in the World*. New York: Columbia University Press.

Tunstall, Jeremy. 2008. *The Media Were American: U.S. Mass Media in Decline*. Oxford: Oxford University Press.

Tyrell, Heather. 1999. "Bollywood versus Hollywood: Battle of the Dream Factories." In Tracey Skelton and Tim Allen, eds., *Cultural and Global Change*. London: Routledge.

Wiggershaus, Rolf. 1994. *The Frankfurt School: Its History, Theories, and Political Significance*. Cambridge, MA: MIT Press.

Yang, M. M.-h. 1996. "Mass Media and Transnational Subjectivity in Shanghai: Notes on (Re) cosmopolitanism in a Chinese Metropolis." In A. Ong and D. Nonini, eds., *Ungrounded Empires: The Cultural Politics of Modern Chinese Transnationalism*. New York: Routledge.

Global Culture and Cultural Flows

Globalization: The Essentials, by George Ritzer
© 2011 John Wiley & Sons Ltd

Because much of it exists in the form of ideas, words, images, musical sounds, and so on, culture tends to flow comparatively easily throughout the world. In fact, that flow is increasingly easy because culture exists increasingly in digitized forms. Thus, the Internet permits global downloading and sharing of digitized cultural forms such as movies, videos, music, books, newspapers, photos, and so on. Further, those who see themselves as part of the same culture can maintain contact with one another through e-mail or via virtual face-to-face contact on Skype. They can also remain immersed within the culture in which they exist and/or from which they come by, for example, reading online newspapers from home. While the global flow of digital culture is increasingly easy, the fact is that there are still barriers to its flow, especially, for many, the lack of access to the Internet, especially in the South (the "global digital divide"; see Chapter 11).

While culture does flow comparatively easily across the globe, not all cultures and forms of culture flow as easily or at the same rate. For one thing, the cultures of the world's most powerful societies (most notably the US) flow around the world much more readily than the cultures of relatively weak and marginal societies. Similarly, some types of culture (pop music, for example) move quickly and easily around the globe, while others (innovative theories in the social sciences, for example) move in slow motion and may never make it to many parts of the world.

This chapter on culture permits the introduction of three theories of globalization (for others see Chapter 2) – **cultural differentialism**, **hybridization**, and **convergence** (Nederveen Pieterse 2004). While these theories are treated here under the heading of culture, they have much broader applicability to many issues covered in this book, such as the previously discussed topics of economics and politics. In politics, for example, it could be argued that nation-states throughout the world remain stubbornly different ("differentialism"), are growing increasingly alike ("convergence"), or involve more and more combinations of various political forms drawn from many different parts of the world ("hybridization"). In spite of this broader applicability, the focus here will be on these three types of theories as they relate to global culture.

> **Cultural differentialism** involves barriers that prevent flows that serve to make cultures more alike; cultures tend to remain stubbornly different from one another.

> **Cultural hybridization** is the mixing of cultures and the integration of the global and the local leading to unique combinations.

> **Cultural convergence** is when cultures are subject to many of the same global flows and tend to grow more alike.

What makes these three theories particularly attractive from the perspective of this book is that they are all about our focal concern with flows and barriers and take very different positions on them and their relationship to one another. In *differentialism*, the focus is much more on barriers that prevent flows that would serve to make cultures (and much else) more alike. In this view, cultures tend to remain stubbornly different from one another. In the *convergence* perspective, the barriers are much weaker and the global flows stronger, with the result that cultures are subject to many of the same flows and tend to grow more alike. In its extreme form, convergence suggests the possibility that local cultures can be overwhelmed by other, more powerful cultures, or even a globally homogeneous culture. Finally, in the hybridization perspective, external flows interact with internal flows in order to produce a unique cultural hybrid that combines elements of the two. Barriers to external cultural flows exist in the hybridization perspective, and while they are strong enough to prevent those flows from overwhelming local culture, they are not strong enough to block all external cultural flows entirely. That which does succeed in gaining entry combines with local culture to produce unique cultural hybrids.

CULTURAL DIFFERENTIALISM

Those who adopt this theory argue that there are lasting differences among and between cultures, largely unaffected by globalization or any other bi-, inter-, multi-, and trans-cultural processes and flows. This is not to say that culture is unaffected by any of these processes, especially globalization, but it is to say that *at their core* they are *largely unaffected* by them; they remain much as they always have been. In this perspective, globalization occurs mainly, if not only, on the surface, with the deep structure of cultures largely, if not totally, unaffected by it. Cultures are seen as basically closed not only to global processes, but also to the influences of other cultures. In one image, the world is envisioned as a mosaic of largely separate cultures. More menacing is an image of a billiard ball table, with billiard balls (representing cultures) seen as bouncing off others (representing other cultures). This is more threatening because it indicates the possibility of dangerous, potentially catastrophic, collisions among and between at least some of the world's cultures.

This theory has a long history, but it has attracted increasing attention and adherents (as well as critics) in recent years because of two sets of events. One is the terrorist attacks on September 11th (and later in London, Madrid, etc.) and the subsequent wars in Afghanistan and Iraq. To many, these events are seen as the product of a clash between Western and Islamic culture and the seemingly eternal differences between them. The other is the increasing multi-culturalism of both the US (largely the growth of the Hispanic population) and Western European countries (largely the growing Muslim populations) and the vast differences, and enmity, between majority and minority populations.

Civilizations

The most famous, and controversial, example of this theory is Samuel Huntington's *Clash of Civilizations and the Remaking of the World Order*. Huntington traces the beginnings of the current world situation to the end of the Cold War and the reconfiguring of the world from one differentiated on a political-economic basis (democratic/capitalist vs. totalitarian/communist) to one based on cultural differences. Such cultural differences are nothing new, but they were largely submerged (as in the old Yugoslavia and the differences between, among others, Serbs and Croats) by the overwhelming political-economic differences of the Cold War era. In the last two decades, ancient identities, adversaries, and enemies have resurfaced. Huntington uses the term *civilization* to describe the broadest level of culture and cultural identities (indeed, to him civilization *is* culture "writ large"). What he sees is the emergence of fault lines among and between these civilizations. Given the historic enmities among at least some of the civilizations involved, these fault lines have created a highly dangerous situation.

Huntington differentiates among seven or eight world civilizations: Sinic (Chinese), Japan (sometimes combined with the Sinic as Far Eastern), Hindu, Islamic, Orthodox (centered in Russia), Western Europe, North America (along with the closely aligned Australia, and New Zealand), Latin America, and (possibly) Africa.

He sees these civilizations as differing greatly on basic philosophical assumptions, underlying values, social relations, customs, and overall outlooks on life. To Huntington, human history is, in effect, the history of civilizations, especially these civilizations. Every civilization shares a number of characteristics including the fact that there is great agreement on what they are (although they lack clear beginnings and there are no clear-cut boundaries between civilizations although they are, nonetheless, quite real). Civilizations are among the most enduring of human associations (although they do change over time); they are the broadest level of cultural identity (short of humanity in its entirety); they are the broadest source of subjective self-identification; they usually span more than one nation-state (although they do not perform state functions); they are a totality, and they are closely aligned with both religion (see below) and race.

Huntington offers a modern grand narrative of the relationships among civilizations. For more than 3,000 years (approximately 1500 BC to AD 1500) civilizations tended to be widely separated in both time and space. As a result, contacts among them were apt to be almost non-existent. The contacts that did occur tended to be limited or intermittent, but when they occurred they were likely to be quite intense.

The next phase, roughly from 1500 to the close of WW II, was characterized by the sustained, overpowering, and unidirectional impact of Western civilization on all other civilizations. Huntington attributes this to various structural characteristics of the West including the rise there of cities, commerce, state bureaucracy, and an emerging sense of national consciousness. However, the most immediate cause was technological, especially in ocean navigation and the military (including a superior military organization, discipline and training, and, of course, weaponry). In the end, the West excelled in organized violence and while those in the West sometimes forget this, those in other parts of the world have not. Thus, by 1910, just before the beginning of World War I, the world came closer, in Huntington's view, than at any other time in history to being one world, one civilization – Western civilization.

The third phase – the multi-civilizational system – is traceable to the end of the expansion of the West and the beginning of the revolt against it. The period after

WW II and until about 1990 was characterized by a clash of ideas, especially capitalist and communist ideologies, but with the fall of communism, the major clashes in the world came to revolve around religion, culture, and ultimately civilizations. While the West continues to be dominant, Huntington foresees its decline. It will be a slow decline, it will not occur in a straight line, and it will involve a decline (at least relatively) in the West's resources – population, economic products, and military capability (traceable to such things as the decline of US armed forces and the globalization of the defense industries making weapons once obtainable only, or largely, in the West generally available). Other civilizations will increasingly reject the West, but they will embrace and utilize the advances of modernization, which can and should be distinguished from Westernization.

While the West declines, the resurgence of two other civilizations is of greatest importance. The first is the economic growth of Asian societies, especially Sinic civilization. Huntington foresees continuing growth of Asian economies which will soon surpass those of the West. Important in itself, this will translate into increasing power for the East and a corresponding decline in the ability of the West to impose itself on the East. He sees the economic ascendancy of the East as largely traceable to the superior aspects of its culture(s), especially its collectivism in contrast to the individuality dominant in the West. Also helpful to the economic rise of the East are other commonalities among the nations of the region (e.g. religion, especially Confucianism). The successes of Asian economies are not only important in themselves, but also for the role they play as models for other non-Western societies.

This first of Huntington's arguments is not that surprising or original. After all, we witnessed the dramatic growth of the post-WW II Japanese economy and we are now witnessing the amazing economic transformation of China and India. Few would disagree with the view that, projecting present economic trends, the Chinese economy will become the largest in the world in the not-too-distant future, and India will experience great economic growth, as well.

More controversial is Huntington's second major contention involving the resurgence of Islam. While the Sinic emergence is based in the economy, Islamic expansion is rooted in dramatic population growth and the mobilization of the population. This has touched virtually every Muslim society, usually first culturally and then socio-politically. It can be seen as part of the global revival of religion. It can also be seen as both a product of, and an effort to come to grips with, modernization.

Huntington goes beyond pointing to these developments to paint a dire portrait of the future of the relations between the West and these other two civilizations, especially Islam. Conflict will occur at the fault lines among and between civilizations, especially the Western, Sinic, and Islamic civilizations. Thus, he foresees dangerous clashes in the future between the West (and what he calls its "arrogance"), Islam (and its "intolerance"), and Sinic "assertiveness." Much of the conflict revolves around the West's view of itself as possessing "universal culture," its desire to export that culture to the rest of the world, and its declining ability to do so. Furthermore, what the West sees as universalism, the rest of the world, especially

Islamic civilization, sees as imperialism. More specifically, the West wants to limit weapons proliferation, while other civilizations want weapons, especially the now-infamous "weapons of mass destruction" thought (erroneously) to be in Iraq. The most notable instance of this at the moment is the great heat associated with the possibility that Iran, with its radical Islamic culture and government, is in the process of constructing nuclear weapons.

The West also seeks to export democracy to, even impose it on, other societies and civilizations (Iraq and Afghanistan are notable examples in the Islamic world), which often resist it as part of the West's idea of universal culture. And, the West seeks to control and to limit immigration (especially from Islamic civilizations), but many from those civilizations have found their way into the West, or want to be there. As this increases, Huntington sees cleft societies developing *within* both Europe and the United States (in the latter, fault lines will develop not only between Westerners and Muslims, but also between Anglos and Hispanics [Huntington 2004: 30–45]).

Huntington's predictions seem to have been borne out, at least in part, in recent years as much tension and conflict has arisen between Muslims and "natives" in Europe (notable instances have occurred in France [*Economist* 2007: November 28], the Netherlands [*Economist* 2004: November 4], and Denmark [*Economist* 2006: February 3]) and between Hispanics and "native" Americans over illegal immigrants from Latin America.

Huntington has earned numerous criticisms and great enmity for his controversial statements about Islamic civilization and Muslims (Huntington 1996). For example, he argues that wherever Muslims and non-Muslims live in close proximity to one another, violent conflict and intense antagonism are pervasive. And Huntington puts much of the blame for this on Muslims and what is, in his view, their propensity toward violent conflict. He argues that, from the beginning, Islam has been a religion of the sword; it glorified military values and there is a history of Islamic conquest. The relationship between Islam and other civilizations has historically been one of mutual indigestibility. (Of course, Western imperialism and military adventurism – often with Islam as a target – has played a key role in this.) Islam also lacks a strong core state to exert control over the various elements that constitute its civilization. But of greatest importance to Huntington are the pressures created by the demographic explosion within Islam. The high birth rate in Islam will force many to move out of the heart of Islamic society in search of income and work. This will serve to bring Muslims and their culture into more and more contact – and conflict – with those in other civilizations.

Huntington is concerned about the decline of the West, especially of the US. He sees the US, indeed all societies, as threatened by their increasing multi-civilizational or multi-cultural character. For him, the demise of the US effectively means the demise of Western civilization. Without a powerful, uni-civilizational US, the West is, in his view, minuscule.

Huntington argues that for the West to survive and prosper the US must do two things. First, it must reaffirm its identity as a Western (rather than multi-civilizational) nation. Second, it must reaffirm and reassert its role as the leader of Western civilization around the globe. The reassertion and acceptance of Western civilization (which would also involve a renunciation of universalism) is the surest way to prevent warfare between civilizations. The real danger, for Huntington, is multiculturalism within the West and all other civilizations. Thus, Huntington ultimately comes down on the side of cultural continuity and something approaching cultural purity within civilizations. Thus, for him, at least in some ideal sense, globalization becomes a process by which civilizations will continue to exist and move in roughly parallel and largely independent fashion in the coming years. This constitutes a reaffirmation of the importance of civilization, that is culture, in the epoch of globalization.

Beyond Huntington's specific and highly controversial arguments is a more general theory of culture, especially of the global flow of culture, as well as of the barriers to that flow. At a general level, cultural differentialism emphasizes the barriers to cultural flows and the ways in which those barriers lead cultures to remain largely distinct from, and potentially in conflict with, one another.

CULTURAL HYBRIDIZATION

The second theory emphasizes the mixing of cultures as a result of globalization and the production, out of the integration of the global and the local (Cvetkovich and Kellner 1997), of new and unique hybrid cultures that are not reducible to either local or global culture. From this perspective, the focus is on the integration of global processes with various local realities to produce new and distinctive hybrid forms that indicate continued global heterogenization rather than homogenization. Hybridization is a very positive, even romantic, view of globalization as a profoundly creative process out of which emerges new cultural realities, and continuing, if not increasing, heterogeneity, in many different locales.

Glocalization is the concept that gets to the heart of cultural hybridization as well as what many contemporary theorists interested in globalization think about the essential nature of global processes (Giulianotti and Robertson 2007: 133–52). **Glocalization** can be defined as the interpenetration of the global and the local, resulting in unique outcomes in different geographic areas.

> **Glocalization**: Interpenetration of the global and the local resulting in unique outcomes in different geographic areas.

Based on the work of Roland Robertson (2001: 458–71; Friedman 1994), the essential elements of the perspective on globalization adopted by those who emphasize glocalization are that the world is growing more pluralistic (glocalization theory is exceptionally alert to differences within and between areas of the world); individuals and local groups have great power to adapt, innovate, and maneuver within a glocalized world (glocalization theory sees individuals and local groups as important and creative agents); social processes are relational and contingent (globalization provokes a variety of reactions – ranging from nationalist entrenchment to cosmopolitan embrace – that produce glocalization); and commodities and the media are *not* seen as (totally) coercive, but rather as providing material to be used in individual and group creation throughout the glocalized areas of the world.

A discussion of some closely related terms (and related examples) will be of considerable help in getting a better sense of glocalization, as well as the broader issue of cultural hybridization (Canclini 1995; Nederveen Pieterse 2004). Of course, **hybridization** itself is one such term, emphasizing increasing diversity associated with the unique mixtures of the global and the local as opposed to the tendency toward *uniformity* often associated with globalization. A cultural hybrid involves the combination of two, or more, elements from different cultures and/or parts of the world. Among the examples of hybridization (and heterogenization, glocalization) are Ugandan tourists visiting Amsterdam to watch Moroccan women engage in Thai boxing, Argentineans watching Asian rap performed by a South American band at a London club owned by a Saudi Arabian, and the more mundane experiences of Americans eating such concoctions as Irish bagels, Chinese tacos, Kosher pizza, and so on. Obviously, the list of such hybrids is long and growing rapidly with increasing hybridization. The contrast, of course, would be such uniform experiences as eating hamburgers in the United States, quiche in France, or sushi in Japan.

> **Hybridization**: External flows interact with internal flows producing a unique cultural hybrid that combines elements of the two.

> **Creolization** involves a combination of languages and cultures that were previously unintelligible to one another.

Yet another concept that is closely related to glocalization is **creolization** (Hannerz 1987: 546–59). The term "creole" generally refers to people of mixed race, but it has been extended to the idea of the creolization of language and culture involving a combination of languages and cultures that were previously unintelligible to one another (Cohen 2007: 369–84).

While all of the above – glocalization, hybridization, creolization – should give the reader a good feel for what is being discussed here under the heading of cultural hybridization, the following example should also help.

Muslim Girl Scouts

An interesting example of hybridization in the US involves Muslim girls (Sarroub 2005) who participate in one of the quintessentially American institutions, the Girl Scouts (Muslim involvement in the Boy Scouts is less significant) (MacFarquhar 2007: A1, A22). Muslim girls are now wearing a Girl Scout sash (with American flag, troop number, and merit badges) along with the flowing headscarf that is traditional Muslim garb. For some Muslim girls, the Girl Scout garb tends to reduce tension when they interact with non-Muslims. At a cookout, hot dogs and s'mores are served, but such food meets the dietary restrictions of Islamic law (the hot dogs are made of beef not pork). One Girl Scout broke the fast of Ramadan with a hot dog and s'mores exclaiming, "It's delicious! … It's a good way to break my fast" (quoted in MacFarquhar 2007: A22). Another won a ribbon, a Bismallah (in the name of God) ribbon, from her group for writing some of God's names in Arabic calligraphy and for memorizing a verse in the Koran that involves protection from gossips and goblins. (Such religious badges are not issued by Girl Scouts, USA, but it does endorse having them issued by specific groups.) However, her favorite badge was awarded for learning "how to make body glitter and to see which colors look good on us and 'how to clean our nails'" (quoted in MacFarquhar 2007: A22).

The Girl Scouts have adapted to Muslims, as well, especially if a given troop is predominantly or wholly Muslim. In one mostly Muslim troop, the Girl Scout Promise is: "On my honor I will try to serve Allah and my country, to help people and live by the Girl Scout law" (quoted in MacFarquhar 2007: A22).

Appadurai's "Landscapes"

Arjun Appadurai's *Modernity at Large: Cultural Dimensions of Globalization* (1996) emphasizes the concept – global flows – that, as we saw in Chapter 1, is central to this book, as well as to the disjunctures among them. These flows and disjunctures serve to produce unique cultural realities around the world; they tend to produce cultural hybrids.

Appadurai discusses five global flows – *ethnoscapes, mediascapes, technoscapes, financescapes*, and *ideoscapes.* The use of the suffix *-scape* allows Appadurai to communicate the idea that these processes have fluid, irregular, and variable shapes and are therefore consistent with the idea of heterogenization and not homogenization. The fact that there are a number of these scapes and that they operate independently of one another to some degree, and are perhaps even in conflict with one another, makes this perspective also in tune with those that emphasize cultural diversity and heterogeneity. Furthermore, these scapes are interpreted differently by different agents, ranging all the way from individuals, to face-to-face groups, sub-national groups, multi-national corporations, and even nation-states. And, these scapes are ultimately navigated by individuals and groups on the basis of their own subjective interpretations of them. In other words, these are imagined worlds and those doing the imagining can range from those who control them to those who live in and traverse them. While power obviously lies with those in control and their imaginings, this perspective gives to those who merely live in these scapes, or pass through them, the power to redefine and ultimately subvert them.

At the center of Appadurai's thinking are the five landscapes mentioned above. **Ethnoscapes** involve those who are mobile, groups and individuals on the move (tourists, refugees, guest

> **Ethnoscapes:** Actual movement, as well as fantasies about moving, of mobile groups and individuals.

workers) that play such an important role in the ever-changing world in which we increasingly live. This involves actual movement as well as fantasies about moving. Furthermore, in an ever-changing world, people cannot afford to allow their imaginations to rest too long and thus must keep such fantasies of movement alive.

Technoscapes: Fluid, global configurations of technology and the wide range of material that moves freely and quickly around the globe.

Technoscapes are the ever fluid, global configurations of high and low, mechanical and informational technology and the wide range of material (downloading files, e-mail) that now moves so freely and quickly around the globe and across borders that were at one time impervious to such movement (or at least thought to be).

Financescapes: Processes by which huge sums of money move through nation-states and around the world at great speed.

Financescapes involve the processes by which huge sums of money move through nation-states and around the world at great speed through commodity speculations, currency markets, national stock exchanges, and the like. The great importance of this scape was highlighted, if it was ever downplayed, by the global recession that spread rapidly throughout the world following its onset in late 2007.

Mediascapes: Electronic capability to produce and transmit information and images globally.

Mediascapes involve both the electronic capability to produce and transmit information around the world as well as the images of the world that these media create and disseminate. Involved here are those who write "blogs" online, citizen journalists who provide news to outlets such as CNN, global film makers and distributors, television stations (SkyNews is a notable example), and newspapers and magazines.

Ideoscapes: Flows of images primarily political in nature.

Ideoscapes, like mediascapes, are sets of images. However, they are largely restricted to either political images produced by states and in line with their ideology, or the images and counter-ideologies produced by movements that seek to supplant those in power, or at least to gain a piece of that power.

Three things are especially worth noting about Appadurai's landscapes. First, they can be seen as global processes that are partly or wholly independent of any given nation-state. Second, global flows not only occur through the landscapes, but also increasingly in and through the *disjunctures* among them. Thus, to give one example of such a disjuncture, the Japanese tend to be open to ideas (ideoscapes, mediascapes), but notoriously closed to immigration (at least one of the ethnoscapes). More generally, the free movement of some landscapes may be at variance with blockages of others. Studies in this area must be attuned to such disjunctures and to their implications for globalization. Third, territories are going to be affected differently by the five landscapes and their disjunctures lead to important differences among and between cultures. The focus on landscapes and their disjunctures points globalization studies in a set of unique directions. However, the key point here is that such a focus is in line with the idea of hybridization.

CULTURAL CONVERGENCE

While differentialism is rooted in the idea of lasting differences among and between cultures, and hybridization emphasizes differences resulting from the interaction of the global and the local, cultural convergence is based on the idea that globalization tends to lead to increasing sameness throughout the world. Those who support this perspective see cultures changing, sometimes radically, as a result of globalization, specifically flows of global culture and the relative weakness of barriers to those flows. The cultures of the world are seen as growing increasingly similar, at least to some degree and in some ways. There is a tendency to see global assimilation in the direction of dominant groups and societies in the world.

While the different perspectives to be discussed in this section do focus on cultural convergence, they certainly do *not* argue that that is all that is happening in globalization or that local cultures (Wherry 2008) are disappearing completely, or even necessarily being altered in some fundamental way. While globalization often overwhelms local realities, or at least changes them dramatically, those realities frequently survive in some form or other.

One example is the delivery of home-cooked meals to workers throughout Mumbai (with an estimated metropolitan population of 25 million) by what are called *dabbawallas* (*dabba* is the food box and *wallas* are the people who deliver them) (Kai 2007: C1, C7). Here is the way the system works:

> A network of wallas picks up the boxes from customers' homes or from people who cook lunch to order, then deliver the meals to a local railway station. The boxes are hand sorted for delivery to different stations in central Mumbai, and then re-sorted and carried to their destinations. After lunch the service reverses, and the empty boxes are delivered back home. (Kai 2007: C7)

Color codes on the boxes are crucial because they tell the *wallas* where the food comes from, which train stations it must pass through, and where it is ultimately to go. Once they arrive at the right station, the boxes are unloaded, sorted, carried by wooden cart, and ultimately personally delivered to each recipient. As the wife who cooks lunch for one of those recipients said, "The old fashioned, inexpensive dabbawalla system is a rare survivor in this fast-paced world" (quoted in Kai 2007: C7).

Cultural Imperialism

The idea of **cultural imperialism** (Tomlinson, forthcoming a) indicates that one or more cultures are imposing themselves, more or less consciously, on other cultures thereby destroying

Cultural imperialism: Cultures imposing themselves, more or less consciously, on other cultures.

local culture, in whole, or more likely in part. There are many examples of cultural imperialism in the world today, with local cultural practices being threatened, or even being destroyed, by the flow of culture from other parts of the world, especially from the North to the South.

Indian sari weavers

One of the traditional crafts being threatened with destruction as a result of globalization is hand-woven silk sari-making in India (Wax 2007: A1, A17). These silk saris can take as much as two months to make by hand. They involve elaborate designs (such as leaves, elephants, and birds) made with strands of gold thread and green silk. There are about a million sari makers in India today and they are threatened by machine-made saris (such technologies have their roots in Western culture). While some of these are made in India – employing far fewer and less skilled workers – others are being made in, where else, China. The head of a local committee in India commented: "This is the ugly, painful side of globalization" (quoted in Wax 2007: A17). As a result, a local cultural product (the silk sari), practice (making such saris by hand), and practitioners (skilled sari makers) are being threatened by mass-manufactured saris (often polyester) made by machine and by less skilled workers in China.

Examples such as this have led to the argument that what we are seeing throughout the world is increasing convergence as a result of cultural imperialism. In fact, UNESCO was sufficiently concerned about the issue of cultural imperialism and its deleterious effect on cultural diversity that on November 2, 2001, it adopted a Universal Declaration on Cultural Diversity.

In spite of many examples of, and much hand-wringing about, cultural imperialism (including UNESCO's great concern about threats to cultural diversity), many observers have argued that the danger of cultural imperialism is greatly exaggerated. Mike Featherstone (1995: 13–14) was an early critic of the idea of a global culture, as well as associated ideas such as cultural imperialism and increasing global homogeneity: "The process of globalization, then, does not seem to be producing cultural uniformity; rather it makes us aware of new levels of diversity. If there is a global culture, it would be better to conceive of it not as a common culture, but as a field in which differences, power struggles and cultural prestige contests are played out."

John Tomlinson (2007: 352–66) sees many obvious examples of increasing similarity around the globe in the operations of the global capitalist system and its effects, but there are also many global differences and countervailing trends. Globalization is uneven and neglects and even excludes some areas. Thus, globalization, to Tomlinson, is not quite global. However, he is critical of the view that a global culture is being formed, most generally by cultural imperialism emanating from the West, especially the United States. Involved in this view is the simultaneous loss of distinct, non-Western cultural traditions. Tomlinson sees this perspective as focusing on the superficial issue of the global distribution of cultural goods (e.g. Coke, Big Macs, iPods, and the like).

Deterritorialization

Central to Tomlinson's (forthcoming b) work is the issue of deterritorialization, or the declining significance of the geographic location in which culture exists; culture is no longer as tied as it once was to the constraints of local geography. This means that in Tomlinson's terms "global connectivity" is reaching into local culture and the localities of everyday life. This transformation is both perplexing/disruptive and exhilarating/empowering (here Tomlinson is following the theorizing of Anthony Giddens). Involved is the penetration of everyday life by distant forces and the dislodging of everyday meanings from the anchors of the local environment. In the long run, it may be that this weakening of traditional bonds between cultural experience and geographic territory will be the most far-reaching effect of cultural globalization. However, Tomlinson is careful to point out that this does not simply involve loss, but localities also thrive on globalization. Yet, he admits that the culture produced by locality (if such a narrow source of production was ever the case) is no longer the single most important factor in our lived reality. It has been attenuated by deterritorialization with the integration of distant events, processes, and relationships into everyday lives. Tomlinson singles out the media and communication technology for their role in deterritorialization (Kellner and Pierce 2007: 383–95). He is very even-handed, arguing that while there might be negatives associated with all of this and its effects on emotions, social relations, and cultural identity, there are also many positive potentialities including a new sensibility of cultural openness, human mutuality, and global ethical responsibility.

World Culture

A distinctive theoretical approach to convergence in general, and cultural convergence in particular, is associated with John Meyer and his colleagues (Meyer et al. 1997: 144–81). They argue that there has developed, especially in recent years, a series of global models in a variety of different domains – politics, business, education (see Chapter 5), family, religion, and so on – and that their spread has led to a surprising amount of uniformity throughout the world. This is, in part, a result of the fact that such global models have become more codified and publicized than at any time in history. In addition, there are more organizations involved, and they are more active, in educating and advising various populations about the models Consequently, there is a striking amount of structural **isomorphism** throughout the world as a result of the spread of these models (DiMaggio and Powell 1983: 147–60). These models have been spread by a wide variety of cultural and associational processes. An assumption behind this approach is the decline of the

> **Isomorphism:** A series of global models has led to a great uniformity throughout the world.

nation-state as a significant player in the global world. Indeed, the authors often describe the world society in terms of "statelessness." As a result, the models of concern in this theory are able to flow relatively freely throughout the world and are not impeded to any great extent by the nation-state.

World culture involves the spread of global models leading to global convergence.

While a variety of forms of isomorphism are discussed by **world culture** theorists, culture is accorded pride of place. In fact, world culture scholars describe the world in terms of an enactment of culture. More specifically, culture is associated with a "cultural order" and "institutions," both of which are seen as "rationalized" (e.g. carried and legitimated by professional and scientific organizations). Culture is seen as shaping (and being shaped by) the macro- (states and the state system), meso- (organizations such as schools and firms, associations including voluntary associations), and micro- (individual citizenship and identity) levels throughout the world.

John Boli and Velina Petrova (2007: 103–24) demonstrate the general tendency in this approach to emphasize homogenization. While they acknowledge the existence of global resistance, their emphasis is on the spread of world culture, standardized cultural models, and the tendency toward organizational isomorphism around the globe. All of this is part of a "soft" model of increasing global homogeneity. These things tend not to be imposed on people, institutions, or societies, but rather are more likely to be welcomed by them. Thus, globalization, in their view, tends to be seen as something legitimate rather than as something that is imposed on people illegitimately. People tend to feel increasingly part of, included in, a global culture. While global culture can be constraining, the emphasis in this approach is on how that culture is enabling; how it permits people to self-actualize.

There has been a globalization of models that place great value on the individual. They are manifest in the educational system (the emphasis on the education and well-being of the individual student), the economy (it is individuals who are to be paid, to have property rights, etc.), an increasingly pervasive ideology of human rights, and so on. Then there are global models for the state that expect it to be responsible to its citizens for schooling, medical care, development, gender empowerment, control over state corruption, etc. We have seen the spread not only of global models for the state, but also of methods for assessing the performance of the state. There is also the spread of methods for deciding whether the state is, in fact, handling its responsibilities, including the possibility that the state can fail to fulfill its responsibilities to such a degree that it can be considered a "failed state." A failed state is characterized by high levels of poverty, violence, and social disorder. In the realm of economic organizations, the corporation has become the globally favored model. A global model of corporate morality has emerged, as well. Fairly standard organizational forms have also developed globally for universities, sports clubs, hobby groups, and professional associations.

The power of globalization from this perspective is that it is *both* internal and external to actors. Culture is manifest cognitively in the individual, but it also exists outside the actor in the form of the larger culture and increasingly isomorphic organizations that reflect that culture. The school is crucial here since it is a prime agent for teaching world culture and it is an organizational form that is both increasingly similar throughout the world and a structural reflection of world culture.

While the thrust of this is to emphasize increasing global homogeneity, there is also diversity, glocalization, and resistance. The emphasis is not on globalized homogeneity inducing resistance, but rather globalization is seen as producing legitimate differences and diversity.

One way of getting at world culture is to examine the INGO as an organizational form that is shaped by it. There is a common set of principles among most INGOs throughout the world (Boli and Thomas 1997: 171–90). They include universalism, individualism (e.g. the one-person, one-vote rule), rational voluntaristic authority (rational individuals organizing themselves on a global basis to undertake purposive action and employing rational procedures; the collectivities in which they exist create and come to employ rules that are efficient, just, and equitable), rational progress (economic development, collective security, justice, and the self-actualization of individuals), and world citizenship (everyone is seen as having various rights and obligations, including the taking of actions to deal with global problems; everyone is seen as a citizen of the global polity).

McDonaldization

The McDonaldization thesis (Ritzer 1997, 2008) is based on Max Weber's classic, turn-of-the-twentieth-century, theory of the rationalization of the West. In fact, Weber's theory of rationalization was, at least in part, an early theory of globalization since he tended to see not only the Occident increasingly dominated by rationalization, but much of the rest of the world as destined to rationalize, as well. Weber's model for the rationalization process was the bureaucracy, while the end-of-the-twentieth-century McDonaldization thesis takes the fast-food restaurant as its model. The McDonaldization thesis also brings the theory into the twenty-first century, and views rationalization extending its reach into more sectors of society and areas of the world than Weber ever imagined. Of greatest concern here is the fact that McDonaldization is a force in global cultural homogenization.

McDonaldization is defined as the process by which the principles of the fast-food restaurant are coming to dominate more and more sectors of American society, as well as the rest of the world. It is the latter aspect of the definition that makes it clear that McDonaldization is a globalizing force.

McDonaldization: Process by which the principles of the fast-food restaurant are coming to dominate more of the world.

The nature of the McDonaldization process may be delineated by outlining its five basic dimensions: efficiency, calculability, predictability, control through the substitution of technology for people, and, paradoxically, the irrationality of rationality. The key point for our purposes is that these five principles, as well as the McDonaldization process of which they are part, are becoming increasing global.

First, a McDonaldizing society emphasizes *efficiency*, or the effort to discover the best possible means to whatever end is desired. Workers in fast-food restaurants clearly must work efficiently; for example, burgers are assembled, and sometimes even cooked, in an assembly-line fashion. Customers want, and are expected, to acquire and consume their meals efficiently. The drive-through window is a highly efficient means for customers to obtain, and employees to dole out, meals. Overall, a variety of norms, rules, regulations, procedures, and structures have been put in place in the fast-food restaurant in order to ensure that *both* employees and customers act in an efficient manner. Furthermore, the efficiency of one party helps to ensure that the other will behave in a similar manner.

Second, great importance is given to *calculability*, to an emphasis on quantity, often to the detriment of quality. Various aspects of the work of employees at fast-food restaurants are timed; this emphasis on speed often serves to affect adversely the quality of the work, from the point of view of the employee, resulting in dissatisfaction, alienation, and high turnover rates. Similarly, customers are expected to spend as little time as possible in the fast-food restaurant. In fact, the drive-through window reduces this time to zero, but if the customers desire to eat in the restaurant, the chairs may be designed to feel increasingly uncomfortable in order to impel them to leave after about 20 minutes. This emphasis on speed clearly has a negative effect on the quality of the dining experience at a fast-food restaurant. Furthermore, the emphasis on how fast the work is to be done means that customers cannot be served high-quality food that, almost by definition, requires a good deal of time to prepare.

McDonaldization also involves an emphasis on *predictability*, meaning that things (products, settings, employee and customer behavior, and so on) are pretty much the same from one geographic setting to another (globalization!) and from one time to another. Employees are expected to perform their work in a predictable manner and, for their part, customers are expected to respond with similarly predictable behavior. Thus, when customers enter, employees ask, following scripts, what they wish to order. For their part, customers are expected to know what they want, or where to look to find what they want, and they are expected to order, pay, and leave quickly. Employees (following another script) are expected to thank them when they do leave. A highly predictable ritual is played out in the fast-food restaurant – one that involves highly predictable foods that vary little from one time or place to another.

In addition, great *control* exists in McDonaldized systems and a good deal of that control comes from technologies. Although these technologies currently dominate employees, increasingly they will be replacing them. Employees are clearly controlled by such technologies as french-fry machines that ring when the fries are done and even automatically lift the fries out of the hot oil. For their part, customers are controlled both by the employees who are constrained by such technologies as well as more directly by the technologies themselves. Thus, the automatic fry machine makes it impossible for a customer to request well-done, well-browned fries.

Finally, both employees and customers suffer from the *irrationality of rationality* that seems inevitably to accompany McDonaldization. That is, paradoxically, rationality seems often to lead to its exact opposite – irrationality. For example, the efficiency of the fast-food restaurant is often replaced by the inefficiencies associated with long lines of people at the counters or long lines of cars at the drive-through window. Another of the irrationalities of rationality is dehumanization. Employees are forced to work in dehumanizing jobs and customers are forced to eat in dehumanizing settings (e.g. in their cars) and circumstances (e.g. on the move). The fast-food restaurant can be a source of degradation for employees and customers alike.

The most important irrationality of rationality, at least from the point of view of globalization, is that McDonaldization is a force for increasing global homogeneity. This is because fast-food restaurants and many other businesses and organizations throughout the world are based on the same fundamental principles – efficiency, predictability, calculability, and control. This serves to give them a high degree of structural similarity even though they may sell (or do) very different things, even things (e.g. foods) that are quite local in nature. They are also similar in the sense that they all tend to spawn various irrationalities of rationality. Thus, the McDonaldization thesis describes a process of increasing global homogenization, but it is critical of that process for helping to reduce global differences and to produce a rather depressing sameness throughout the world.

McDonaldization, expansionism, and globalization

The fast-food restaurant in general, and McDonald's in particular, has been a resounding success in the international arena. Over 43 percent of McDonald's restaurants are outside the US (in the mid-1980s only 25 percent of McDonald's were outside the US). The vast majority of new restaurants opened each year are overseas – in 2006, 233 of the 280 new restaurants opened were overseas. Well over half of McDonald's profits come from its overseas operations. The highly McDonaldized Starbucks has also become an increasingly global force, at least until its setback in mid-2008, with locations in 36 countries besides the US, and serving as a strong presence in Latin America, Europe (it is particularly visible in London), the Middle East, and the Pacific Rim.

Many highly McDonaldized firms outside of the fast-food industry have also had success globally. In addition to its 9,000-plus stores in the US, Blockbuster now has just over 2,000 sites in 24 other countries. Although Wal-Mart opened its first international store (in Mexico) in 1991, it now operates over 2,700 units in 15 countries.

Another indicator of globalization is the fact that other nations have developed their own variants of McDonaldized fast-food restaurants. Canada has a chain of coffee shops, Tim Hortons (merged with Wendy's in 1995), with 2,711 outlets (336 in the United States). Paris, a city whose love for fine cuisine might lead one to think it would prove immune to fast food, has a large number of fast-food croissanteries; the revered French bread has also been McDonaldized. India has a chain of fast-food restaurants, Nirula's, which sells mutton burgers (about 80 percent of Indians are Hindus, who eat no beef) as well as local Indian cuisine. Mos Burger is a Japanese chain, with over 1,600 restaurants, which, in addition to the usual fare, sells Teriyaki chicken burgers, rice burgers, and Oshiruko with brown rice cake. Russkoye Bistro, a Russian chain, sells traditional Russian fare such as pirogi (meat and vegetable pies), blini (thin pancakes), Cossack apricot curd tart, and, of course, vodka. Perhaps the most unlikely spot for an indigenous fast-food restaurant, in 1984 war-ravaged Beirut witnessed the opening of Juicy Burger, with a rainbow instead of golden arches and J.B. the Clown standing in for Ronald McDonald. Its owners hoped that it would become the McDonald's of the Arab world. After the 2003 war, a number of clones of McDonald's ("Madonal," "Matbax") quickly opened in Iraq. In spite of the great hostility between the governments of Iran and the US, many Iranians are very positive toward Americans and America and this is reflected in their fast-food restaurants. While there were no American chains there as of 2008, there are local shops that are modeled after them such as an ice-cream shop that emulates Baskin-Robbins down to its 31 flavors, a T.G.I. Friday's clone featuring burgers, Cobb Salad, and waiters with familiar Friday's garb, as well as "Starcups and Kabooky Fried Chicken" (Blackman 2008: A11).

Now McDonaldization is coming full circle. Other countries with their own McDonaldized institutions are beginning to export them to the US. The Body Shop, a British cosmetics chain, had over 2,100 shops in 550 nations in 2006. Three hundred of them were in the US. Furthermore, American firms are now opening copies of this British chain, such as Bath and Body Works. Pollo Campero, a Guatemalan chain specializing in fried chicken, is currently in six countries and is spreading rapidly throughout the US.

As the model of the process, McDonald's has come to occupy a central position throughout the world. At the opening of McDonald's in Moscow, it was described as the ultimate American icon. When Pizza Hut opened in Moscow in 1990, customers saw it as a small piece of America. Reflecting on the growth of fast-food restaurants in Brazil, an executive associated with Pizza Hut of Brazil said that his nation was passionate about things American.

Beyond fast food

While the fast-food restaurant is the model for the process of McDonaldization, the process extends far beyond it. A wide range of studies have analyzed the McDonaldization of higher education (Hayes and Wynyard 2002), the church (Drane 2000, 2008), social work (Dustin 2007), and much else. The point is that not only have many sectors of society been McDonaldized, but those sectors, like McDonald's itself, are increasingly global in character.

Let us close this section with an unusual example of McDonaldization, this time as it relates to the globally distributed drug, Viagra. Viagra is designed to help deal with erectile dysfunction (ED), but it could be argued that it also serves in many ways to McDonaldize sex (e.g. by making more predictable the ability of males to perform sexually). Viagra, and its use, have become global phenomena. Wide-scale use of Viagra has become a subject of concern (and some humor), not only in the US, but elsewhere in the world. In Spain, Viagra has been stolen from pharmacies; it has become a recreational drug demanded even by young people; and this has led to enormous sales even at high retail prices ($104 for a box of eight), and illegal sales (at discos, for example) of a single pill for as much as $80. Why this great demand for Viagra in a society noted for its macho culture? According to a spokesperson for the company that makes Viagra, it is linked to McDonaldization: "We used to have a siesta, to sleep all afternoon.... But now we have become a *fast-food nation* where everyone is stressed out, and this is not good for male sexual performance" (quoted in Bilefsky 2007: 14, italics added).

McDonaldization, as a theory of globalization, certainly emphasizes convergence, but it does *not* argue that everything throughout the world is growing increasingly homogeneous. Overall, we do see the global proliferation of systems that operate on the basis of the basic principles of McDonaldization. However, while that represents some degree of convergence, there is considerable variation around the world in terms of the degree to which, and the way in which, McDonaldized systems operate efficiently, predictably, and so on. Further, McDonaldized systems often provoke resistance and this helps to lead to continued, or even greater, differences in many parts of the world.

Interestingly, most of the debate over McDonaldization and globalization has focused on the wrong issue. In the main, it has focused on the end-products, arguing against convergence because the products differ, at least to some degree, from one geographic locale to another. However, McDonaldization is *not* about end-products (e.g. Big Macs), but rather about the system and its principles. That system has been globalized, and in many different domains, but it operates at least slightly differently from sector to sector and in different parts of the world. There is convergence, but it does not result in uniformity and homogeneity.

The Globalization of Nothing

The globalization of nothing (Ritzer 2007), like McDonaldization, implies growing convergence as more and more nations around the world are increasingly characterized by various forms of nothing (see below for the definition of this concept). The argument is that there is an *elective affinity*, using a term borrowed from Weber (1921/1968), between globalization and nothing. That is, one does not cause the other, but they do tend to vary together. Note: the argument is *not* that globalization is nothing; indeed it is clear, if for no other reason than this book, that the process is of enormous significance.

Central to this argument is the idea of **grobalization** (a companion to the notion of glocalization) which is defined as the imperialistic ambitions of nations, corporations, organizations, and the like and their desire, indeed

Grobalization: Imperialistic ambitions of nation-states, corporations, and organizations, and their imposition throughout the world.

need, to impose themselves on various geographic areas throughout the world (Ryan 2007: 2022–3). Their main interest is in seeing their power, influence, and in some cases profits *grow* (hence the term *grobalization*, a combination of grow and globalization) throughout the world. Grobalization involves a variety of sub-processes, three of which – capitalism, Americanization, as well as McDonaldization – are not only central driving forces in grobalization, but also of great significance in the worldwide spread of nothingness.

Nothing: Social forms largely devoid of distinctive content.

Something: Largely full social forms; those rich in distinctive content.

Nothing involves (largely) empty forms; forms largely devoid of distinctive content. (Conversely, **something** is defined as [largely] full forms; forms rich in distinctive content.) It is easier to export empty forms (nothing) throughout the globe than it is forms that are loaded with distinctive content (something). The latter are more likely to be rejected by at least some cultures and societies because the content conflicts, is at variance, with local content. In contrast, since they are largely devoid of distinctive content, empty forms are less likely to come into conflict with the local. In addition, empty forms have other advantages from the point of view of globalization including the fact that since they are so minimalist, they are easy to replicate over and over and they have a cost advantage since they are relatively inexpensive to reproduce.

A good example of nothing in these terms is the shopping mall (especially chains of malls) which is an empty (largely) structure that is easily replicated around the world. These malls could be filled with an endless array of specific content (e.g. local shops, local foods, etc. – something!) that could vary enormously from one locale in the world to another. However, increasingly they are filled with chain stores, themselves meeting the definition of nothing, carrying a wide range of various types of … nothing! That is, chain stores throughout the world sell goods that are more or less the same everywhere they are sold. Since more and more countries in the world have these malls, chain stores, and chain-store products, this is an example of the grobalization of nothing and of increasing global convergence.

Non-places: Settings largely devoid of distinctive content.

Non-things: Objects largely devoid of distinctive content.

Non-people: Those who occupy positions that lead them to be devoid of distinctive content at least in those positions.

There are four sub-types of nothing and all of them are largely empty of distinctive content and are being grobalized. The four types are: **non-places**, or settings that are largely empty of content (e.g. the malls and chain stores discussed above); **non-things** such as chain-store products and credit cards (there is little to distinguish one credit card from the billions of others, all of which work in exactly the same way for all who use them anywhere in the world); **non-people**, or the kind of employees associated with non-places, for example, telemarketers (who may be virtually anywhere in the world) who interact with all customers in much the same way relying heavily on scripts; and **non-services** such as those provided by ATMs (the services provided are identical; the customer does all the

> **Non-services**: Services largely devoid of distinctive content.

work involved in obtaining the services) as opposed to human bank tellers. The grobal proliferation of non-places, non-things, non-people, and non-services is another indication of increasing convergence.

Cricket: local, glocal, or grobal?

The sport of cricket has attracted a lot of attention from those interested in globalization in general and of sport in particular (Kaufman and Patterson 2005: 82–110), with perhaps the best-known work on it done by Appadurai (1996). His argument is that cricket has become decolonized, indigenized in India so that it is "no longer English-mediated" (Appadurai 1996: 104). That is, it has been glocalized, if not localized. Appadurai recognizes that cricket was brought to India by England; it was one aspect of colonization. England needed to create teams that it could play against. India and the other colonies were perfect for this role. However, the Indians have transformed cricket (just as the Japanese transformed baseball) and made it their own.

Of particular importance has been the role played by the media and language in the transformation of cricket in India. Mass Indian publications – books, magazines, and pamphlets – liberated cricket from its "Englishness" and dealt with cricket matches in native terms; they "vernacularized" cricket. The game came to be played widely in the streets, playgrounds, and villages of India so that it became inculcated in the bodily practice of many Indians. Indians also read about their favorite teams and stars and heard about them on the radio and saw them on TV. This served to make cricket an important part of the fantasy lives of many Indians.

In India, and elsewhere in former English colonies, cricket has come to be dominated by the locals and not by England; they have "hijacked" the game from the English. In the process, they have transformed cricket, making it a much more aggressive game, one that is less "sportsmanlike," and perhaps most importantly, much more spectacular (just as the Japanese game of baseball is more spectacular than the American version). To Appadurai (1996: 107), cricket "now belongs to a different moral and aesthetic world." It has become an "instrument for mobilizing national sentiment in the service of transnational spectacles and commoditization" (1996: 109). Thus, to take one example, cricket matches between rivals India and Pakistan resemble a war. As a result, in such matches, as well as in many other international cricket matches, "England … is no longer part of the equation" (1996: 109).

While there is much merit in Appadurai's analysis, it is important to remember that cricket was grobalized by the English. It was out of the interaction between the cricket grobalized by the English that was centrally conceived, controlled, and lacking in distinctive content ("nothing") and the indigenously conceived, controlled, rich-in-distinctive-content cricket ("something") produced by glocalization in India, that the distinctive form of Indian cricket emerged. As with all other cultural forms, cricket cannot be reduced to glocalization or grobalization, or something or nothing. In today's world, all cultural forms involve elements of all of these.

CHAPTER SUMMARY

This chapter examines the global flows of culture, which tend to move more easily around the globe than ever before, especially through non-material digital forms. Three perspectives on global cultural flows are examined – differentialism, hybridization, and convergence.

Cultural differentialism emphasizes the fact that cultures are essentially different and are only superficially affected by global flows. The interaction of cultures is deemed to contain the potential for "catastrophic collision." Samuel Huntington's theory of a clash of the civilizations best exemplifies this approach. According to Huntington, after the Cold War, political-economic differences were overshadowed by new fault lines which were primarily cultural in nature. Increasing interaction among different "civilizations" (such as the Sinic, Islamic, Orthodox, Western) would lead to intense clashes, especially economic conflict between the Western and Sinic civilizations and bloody political conflict between the Western and Islamic civilizations. This theory has been critiqued for a number of reasons, especially its portrayal of Muslims as being "prone to violence."

The cultural hybridization approach emphasizes the integration of local and global cultures. Therefore, globalization is considered to be a creative process which gives rise to hybrid entities that are not reducible to either the global or the local. A key concept is "glocalization," or the interpenetration of the global and local resulting in unique outcomes in different geographic areas. Another key concept is Arjun Appadurai's "scapes" (global flows involving people, technology, finance, political images, and media) and the disjunctures between them, which lead to the creation of cultural hybrids.

The cultural convergence approach stresses homogeneity introduced by globalization. Cultures are deemed to be radically altered by strong flows. Cultural imperialism, wherein one culture imposes itself on and tends to destroy at least parts of another culture, is also analyzed under this heading. One important critique of cultural imperialism is based on the idea of "deterritorialization" of culture. This means that it is much more difficult to tie culture to a specific geographic point of origin.

McDonaldization, based on the principles of fast-food restaurants, involves the global spread of rational systems, such as efficiency, calculability, predictability, and control. This process is extended to other businesses, sectors, and geographic areas. Grobalization (in contrast to glocalization) is a process wherein nations, corporations, etc. impose themselves on geographic areas in order to gain profits, power, and so on.

Globalization can also be seen as a flow of "nothing" (as opposed to "something"), involving the spread of non-places, non-things, non-people, and non-services. The interplay between these processes (grobalization and glocalization; nothing and something) can be clearly seen in the globalization of sports, a phenomenon that is an important part of culture.

DISCUSSION QUESTIONS

1. Analyze the three main perspectives discussed in this chapter with respect to the deterritorialization of culture.

2. Analyze "clash of the civilizations" as a perspective on globalization. What are the advantages and disadvantages of utilizing a "civilizational" approach?

3. Critique "differentialism" and "convergence," using the concept of "scapes."

4. Make a case for cultural hybridization in the study of culture.

5. Contrast glocalization with grobalization. Examine the relative significance of each to the study of globalization.

FURTHER READING

Jan Nederveen Pieterse. *Globalization and Culture: Global Melange*. Lanham, MD: Rowman and Littlefield, 2004.

Nestor Garcia Canclini. *Hybrid Cultures: Strategies for Entering and Leaving Modernity*. Minneapolis: University of Minnesota Press, 1995.

Frederick F. Wherry. *Global Markets and Local Crafts: Thailand and Costa Rica Compared*. Baltimore: Johns Hopkins University Press, 2008.

Benjamin Barber. *Jihad vs. McWorld*. New York: Times Books, 1995.

Samuel P. Huntington. *The Clash of Civilizations and the Remaking of the World Order*. New York: Simon and Schuster, 1996.

John Drane. *The McDonaldization of the Church*. London: Darton, Longman and Todd, 2000.

George Ritzer. *The McDonaldization of Society*, 5th edn. Thousand Oaks, CA: Pine Forge Press, 2008.

George Ritzer. *The Globalization of Nothing*, 2nd edn. Thousand Oaks, CA: Pine Forge Press, 2007.

John Tomlinson. *Cultural Imperialism: A Critical Introduction*. London: Cassell, 1991.

John Tomlinson. *Globalization and Culture*. Cambridge: Polity, 1999.

REFERENCES

Appadurai, Arjun. 1996. *Modernity at Large: Cultural Dimensions of Globalization*. Minneapolis: University of Minnesota Press.

Bilefsky, Dan. 2007. "Spain Says Adios Siesta and Hola Viagra." *New York Times*. February 11.

Blackman, Michael. 2008. "Warmth for Americans in Once Hostile Tehran." *New York Times*. February 13.

Boli, John, and Velina Petrova, 2007. "Globalization Today." In George Ritzer, ed., *The Blackwell Companion to Globalization*. Malden, MA: Blackwell.

Boli, John, and George M. Thomas. 1997. "World Culture in the World Polity: A Century of International Non-Governmental Organization." *American Sociological Review* 62, 2.

Canclini, Nestor Garcia. 1995. *Hybrid Cultures: Strategies for Entering and Leaving Modernity*. Minneapolis: University of Minnesota Press.

Cohen, Robin. 2007. "Creolization and Cultural Globalization: The Soft Sounds of Fugitive Power." *Globalizations* 4, 3.

Cvetkovich, Ann, and Douglas Kellner. 1997. *Articulating the Global and the Local: Globalization and Cultural Studies*. Boulder, CO: Westview Press.

DiMaggio, P. J., and W. Powell. 1983. " 'The Iron Cage Revisited': Institutional Isomorphism and Collective Rationality in Organizational Fields." *American Sociological Review* 48.

Drane, John. 2000. *The McDonaldization of the Church*. London: Darton, Longman and Todd.

Drane, John. 2008. *After McDonaldization: Mission, Ministry, and Christian Discipleship in an Age of Uncertainty*. Grand Rapids, MI: Baker Academic.

Dustin, Donna. 2007. *The McDonaldization of Social Work*. Burlington, VT: Ashgate.

Economist. 2004. November 4. "Another Political Murder."

Economist. 2006. February 3. "A Growing Furore Over Denmark's Satanic Sketches."

Economist. 2007. November 28. "On the Streets, Again."

Featherstone, Mike. 1995. *Undoing Culture: Globalization, Postmodernism and Identity*. London: Sage.

Friedman, Jonathan. 1994. *Culture Identity and Global Processes*. London: Sage.

Giulianotti, Richard, and Roland Robertson. 2007. "Forms of Glocalization: Globalization and the Migration Strategies of Scottish Football Fans in North America." *Sociology* 41, 1.

Hannerz, Ulf. 1987. "The World in Creolisation." *Africa* 57.

Hayes, Dennis, and Robin Wynyard, eds. 2002. *The McDonaldization of Higher Education*. Westport, CT: Bergin and Garvey.

Huntington, Samuel P. 1996. *The Clash of Civilizations and the Remaking of the World Order*. New York: Simon and Schuster.

Huntington, Samuel P. 2004. "The Hispanic Challenge." *Foreign Policy* (March/April).

Kai, Saritha. 2007. "Grandma Cooks, They Deliver." *New York Times*. May 29.

Kaufman, Jason, and Orlando Patterson. 2005. "Cross-National Cultural Diffusion: The Global Spread of Cricket." *American Sociological Review* 70.

Kellner, Douglas, and Clayton Pierce. 2007. "Media and Globalization." In George Ritzer, ed., *The Blackwell Companion to Globalization*. Malden, MA: Blackwell.

MacFarquhar, Neil. 2007. "To Muslim Girls, Scouts Offer a Chance to Fit in." *New York Times*. November 28.

Meyer, John W., John Boli, George M. Thomas, and Francisco O. Ramirez. 1997. "World Society and the Nation-State." *American Journal of Sociology* 103.

Nederveen Pieterse, Jan. 2004. *Globalization and Culture: Global Melange*. Lanham, MD: Rowman and Littlefield.

Ritzer, George. 1997. *The McDonaldization Thesis*. London: Sage.

Ritzer, George. 2007. *The Globalization of Nothing*, 2nd edn. Thousand Oaks, CA: Pine Forge Press.

Ritzer, George. 2008. *Modern Sociological Theory*, 7th edn. New York: McGraw-Hill.

Robertson, Roland. 2001. "Globalization Theory 2000 Plus: Major Problematics." In George Ritzer and Barry Smart, eds., *Handbook of Social Theory*. London: Sage.

Ryan, J. Michael. 2007. "Grobalization." In George Ritzer, ed., *Encyclopedia of Sociology*. Malden, MA: Blackwell.

Sarroub, Loukia K. 2005. *All American Yemeni Girls: Being Muslim in a Public School*. Philadelphia: University of Pennsylvania Press.

Tomlinson, John. 2007. "Cultural Globalization." In George Ritzer, ed., *The Blackwell Companion to Globalization*. Malden, MA: Blackwell.

Tomlinson, forthcoming a. In George Ritzer, ed., *Blackwell Encyclopedia of Sociology Online*. Oxford: Wiley-Blackwell.

Tomlinson, forthcoming b. In George Ritzer, ed., *Blackwell Encyclopedia of Sociology Online*. Oxford: Wiley-Blackwell.

Wax, Emily. 2007. "An Ancient Indian Craft Left in Tatters." *Washington Post*. June 6.

Weber, Max. 1921/1968. *Economy and Society*, 3 vols. Totowa, NJ: Bedminster Press.

Wherry, Frederick F. 2008. *Global Markets and Local Crafts: Thailand and Costa Rica Compared*. Baltimore: Johns Hopkins University Press.

Global Flows of Migrants

Globalization: The Essentials, by George Ritzer
© 2011 John Wiley & Sons Ltd

The term **migrants** encompasses both vagabonds and tourists (Bauman 1998), although it will most often be used in association with vagabonds. **Vagabonds** are often impoverished itinerants on the move *because they have to be*; because, for example, they find their environs unbearable, inhospitable for any number of reasons, and are forced to find better circumstances elsewhere. In contrast, **tourists** are those who are on the move *because they want to be*. It is also the case that tourists move because they can afford to, while vagabonds feel they cannot afford to remain where they are. These are unique definitions that focus on our key interest in this chapter on global flows and barriers. Thus, because they are "light" (e.g. well educated), tourists flow around the world easily and they encounter comparatively few barriers (although there have been more barriers erected in their way in recent years, especially in the US). In contrast, vagabonds, especially if they are illegal, have great, and increasing, difficulty moving about the world because they are "heavy" (e.g. they lack education, training) and because they encounter many structural barriers that impede their movement (Cohen 1995). While this distinction is important, most of our attention here will be on vagabonds, especially illegal migrants.

> **Migrants**: Populations on the move, both vagabonds and tourists.

> **Vagabonds**: Those likely to move because they are forced to.

> **Tourists**: People who move about the world because they *want to*; because they are "light."

MIGRANTS

There has undoubtedly been a great deal of population movement associated with globalization. A UN estimate puts the number of international migrants (tourists and vagabonds who live outside their country for at least a year) at just over 190 million (Kritz, Lim, and Zlotnik 1992; Kritz 2008). As large as that number seems, it is only about 3 percent of the global population (*Economist* 2008: January 3 ["Open Up"]). To some observers, this represents a large and growing number, and, in fact, it constitutes an increase of 36 percent since 1990. However, to other observers, the sense that we live in a global era of unprecedented international migration is exaggerated (Guhathakurta, Jacobson, and DelSordi 2007: 178–200). While international migration has ebbed and flowed over time, the current rate is unspectacular in comparison to at least some other periods in the recent past. Further, rates of migration in order to find work, while high and the subject of much media interest, lag behind the mobility rates for goods, services, and technologies.

While the contemporary numbers may not be impressive in comparison to those in the past, migrants do make up a significant percentage of the population of many countries. For example, among OECD nations, almost a quarter of the population of Australia and Switzerland are migrants, just under 20 percent of Germany's population are migrants, and 12 percent of the US population (in 2005) were migrants (Roberts 2008: A11), while in Great Britain and France migrants comprise just under 10 percent of the population (*Economist* 2008: January 3 ["Of Bedsheets and Bison Grass Vodka"]). In the case of the US, the percentage of migrants in the total population will reach 15 percent between 2020 and 2025 (and it will reach 19 percent by 2050), exceeding for the first time the previous high of nearly 15 percent achieved in the late nineteenth century (Roberts 2008: A11).

MIGRATION

International migration has four components – "the in-migration of persons to a country other than that of their place of birth or citizenship; the return migration of nationals to their home country after residing abroad; the out-migration of nationals from their home country, and the out-migration of foreigners from a foreign country to which they had previously immigrated" (Kritz 2008). Our primary concern in this section will be with the out-migration of nationals and their in-migration to other countries.

There are interesting and important changes in the nature of today's migrants. First, the proportion of international migrants from the developed world has actually declined. Second, there has been a large increase in the number of migrants from the developing world and a very significant proportion of them (70–90 percent) are moving to North America.

Our ability to discuss migration is hampered by the fact that there are great difficulties in tracking population flows. First, many countries do not collect such data. Second, those countries that do collect such data do not report them to international agencies. Third, population flows are defined differently in different countries; there are also differences in defining the permanency of a move and the residency period required for migrant status. Fourth, few countries keep track of their expatriates. Finally, there are overwhelming difficulties in keeping tabs on illegal migrants. One must keep these limitations on data clearly in mind in discussing migration.

Unlike much else in the modern world (trade, finance, investment), restrictions on the migration of people, especially labor migration, have *not* been liberalized (Tan 2007: 735–9). The major exception is in the European Union, but elsewhere in the world restrictions on migration remain in place. How do we explain this anomaly?

For one thing, in order to prosper economically, a nation must try to keep the labor it needs, both highly paid skilled workers and professionals of various types and masses of low-paid semi-skilled and unskilled workers. If nations routinely lost large numbers of such workers, their ability to compete in the global marketplace would suffer.

For another, the influx of large numbers of migrants into another country often leads to conflict of various types, usually between the newcomers and those who have been in place for quite some time, although there may also be conflict between different groups of newcomers. Thus, many nations prefer to maintain significant barriers to migration.

Finally, the concern over terrorism in many parts of the world, especially in the United States and in many European nations, has served to reinforce, if not increase, the restrictions on migration. This is especially clear in the immense difficulties involved in migrating to the United States today. This difficulty has even been extended to people traveling on business and to students wishing to study in the US ("tourists" in the terms used in this chapter). Even those who are tourists in the conventional sense of the term (vacationers) now often find the process of clearing border control in the US burdensome and even offensive. There is concern that these barriers and difficulties will cause people to take their business elsewhere and the best students to study in other countries, as well as lead to a significant decline in tourism and the income to be earned from it.

Shamir (2005) discusses the emergence of a "mobility regime" which seeks to contain the movement of migrants not only between, but even within, national borders. For example, by late 2008 Great Britain began issuing identity cards to foreigners from outside the EU in order to be better able to track their movement within the country, and therefore better able to contain their movement, should the need arise (*New York Times* 2008: March 7, A7). This desire for surveillance and containment is traceable to fear, real or imagined, of the dangers of terrorism (and crime) associated with immigrants.

While much attention has been devoted in recent years to barriers to the movement of migrants, it is important to note that at the same time barriers have been reduced in terms of movement between, for example, the EU nations (this was predated by the 1985 Schengen agreements – now part of EU law – which eased border controls among the European signatories). In the case of NAFTA, some restrictions on movement have been eased between the US, Canada, and Mexico (e.g. for business executives and highly skilled workers), while other barriers remain in effect and, in fact, have been strengthened and increased.

Since many of these barriers are created by nation-states, it is clear that they are a product of the Westphalian era (see Chapter 3) of the preeminence of the nation-state. Prior to that era, people moved about geographic space fairly freely, but with the rise of the nation-state much more notice was taken of such movement and many more barriers were erected to limit and control it. However, as late as the end of the nineteenth century, there was still much freedom of movement, most notably in the great Atlantic migration to the US from Europe. It is estimated that about 50 million people left Europe for the US between 1820 and the end of the nineteenth century (Moses 2006: 47). Prior to 1880, entry into the US was largely unregulated; anyone who wanted to get in, could get in. In 1889 an International Emigration Conference declared: "We affirm the right of the individual to the fundamental liberty accorded to him by every civilized nation to come and go and dispose of his person and his destinies as he pleases" (cited in Moses 2006: 47). It was WW I that changed attitudes and the situation dramatically; nation-states began to impose drastic restrictions on the global movement of people. Today, while there is variation among nation-states, "there is not a single state that allows free access to all immigrants" (Moses 2006: 54).

However, while legal migration is restricted in various ways (although there are exceptions in some locales for skilled people, "guest worker programs" are in existence in other locations, etc.), there seems to have been an increase in illegal immigration, even in the smuggling of people into (and out of [Shane and Gordon 2008: 1, 17]) various nations. In some cases, nations have laws requiring them to accept refugees (see below) escaping war, political persecution, and so on. For those who make it legally or illegally into another country, the burgeoning business of global remittances (see below), as well as technological developments that have made such transfers of funds quicker and easier, has tended to encourage and support migration.

A combination of push and pull factors is usually used to explain migration. Among the *push* factors are the motivations of the migrants, contextual issues in the home country (e.g. unemployment, low pay) making it difficult or impossible for them to achieve their goals, and major disruptions such as war, famine, political persecution, or an economic depression. Then there are *pull* factors such as a favorable immigration policy in the host country, higher pay and lower unemployment, formal and informal networks in such countries that cater to migrants, labor shortages, and a similarity in language and culture between home and host country.

To these traditional factors are added new ones in the global age. There is, for example, the global dispersion of information which makes it easier to find out about, and become comfortable in, a host country. Then there is the interaction of global–local networks, either through formal networks mediated by modern technologies such as mobile phones and the Internet (especially e-mail and Skype), or through more informal family and social networks that might well employ the same technologies. All of this makes it much easier to migrate and to be comfortable in new settings. The presence of diasporic communities in such settings makes it easier for migrants to find housing and work. At the same time, remittances have become an increasingly significant factor in the economies of many home countries.

While in general migration policies have not been liberalized, there has been a selective reduction in barriers to migration in many countries. This is driven by various factors in host countries, including labor shortages, the needs of MNCs for workers, aging populations, and new tax revenues from migrants to be used to help support state welfare systems.

Refugees: Those forced to leave their homeland, or who leave involuntarily, because they fear for their safety.

Asylum seekers: Refugees who seek to remain in the country to which they flee.

Labor migrant: One who is forced to search for work outside his/her home country by "push" and "pull" factors.

Various types of migrants could be dealt with in this section, but our focus will be on vagabonds, especially those who are **refugees** (Haddad 2003: 297–322); i.e., those who are forced to leave their homeland, or leave involuntarily, because they fear for their safety; **asylum seekers** – refugees who seek to remain in the country to which they flee; as well as **labor migrants** who are driven by "push" factors (e.g. a lack of work, low pay) in their homeland and "pull" factors (jobs and higher pay available else-where) (Kritz 2008).

There were about 10 million refugees in the world in 2006 and while many of them moved legally, many others joined the flow of illegal immigrants (*Economist* 2008: January 3 ["Open Up"]). Many sociological concepts relate to the refugee including the "stranger," the "marginal man," the "outsider within," and so on. All point to the idea that the refugee is, at least structurally, in an uncomfortable position since he/she is no longer in, or part of, his/her home country, but is also not, or at least not yet, truly part of the country to which he/she has emigrated. Of course, refugee status is generally only a temporary state and it is possible that the refugee can, among other things, become a citizen of the new country, return to their country of origin, or move on to some other locale. Of course, in this last case, the status of refugee is retained, albeit in a new country.

The migrants from the less developed world to the North (there is also significant migration from one less developed country to another: South-to-South migration) who are of interest to us in this section are the often unwelcome, less skilled and unskilled workers. Of special interest are those who are illegal migrants and who are therefore likely to exist at the margins of the North and who are apt to fare poorly there. Since the 1970s the number of such migrants has increased dramatically.

Flow of Migrants to and from the US

Illegal Mexican migrants to the US

More than one-tenth of the US population (37 million out of a total of about 300 million) were born outside the US and many of them arrived after a(nother) great boom in immigration (Barkan, Diner, and Kraut 2008) that began in the early 1990s. Many entered the US illegally. They come from various countries (Philippines, China, El Salvador), but the largest number (at least one-third) come from Mexico (in 2008 about 6 million Mexicans were in the US illegally [Thompson 2008: A17]). (It is estimated that more than 10 percent of Mexico's total population [116 million] live in the United States.) In fact, the majority of Mexican immigrants are in the US illegally (they may have crossed the border ille-gally [about 85 percent of those who cross the border do so illegally], or they may have remained after their visas expired). They come (and often stay) because while they may be paid poverty wages by US standards (approximately $300 per week), that may be as much as four times what they could earn in Mexico (Preston 2006a: A24). Furthermore, there are more jobs and better future job opportunities in the US than in Mexico.

Life is not easy for illegal Mexican immigrants in the United States (Preston 2006b: A1, A24, A25). While they may be better off economically than they were in Mexico, and than those who remained in or returned to Mexico, their life is problematic in various ways. First, while they have improved their lives from an economic point of view, they remain largely marginal economically in the US context. Second, their family life is often in shreds, with many family members (and friends) still in Mexico (Navarro 2006a: A1, A20, A21). They are separated from them by a border that has recently become increasingly difficult to breach from the Mexican side for those who are not entering the US legally. These new restrictions seem to have deterred few, but it "has resulted in a greater demand for smugglers, higher prices for smuggling and more deaths from crossing the border. It has also discouraged people from going back home" (Alvarez 2006a: A20). The economic situation of immigrants is complicated by the fact that they are asked for, and often feel obligated to give, financial aid (remittances) to relatives (and friends) who remain in Mexico (roughly $20 billion in 2005 [Preston 2006a: A24]) and who are worse off than they are. Third, those who are in the US illegally are haunted by the possibility of being apprehended by the immigration authorities, "*la migra*" (Alvarez 2006b: A1, A20, A21).

The life of illegal Mexican immigrants in the US often shrinks to just the few square blocks of their immediate neighborhood where they feel safe from *la migra*. This is also an area where they are not asked for what they do not have – the crucial indicators of legitimacy – insurance cards, credit cards, Social Security cards, and "Green" cards (which offer legal permanent residence in the US and enable immigrants to get a job legally; people often pay large sums for illegal Green cards). Local information networks warn them of the presence of government authorities. Some places (e.g. the nearby Wal-Mart) become no-go zones when there is word that they are being watched by *la migra*. It is even deemed a good idea to be wary of neighbors who just might inform on them. Illegal Mexican immigrants rely heavily on the underground economy. When they need to cash a check, they often rely on check-cashing enterprises that charge exorbitant fees. Yet, with all these problems (and more), many prefer life in the US to their old life in Mexico. To quote one, "Living here without papers is still better than living there" (quoted in Alvarez 2006b: A20).

One woman who had lived (illegally) in the US for six years returned to Mexico distressed about what was happening to her family there. Three years later, however, she was forced to exclaim: "Look how I live … I was used to something else" (quoted in Navarro 2006a: A1). She now lives in a cinderblock house in Mexico that has been carved into four tiny apartments. The family shares two toilets and two showers outside the house. Her bedroom lacks a window. The kitchen has no refrigerator or sink. To do the dishes she needs to fill buckets with water from a faucet also found outside the house.

Many, including the woman described above, leave the US because they regret the inability to interact with family members who remain in Mexico and the loss of their support network. However, upon their return to Mexico, many of these people must deal with the separation from family and friends who remain behind in the US. And, they are now separated by the newly reinforced border as well as the difficulty in obtaining the funds necessary to finance an illegal trip across it to visit those still in the US. Adding to the dissatisfaction of many who return to Mexico are the relatively poor wages and occupational prospects there. Furthermore, they now have the experience of life in the US to compare with what it is like in

Mexico. For many, the life they left in the US seems far better than the way they now live in Mexico. This led the woman described above to exclaim: "If I had the money, I'd leave today" (quoted in Navarro 2006a: A21).

Migrants through Mexico and to the US

In addition to the large number of illegal immigrants from Mexico, many others (an estimated 170,000 in 2006) make their way illegally from various Central American nations to the US. As of 2008, there were 2.7 million of these immigrants in the US, up from 1.8 million in 2000, but down from 3 million in 2007 (Thompson 2008: A17). To get to the US, the vast majority must travel through much of Mexico and across the Mexico–US border. One route is through Mexico's southern neighbor, Guatemala, wading across the Suchiate River (an "open border"), on to the city of Tapachula, and from there undertaking an arduous 1,500-mile trip to the US border. This last stage involves a 250-mile walk along the Chiapas coast to Arriaga where they swarm aboard moving trains (an average of 300–500 people per day find their way on to such trains) and hang precariously from them en route to the US. Many are injured or die falling from the moving trains. One Honduran migrant, Donar Antonio Ramirez Espinas, had both of his legs sheared off above the knees when, riding between cars, he dozed off and fell from the train. "I fell face down, and at first I didn't think anything had happened. … When I turned over, I saw, I realized, that my feet didn't really exist" (quoted in McKinley 2007: 12). Before getting to the train, migrants must run a gauntlet of crooked federal police and robbers (and rapists) who are likely to steal most of their already meager amount of money and other possessions.

In early 2007, Misael Mejia (27 years old) made this trek from Comayagua, Honduras. It took him 11 days to walk from the Suchiate River to Arriaga to await the train. While there, he and several others were ambushed by three men, one with a machine gun. "They told us to lay down and take off our clothes. … I lost my watch, about 500 Honduran lempiras, and 40 Mexican pesos,' about $31" (quoted in McKinley 2007: 12). Yet, Mejia was undeterred, driven by hope of higher pay (he earned $200 a month as a driver in Honduras, but his brother in Arizona earned $700 a week as a carpenter). Mejia said, "I felt hopeless in Honduras. … Because I could never afford a house, not even a car. There is nothing I could have" (quoted in McKinley 2007: 12).

Increased law enforcement

In the past, most migration, especially from Mexico, was a round-trip journey. However, it is increasingly becoming one-way as migrants settle, often illegally, into life in the US (and elsewhere in the world). There are several reasons for this. First, they are more likely to be able to get jobs outside of the agricultural sector. Such work is less seasonal and more likely to be regular and stable. Second, many are moving beyond the southwestern border states and deeper into the US, thereby making a return to Mexico more difficult and more expensive. Third, with the tightening of border controls since the 1980s, and especially after 9/11, it is simply more difficult and more expensive to find a way to return to Mexico. According to one sociologist, "Having run the gauntlet of enforcement resources at the border, migrants grew reluctant to repeat the experience and hunkered down to stay, causing rates of return migration to fall sharply" (quoted in Navarro 2006b: A20). Another expert commented, "The primary effect of hardening the border has been one of locking people in" (quoted in Navarro 2006b: A20). About 47 percent of illegal immigrants returned to Mexico between 1979 and 1984, but the percentage of returns had declined to 27 percent between 1997 and 2003. And the longer immigrants stay in the US, the lower the probability that they will return. Thus, one of the ironies of increased US border controls is that *more* illegal immigrants from Mexico remain in the US rather than returning (as many would have in an earlier era of easier border-crossing).

The controls on the 2,000-mile Mexican border have continued to increase, with thousands of new border patrol agents and national guardsmen. That control will increase still further when the 700-mile, 12- to 15-foot-high steel fence is completed (Fletcher and Weisman 2006: A4; Archibold 2007: A16). The fence was supposed to be completed by the end of 2008, but progress has been slower than expected.

The fence between the US and Mexico that was in existence in late 2007, as well as increased border patrols, was said to have produced a 22 percent drop in apprehensions of illegal immigrants at the border, but others claim that the drop may be, at least in part, the result of other factors. There are real questions, however, as to whether such a fence is really useful given the terrain. Limited experience with a far less lengthy fence near San Diego is not encouraging for supporters of such a fence. That fence merely led many illegal immigrants to use other, more dangerous, routes into the US.

Simultaneously, there are proposals to make it tougher for legal immigrants to become US citizens, by increasing fees, making the English and history exams more difficult, and by delving more deeply into applicants' past lives (Fears 2006: A4). While such changes may never occur, they reflect the current mood in the US, at least among more conservative politicians and citizens.

In addition to the fence, the US employs many other tools to police its borders with Mexico:

Unmanned Predator Bee drones float at 12,000 feet, helping to guide officers in bulletproof helicopters, in jeeps, on horseback, on mountain bikes and all-terrain buggies towards any would-be migrants. Seismic sensors catch footfalls, magnetic ones notice cars, infra-red beams are useful for tunnels. Some 18,000 officers man the border crossings and a further 15,000 (due to rise to 18,000 by the end of 2008) patrol in between them. (*Economist* 2008: January 3 ["Keep Out"])

The impact of increased enforcement of immigration laws is being felt throughout the US even as far north as upper New York State where natives engaged in already marginal farming are increasingly threatened by the loss of their low-paid illegal immigrant workers from Mexico (Bernstein 2006: 20). Not only are the workers more likely to be picked up by immigration authorities, but the farm owners themselves now worry about criminal prosecution. There is a pervasive climate of fear as illegal workers are suspicious of everyone and farmers fear that jealous neighbors might inform on them for employing such people. The result of increased law enforcement is that deportation rates are up dramatically.

Some of those who support the more stringent law enforcement do so out of a concern for the immigrant workers, their low wages, and their otherwise highly exploited status as farm workers. However, others do so because they feel illegal immigrants drag down wages for everyone and they resent the costs associated with public services accorded to them. In contrast, native farmers (among others) tend to support the immigrant workers because they contend that they are unable to find anyone else to do the work. Migrants are also supported by those who are concerned that the human rights of illegal immigrants are being abused (e.g. fathers being arrested and leaving behind wives and American-born children to fend for themselves) in the current crack-down.

Flow of Migrants Elsewhere in the World

It is not only in the US that control over borders is a major issue.

Illegal immigrants in Europe

Since the ratification of the Maastricht Treaty, a number of nations have been added to the EU including less developed Eastern European nations such as Poland in 2004 and Bulgaria and Romania in 2007. One of the key points of the Maastricht Treaty was to move toward Europe as an increasingly borderless society, at least as far as the member nations and their citizens are concerned. However, the influx of immigrants from the less developed east to the more developed west has led to major concerns in a number of countries in Western Europe and calls by many for a reassertion of border controls. As in the US, there is growing concern about illegal immigration in Europe and increasing efforts to reduce or eliminate the flow of illegal immigrants.

GREAT BRITAIN   In Great Britain, there is great public debate over various aspects of the EU, but especially about the impact of the free movement of workers from Eastern Europe. After the admission of new members (including Poland) to the EU, Great Britain (and a few other EU nations) opened their doors to immigrants from those nations and the result was an influx of over half a million people. Predictably, these immigrants took many low-paying jobs and were perceived as a threat because the jobs they obtained might have gone to British workers and because of their overall impact in driving down wages for all, especially at the lower end of the occupational hierarchy. These fears resurfaced with the admission of Bulgaria and Romania to the EU; perhaps the ultimate fear for many is the proposed admission of Turkey to the EU.

Many larger issues are involved in this debate. There are those who argue that the influx of low-wage immigrants aids a country like Great Britain by making its products less expensive and therefore more competitive in the global marketplace. These immigrants also often take jobs that natives are reluctant to take because of the low wages or the intrinsic nature of the work. Their low wages are also seen as tending to dampen the tendency toward inflation. And, the taxes paid by immigrant workers help pay for public services. In spite of such advantages, in 2008 the prime minister (Gordon Brown) issued a call for "British jobs for British workers," while the then opposition leader of the Conservative Party (David Cameron) was in favor of much lower rates of immigration into Great Britain (*Economist* 2008: January 3 ["The Politics of the Gun"]).

SWITZERLAND   To take another example, in the 2007 national elections in Switzerland, the most powerful party (Swiss People's Party) widely distributed a poster that depicted three white sheep standing on a flag, with one of the white sheep kicking a black sheep away. The words on the poster were: "To Create Security" (Sciolino 2007: A1, A7). Then there was a campaign film with the following three segments:

> In the first segment, young men inject heroin, steal handbags from women, kick and beat schoolboys, wield knives and carry off a young woman. The second segment shows Muslims living in Switzerland – women in head scarves; men sitting, not working. ... The third segment shows "heavenly" Switzerland: men in suits rushing to work ... harvesting on farms ... lakes, mountains, churches and goats. (Sciolino 2007: A7)

These kinds of sentiments exist in a nation that is traditionally associated with "peaceful consensus in politics, neutrality in foreign policy and tolerance in human relations" (Sciolino 2007: A1). (Similar events have occurred in Denmark [*Economist* 2007: November 22 ("The Trouble with Migrants")], which has passed strong anti-immigrant laws.) Over 20 percent of Switzerland's 7.5 million inhabitants (and a quarter of the work force) are foreign nationals. While Swiss People's Party officials claim their focus is on foreign criminals (and their families – it wants whole families deported if the criminal is a minor), the underlying message is "that the influx of foreigners has somehow polluted Swiss society, straining the social welfare system and threatening the very identity of the country" (Sciolino 2007: A7).

In the election held in late 2007, the Swiss People's Party received almost 30 percent of the vote and gained seven seats to reach a total of 62 of the 200-seat Parliament. Its closest competitor, the leftist Social Democratic Party, received less than 20 percent of the vote and lost nine seats and was left with a total of 43 seats. This vote was likely seen as an endorsement of the Swiss People's Party and was likely to lead it to push forward its conservative agenda, including more conservative policies in general, as well as toward immigration and asylum, in particular (Cumming-Bruce 2007: A4).

GREECE   EU countries are involved in a system, Frontex, designed to police their borders. Frontex has patrol boats, spotter airplanes, radar on land, and other high-tech devices (*Economist* 2008: January 3 ["Keep Out"]). A traditional route for illegal immigrants to EU countries was to travel, perhaps hundreds of miles, by flimsy boat, to places like the island of Lampedusa off Italy, or Spain's Canary Islands. A newer, and much shorter, route is from Turkey to three Greek islands – Lesbos, Chios, and especially Samos – that lie very close to Turkey and therefore the gateway to the Middle East and Asia. Although it is a short dinghy ride from Turkey to Chios, the waters there are treacherous and the trip is quite dangerous (in 2006, 24 bodies washed up on the shore of Samos, or were found in fishing nets offshore; one estimate put the number of dead or missing at about 100 on such voyages in that year). In spite of the danger (and the cost of using intermediaries such as smugglers and lawyers), many have used this route including migrants from "Iraq, Afghanistan, Somalia, Libya, Lebanon, Eritrea, the Palestinian territories and Iran" (Brothers 2008: A3). While clandestine arrivals to other locales have declined, they more than doubled in the Greek island chain from about 4,000 in 2006 to over 10,000 in 2007. To deal with such increases, a $3.5 million detention center has been built and there are plans to increase the islands' police force from 500 to 800. The islanders (as well as Greece more generally) want more help from the EU on this problem, especially in terms of putting pressure on Turkey to better police its borders.

Among those that suffer in this are those who have a legitimate reason to seek asylum in Greece. In fact, Greece has been criticized by the EU for not dealing adequately with the issue of asylum seekers. EU rules state that the first country reached by an immigrant is the one that is supposed to deal with asylum issues. The islanders seem more interested in stemming the tide of illegal immigrants and getting those who arrive in the islands to leave than they are in the immigrants' rights to a hearing on requests for asylum.

One of the ironies in this case is that it was not too long ago that it was large numbers of Greeks who were emigrating from their homeland. Further, during WW II the three islands in question were often sites for the debarkation of Greeks seeking to escape the German army by taking small boats to Turkey.

As the flow of illegal immigrants to Greece has increased, so has Greek resistance to it. Those illegal immigrants who are caught are put in detention for three months and then forced to leave Greece within 30 days. According to the chief of police for the three Greek islands: "Greece was not ready to accept such vast numbers of immigrants" (quoted in Brothers 2008: A3). The example of an Ethiopian law student is illustrative of the problems of even highly desirable illegal immigrants:

> He bribed Ethiopian border officials, hid in a truck carrying coffee to Sudan, endured seven days in the Sahara, spent months in a grim camp in Libya, suffered a terrifying voyage across the Mediterranean, hitched a lift in a frozen-meat lorry in Turkey, scavenged in a forest for days and feared he would drown in a fishing boat that carried

him into the EU. He paid several thousand dollars for the journey and ended up locked in a cramped and stinking warehouse on the island of Samos, crammed with asylum-seekers. Dejected, he says he wants to go home. (*Economist* 2008: January 3 ["Keep Out"])

Yet, large numbers of illegal migrants still make it to Europe, as well as to the US. In the end, these barriers will not keep out those who are desperate to get to these destinations (and they likely keep in those who might want to leave). There is some evidence of a decline of illegal immigration in Europe, especially those coming from Africa. However, the issue is whether the decline will continue in the long term, or whether it is nothing more than a blip on the otherwise upward trend in migration from Africa. The latter appears more likely given the problems seemingly endemic to Africa – warfare, poverty, and ethnic and religious conflict. One migrant from Darfur said, "We were already dead when we were in Sudan and Libya. If we died on the boat, it's all the same" (quoted in Fisher 2007: 10).

A US immigration expert commented: "Our politicians are not stupid. They know that walls do not stop people. It is a loser's game." Similarly an expert in Europe said: "It is playing King Canute to say that you can stop illegal immigration. It has never worked. It is no easier to stop than prostitution" (quoted in the *Economist* 2008: January 3 ["Keep Out"]). Yet, efforts continue in Europe, and elsewhere, to do just that. For example, in addition to Great Britain many countries have begun, or are planning soon, to collect biometric information (e.g. fingerprints) on all visitors and immigrants (*Economist* 2007: November 22 ["Giving You the Finger"]).

Illegal immigrants in Asia

The problem of illegal immigrants is not restricted to the EU and the US. It is an issue elsewhere, including Asia. For example, there are as many as three million immigrants in Malaysia and about half of them are there illegally. Most are from Indonesia, but others come from Bangladesh, India, Nepal, Vietnam, and Myanmar. They are there to work in various manual occupations, as well as to labor in the service industry. However, many, especially those who are there illegally, live in fear of harassment, arrest, whippings, imprisonment, and deportation.

In 2005 a group, created in the 1960s to combat communism, was deputized and transformed into a strike force ("Rela" – People's Volunteer Corps) to search out illegal immigrants throughout Malaysia. They are permitted to stop a "suspect" on the streets or to enter the homes of suspects. Rela's leaders are armed. Rela has grown to about half a million uniformed volunteers and is larger than Malaysia's police and armed forces. Official counts indicate that it carries out 30 to 40 raids per night. Human rights groups accuse it of various abuses such as "violence, extortion, theft, and illegal detention." A 2007 Human Rights Watch report said: "They break into migrant lodgings in the middle of the night without warrants, brutalize inhabitants, extort money and confiscate cell phones, clothing, jewelry, and household goods before handcuffing migrants and transporting them to detention camps for illegal immigrants" (quoted in Mydans 2007: A4). Rela's director-general responded: "… if you talk about human rights, you cannot talk about security" (quoted in Mydans 2007: A4). Those who are caught and detained (over 30,000 in 2007) are tried and, if convicted, can get up to five years in prison, or a whipping followed by deportation. One illegal immigrant serving as lookout for an apartment he shares with several other illegal immigrants said: "We always fear, especially at night. … Maybe there will be a raid. Where will we run? I worry for my wife and children. I've been thinking of moving to the jungle [many have done just that]" (quoted in Mydans 2007: A4). Rela's director-general responds by saying that illegal immigrants are Malaysia's enemy number two. The first? Drugs.

The issue of immigration, often illegal, is also of concern in central Asia where large numbers of people are moving north from impoverished and declining countries such as Uzbekistan and Tajikistan to comparatively oil-rich Kazakhstan and Russia (Greenberg 2007: A4). According to Russian estimates, approximately 2.5 million Uzbeks, 1 million Tajiks, and nearly as many Kyrgyz nationals are currently working, some of them seasonally, in Russia, either legally or semi-legally.

Problems arise because receiving nations do not seem to know how to categorize such immigrants and they are often treated very badly, sometimes even turned into slaves or semi-slaves. One Uzbek immigrant contended that immigrants were being sold in an open public market. In spite of such treatment, the immigrants keep coming because economic conditions are so poor back home. They take jobs in construction (buildings, roads), in factories, or in market stalls of various types. While the immigrants already encounter personal problems, there has been a rise in Russia in anti-immigration sentiments and demonstrations, and there is the potential there, and elsewhere in the region, for even greater problems (e.g. a rise in ethnic tensions and violence). However, there are also gains for immigrants such as improved conditions at home as a result of remittances (see below) from immigrant workers. While the borders in the region remain open, there has been an increase in the smuggling of illegal immigrants because the borders are more difficult to cross.

The Case Against the Backlash to Illegal Immigration

A number of arguments have been made against the various roadblocks currently being erected in the path of immigrants (*Economist* 2000, January 5 ["Keep the Borders Open"]). From the point of view of the South, immigrants from there to the North have benefited enormously and many have sent money back home. Those who return eventually bring with them money saved while working in the North, new skills and technical expertise, and innovative new ideas.

Of course, it could be argued that it is the North that benefits more from immigration, legal or illegal. It is this that makes the growing opposition in the North even more incomprehensible. Among other things, the North usually gains youthful, vigorous, and ambitious new workers of all types. This factor is especially important to the graying, and perhaps shrinking, work forces in the EU and the US. In some cases, there are few alternatives to hiring immigrants. For example, a hotel owner in Ireland recently advertised for a hotel receptionist. Two hundred people applied, but *none* were Irish. Immigrants often do work (e.g. farm labor, care for the elderly) that natives eschew. Migrant workers are generally more flexible than natives, willing to go almost anywhere and do anything. Additional flexibility is made possible by the fact that migrants may free up natives to take other jobs (e.g. by taking on low-paid jobs working in day care), or to move on to higher-status, better-paying jobs. Migrant workers also better protect the economy from inflation because of the mixed blessing of their low wages. The North may even see an influx of the best-trained, elite workers from the South. Then there is the fact that migrants are consumers and the more they are paid, the more they spend. As consumers, they contribute to the growth of the local economy in another way (although there is a debate about just how much they contribute and their contribution is difficult to measure precisely). Related to this is the fact that as they open their own shops and restaurants, they contribute to the diversity of the host country. Overall, the economies of the North have grown historically, and are likely to continue to grow, as a result of immigration, legal and illegal (*Economist* 2007: November 1).

Why, then, the fears (*Economist* 2007: November 22 ["Fear of Foreigners"]) in the North? Politicians gain much notoriety and support by focusing national attention on illegal immigration and immigrants. After all, the latter are safe to attack, especially the illegals who cannot vote. Further, they represent a convenient scapegoat for both politicians and much of the public. Few members of the public support illegal immigrants, or at least want to be seen as supporting them, and many fear them for various reasons. Thus, they are receptive to the arguments of ambitious politicians.

There are also a number of more practical reasons why there is such fear of illegal immigrants in the North. Some may simply find it disturbing to see a significant influx of people from other cultures, especially dramatic increases in the number of such people that they come in contact with on a daily basis. It is difficult for such immigrants to integrate into the larger culture and some may not want to. For their part, Northerners may not want, or allow, them to integrate. The least skilled workers in the North are the ones who may see their jobs threatened or a decrease in pay as a result of competition from illegals, and this fear has been heightened by the Great Recession. However, there is evidence that the decline in pay traceable to immigration is relatively small and that over time the wages recover. Furthermore, there is at least some job creation that occurs as a result of immigration – employers move in to take advantage of their low wages, distinctive skills, etc. There is also a fear, especially in the US and the EU, that illegals will become reliant on state welfare systems and strain school systems, public housing, and hospitals. Of course, fears in the North of all types of immigration were exacerbated by terrorist attacks on or after 9/11.

The most complete case against restrictions on international migration is made by Jonathon W. Moses in *International Migration* (2006). He divides his argument into economic, political, and moral dimensions.

Economically, Moses argues that immigration has had a positive, *not* a negative, effect on the economy of the US (and other developed nations). In one estimate, an increase in foreign workers would lead to great global economic gains. An increase of 500,000 immigrants a year would lead to a global gain of $675 billion a year by 2025 (*Economist* 2008: March 27 ["How to Smite Smoot"]). Contrary to what many believe, it is not clear that immigrants compete with natives for jobs. It is also not clear that immigrants have less skill than natives; in any case, there is great variation in this from nation to nation and from immigrant group to immigrant group. While the wages of native, less-skilled workers may be negatively affected, overall wages are not affected, or may even increase. Immigrants are not a drain on public finances and may even pay more in taxes than they cost in services (one reason for this is that immigrants are usually young and in their prime as far as work is concerned). A very strong economic argument in support of more open immigration in developed countries is the fact that these countries are dominated by aging work forces and they need an influx of young, vibrant, and "hungry" workers. Yet another economic argument relates to the high (and increasing) cost of restricting immigration through border controls – money that would be saved and could be put to other uses if border controls were eased.

The above relates to economic benefits to receiving countries, but sending countries benefit economically, as well. Those workers who remain behind are in an improved bargaining position and can better their economic situation and their lives more generally. Remittances can provide capital that can be used by the countries receiving the money for investments in economic development.

In the political realm, freer immigration can contribute in various ways to greater democratization, less authoritarianism. In terms of sending countries, the fact that people (especially the most highly educated and skilled) can and do leave because of a lack of democracy puts pressure on the political system to reform itself. More generally, it strengthens the ability of individuals to influence political regimes and to push them in the direction of increased democratization. In short, with free(r) migration, nation-states need to be more responsive to their citizens. In a world of freer movement, nation-states would also compete with one another in order to be better able both to keep their best people and to attract those from elsewhere. This could improve nation-states the world over and enhance international exchanges.

There are two basic moral arguments in support of freer migration. First, as an end in itself, free mobility is "a universal and basic human right" (Moses 2006: 58). Second, instrumentally, "free migration is seen as a means to achieve greater moral ends (in particular, economic and political justice)" (Moses 2006: 59). In terms of the latter, greater freedom of movement would lead to a reduction in global economic inequality and would mitigate global tyranny. Overall, Moses emphasizes the moral aspect of freer migration: "Today's migration regime is terribly unjust: it distributes opportunity by fate, and has the effect of condemning people to life sentences in their country of birth. As such, the current regime tends to prioritize the rights of an imagined community (the nation), at the expense of sometimes desperate individuals" (Moses 2006: 9).

Of course, all of this challenges much conventional wisdom today about migration and open borders. However, Moses shows that most of that conventional wisdom is erroneous or, at best, only partially correct. There is much fear these days over the crime and terrorism that might be associated with free, or even just freer, global migration. However, Moses argues that freer migration would bring with it greater global cooperation, and global systems, that would allow for greatly improved tracking of flows of people and a much-improved ability to identify and apprehend those intent on criminal or terroristic activities.

Remittances

The issue of remittances is increasingly important as more and more immigrants, legal and illegal, make their way into developed countries in order to find work. Those who are successful often end up sending money back to their country of origin for the care and support of various family members. While they are often poorly paid by the standards of developed countries, they are better off than many in their country of origin. Further, they are aware that their absence makes it harder for family members left behind to survive. Thus, remittances have become an increasing reality, and of increasing importance, to developing countries. According to one estimate, some 200 million migrants in the world are supporting a roughly equal number who remain at home (if the population of migrants was a nation-state, it would be one of the largest in the world). It is also estimated that in 2006 remittances amounted to an estimated $300 billion (almost three times the total of all of the world's foreign aid budgets combined) (DeParle 2007a: 50ff.). More conservatively, the World Bank estimates that remittances were $208 billion in 2006 (up from less than $40 billion in 1990), but it only counts transfers recorded by central banks and concludes that the real total is about $300 billion (DeParle 2007b: 3; Davis 2006: A1, A12).

Thriving businesses have arisen in the North to handle the large numbers of transfers of relatively small amounts of funds that banks generally are unwilling to bother with. In addition, banks lack the infrastructure to handle such transfers. The small businesses that handle most of these transfers (as we will see, large businesses are also involved) generally use the Internet for the transfers and can function with small offices in cities in the North (London has a large number of them) and in the South to which they send money (*Economist* 2008: January 3 ["Send Me a Number"]).

Remittances constitute *the largest source of money* flowing into developing countries from the rest of the world. In some countries in the South remittances constitute a substantial, even stunning, proportion of GNP (31 percent in Tonga, 27.1 percent in Moldova, 24.8 percent in Haiti, 17.4 percent in Jamaica, and about 16 percent in El Salvador). Remittances are most likely to go to Asia (almost $114 billion); Central and South America and the Caribbean are next with just over $68 billion. In terms of specific countries, the leaders are India (receiving $24.5 billion), China ($21.1 billion), and the Philippines ($14.7 billion) (Malkin 2007: A10).

This is usually seen as a boon to those who receive remittances, as well as to the economies of the societies in which they live. Recipients are better able to survive, to buy the basics they need, and even to afford a few luxuries (a TV set, a cell phone). More generally, remittances can

- reduce poverty rates;
- go directly to those in need and give them experience with banks and in saving;
- help deal with emergencies because flows of money can be increased easily and quickly because virtually all of the money goes to satisfy important needs for "food, clothes, housing, education and health" (*Economist* 2008: January 3 ["Send Me a Number"]);
- be used to raise educational levels,
- be a source of pride and confidence in the receiving community over the success of those able to send remittances;
- be countercyclical, that is remittances can be increased as a result of an economic slump at home (or a natural disaster) (in contrast to money from investors that declines during a slump);
- be preferable to foreign aid because they are more predictable, better aimed at those in need, and less susceptible to corruption (since they go directly to recipients, officials cannot skim money from them);
- increase a nation's foreign reserves and thereby reduce its borrowing costs;
- be monitored better by intimates than by officials.

Overall, as the Minister of Émigrés in Morocco put it: "The impact [of remittances] is decisive, enormous, we have a construction boom across the country. This is an important safeguard against poverty and helps to modernize our rural society" (quoted in the *Economist* 2008: January 3 ["Send Me a Number"]).

There are negatives associated with remittances, as well as the immigration they help to encourage, that are more difficult to rebut. First, the most skilled and educated in less developed countries (tourists) are the ones most likely to leave, and to remain in developed countries, because of the greater earnings and the resulting ability to remit money to loved ones in their home countries. This creates a drain on the economy of the home countries; those most likely to succeed in it are precisely those most likely to emigrate. Overall, it is estimated that a startling one-sixth of the population of El Salvador (to take one example) now live (and work) abroad, in many cases as illegal immigrants in the US. While many of these immigrants are among the better trained and educated Salvadorans, the sheer numbers themselves represent a significant drain on the Salvadoran economy.

Second, the money that is infused into the local economy does not necessarily translate into economic growth and development. The increases in personal consumption made possible by remittances do not lead to greater investment in the economic infrastructure that could fuel economic development. As one scholar said: "If I ask can you name a single country that has developed through remittances, the answer is no – there's none" (quoted in DeParle 2008: A9). However, some Southern countries (e.g. India, Morocco, Mexico) are making greater efforts to ensure that more of this money is being invested in infrastructure and industry. In any case, greater consumption among the poor can be seen as a good thing.

Third, those who receive remittances can become targets of local gangs interested in stealing either the cash received or the products purchased with that cash.

Fourth, the money sometimes goes to countries that have regimes that are highly dubious, such as Zimbabwe and North Korea. That is, while those who send the money are supporting, perhaps only indirectly, regimes of choice, it may be that from a broader global perspective those regimes should not be supported.

Fifth, it is surprisingly costly (although that cost has been declining) to send remittances and those who process such payments also manipulate exchange rates to further enhance their profits and thereby reduce the actual amount of money being remitted to developing countries.

Sixth, while they may help, remittances are no cure for poverty. On their own, they are unable to lift a country out of poverty. And there is a fear that those who receive remittances will become dependent and reduce their efforts to find ways to make it on their own.

Seventh, there are the problems of those left behind by those who migrate in search of work, such as broken families, delinquent children, and the like. A UNICEF official said: "Behind every remittance, there's a separated family" (quoted in DeParle 2008: A9). Remittances can also be a source of divisiveness within families (Schmalzbauer 2008: 329–46). Those who go abroad in search of work may also be abused, forced into sex work, beaten, or even killed.

Eighth, the poorest nations are not the greatest recipients of remittances. In fact, it is middle-income countries that are the largest recipients. Similarly, within the poorest countries, the poorest people are *not* the most likely to receive remittances.

Finally, in the end, we are still talking about relatively small sums of money and it tends to obscure the problem of the exploitation of migrants. It also "tends to justify the way the world is being restructured for the benefit of a small elite" (quoted in DeParle 2008: A9).

Overall, then, remittances have been an increasing reality (although declining rapidly, at least for the time being, in the Great Recession), but perhaps not an unmitigated boon to the economies of developing countries and to the people who remain behind. Yet, there are many whose lives are materially better as a result of remittances. As a pioneer in the area of remittances put it, "Let's not forget, a billion dollars in the hands of poor people is a lot of money" (quoted in DeParle 2008: A9).

Increasing barriers to immigration into the US, especially from Mexico, have affected remittances from the US to Mexico. From 2000 to 2006 such remittances grew from $6.6 billion to $24 billion, at times reaching increases of 20 percent per year. However, in late 2007 the increase was below 2 percent (Malkin 2007: A1, A10). In addition to increased border restrictions (and the resulting higher cost of an illegal crossing), other reasons for this decline include a dramatic drop in American housing construction where many illegal immigrants could get work more easily, the return by many to Mexico, and the fact that those who remain are sending smaller amounts of money back home. Many communities in Mexico are being hurt economically as a result of the decline in remittances.

Remittances to Mexico, and to many other places, are being hard hit by the global economic decline, especially in the US. The Mexican government projected a 12 percent decline in remittances in 2008 and that decline is likely to accelerate for the foreseeable future. This is a serious matter since remittances are Mexico's second largest source of income from outside the country (Thompson 2008: A17).

Diaspora

The term **diaspora** has a long and rather specific history, but it has come to be adopted by various groups to describe their situation (and that of others); it has also come to be used widely in the popular media to describe a range of population movements (Bernal 2006; Mavroudi 2007; McAuliffe 2007; Braziel 2008). The term is, of course, most asso-

> **Diaspora**: The large-scale dispersal of a population.

ciated with the dispersion of Jews to many places in the world in the years both before and after the birth of Christ. In 586 BC, the Babylonians dispersed the Jews from Judea and in AD 136 it was the Romans who chased the Jews out of Jerusalem (Armstrong 1996). In recent years, however, the use of the term has broadened to include the dispersion, dislocation, and de-territorialization of *any* population (Bauman 2000: 314). Most frequently, a diaspora involves the large-scale dispersal of a religious, ethnic, racial, or national group. In addition to the Jews, other groups that have experienced diasporas include the Lebanese, Palestinians, Armenians, and the Irish. In fact, the term has come to be used so widely and loosely that many complain that diaspora discourse has lost a consensus on the meaning of the term (Lie 1995), its meaning has in fact become *less* clear, and it is in danger of becoming little more than a "buzzword" (Cohen 1999: 3). It seems clear that it is best to differentiate among the various diasporas rather than to combine them all under one all-encompassing heading.

Nevertheless, there have been a number of efforts to develop an ideal typical diaspora by enumerating its various characteristics. Safran, for example, discusses "expatriate minority communities" that are dispersed from some original central location to two or more peripheral locations; have a collective memory or mythology of their homeland that is maintained by the community and that binds them together; involve people who are alienated from the country from which they emanated and are not – and may never be – fully accepted there; involve people who nevertheless idealize a return to their ancestral homeland and maintain a commitment to restore their homeland to its former glories (e.g. independence, prosperity);

maintain a relationship to the homeland not only through a commitment to its restoration, but also through group solidarity and consciousness resulting from this commitment. Of course, since this is an ideal type, no single diaspora conforms to all of these dimensions, nor could any of them (Clifford 1994).

In another approach, a diaspora can be seen as involving one, several, or all of the following (Vertovec 1999). First, it is a social form. That form is defined by the fact that relationships are maintained even though the population has been dispersed. The population spans transnational borders; they constitute transnational communities. They involve a group of people who collectively define themselves as such even though they may be widely dispersed, perhaps even globally. While they reside in a different locale, they relate to the homeland from which they and/or their forebears came. Second, a diaspora involves a type of consciousness. Those involved have great sensitivity to various interconnections, especially those that span borders, and to attachments that are decentered. They are aware of being different from those around them and of the fact that those they identify with exist in multiple locales, as well as in the homeland. Third, diaspora is a mode of cultural production. The diaspora's cultural objects, meanings, and images are produced in, and involve, global flows. Thus, they are highly fluid and subject to many mutual influences, negotiations, transformations, and contestations. Fourth, a diaspora is political. Individuals and/or collectivities involved in diasporas often become important political players in both their host country as well as internationally (prominent examples include Palestinians and Tibetans) (Bruneau 1995).

However, the preceding are rather static approaches to diaspora that are inconsistent with the more fluid orientation to globalization adopted in this book. A better approach, at least for our purposes, is to be found in Paul Gilroy's (1993: 190) *The Black Atlantic* which, most generally, is concerned with "flows, exchanges and in-between elements." Implied here is a sense of diaspora as process, specifically a transnational process. It is not tied to any specific locale (especially nation-state) but involves a constant dialogue with both real and imagined locales. Thus, the Black Atlantic (Black cultures in the Atlantic basin) cannot be understood as West Indian, British, or American, but as an ongoing relationship involving the Black Atlantic in its entirety. The Black Atlantic (and diasporas in general) is therefore an imagined (and contested) community rather than a specific geographic space(s). Thus, Gilroy (1993: 18) concludes that the Black Atlantic should be seen as "a deterritorialised, multiplex and anti-national basis for the affinity or 'identity of passions' between diverse black populations."

The use of the term diaspora has expanded with the process of globalization. There are not only more diasporas, but more people describe themselves and their relationships with others in these terms. This relates, in Dufoix's (2007: 311–16) view, to the expansion of "trans-state collective experiences linked to an organized referent (e.g., a state, a land, a nation, a people, a language, a culture)." In fact, the use of the term has become so common that Dufoix (2007: 314) describes the "diasporization" of the world. It shares with globalization "processes such as the shrinking of the world, a disembeddedness of time and space, glocalization, instantaneous communication, the reshaping of geography, and the spatialization of the social." While diasporas were relatively unusual in a world dominated by powerful nation-states and territories, they have proliferated with the decline of the nation-state and deterritorialization. Furthermore, the trans-state community networks that characterize diasporas today are made possible by a wide range of technologies (e.g. inexpensive air travel, cheap international phone calls and phone cards [Vertovec 2004], cell phones, the Internet, Skype) that make communication among far-flung people possible. Thus, diasporization and globalization are closely linked today, and since the latter will continue to develop and expand, we can expect more and more dispersals that are, or at least are called, diasporas.

New technologies are playing such an increasing role in diasporas that it could be argued that we have seen the emergence of "virtual diasporas" (Laguerre 2002). These virtual worlds have been created through "international calls, faxes, emails, satellite TV broadcasting, simultaneous media access through the Internet" (Grainger 2008: 47). These technologies have provided new ways for people to maintain links with one another and for communities to maintain themselves and even to create new communities (Spoonley 2001). Of course, a virtual diaspora requires the prior existence of a real diaspora, the real dispersal of a given population.

CHAPTER SUMMARY

This chapter analyzes the global flow of people through the categories of migrants – "vagabonds" and "tourists." Vagabonds are on the move because they have to be – they are not faring well in their home countries and are forced to move in the hope that their circumstances will improve. Tourists, on the other hand, are on the move because they want to be and because they can afford it.

Refugees are vagabonds forced to flee their home countries due to safety concerns. Asylum seekers are refugees who seek to remain in the country to which they flee. Those who migrate to find work are involved in labor migration. Labor migration is driven by "push" factors (for instance lack of employment opportunities in home countries), as well as "pull" factors (work available elsewhere). Labor migration mainly involves the flow of less- and un-skilled workers, as well as illegal immigrants who live on the margins of the host society.

Unlike other global flows, labor migration still faces many restrictions. Many of these barriers are related to the Westphalian conception of the nation-state and are intimately associated with it. The state may seek to control migration because it involves the loss of part of the work force. An influx of migrants can lead to conflicts with local residents. Concerns about terrorism also affect the desire of the state to restrict population flows.

Migration is traditionally governed either by "push" factors such as political persecution, economic depression, war, and famine in the home country; or by "pull" factors such as a favorable immigration policy, a labor shortage, and a similarity of language and culture in the country of destination. Global factors which facilitate easy access to information about the country of destination also exert a significant influence.

Many countries face issues of illegal migration. The US faces a major influx of illegal immigrants from Mexico and other Central American states. A fence is being constructed on the US–Mexico border to control this flow of people. However, its efficacy is questioned and it is thought that it will only lead illegal immigrants to adopt more dangerous methods to gain entry. In addition, tighter borders have also had the effect of "locking in" people who might otherwise have left the country. Other countries with similar concerns about illegal immigration include Great Britain, Switzerland, and Greece as well as countries in Asia.

A strong case can be made against the backlash against illegal immigrants. In the North, such immigrants constitute a younger work force which does work that locals may not perform, and they are consumers who contribute to growth. They also send remittances back to family members in the country of origin, which improves the lives of the recipients, reduces poverty rates, and increases the level of education as well as the foreign reserves of the home country. Banks are often unwilling or unable to handle the type (small amounts of money) and volume of remittances. As a result, specialized organizations play a major role in the transmission of remittances.

The term diaspora is increasingly being used to describe migrant communities. Of particular interest is Paul Gilroy's conceptualization of the diaspora as a transnational process, which involves dialogue with both imagined and real locales. Diasporization and globalization are closely inter-connected and the expansion of the latter will lead to an increase in the former. Today there exist virtual diasporas which utilize technology such as the Internet to maintain the community network.

DISCUSSION QUESTIONS

1. Is the heightened flow of people a unique feature of the current global era?

2. Analyze the concept of an "illegal migrant." How does a migrant become "illegal"? Trace the repercussions of such labeling.

3. Has globalization facilitated or obstructed greater labor migration?

4. Examine the concept of "diaspora as a transnational process," in the context of global technological flows.

FURTHER READING

Jonathon W. Moses. *International Migration: Globalization's Last Frontier*. London: Zed Books, 2006.

Jana Evans Braziel. *Diaspora: An Introduction*. Malden, MA: Blackwell, 2008.

Paul Gilroy. *The Black Atlantic: Modernity and Double-Consciousness*. Cambridge, MA: Harvard University Press, 1993.

Uri Ram. *The Globalization of Israel*. New York: Routledge, 2008.

Annalee Saxenian. *The New Argonauts: Regional Advantage in a Global Economy*. Cambridge, MA: Harvard University Press, 2006.

Chris Rojek and John Urry, eds. *Touring Cultures: Transformations of Travel and Theory*. London: Routledge, 1997.

John Urry. *The Tourist Gaze*. 2nd edn. London: Sage, 2002.

Dean McCannell. *The Tourist: A New Theory of the Leisure Class*, 2nd edn. New York: Schocken, 1989.

REFERENCES ···

Alvarez, Lizette. 2006a. "A Growing Stream of Illegal Immigrants Choose to Remain Despite the Risks." *New York Times*. December 20.

Alvarez, Lizette. 2006b. "Fear and Hope in Immigrant's Furtive Existence." *New York Times*. December 20.

Archibold, Randal C. 2007. "Border Fence Project Raises Environmental Concerns." *New York Times*. November 21.

Armstrong, Karen. 1996. *Jerusalem: One City, Three Faiths*. New York: Ballantine Books.

Barkan, Elliott R., Hasia Diner, and Alan M. Kraut, eds. 2008. *From Arrival to Incorporation: Migrants to the US in a Global Era*. New York: New York University Press.

Bauman, Zygmunt. 1998. *Globalization: The Human Consequences*. New York: Columbia University Press.

Bauman, Zygmunt. 2000. *Liquid Modernity*. Cambridge: Polity.

Bernal, Victoria. 2006. "Diaspora, Cyberspace and Political Imagination: The Eritrean Diaspora Online." *Global Networks* 6, 2.

Bernstein, Nina. 2006. "A Climate of Fear as Immigration Agents Raid New York Farms." *New York Times*. December 24.

Braziel, Jana Evans. 2008. *Diaspora: An Introduction*. Malden, MA: Blackwell.

Brothers, Caroline. 2008. "Unwilling New Frontier for Migrants: 3 Greek Isles." *New York Times*. January 3.

Bruneau, Michel. 1995. *Diasporas*. Montpellier: GIP Reclus.

Clifford, James. 1994. "Diasporas." *Cultural Anthropology* 9, 3.

Cohen, Phil. 1999. "Rethinking the Diasporama." *Patterns of Prejudice* 33, 1.

Cohen, R., ed. 1995. *The Cambridge Survey of World Migration*. Cambridge: Cambridge University Press.

Cumming-Bruce, Nick. 2007. "Far-Right Party Posts Gains in Voting for Swiss Parliament." *New York Times*. October 22.

Davis, Bob. 2000. "Migrants' Money Is Imperfect Cure for Poor Nations." *Wall Street Journal*. November 1.

DeParle, Jason. 2007a. "A Good Provider Is One Who Leaves." *New York Times Magazine*. April 22.

DeParle, Jason. 2007b. "Migrant Money Flow: A $300 Billion Current." *New York Times – Week in Review*. November 18.

DeParle, Jason. 2008. "World Banker and His Cash Return Home." *New York Times*. March 17.

Dufoix, Stephane. 2007. "Diasporas." In Jan Aart Scholte and Roland Robertson, eds., *Encyclopedia of Globalization*. New York: MTM Publishing.

Economist. 2007. November 1. "Illegal, but Useful."

Economist. 2007. November 22. "Fear of Foreigners."

Economist. 2007. November 22. "Giving You the Finger."

Economist. 2007. November 22. "The Trouble with Migrants."

Economist. 2008. January 3. "Keep Out."

Economist. 2008. January 3. "Keep the Borders Open."

Economist. 2008. January 3. "Of Bedsheets and Bison Grass Vodka."

Economist. 2008. January 3. "Open Up."

Economist. 2008. January 3. "Send Me a Number."

Economist. 2008. January 3. "The Politics of the Gun."

Economist. 2008. March 27. "How to Smite Smoot."

Fears, Darryl. 2006. "Citizenship Changes Draw Objections." *New York Times*. October 27.

Fisher, Ian. 2007. "For African Migrants, Europe Becomes Further Away." *New York Times*. August 26.

Fletcher, Michael A., and Jonathan Weisman. 2006. "Bush Signs Bill Authorizing 700-Mile Fence for Border." *New York Times*. October 27.

Gilroy, Paul. 1993. *The Black Atlantic: Modernity and Double Consciousness*. Cambridge, MA: Harvard University Press.

Grainger, Andrew David. 2008. "The Browning of the All Blacks: Pacific Peoples, Rugby, and the Cultural Politics of Identity in New Zealand." PhD dissertation, University of Maryland, College Park, MD.

Greenberg, Ilan. 2007. "Central Asians Chase Jobs, and Endure Exploitation." *New York Times*. May 15.

Guhathakurta, Subhrajit, David Jacobson, and Nicholas C. DelSordi. 2007. "The End of Globalization? The Implications of Migration for State, Society and Economy." In George Ritzer, ed., *Blackwell Companion to Globalization*. Malden, MA: Blackwell.

Haddad, Emma. 2003. "The Refugee: The Individual between Sovereigns." *Global Society* 17, 3 (July).

Kritz, Mary M. 2008. "International Migration." In George Ritzer, ed., *Blackwell Encyclopedia of Sociology Online*. Submitted February. Malden, MA: Blackwell.

Kritz, Mary M., L. I. Lim, and H. Zlotnik. 1992. *International Migration Systems: A Global Approach*. Oxford: Oxford University Press.

Laguerre, M. S. 2002. *Virtual Diasporas: A New Frontier of National Security*. The Nautilus Project on Virtual Diasporas. www.nautilus.org/archives/virtual-diasporas/paper/Laguerre.html.

Lie, John. 1995. "From International Migration to Transnational Diaspora." *Contemporary Sociology* 24, 4.

Malkin, Elisabeth. 2007. "Mexicans Miss Money from Workers up North." *New York Times*. October 26.

Mavroudi, Elizabeth. 2007. "Learning to Be Palestinian in Athens: Constructing National Identities in Diaspora." *Global Networks* 7, 4.

McAuliffe, Cameron. 2007. "A Home Far Away? Religious Identity and Trans National Relations in the Iranian Diaspora." *Global Networks* 7, 3.

McKinley, Jr., James C. 2007. "Despite Crackdown, Migrants Stream into South Mexico." *New York Times*. January 28.

Moses, Jonathon W. 2006. *International Migration: Globalization's Last Frontier*. London: Zed Books.

Mydans, Seth. 2007. "A Growing Source of Fear for Migrants in Malaysia." *New York Times*. December 10.

Navarro, Mireya. 2006a. "For Divided Family, Border Is Sorrowful Barrier." *New York Times*. December 21.

Navarro, Mireya. 2006b. "Traditional Round Trip for Workers Is Becoming a One-Way Migration North." *New York Times*. December 21.

New York Times. 2008. March 7. "Britain to Issue Identity Cards for Foreigners in November."

Preston, Julia. 2006a. "Low-Wage Workers from Mexico Dominate Latest Great Wave of Immigrants." *New York Times*. December 19.

Preston, Julia. 2006b. "Making a Life in the United States, but Feeling Mexico's Tug." *New York Times*. December 19.

Roberts, Sam. 2008. "Study Foresees the Fall of an Immigration Record that Has Lasted a Century." *New York Times*. February 12.

Schmalzbauer, Leah. 2008. "Family Divided: The Class Formation of Honduran Transnational Families." *Global Networks* 8, 3.

Sciolino, Elaine. 2007. "Immigration, Black Sheep and Swiss Rage." *New York Times*. October 8.

Shamir, Ronen. 2005. "Without Borders? Notes on Globalization as a Mobility Regime." *Sociological Theory* 23, 2 (June).

Shane, Scott, and Michael Gordon. 2008. "Dissident's Tale of Epic Escape from Iran's Vise." *New York Times*. July 13.

Spoonley, Paul. 2001. "Transnational Pacific Communities: Transforming the Politics of Place and Identity." In Cluney Macpherson, Paul Spoonley, and Melani Anae, eds., *Tangata O Te Moana Nui: The Evolving Identities of Pacific Peoples in Aotearoa New Zealand*. Palmerston North, NZ: Dunmore Press.

Tan, Celine. 2007. "Liberalization." In Jan Aart Scholte and Roland Robertson, eds., *Encyclopedia of Globalization*. New York: MTM Publishing.

Thompson, Ginger. 2008. "Fewer People Are Entering US Illegally, Report Says." *New York Times*. October 3.

Vertovec, Steven. 1999. "Conceiving and Researching Transnationalism." *Ethnic and Racial Studies* 22, 2.

Vertovec, Steven. 2004. "Cheap Calls: The Social Glue of Migrant Transnationalism." *Global Networks* 4, 2.

Global Environmental Flows

Globalization: The Essentials, by George Ritzer
© 2011 John Wiley & Sons Ltd

n this chapter and the next we deal with what can be termed "negative global flows." As we saw in Chapter 1, the idea of flows owes a large debt to Zygmunt Bauman and his thinking on the liquid society (as well as to the work of others including Arjun Appadurai [Chapter 7]). This analysis now owes a further debt to Bauman (2006: 96) for his discussion of "negative globalization." We will discuss this idea at the beginning of the next chapter where it has greater and more specific relevance to the issues discussed there. While Bauman does not discuss environmental issues under the heading of negative globalization, it is clear that adverse environmental flows are among the most, if not the most, negative aspects of globalization.

One of the most enduring and important issues in the study of globaliztion involves its relationship to the environment (Stevis 2005: 323–33). The environment is inherently, and has always been, global. That is, we all share the atmosphere, are warmed by the sun, and are connected by the oceans (Yearley 2007: 239–53). Further, much that relates to the environment has an impact on, and flows around (e.g. weather patterns), the world, or at least large portions of it.

In spite of this, the earliest thinking on globalization tended to ignore the environment, or at least to underplay its significance. There was some early concern for the environmental impact of fallout from nuclear testing and acid rain (Munton and Wilkening 2007: 7–9). However in the 1980s and 1990s the environmental movement (Rootes 1999) made great progress and a number of notable problems, especially the depletion of the ozone layer (Liftin 2007: 927–30) and global climate change, brought the environment to the fore as a global issue and problem. In the case of these two issues, and many others, it is clear that many throughout the world play a major role in the creation of these problems and that virtually everyone in the world will suffer their adverse consequences. In that sense they are clearly global in nature.

However, while the idea that environmental problems are global problems seems indisputable, it can be challenged in various ways.

- Not everyone or every part of the world is equally responsible for the most pressing global environmental problems. It is clear that those from the most developed countries are disproportionately responsible for them.
- Such problems do not, and will not, affect everyone and all areas of the world in the *same way*. For example, the rise in the sea level as a result of global warming will most affect those who live in coastal areas or on islands (see below). Such areas will also be most affected by the expected increase in the number and severity of hurricanes. Tornados are also expected to increase, although they are likely to affect different geographic areas (e.g. the American Midwest more than American coasts). To take another example, those in the North will be better able to find ways of avoiding or dealing with all but the most catastrophic of the problems caused by global warming. On the other hand, those in the South will be far more defenseless and have fewer options (e.g. selling their homes and moving to a less threatened locale). Therefore, they will suffer more from environmental problems of various kinds.

- There are global differences in the importance accorded to, and the dangers associated with, these problems. For example, the developed North is highly concerned about global warming, while much of the South feels that it is faced with so many more pressing problems (e.g. health problems such as malaria, HIV, hunger and malnutrition, etc.) that global warming seems, at best, a remote difficulty that will need to be confronted later, if at all.
- Many in various other parts of the world have different candidates for the most important global environmental problems than those that are of focal concern in the North (e.g. the decline of available drinking water, although as we will see, this is an increasing issue in the North, as well).
- The main sources of environmental problems will change – for example, as the center of manufacturing (with its associated pollutants) moves from the US to China.

The free trade that is so central to economic globalization today from a neo-liberal perspective is generally seen as the enemy of the environment. For one thing, a free-trade policy leads to the expansion of manufacturing and to the wide range of pollutants produced by it. For another, it leads to the view that the efforts favored by environmentalists to limit industrial pollution are impediments to free trade and need to be opposed; and if efforts to reduce pollution are implemented, they need to be watered down and, if possible, eventually eliminated. In effect, environmentalists offer an alternative model of globalization to that of the neo-liberals (Harvey 2005; Antonio 2007: 67–83). To environmentalists, environmental issues are not only global in nature, but they also should be accorded priority over economic considerations. The priorities are clearly reversed by neo-liberals, especially economists and capitalists.

While the environmental and neo-liberal economic paradigms are clearly opposed to one another, there are efforts to create models that integrate the two. One example is **ecological modernization theory** (Yearley 2007: 239–53), which argues that the economic and technological development favored by neo-liberal economists can go hand-in-hand with a decline in the negative effects on the environment that are the focal concerns of environmentalists. Examples include the creation of low-odor paints and less environmentally destructive pesticides. Central to ecological modernization theory are environmental NGOs that put pressure on nation-states and other entities to move toward policies that are less slavishly devoted to neo-liberal economic development and more attuned to the environment, its protection, and even its enhancement. In other words, globalization need not be a "race to the bottom" (see Chapter 4) ecologically (and in many other senses), but can be a process that protects and enhances the environment as well as much else that is of importance to all of us and that all of us value greatly (or at least should).

> **Ecological modernization theory**: Economic and technological development hand-in-hand with a decline in negative effects on the environment.

DIFFERENCES AMONG NATION-STATES

Many of the nations of the world, 149 of them, were ranked in 2006 in terms of their environmental performance on a number of dimensions, such as air pollution, greenhouse gas emissions, sanitation, agricultural policies, and many others. The highest-ranking nations in terms of friendliness to the environment were Switzerland, Sweden, Norway, Finland, Austria, France, Latvia, Costa Rica, Columbia, and New Zealand. The US ranked thirty-ninth.

The issue of climate change was given more attention in this evaluation than in previous ones. Here, too, Switzerland was at the top because of its system of hydro-electric power and because its extensive train system tends to reduce the use of cars and trucks. The US performs poorly on greenhouse gas (e.g. carbon dioxide) emissions that contribute to global warming (the US alone contributes 25 percent of all of the world's emissions of this type); the rising industrial powers, China and India, ranked lower than the US and were among the worst 25 nations on such emissions (Barringer 2008: A8).

COLLAPSE

Jared Diamond has written a popular book – *Collapse* (2006) – about societal collapse and the role of environmental factors in that collapse. He concludes that not all civilizations that collapsed in the past have done so because of environmental causes, but at least some have. One factor in collapse due to environmental causes is the amount and type of damage that people inadvertently inflict on their environment. Damage will depend, in part, on what people do, and in part on the degree of fragility or resilience of the environment (e.g. its ability to restore itself). Another factor affecting degree of damage is the way in which different societies respond to these environmental problems. For example, historically those societies (e.g. Highland New Guinea) that developed sound forest management policies and procedures continued to survive, while others that did not (e.g. Easter Island) collapsed.

What is unique about the global era is the fact that unlike in the past societies are not likely to collapse in isolation from others (as Easter Island did). On the one hand, globalization can be a cause of optimism in the sense that other parts of the world will be alerted to dangers elsewhere long before the dangers are critical to them. Those in other parts of the world can, therefore, act to ward off or reduce the problem and help their societies avoid collapse. On the other hand, global interconnectedness means that ecological problems in one part of the world are likely to affect others, perhaps the entire planet. Thus, profligate use of fossil fuels (especially oil) by the US has played a huge role in the global warming that is threatening large portions of the globe. Similarly, the emergence of China as an economic superpower means that it will soon supplant the US in the dubious position of being the leading contributor to global warming and therefore as a threat to the ecology of the world. The nature of the problem makes it impossible for significant ecological problems, including collapse, to be isolated to one locale in the global age.

THE LEADING ENVIRONMENTAL PROBLEMS

Diamond does a good job of enumerating today's leading global environmental problems. Most, if not all, of them are global in the sense that many of them flow readily around the world and there are few barriers to those flows. His list, with some additions, will be used to orient the discussion in this section of this chapter.

Destruction of Natural Habitats

This involves, according to Diamond, the destruction, or conversion into human habitats, of natural habitats such as the "forests, wetlands, coral reefs, and the ocean bottom" (Diamond 2006: 487). In fact, deforestation was a, or perhaps the, major factor in the collapse of the past societies analyzed by Diamond. Today, the most notable deforestation in the world is taking place in the Amazon rainforest (mostly in Brazil) (*Economist* 2008: June 5), but other parts of the world are also destroying/ losing their forests. The Amazon forest is being decimated to allow the area to be "developed" (to create farms and areas for livestock to graze) and for the creation of more human settlements. What is different about Brazil today is that its forest is so huge and it plays such a large role in the global ecology, that its destruction will have negative effects on the world as a whole. For example, the burning of all of those felled trees releases large amounts of carbon dioxide that flow around the globe, contributing to global warming. The loss of the forest leads to other problems for humans including the loss of timber and other raw materials. It is also of great concern, especially in the areas undergoing deforestation, because forests "provide us with so-called ecosystem services such as protecting our watersheds, protecting soil against erosion, constituting essential steps in the water cycle that generates much of our rainfall, and providing habitat for most terrestrial plant and animal species" (Diamond 2006: 487). The loss or decline of the other natural habitats (wetlands, coral reefs, the ocean bottom) will also have a variety of negative consequences for life on earth. For example, the decline of coral reefs (due, for example, to runoffs from agriculture) adversely affects the sea life that exists in and around them.

Decline of Fish

A large fraction of the protein consumed by humans comes from fish and, to a lesser extent, shellfish. However, many fishing areas (e.g. the Mediterranean) are in decline or have collapsed. Without seafood, more people would need to rely on meat for protein and livestock can only be reared at great cost, and with great damage to the environment. Aquaculture is not an adequate replacement for the loss of natural fishing areas because it causes a series of ecological and other problems (Goldburg 2008: 183–94).

Marine life in the world's oceans has been greatly diminished by over-fishing. According to the United Nations Food and Agricultural Organization, 69 percent of the world's most important fisheries can be considered either "fully exploited" or "overexploited" (Khatchadourian 2007: 69). An early twenty-first-century study concluded that industrial fishing had led to a 90 percent decline in large predatory fish such as swordfish, tuna, and marlin. In 2007, over one hundred scientists signed a letter to the WTO saying that unless subsidies to the fishing sector were scaled back: "There are only decades before the damage we have inflicted on the oceans becomes permanent" (quoted in Khatchadourian 2007: 69).

A major culprit in the decimation of marine life is industrial fishing. As the amount of sea life declines, the techniques involved compensate by becoming that much more industrialized and intensive. Drift nets were in use until 1992 when they were banned on the high seas by the UN. They were "free-floating veils of monofilament webbing that can be as long as twenty-five miles … at the peak of their use in the eighties, there was enough drift netting in the ocean on any given day to encircle the planet, if measured end to end" (Khatchadourian 2007: 68). Clearly, such a technology was capable of ensnaring innumerable forms of marine life, some wanted, others unwanted – with the latter unceremoniously discarded into the sea. Bottom trawling continues and it "involves raking the ocean floor for food on a large scale." Not only does this contribute to over-fishing, but it destroys complex ecosystems in the process (Khatchadourian 2007: 68). Longlines are what they sound like and can employ thousands of hooks at a time. They, too, catch lots of unwanted fish that are discarded. In fact, over 20 percent of the fish hauled out of American waters – over a million tons – is discarded as bycatch. One of the worst examples of bycatch occurs as a result of the use of bottom trawling in the harvesting of shrimp in the Gulf of Mexico. That method leads to over 80 percent bycatch. Furthermore, innumerable plants and corals are uprooted, caught in the trawling and destroyed in the process.

Decline in Fresh Water

Water is becoming an increasingly important global issue, or rather it raises a number of different issues (Conca 2006). Among the concerns are water pollution (with one result being water-borne diseases), flooding (especially as a result of global warming), the increasing scarcity of water, the need to choose between water (to drink) and the crops (food) that can be produced with it (Martin 2008: A1, A8), and the possibility that the flow of water could slow or stop completely, at least in some locales. This last concern involves "desertification" (Glantz 1977) or the decline in the water supply as a result of the degradation and deterioration of soil and vegetation. Indeed, because of the latter, water, once considered a public good, is increasingly becoming a valuable and privatized commodity as many places run low on, and in some cases begin to run out of, drinkable water. (Much water – perhaps two-thirds of all water used for irrigation, and as much as half of city water supplies – is simply wasted, due, among other things, to leaky pipes.) There is likely to be an increase in the number, and an escalation of the actions, of social movements involved in efforts to deal with various issues that relate to water.

While we usually think of water as abundant and readily accessible, the fact is that about "1.3 billion people currently lack reliable access to safe drinking water; a staggering 2.6 billion lack adequate sanitation systems, putting whatever local water supplies they do have at great risk" (Conca 2007: 1245–50). The poorest areas of the globe (largely in the South), and the poorest people within those areas, especially children and women, experience a disproportionate share of water-related problems. The situation is apt to grow worse in coming years with the possibility that as much as half the world's population will be faced with water security problems by the 2030s.

Fresh water ecosystems (rivers, lakes, wetlands, etc.) are under increasing stress (from dams, pollution, etc.), as are the invaluable services they provide, "including controlling floods, filtering water supplies, diluting pollutants, cycling sediments and critical nutrients, and providing rich storehouses of biodiversity" (Conca 2007: 1246).

A less visible water problem involves international trade, especially in agricultural and industrial products. For example, when Japan buys crops (which are water-intensive) produced in the US, pressure is put on American water supplies. In other words, Japanese consumers (to use just one example) contribute to the "mining of aquifers and emptying of rivers in North America" (Hoekstra and Chapagain 2008: 1). Without realizing it, people throughout the world are using water from elsewhere in the world ("virtual water"). If they do not realize they are using (or abusing) it, how can they do anything about it?

Astounding quantities of water can be used to produce commodities consumed as far away as half way around the world. For example, according to one estimate, it takes about 140 liters of rainwater to produce enough coffee beans to make one cup of coffee! We begin to get a sense of the magnitude of the water problem produced by the consumption of "virtual water" when we multiply that level of water consumption by the many cups of coffee, to say nothing of all the other commodities, that people consume on a daily basis throughout the world (Hoekstra and Chapagain 2008: 7).

Global climate change will make some parts of the world wetter, but other parts will grow drier (as a general rule, already wet areas will grow wetter, already dry areas drier; both floods and droughts will intensify), and it is in the latter that we are likely to see increasingly desperate and expensive efforts to find water (e.g. by drilling ever-deeper in the earth for underground water supplies) (Struck 2007b: A8). Among the areas likely to grow drier are southern Europe (in May, 2008, Barcelona became the first major city in the world to begin bringing in large amounts of water by ship to help deal with a long-term drought and a precipitous drop in water resources), the Middle East, South Australia, Patagonia, and the southwestern US. There are predictions of a dust-bowl-like situation in the American southwest and the resulting possibility of mass migrations. A similar situation, with potentially even more dire implications, is forecast for Mexico where similar conditions will lead to mass migrations to Mexican cities *and* to still more, likely illegal, migration to the US. Such an increase threatens to create even greater problems and animosities than already exist in the US as a result of legal, and especially illegal, immigration from Mexico. In more general terms, we are increasingly likely to see the emergence of an entirely new group of people in the world, *climate refugees*.

Another water-related problem is the melting, due to global warming, of mountain-top glaciers which are an important source of the flow of drinking water to many people in the world. As those glaciers melt and fail to re-form fully, they will produce less and less water for those below them who need the water to survive. The affected populations, too, are likely to become climate refugees and they are likely to come into conflict with residents of the still water-rich areas to which they are likely to move. Furthermore, various areas and countries around the world are already trading threats over common or disputed water supplies (as are various areas within countries; in the US – Georgia vs. Florida, and the states in the southwestern US, to take two examples). We will likely see more barriers erected by territories interested in retaining their water supplies and preventing their flow to neighboring territories. Tensions will increase in the future leading, perhaps, to open national and global warfare over water!

The paradox of bottled water

Water is becoming an increasingly important global commodity as many places run low on, and in some cases begin to run out of, drinkable water. At the same time, there has been an enormous growth in the global distribution and sale of bottled water; bottled water has become a global commodity commanding relatively high prices. However, it is too expensive for the poorest people in the world who may be most in need as a result of the decline in available water supplies. Sales of bottled water are most likely to thrive in the relatively well-off areas of the world where there is still plenty of drinkable water freely available. But instead of using this inexpensive and accessible water, increasing numbers of people, especially in the North, are buying bottled water, which is sometimes shipped in, at great cost and with profoundly negative effects on the environment, from distant locales. All sorts of environmental problems are related to, for example, the great use of fuel by airplanes and ships that transport the bottled water.

One of the most outrageous examples of this is Fiji Water, with $150 million in sales per year. The water is produced and bottled in Fiji in the South Pacific and transported thousands of miles to places like New York and London. Aware of the danger it poses to the environment, Fiji Water has announced plans to use renewable energy (it plans to build a windmill to power its bottling plant), preserve forests, and cut its carbon footprint by, for example, shipping its bottles of water by sea to the East Coast of the US rather than by truck from Los Angeles (after it gets there by ship). Of course, this says nothing about the environmental cost of shipping to Los Angeles or to the East Coast. In spite of actions like these, the executive director of the Rainforest Action Network said: "Bottled water is a business that is fundamentally, inherently and inalterably unconscionable. ... No side deals to protect forests or combat global warming can offset that reality" (Deutsch 2007: C3).

Toxic Chemicals

Various industries, especially the chemical industry, "manufacture or release into the air, soil, oceans, lakes, and rivers many toxic chemicals" (Diamond 2006: 491). Among the culprits are "insecticides, pesticides, and herbicides ... mercury and other metals, fire-retardant chemicals, refrigerator coolants, detergents, and components of plastics" (Diamond 2006: 491). All of these have a variety of immediate, and more usually long-term, negative effects on humans and other forms of life.

There is, for example, the issue of persistent organic pollutants (POPs), which are highly toxic, human-made chemicals. Among these are polychlorinated biphenyls (PCBs), once used as coolants, and various pesticides (especially DDT, dichlorodiphenyltrichloroethnane) (Dinham 1993, 2007: 955–7). POPs have four characteristics in common – they are highly toxic; they are persistent, remaining in the environment for years before breaking down and becoming less harmful; they can travel great distances (thus, what is locally produced and may create local problems can easily become a global problem – for example, the role of PCBs in the decline of the ozone layer and the relationship of that to global health problems resulting from increased exposure to ultraviolet radiation); and the "impact of POPs can be magnified through processes of bioaccumulation and biomagnification, in which their concentrations build up along food chains."

Greenhouse Gases and Global Warming

Humans have produced gases that have damaged the atmosphere. Now-banned refrigerator coolants damaged the protective ozone layer and served as greenhouse gases that absorbed sunlight and contributed to global warming. Great concern these days is focused on the emission of carbon dioxide and the role it plays in global warming.

Several of the more specific problems enumerated by Diamond involve the general environmental problem of global warming. There is little or no doubt any longer, at least among scientists, that global warming is a real phenomenon with man-made causes, most notably the huge increase in greenhouse gases. Furthermore, the predominant view is that global warming is already well-advanced and is moving ahead rapidly.

However, there are still a few scientists and many lay dissenters who adhere to the view that the global warming and resulting climate changes that are now occurring are not the result of human actions but simply part of a natural cycle. Further, they argue that we will soon return to the cold part of the cycle when, for example, much of the ice in the Arctic and Antarctica will refreeze, as will the glaciers atop the world's highest mountains. The dissenters' view seemed to be supported by an unusually cold winter in both hemispheres in 2007–8. There were even signs of some refreezing of the Arctic sea ice. However, that new ice is quite thin in comparison to the ice that had accumulated previously and that had melted in the last few decades. Most scientists were unimpressed by the recent cold weather and saw it as little more than a brief respite from the continuing progress of global warming (Revkin 2008: 14).

As a result of global warming, various changes (e.g. the melting of Greenland's ice) are occurring so rapidly that geographers are re-thinking their sense of the globe's geographic parameters. That is, as the ice melts, aspects of the landmass of Greenland (to take one example) are being revealed that could never be seen before because they were covered in ice. Thus, for example, tracts of land are being uncovered that were previously thought to be sea (and vice versa) and islands have been revealed for the first time as a result of the melting of surrounding icebergs.

Rising seas

The big factor in the degree to which the seas will rise as a result of global warming is the degree and rapidity with which the huge ice sheets that cover Greenland, the Arctic, and Antarctica will melt (Struck 2007a). It seems clear that ice sheets throughout the world are melting far more rapidly than was previously believed possible. This has potentially dire consequences because the melting of land-based ice, unlike the melting of icebergs, raises the level of the sea. If all of the ice on Greenland *alone* was to melt, global sea levels would rise 23 feet; another 17-foot rise would be associated with similar disintegration in Antarctica. Such a rise would be a global catastrophe leading to the end of life on many islands and in coastal civilization throughout the world. With the sea level likely to rise much more rapidly than was previously believed, vulnerable areas around the world near, at, or below sea level are likely to be swamped much sooner than was previously forecast (Rudolph 2007: D1, D4).

Scientists know that the ice, not only in Greenland, but elsewhere, is melting and that the melt will accelerate as global temperatures rise and that this will lead to a rise in the sea levels. However, it is difficult to find much agreement among scientists beyond that. For example, the Intergovernmental Panel on Climate Change estimated in 2007 that there was a 50–50 probability that by the end of the twenty-first century temperatures would increase by between 1.8 and 7.2 degrees Fahrenheit and that the sea level, as a result, would rise by between 7.8 inches and two feet (Eilperin 2007: A6). Indeed, temperatures have already been rising by 0.2 degrees Fahrenheit every decade (Fahrenthold 2007: A7). However, the consensus among scientists is that they are unable to predict sea levels, with the result that they (and we) will need to be content to simply measure the increase in sea levels as it happens, giving the world far less lead time to act to prevent it (if possible), reduce it, or reduce its impact (e.g. 60 million people are predicted to become refugees with only a 3-foot rise in the sea level).

Global warming and health

Global warming is expected to adversely affect health in a number of different ways (Brown 2007: A7). Global warming will bring with it more, and more intense, heat waves, and excessive heat can be deadly. A heat wave in Europe in 2003, the worst in almost 500 years, caused about 30,000 deaths from heat-related illnesses. The aging of the population throughout much of the developed world makes more people vulnerable to becoming ill and dying due to excessive heat. Increasing urbanization also increases the likelihood of death since cities become "heat islands." Death from excessive heat is also more likely among the very young, those who are ill, the poor, and those who lack the ability to move away from super-heated areas. However, there are steps that can be taken to mitigate the dangers of heat stress, such as more use of air conditioning (although many people in the world have no access to it or cannot afford it; furthermore it causes other problems such as great demand on energy sources), greater awareness of the dangers associated with excessive heat, and better medical treatment of those afflicted with heat stress. Of course, those in the North are much more likely to be able to avail themselves of these mechanisms.

More severe storms will lead to more deaths, especially from increased flooding due to the storms (e.g. the massive death toll in Myanmar as a result of a typhoon, especially its storm surge, in May, 2008). The residents of coastal areas are in particular danger due to storm surges. Extreme variations in weather may lead to more droughts and shortages of water. Food production may not increase as rapidly as expected, with the result that the long-term decline in the number of the world's hungry will slow.

Increased heat will speed up chemical reactions and pollution from ozone and soot will be made worse. Deaths from ozone pollution (mostly among those with lung or heart problems) could rise by 5 percent by 2050. Pollen production could increase, adversely affecting those with asthma and other allergies.

Water-borne diseases (e.g. cholera) will increase with higher temperatures and more torrential rains. Food-borne infections (e.g. salmonella) will also increase with hotter weather.

Diseases caused by animals and insects may increase, although there is less certainty on this than on the other health issues discussed above. For example, it is expected that there will be an increase in malaria and dengue borne by mosquitoes. Exposure to malaria is expected to increase by 25 percent in Africa by 2100. However, here, as elsewhere, actions can be taken to mitigate the problem, such as controlling the mosquito population with pesticides (although these pose many other hazards [Carson 1962]), greater use of bed nets (especially by pregnant women and children), and better medical care. Other diseases of this type that are likely to become more prevalent are "yellow fever (also carried by mosquitoes), schistosomiasis (by snails), leishmaniasis (sand flies) and Lyme disease (ticks)" (Brown 2007: A7).

Population Growth

Significant population growth, especially in the South (populations will remain stable or decline in much of the North), will exacerbate the kinds of ecological problems discussed above and produce new ones.

In terms of the latter, it is not sheer numbers themselves that matter, or matter most, but rather what the population consumes, and there are huge variations around the world in consumption (see Chapter 4) (Diamond 2008: A19). The roughly one billion people who live in the developed countries, especially the 300 million or so in the United States, have a per capita consumption rate of 32, while it is much less in the less developed world, with many countries located there (e.g. Kenya) approaching a rate of 1, or *32 times less* than that in the US. Thus, from an ecological point of view, the greatest problems are produced by those nations (especially the US) with both the largest populations *and* the highest consumption rates.

The latter also points to the looming increase in ecological problems traceable to the booming populations and economies of India and especially China (its 1.3 billion people give it a larger population than the developed world). Their consumption rates still rank far below those in the developed world, but clearly they are increasing rapidly. Enormous strain would be placed on the resources and the ecology of the planet, should (as seems likely) China's consumption rate (and that of India) approach that of the developed countries. Of course, this could be compensated for by a decline in the consumption rate in the developed world (perhaps inevitable with the ongoing global redistribution of wealth), as well by various conservation efforts. The latter would not be too painful in those countries since it would mainly focus on the many wasteful aspects of consumption (e.g. reduction in at least the excessive rate of growth of oil, forest, and fish consumption).

The Global Flow of Dangerous Debris

All parts of the world produce detritus that is dangerous, or at least potentially so. Examples of concern here include "e-waste" such as discarded television sets, computers, printers, cell phones, and so on. However, it is the highly developed Northern countries that produce a disproportionate amount of such debris. Once products have outlived their usefulness (or even long before that) and are reduced to detritus, the developed nations want no more to do with them. They seek to send much of the detritus to less developed countries which, for their part, are anxious to receive the debris since it can be transformed into work, jobs, and profits. Very often the debris that is unloaded on these countries has components and elements (gold, silver, copper) that are of value. However, they are difficult and time-consuming to extract. The poorly paid workers of less developed countries are ideal for this unskilled work. Few in the developed world want to do this work, especially for the pay those in the less developed world receive.

Furthermore, many of the things that are found in e-waste are dangerous. For example, a cell phone contains about 200 chemical compounds and it is not clear which are hazardous and which are not. When workers in developing countries dismantle, burn, or pour acids on cell phones, it is unclear what toxic chemicals are released and how they are affected by the processes that release them. What is clear is that there are many toxic elements involved and it is the workers in less developed countries who are being exposed to them. Furthermore, the population as a whole in those areas is being endangered since what remains after the valuable e-waste is removed is often carelessly discarded to poison the land, crops, and so on.

One of the roots of this problem is the fact that those in developed countries are discarding electronics of all sorts long before the equipment has exhausted its useful life. Thus, for example, people buy new cell phones – and discard old ones (often, at least initially, by just dumping them in a drawer at home) – not because the old ones have ceased functioning, but because they like the color, design, or additional functions of new ones. Thus, much e-waste is unnecessary. Furthermore, many of the older phones could be recycled, but few people have any interest in doing what is necessary to recycle old phones (Mooallem 2008: 38–43).

GLOBAL RESPONSES

Many global environmental problems, especially global warming, are traceable to economic development. That is, as economies grow larger and more successful they are likely to do increasing damage to the environment in, for example, the ways in which they produce things (factories that pollute) and what they produce (automobiles that pollute still further). As concerned as nation-states are becoming about damage to the environment, they are not about to either give up the fruits of development or cease seeking to become more developed. This leads to the important concept of sustainable development (Borghesi and Vercelli 2008; Dietsch and Philpott 2008: 247–58; Kasa 2008: 151–63; Linton 2008: 231–45; Park, Conca, and Finger 2008).

Sustainable Development

The origin of this concept is a 1987 report to the UN by the World Commission on Environment and Development, entitled "Our Common Future." In the view of the authors of the report, **sustainable development** (which should apply to all countries) involves economic and environmental changes that meet the needs of the present, especially of the world's poor, without jeopardizing the needs of the future. While the focus of sustainable development is on physical sustainability, there must also be a concern for equity within the current generation and for future generations.

> **Sustainable development**: Economic and environmental changes that meet the needs of the present without jeopardizing the future.

A key event in the history of global environmentalism, indeed of globalization, was the 1992 meeting in Rio de Janeiro, Brazil, labeled the "Earth Summit," but formally titled the United Nations Conference on Environment and Development (Najam 2007: 345–7). It is known for legitimizing and advancing the concept of sustainable development.

While "sustainable development" was focused on the environment (although not exclusively, given the concern for economic development), the term has come to be used much more broadly, even indiscriminately, to include "using renewable energy and farming organically to increasing local self-sufficiency and undertaking radical political decentralization" (LeLe 2007: 1103).

Globalization can be seen as either a threat or a boon to sustainability. As a threat, globalization can be seen as leading to unsustainable development by "undermining of the regulatory capacities of nation-states and local communities, and the depletion of biological and social diversity in favor of an overconsuming and culturally homogenized lifestyle" (LeLe 2007: 1103). Globalization can aid sustainable development through the "enhanced penetration of markets, diffusion of modern technologies, and globalization of standards," which, in turn, lead to "enhanced efficiency of resource use and demand for cleaner environments" (LeLe 2007: 1103).

While virtually everyone today would be in favor of sustainable development, there are at least three key issues involved in such a notion. The first is the difficulty involved in developing reliable projections about what is likely to happen to an ecosystem in the future. Second, should we simply seek to maintain the current ecosystem (e.g. the rainforests), or can we rely on advances in knowledge and production to compensate, perhaps more than compensate, for what is lost as a result of declines in the ecosystem? The third, and biggest, debate is over the causes of the current unsustainability of our ecosystem. The main difference is between those who argue that the main cause is population growth and those who contend that it is high levels of production and consumption (Dauvergne 2008) in developed countries (as well as China and India). Overall, there is a strong relationship in the debate over sustainability between the environment and economic development. The issue, of course, is whether economic development is possible without causing substantial, if not overwhelming, damage to the environment.

There are a number of dimensions to the relationship between globalization and sustainability. First, there is the *economic* dimension and the issue of whether economic development irretrievably destroys the environment or whether with economic development comes the desire and the ability to better control the factors that are adversely affecting the environment. Second, *technology* can be seen as both producing environmental degradation and creating the possibility (e.g. through dissemination of information about environmental problems and their causes via the mass media or the global spread of green technologies) of limiting the damage. Third, there is the dimension of *awareness* and whether the global media have led to greater awareness of environmental problems and their causes, or whether consumerism, also pushed by the global media, increases people's blindness to these issues. Finally, there is the *politics* of environmentalism, with some global organizations (e.g. the WTO) pushing for more economic growth, while many others (environmental INGOs such as Greenpeace) are seeking to reduce it or to limit its negative impact on the environment. Overall, then, "[w]hile many elements of globalization are clearly detrimental to already fragile efforts at environmental protection, there are those who believe that the economic benefits resulting from globalization will increase societal capacity to deal with environmental problems" (LeLe 2007: 1106).

Dealing with Climate Change

In spite of mounting evidence that fossil fuels are the major factor in global warming, many major corporations and some governments, especially in the US (Armitage 2005: 417–27), have resisted taking action to limit fossil-fuel emissions.

Take, for example, the 1997 Kyoto Protocol, a major effort to deal with climate change due to carbon emissions. Ratifying nations would have been required by 2012 to reduce their emissions to 5 percent below what they were in 1990. The agreement created ceilings for the carbon emissions of developed countries, but none for developing countries, especially China and India. Many nations ratified the Kyoto Protocol, but it required that countries that were responsible for a total of 55 percent of the emissions be signatories; it did not reach the required percentage. Especially notable is the fact that the US did not ratify the Kyoto Protocol and in 2001 it was finally rejected by President George W. Bush. Arguments against the treaty were that it was based on questionable science, that it would hurt the American economy, and that it was not fair and would not be successful because the rapidly developing nations, especially China (and India), were not restricted in terms of their emissions. In spite of the failure to ratify the Kyoto Protocol, many believe that something like it will need to be negotiated (Zedillo 2008). After all, the evidence on global climate change, especially global warming, seems even clearer and stronger today than it did in the late 1990s.

There are signs that the reluctance of developed nations, especially the US, and their political and corporate leaders, is giving way to the increasingly clear reality that global warming is here and its adverse effects are already being felt. In early 2007 ten large corporations joined many environmental groups and called for "federal law to slow, stop and reverse the growth" of global-warming emissions "over the shortest period of time reasonably achievable" (Ball 2007: A1, A17). At the same time, President Bush, as we saw above, no friend of the environment, called for a greater effort to find low-emission alternatives to gasoline. He announced a goal of cutting US gasoline consumption by 20 percent over the next ten years and, more importantly, he publicly acknowledged "the serious challenge of global climate change," and the need to deal with the fact that the US is "addicted to oil" (Sanger and Rutenberg 2007: A1 [and A14]; Andrews and Barringer 2007: A14). Critics, however, argued that this does not go nearly far enough and, for example, does not deal with the energy from electric power plants (they produce 40 percent of these emissions) and other "smokestack industries." The President of the National Environmental Trust pointed out that even with the suggested cuts, carbon emissions would *increase* by 14 percent in the next decade.

Of course, a cynic might wonder what took corporate leaders and politicians so long to realize what was abundantly obvious not only to scientists but to increasing numbers of laypeople. Furthermore, there is the suspicion that, sensing that change was coming, corporations simply acted so that they would be included in the deliberations and could limit the costs to them. In many cases, it appears that corporations are jumping on the ecological bandwagon largely because it is good public relations (this is known as "greenwashing"). Furthermore, some of these corporations sense that there is money to be made in clean-energy technologies and they want a piece of the action. For example, some corporations have invested heavily in wind, hydroelectric, and nuclear power and they would gain business if there are cuts in those power sources that emit large amounts of carbon dioxide (Strassel 2007: A10). Furthermore, various industries are jockeying for position in order to force others to absorb the costs associated with change. For example, the auto industry wants the oil industry to produce more low-carbon alternatives, and the oil industry, for its part, wants the auto industry to produce more efficient automobiles.

In spite of the beginning of momentum in the direction of corporate concern about global warming, the majority of chief executives surveyed, especially in the US, were neither "somewhat" nor "extremely concerned" about it. Concern about global warming was highest in Japan, with 70 percent of executives expressing concern; in Europe it was German executives who were most likely to express concern; but only 18 percent of US executives manifested such a concern. This figure was considerably below the overall average for all countries surveyed, of 40 percent (Norris 2007: B3).

While the US wants to see developing countries, especially China (and India), limit their emissions, China (and other developing countries) tends to take the view that many of today's problems are a result of what the developed countries have done, and are doing, to the environment. Furthermore, it is China's view that it is now its time to develop, to catch up, and in order to do so, it must both industrialize further and develop more of a consumer society (including many more highly polluting private automobiles). The result, of course, would be a great increase in both China's absolute and relative contribution to global pollution. Indeed, China is already the second largest producer of greenhouse gases. This is largely traceable to China's extremely rapid industrial development and the fact that almost 70 percent of the nation's energy comes from coal-fired power plants, many with poor and outmoded devices to limit pollution. Furthermore, everyone agrees that in the not-too-distant future China will supplant the US as the world's worst emitter of greenhouse gases. Thus, the US wants to see limits on China before it reaches this point, but for its part, China is determined to develop economically (Yardley 2007: A9).

Carbon Tax

A more recent proposal for helping to reduce the emission of greenhouse gases is the carbon tax. Businesses would pay a tax based on the amount of their carbon emissions from the use of fossil fuels (e.g. oil, coal, and natural gas). The idea is that the economic costs involved in paying the tax would motivate them to modify their production processes in order to reduce emissions and therefore the taxes they would need to pay. The ideal scheme would be a global carbon tax so that all nations of the world would participate. Clearly, the effectiveness of the system would be reduced if some areas of the world participated and others did not. However, the participation of any nations, especially major polluters such as the US and China, would help to reduce global carbon emissions and thereby ultimately global warming.

Carbon Neutral

The difficulty of actually reducing carbon emissions is reflected in the case of Norway which announced in 2007 that it would be "carbon neutral" by 2050. That is, it would generate no *net* greenhouse gases into the atmosphere by that date. By early 2008 the Norwegian government announced that the date for carbon neutrality had been moved forward two decades to a startling 2030. However, it turns out that these gains are the result not so much of reducing carbon emissions in Norway, but of canceling them out by, for example, "planting trees or cleaning up a polluting factory in a country far away" (Rosenthal 2008a: A6). This kind of accounting sleight of hand is allowable under the environmental accounting policy of the UN. Even with its limitations, Norway's method of dealing with carbon emissions is costly, and few other nations can afford it (Norway is awash with oil income). More importantly, it is not sustainable since there are just not enough trees to plant and factories to clean up in the less developed world to compensate for carbon emissions in developed (and some developing) countries. Critics of Norway and other countries engaging in these practices argue that they conceal the fact that much more needs to be done at home to cut carbon emissions (e.g. cutbacks in heavy industries).

Alternate Fuels and Power Sources

The global problems associated with the extraordinary use, especially in the US, of gasoline to power automobiles have finally led to the beginnings of a serious effort to find alternatives to it, especially in the US, the world leader in automobile and gasoline use.

Hybrid technology

One development of note is the increasing importance of hybrid automobiles that derive at least part of their power from electricity. Then there is an all-electric car that, in order to be re-energized, would simply be plugged into an electrical outlet (*Economist* 2008: June 19). With future sources of oil dwindling, demand rising, and growing concern about global warming, we will see more and more efforts to create alternatives to the gasoline-powered automobile.

Ethanol

There is also growing interest in alternative fuels to gasoline, with the greatest attention these days focused on ethanol (Barrionuevo 2007: C1). The US is a large and growing producer of ethanol, but it trails Brazil in both production and use (40 percent of Brazil's non-diesel gasoline consumption is ethanol and 70 percent of new automobiles sold in Brazil can use either gasoline or ethanol [Reel 2007: A14]). The major current source of ethanol is corn, but it can be made from other agricultural products (e.g. cellulosic sources such as switchgrass or wood chips). Ethanol, however, is a third less efficient than gasoline and in the US a federal subsidy of 51 cents a gallon is required to make it competitive with gasoline.

While ethanol promises to help with various global problems – dependence on oil produced and controlled elsewhere in the world, a reduction in carbon dioxide emissions – it creates other problems. First, the growing interest in ethanol has already driven up corn prices and this threatens American exports of corn to many parts of the world. Second, it is also a threat in other parts of the world, such as Mexico, where there is great reliance on corn for food staples like tortillas. Because of globalization, Mexico has grown increasingly reliant on American corn and is therefore directly affected by the increase in price. Furthermore, because there is a global market for corn, the price of Mexican corn has risen as well.

Ethanol has become a global political football. For example, the US is seeking to forge a partnership with Brazil on ethanol. This is deemed important in terms of reducing US dependence on gasoline, but it is also a result of the US effort to counter the growing power of Hugo Chávez and oil-rich Venezuela in Latin America (Reel 2007: A14). (With the recent discovery of a potentially huge new oil field in Brazil, it remains to be seen how long its interest in ethanol will be sustained.)

Interestingly, in one of many actions that contradict its neo-liberal orientation to free trade, the US levies a 54-cent-a-gallon tariff on most ethanol imported into the country. This serves to protect American corn growers, and to punish those in other countries, especially Brazil. There is hope that in the long run the talks between Brazil and the US will lead to a reduction or elimination of those tariffs.

However, concern has surfaced recently that biofuels such as ethanol may exacerbate the problem of greenhouse gas emissions rather than reduce them. While biofuels on their own produce fewer such emissions than fossil fuels, they cause *more* when we adopt a broader view. It has been known for quite some time that the refining and transportation of these fuels produce carbon emissions. What is new is the realization that in order to produce biofuels, rainforests, grasslands, and other natural ecosystems are reduced or destroyed and that the burning or plowing of those systems releases greenhouse gases. Further, the problem is exacerbated because natural ecosystems act like sponges in absorbing carbon emissions, and the cropland that replaces these natural systems absorbs much less carbon.

The global reverberations associated with producing biofuels can eventually be immense. Already, as the US devotes more farm land to producing corn, countries like Brazil are responding by producing more soybeans to compensate for the decline in American production of that crop. This leads to more deforestation in

Brazil to create new farm land and that, in turn, leads as we saw above to more carbon emissions and less ability to absorb them. Sugar cane seems to offer some hope because it requires little energy to grow and it can easily be made into fuel. A better possibility would be agricultural waste products because they would not require more farm land in order to produce fuel (Rosenthal 2008b: A9).

Other problems associated with ethanol are becoming increasingly clear. For example, as more land is devoted to the crops needed to produce it, less is devoted to growing food. This serves to increase food prices not only for Mexico and its corn, but around the world. Another problem is that factories that produce ethanol use huge amounts of water and, as is discussed above, water is itself an increasingly endangered resource (*Economist* 2008: February 28).

Solar power

A better alternative source of energy is solar power. One of its attractions is that it produces no greenhouse gases. Another, especially in warmer climes, is that it produces its maximum energy just when it is needed. That is, it produces the most energy on hot, sunny days and those are the times of the greatest demand for energy to run air conditioners. Some of the technologies needed to use solar energy are able to store it and are therefore able to operate at night and on cloudy days. Solar power remains more expensive than using fossil fuels, but as the costs of the latter continue to rise (as they must given increasing demand and declining supply) and the costs of the former decline (as technologies improve and economies of scale kick in), we may see more and better use of solar power (*Economist* 2008: February 21).

A Technological Fix?

Talk of increased use of solar power is related to the growing interest these days in a "technological fix" for at least some global environmental problems such as global warming. There is a longstanding attraction to finding technological solutions to all social problems. To many, finding new technologies seems far easier and less painful than the much harder task of getting large numbers of people to change longstanding behaviors. That is, people tend to be loath to change their consumption patterns and thus prefer the hope of technological fixes to the ecological problems they play a large role in causing. Furthermore, many industries have a vested interest in people continuing to consume at high levels. Thus, a major cause of global warming is the ever-increasing burning of fossil fuels, but innumerable industries and people are wedded to it and many people in other parts of the world would dearly like to do more of it. This is especially the case with the use of gasoline in automobiles in highly developed countries, the increasing number of people in countries like China and India who can now afford automobiles, and the large numbers in less developed countries who would dearly love to drive automobiles. In the face of this huge and growing demand, it is unlikely that calls to cut back on gasoline use are going to be heeded (although the Great Recession is forcing people to cut back). Hence the attraction of the search for a technological fix that will solve the problems caused by the burning of gasoline and, more generally, fossil fuels. With such a fix, production and consumption throughout the world can not only continue, but expand further.

Enter "geoengineering" and a series of relatively new proposals for dealing with global ecological problems while leaving untouched and unaddressed the underlying and growing causes of global warming. Among the ideas being discussed are "injecting chemicals into the upper atmosphere to cool the poles, or blocking sunlight by making clouds more reflective or stationing mirrors in space" (Dean 2007: A11). Scientific support for these possibilities has been muted for several reasons: there is fear that talk of such solutions would encourage people to continue, if not increase, their use of fossil fuels; there is great fear that even if some of the proposals do work, they might have a series of unanticipated consequences that will pose as great, or greater, problems than the problems they are designed to help deal with; these innovations in geoengineering are untried, incredibly difficult, and likely to be extraordinarily expensive; and there are many other climate-related problems (e.g. the increasing acidity of the oceans) which would be unaffected by global climate changes produced by such technologies. Undertaking such projects would require truly global efforts and a massively funded global governance structure. The hope here is that already functioning systems of global governance that "regulate the use of radio frequencies, organize air traffic control, track space" (Dean 2007: A11) will be a model for what is needed to deal with global climate problems.

While geoengineering technologies are little more than vague ideas at this point and a long way from anything approaching functionality, a leading expert in the area predicted that within two centuries the earth will be "an artifact," that is, it will be a product of human design and geoengineering. Already underway are efforts to respond to the adverse effects of global warming on agriculture and crops. This involves new aspects of the "green revolution" such as the creation of crops, through selective breeding and genetic engineering, that can survive in warmer climates, that can use increased salinity rather than being destroyed by it, that are not desiccated by droughts, and that can even thrive while submerged under water (Weiss 2007: A6). Less dramatic responses include reducing plowing and tilling (to reduce evaporation and the amount of carbon dioxide released), reducing the amount of fertilizer used (fertilizer produces nitrous oxide which is far more harmful to the atmosphere than carbon dioxide), the planting of shade trees, and the addition of fruit trees better able to survive climate change than subsistence crops.

There is even a "doomsday vault" in a Norwegian mountainside which is being stocked with seeds from around the world. The idea is that in the event of dramatic and unexpected climate changes, we cannot know in advance which seeds will survive and thrive. Even in worst case scenarios, the hope is that some of these seeds stored in the Norwegian vault will be the ones that save humanity from starvation.

Economic Issues

Long-term solutions, and even very short-term solutions, to environmental problems in general, and the problems of climate change in particular, are likely to be hugely, if not monumentally, expensive (Mufson 2007: A1, A9). The kinds of advanced scientific efforts outlined above will cost huge sums just to research, let alone to implement. Even less innovative changes such as more wind turbines, solar panels, reforestation, retooling large industries, building power plants able to recapture carbon dioxide, and, most controversially, lots more nuclear power plants, involve unimaginable costs. Furthermore, these efforts need to be undertaken globally and that would involve many nations without the resources to do much, if anything, about these problems. Even in the highly developed countries, it is not clear that people understand the costs involved in these efforts, let alone being willing to pay for them. This is especially the case in the United States which lags behind Europe in implementing and paying for even the most rudimentary of these changes. Germany, for example, is the European leader in the use of wind and solar power and the US lags far behind in this. And, of course, the ongoing recession makes it even less likely that such massive, and hugely expensive, programs will be undertaken.

Opposing Environmentalism

While it seems like an unmitigated good, it is not unusual for there to be opposition to environmentalism. Most generally those interested in economic development have little patience for environmentalists, especially when environmental concerns slow down, or stop, such development. An interesting example of this involves efforts by the World Wildlife Fund (WWF), beginning in 2003, to create parks and reserves in Brazil in a program known as Amazon Region Protected Areas (Rohter 2007: A4). A great concern there is the limiting of further deforestation. As discussed above, the Amazon has already been deforested to a great degree. The Amazon forest was, and is, important to the world for its innumerable trees that absorb enormous quantities of carbon dioxide. That capacity has declined dramatically and, instead, decaying plant life in the Amazon is contributing heavily to the production of carbon dioxide and therefore to global warming. As of this writing, the area of deforestation in Brazil is larger than New York, Connecticut, and New Jersey *combined*. The goal of the WWF is to protect not only the trees in Brazil but also its biodiversity. However, some businessmen have reacted negatively to this for two basic reasons. First, it is seen as impeding their ability to develop the region and its natural resources and thereby to increase their business and profits. Second, it is seen as, itself, a kind of colonialism and perhaps a precursor to the re-emergence of a more traditional kind of colonialism, in which foreign (especially American) entrepreneurs come in to develop the area, perhaps preceded by the military. The WWF denies such interests and associations and says that it is simply seeking to protect land that the Brazilian government has failed to protect.

CHAPTER SUMMARY

This chapter examines the detrimental impact of negative global flows on the environment. The most developed countries are disproportionately responsible for the current environmental problems. These countries are also better equipped to deal with these problems.

Neo-liberals and environmentalists debate the impact of free trade on the environment. Environmentalists argue that environmental issues should be given priority over economic issues. Free trade, through its emphasis on the expansion of manufacturing, is associated with environmental damage. For their part, neo-liberals see the efforts of the environmentalists as serious impediments to trade. Some seek to integrate these approaches. For instance ecological modernization theory sees globalization as a process that can both protect and enhance the environment.

The relationship between environmental damage and societal collapse is examined in this chapter. It is argued that, unlike in the past, global interconnectedness ensures that damage to nature will not be confined to isolated geographical areas.

A major environmental problem is the destruction of natural habitats, particularly through deforestation. Industrial fishing has contributed to a significant destruction of marine life and ecosystems. Biodiversity and usable farmland have also declined at a rapid pace.

A significant environmental challenge is that of the decline in the availability of fresh water. The decline in the water supply as a result of degradation of the soil, or desertification, has transformed what was once considered a public good into a privatized commodity. The poorest areas of the globe experience a disproportionate share of water-related problems. The problem is further intensified by the consumption of "virtual water," wherein people inadvertently use up water from elsewhere in the world through the consumption of water-intensive products. The destruction of the water ecosystem may lead to the creation of climate refugees, people who are forced to migrate due to lack of access to water or due to flooding.

Pollution through toxic chemicals has had a long-term impact on the environment. The use of persistent organic pollutants (POP) has led to significant industrial pollution. Greenhouse gases, gases that trap sunlight and heat in the earth's atmosphere, contribute greatly to global warming. In turn, this process causes the melting of land-based and glacial ice with potentially catastrophic effects. Apart from the possibility of substantial flooding, global warming causes a reduction in the alkalinity of the oceans as well as the destruction of existing ecosystems. Global warming also poses a threat to the global supply of food as well as to human health.

Population growth and the attendant increase in consumption intensify ecological problems. The global flow of debris is another major concern, with e-waste often being dumped in developing countries.

Degradation of the environment has elicited significant global responses. One approach is that of sustainable development, which seeks to chart a middle path between economic growth and a sustainable environment. The relationship between globalization and sustainability is multi-dimensional – it involves economic, political, and technological aspects.

Various efforts are underway to deal with climate change. However, these are countered by strong resistance on the part of governments and corporations. For instance the Kyoto Protocol, aimed at a reduction of global carbon emissions, failed to take off largely because it was not ratified by the US. However, some momentum is being built up in corporate circles regarding dealing with environmental problems.

There are significant challenges involved in implementing various measures (e.g. carbon tax, carbon neutrality) to deal with environmental problems. It is also difficult to find alternatives to fossil fuels. For instance, the use of ethanol as an alternative to gasoline has an attendant set of problems – it is less efficient and it has led to an escalation in the price of corn (which currently serves as a major source of ethanol). Although biofuels themselves produce lower emissions, their extraction and transport contribute significantly to total emissions.

Previous experience in dealing with environmental issues indicates that a global view of the problem is required. A focus on specific regions, such as Europe, overlooks impacts in other regions. Instead of dealing with the causes of global warming, there is some interest in "technological fixes" such as geoengineering.

DISCUSSION QUESTIONS

1. Outline as many connections as possible among the world's leading environmental problems.

2. Examine the influence of various consumption practices on environmental degradation.

3. Examine the role of global corporations in causing and alleviating environmental problems.

4. Do you think that the world may someday "collapse" because of accelerating environmental problems? Why? Why not?

5. In what ways can global flows positively affect the environment.

6. Analyze the various global responses to environmental degradation.

7. Examine the feasibility of sustainable development as a global project.

FURTHER READING

Zygmunt Bauman. *Liquid Fear*. Cambridge: Polity, 2006.
Jared Diamond. *Collapse: How Societies Choose to Fail or Succeed*. New York: Penguin, 2006.

Arjen Y. Hoekstra and Ashok K. Chapagain. *Globalization of Water: Sharing the Planet's Freshwater Resources*. Malden, MA: Blackwell, 2008.

Rachel Carson. *Silent Spring*. Boston: Houghton Mifflin, 1962.

Ernesto Zedillo, ed. *Global Warming: Looking Beyond Kyoto*. Washington, DC: Brookings, 2008.

Simone Borghesi and Alessandro Vercelli. *Global Sustainability: Social and Environmental Conditions*. New York: Palgrave Macmillan, 2008.

Jacob Park, Ken Conca, and Matthias Finger, eds. *The Crisis of Global Environmental Governance: Towards a New Political Economy of Sustainability*. New York: Routledge, 2008.

REFERENCES ···

Andrews, Edmund L., and Felicity Barringer. 2007. "Bush Seeks Vast, Mandatory Increase in Alternative Fuels and Greater Vehicle Efficiency." *New York Times*. January 24.

Antonio, Robert J. 2007. "The Cultural Construction of Neoliberal Globalization." In George Ritzer, ed., *The Blackwell Companion to Globalization*. Malden, MA: Blackwell.

Armitage, Kevin C. 2005. "State of Denial: The United States and the Politics of Global Warming." *Globalizations* 2, 3.

Ball, Jeffrey. 2007. "In Climate Controversy, Industry Cedes Ground." *Wall Street Journal*. January 23.

Barringer, Felicity. 2008. "US Given Poor Marks on the Environment." *New York Times*. January 23.

Barrionuevo, Alexei. 2007. "Springtime for Ethanol." *New York Times*. January 23.

Bauman, Zygmunt. 2006. *Liquid Fear*. Cambridge: Polity.

Borghesi, Simone, and Alessandro Vercelli. 2008. *Global Sustainability: Social and Environmental Conditions*. New York: Palgrave Macmillan.

Brown, David. 2007. "As Temperatures Rise, Health Could Decline." *Washington Post*. December 17.

Carson, Rachel. 1962. *Silent Spring*. Boston: Houghton Mifflin.

Conca, Ken. 2006. *Governing Water: Contentious Transnational Political and Global Institution Building*. Cambridge, MA: MIT Press.

Conca, Ken. 2007. "Water." In Jan Aart Scholte and Roland Robertson, eds., *Encyclopedia of Globalization*. New York: MTM Publishing.

Dauvergne, Peter. 2008. *Shadows of Consumption: Consequences for the Global Environment*. Cambridge, MA: MIT Press.

Dean, Cornelia. 2007. "Experts Discuss Engineering Feats, Like Space Mirrors, to Slow Climate Change." *New York Times*. November 10.

Deutsch, Claudia H. 2007. "For Fiji Water, a Big List of Green Goals." *New York Times* November 7.

Diamond, Jared. 2006. *Collapse: How Societies Choose to Fail or Succeed*. New York: Penguin.

Diamond, Jared. 2008. "What's Your Consumption Factor?" *New York Times*. January 2.

Dietsch, Thomas V., and Stacy M. Philpott. 2008. "Linking Consumers to Sustainability: Incorporating Science into Eco-friendly Certification." *Globalizations* 5, 2.

Dinham, Barbara. 1993. *The Pesticide Hazard: A Global Health and Environmental Audit*. London: Zed.

Dinham, Barbara. 2007. "Pesticides." In Jan Aart Scholte and Roland Robertson, eds., *Encyclopedia of Globalization*. New York: MTM Publishing.

Economist. 2008. February 21. "The Power of Concentration."

Economist. 2008. February 28. "Ethanol and Water Don't Mix."

Economist. 2008. June 5. "Welcome to Our Shrinking Jungle."

Economist. 2008. June 19. "The End of the Petrolhead."

Eilperin, Julie. 2007. "Clues to Rising Seas Are Hidden in Polar Ice." *Washington Post*. July 16.

Fahrenthold, David. 2007. "Climate Change Brings Risk of More Extinctions." *Washington Post*. September 17.

Glantz, M. 1977. *Desertification*. Boulder, CO: Westview.

Goldburg, Rebecca J. 2008. "Aquaculture, Trade, and Fisheries Linkages: Unexpected Synergies." *Globalizations* 5, 2.

Harvey, David. 2005. *A Brief History of Neoliberalism*. Oxford: Oxford University Press.

Hoekstra, Arjen Y., and Ashok K. Chapagain. 2008. *Globalization of Water: Sharing the Planet's Freshwater Resources*. Malden, MA: Blackwell.

Kasa, Sjur. 2008. "Globalizing Unsustainable Food Consumption: Trade Policies, Producer Lobbies, Consumer Preferences, and Beef Consumption in Northeast Asia." *Globalizations* 5, 2.

Khatchadourian, Raffi. 2007. "Neptune's Navy." *New Yorker*. November 5.

LeLe, Sharachchandra. 2007. "Sustainability." In Jan Aart Scholte and Roland Robertson, eds., *Encyclopedia of Globalization*. New York: MTM Publishing.

Liftin, Karen T. 2007. "Ozone Depletion." In Jan Aart Scholte and Roland Robertson, eds., *Encyclopedia of Globalization*. New York: MTM Publishing.

Linton, April. 2008. "A Niche for Sustainability? Fair Labor and Environmentally Sound Practices in the Specialty Coffee Industry." *Globalizations* 5, 2.

Martin, Andrew. 2008. "Mideast Facing Difficult Choice, Crops or Water." *New York Times*. July 21.

Mooallem, Jon. 2008. "The Afterlife of Cellphones." *New York Times Magazine*. January 13.

Mufson, Steven. 2007. "Climate Change Debate Hinges on Economics." *Washington Post*. July 15.

Munton, Don, and Ken Wilkening. 2007. "Acid Rain." In Jan Aart Scholte and Roland Robertson, eds., *Encyclopedia of Globalization*. New York: MTM Publishing.

Najam, Adil. 2007. "Earth Summit." In Jan Aart Scholte and Roland Robertson, eds., *Encyclopedia of Globalization*. New York: MTM Publishing.

Norris, Floyd. 2007. "Not Much Market for Worry Beads in the Executive Suites." *New York Times*. January 27.

Park, Jacob, Ken Conca, and Matthias Finger, eds. 2008. *The Crisis of Global Environmental Governance: Towards a New Political Economy of Sustainability*. New York: Routledge.

Reel, Monte. 2007. "US Seeks Partnership with Brazil on Ethanol." *Washington Post*. February 8.

Revkin, Andrew C. 2008. "Skeptics on Human Climate Impact Seize on Cold Spell." *New York Times*. March 2.

Rohter, Larry. 2007. "In the Amazon: Conservation or Colonialism?" *New York Times*. July 27.

Rootes, Christopher, ed. 1999. *Environmental Movements: Local, National and Global*. London: Routledge.

Rosenthal, Elisabeth. 2008a. "Lofty Pledge to Cut Emissions Comes with Caveat in Norway." *New York Times*. March 22.

Rosenthal, Elisabeth. 2008b. "Studies Call Biofuels a Greenhouse Threat." *New York Times*. February 8.

Rudolph, John Collins. 2007. "The Warming of Greenland." *New York Times*. January 16.

Sanger, David E., and Jim Rutenberg. 2007. "Bush, Pressing Modest Agenda, Insists US Must Not Fail in Iraq." *New York Times*. January 24.

Stevis, Dimitris. 2005. "The Globalizations of the Environment." *Globalizations* 2, 3.

Strassel, Kimberly A. 2007. "If the Cap Fits." *Wall Street Journal*. January 26.

Struck, Doug. 2007a. "At the Poles, Melting Occurring at Alarming Rate." *Washington Post*. October 22.

Struck, Doug. 2007b. "Warming Will Exacerbate Global Water Conflicts." *Washington Post*. August 20.

Weiss, Rick. 2007. "Facing a Threat to Farming and Food Supply." *Washington Post*. November 19.

World Commission on Environment and Development. 1987. *Our Common Future*. New York: Oxford University Press.

Yardley, Jim. 2007. "China Says Rich Countries Should Take Lead in Global Warming." *New York Times*. February 7.

Yearley, Steve. 2007. "Globalization and the Environment." In George Ritzer, ed., *Blackwell Companion to Globalization*. Malden, MA: Blackwell.

Zedillo, Ernesto, ed. 2008. *Global Warming: Looking Beyond Kyoto*. Washington, DC: Brookings.

Negative Global Flows and Processes

Dangerous Imports, Diseases, Crime, Terrorism, War

Globalization: The Essentials, by George Ritzer
© 2011 John Wiley & Sons Ltd

Chapter 9 on environmental problems began with, and was informed by, Zygmunt Bauman's (2006: 96) concept of negative globalization. That idea is even more relevant to this chapter since Bauman enumerates a number of issues under that heading that will be of concern to us here. While there are many negative flows that could concern us in this chapter, the discussion will be limited to the global flows associated with dangerous imports, borderless diseases, crime, corruption, terrorism, and war.

While we recognize these negative flows, and agree with Bauman on the idea of increasing global liquidity, he goes too far with the idea of negative globalization, or at least farther than we are prepared to go. That is, in his view "ours is a wholly *negative* globalization: unchecked, unsupplemented and uncompensated for by a 'positive' counterpart which is still a distant prospect at best, though according to some prognoses already a forlorn chance" (Bauman 2006: 96). While there are certainly many negative aspects, flows, and processes associated with globalization, we would not accept the view that globalization is wholly negative. A discussion of the problems associated with globalization and of the kind offered in both this chapter and the preceding one should not blind us to its positive side (e.g. the flow of life-saving pharmaceuticals, or of medical personnel to check the outbreak of a new pandemic, and so on).

Another key point is that the issue of what is regarded as positive or negative about globalization often depends on one's perspective and position. Thus, while most of us would agree that terrorism is a negative process, those who are involved in it, and support it, disagree. To take another example, many in the US see neo-liberalism as a good thing, but there is no shortage of others (including Bauman and this author) who see it as creating problems for large parts of the world and therefore, from that perspective, an example of negative globalization. This general orientation applies to the examples of negative globalization discussed throughout this chapter. That is, while many, perhaps most, would agree with this characterization, others would adopt a more positive view toward them.

Finally, it needs to be pointed out that negative globalization does not merely involve negative flows and processes, but also structures whose effects at least some would regard as largely, if not totally, negative. Thus, for those (the vast majority of people in the world) who take a negative view of terrorism, the cellular organization of al-Qaeda would be considered a negative structure; if one thinks of neo-liberalism as a negative global process, then the structures associated with it, such as the IMF and the World Bank, would be seen as negative structures. Of course, as was pointed out early in this book, the distinction between structure and process is, in many ways, a false one. Among the many reasons for this argument is that any structure is made up of a series of processes and those processes are affected by, and affect, a series of larger processes.

It is also worth noting that negative global flows of various kinds lead to global counter-reactions; to global efforts, both processes and structures, to deal with those flows. In terms of processes, one example is the development of increasingly sophisticated, often continuous, global surveillance techniques to deal with, among other things, terrorism (Lyons 2004: 135–49). As to structures, the World Social Forum is the broadest example of a structure created to centralize efforts to deal with the negative flows associated with globalization, especially those associated with neo-liberal globalization.

DANGEROUS IMPORTS

The flow of all sorts of products from every corner of the world has made it near-impossible to know precisely the true nature of the products entering a country (Barrionuevo 2007: B1, B9). Furthermore, products produced locally contain ingredients from many parts of the world. Take the case of Sara Lee's Soft&Smooth Whole Grain White bread which includes the following ingredients (with the nations supplying each indicated): guar gum – India; calcium propitionate – Netherlands; honey – China, Vietnam, Brazil, Uruguay, India, Canada, Mexico, Argentina; flour enrichments – China; beta-carotene – Switzerland; vitamin D3 – China; wheat gluten – France, Poland, Russia, Netherlands, Australia (Schoenfeld 2007: B9).

The greater the use of global ingredients, the greater the difficulty in ensuring that no contaminants find their way into finished products. Further, when finished products include numerous ingredients from many different locales throughout the world, it becomes difficult, if not impossible, to locate the source of the contamination. Thus, if, for example, Sara Lee's bread were to make people sick, there are many potential sources of the contamination. Furthermore, many of the ingredients come from nations whose food safety standards are not likely to equal those in the US and other nations in the North. And, consumers are helpless since food labels are silent on where such ingredients come from (although some labeling on country of origin of fruits and meat began in the US in late 2008). Thus involved here is *both* a global value chain involving the ingredients in various foods *and* the possibility, because the chain is so long and diverse, of the spread of contaminants associated with at least some of them.

Globalization has led to an increase not only in imports of all kinds, but in imports that are dangerous to a nation and its citizens. This issue has gained much notoriety lately in the case of Chinese imports, especially into the US. As the quantity and diversity of products imported from China by the US and many other nations has exploded in the past two decades, and then exploded again, outcries over problems associated with them have increased proportionately. In 2007 there were scandals associated with pet food made in China (poisons in dog food [e.g. melamine, an industrial chemical]) that made pets ill (some pets died from ingesting the food); toys coated with lead paint; and toothpaste made in China that was making people ill; and in 2008, further scandals involving food for humans, especially infants (also laced with melamine).

While we focus on Chinese imports, it is important to remember that many other countries have been, and still are, involved in the global exportation of dangerous products. For example, American companies have exported pharmaceuticals that were banned in the US to other countries. Many Western countries, especially the US, send their decommissioned ships to South Asia to be dismantled. This involves hard, dirty, polluting, and highly dangerous work. The Swiss company Nestlé was guilty of aggressively exporting baby formula to the South, especially Africa, even though it had adverse effects on infants. Among other things, the water needed to mix the formula could well have been contaminated and the formula replaced nutritious breast milk.

BORDERLESS DISEASES

While borderless diseases have become much more common in recent years, they are not a new phenomenon. Diseases such as plague, malaria, tuberculosis (TB), and sexually transmitted infections (STIs) of various types have long spread globally. A specific example of an STI is syphilis which is now spreading mainly throughout a number of less developed countries. However, the roots of the disease were probably in Europe and it was spread by European colonialism and military exploits. In fact, for many, the disease was closely associated with French soldiers and it came to be known in some parts of the world as the "French Disease."

Then there is the increasing prevalence of other borderless diseases, many of them relatively new, such as severe acute respiratory syndrome (SARS), bovine spongiform encephalopathy (BSE) (or "mad cow disease," a disease often found in cattle that can cause a brain disease, Creutzfeldt-Jakob disease, in humans – outbreaks of this disease in cattle in, for example, Great Britain have led to periodic halts in the exportation of beef [Ong 2007: 102–6]), avian flu, Ebola virus, and HIV/AIDS. The nature of these diseases and their spread either in fact (HIV/AIDS [Patton 2002]), or merely (so far) as a frightening possibility (avian flu), tell us a great deal about the nature and reality of globalization in the twenty-first century. The pathogens that cause these diseases flow, or have the potential to flow, readily throughout the globe and it is very difficult, if not impossible, to erect barriers to many, if not any, of them.

In fact, a WHO report issued in August of 2007 argued that new infectious diseases are emerging at an "unprecedented rate" and are being spread globally because of the much greater mobility of people associated with the expansion of all sorts of means of transportation (quoted in Rosenthal 2007b: A9). As a result, the flow of responses to outbreaks of these diseases must be equally global. WHO urged global responses to the increasing likelihood of the spread of various diseases. However, some nations have proven unable or unwilling to be responsive to this global need. For example, China and Vietnam have been unwilling to provide WHO with samples of the avian flu virus that is a serious problem in those countries, at least among birds. WHO needs such samples in order to study the spread of the disease and the ways in which the flu is evolving. Such information can be useful in heading off the further spread of the disease, especially to humans, and in ultimately developing a vaccine to prevent it.

HIV/AIDS

HIV/AIDS spreads in various ways (e.g. blood transfusions), but it is its spread through sexual human contact (as an STI) that is especially relevant in the context of this book (Follér and Thörn 2008). The globalization of the disease is a result of the increasingly heightened flow, or movement, of people throughout much of the world. Unlike the other diseases to be discussed below, HIV/AIDS cannot be contracted through casual contact with people who have the disease. Thus, passengers on an international flight will not contract AIDS simply because they sit next to, or converse with, a fellow passenger with the disease.

The spread of AIDs is closely linked with globalization, especially the increased global mobility associated with tourism (including, and perhaps especially, sex tourism), the greater migration rates of workers, increased legal and illegal immigration, much greater rates of commercial and business travel, the movements (sometimes on a mass basis) of refugees, military interventions and the movement of military personnel, and so on.

People who have the disease can travel great distances over a period of years without knowing they have it and therefore have the ability to transmit the disease to many others in a number of widely scattered locales. Thus, when those with HIV/AIDS have unprotected sexual contact with people in other countries, they are likely to transmit the disease to at least some of them. Similarly, those without the disease can travel to nations where HIV/AIDS is prevalent, contract it, and then bring it back to their home country. In either case, the disease moves from region to region, country to country, and ultimately globally, carried by human vectors.

More and more people, especially in the South, are contracting the disease, but it is initially largely symptom-less. In the early stages of the disease people move freely around their communities, cities, countries, continents, and in some cases the world, carrying it with them. For example, in Africa one well-known way in which the disease has spread across the continent is through truck drivers who work their way from country to country. If they have the disease, they may infect those who live in areas that were previously free of the disease.

In fact, no area of the world has been more devastated by AIDS than Africa (Nolen 2006: A7), with some nations having infection rates approaching 50 percent of the adult population. The disease, as well as the many burdens associated with it, is having an adverse effect on all aspects of social and economic life throughout Africa. Some even predict the failure of at least some African states and their complete economic collapse as a result of the spread of the disease. The economies of many African nations have already contracted as average life expectancy declines and it becomes harder to find healthy adults to perform basic work-related tasks.

The greater prevalence of AIDS in Africa is just one example of the greater vulnerability of the world's have-nots to this and many other borderless diseases. This is not just a question of economic marginality, but also social and political marginality. Compounding the problem is the fact that it is precisely this *most* vulnerable population that is also *least* likely to have access to the high-quality health care and the very expensive drugs that can slow the disease for years, or even decades.

Avian Flu

For over a decade (since the late 1990s), there has been fear of a pandemic of avian flu that, because of globalization, would spread faster and affect (and kill) more people and more parts of the world than the last flu pandemic, the Spanish flu of 1918. It is hard to know exactly how many people were killed worldwide by the Spanish flu pandemic (somewhere between 20 million and more than 100 million), but we do know that about half a million Americans died from the disease; and more than a quarter of the American population were made ill by the disease (Kolata 1999). Whether or not it is caused by avian flu, when the next flu pandemic occurs (and most experts agree that it is a matter of when and not whether it will occur), it seems clear that far more people throughout the world will be made sick and die as a result of it. However, it is also the case, as will be discussed below, that the ability to deal with such a pandemic has been enhanced as a result of globalization (for example, global monitoring and the ability to get health workers and pharmaceuticals rapidly to the site of an outbreak).

As we saw above, HIV/AIDS can only be spread by intimate human contact, but avian flu has the potential, like other strains of flu before it, to spread through casual human contact. At the moment, there is little evidence of human-to-human spread of the virus that causes avian flu. The relatively small number of humans in the world who have gotten the disease, and the even smaller number who have died from it, contracted the disease mainly through direct contact with infected birds. Those in less developed nations are more likely to have such direct contact with birds (some literally live with their birds) since consuming them and their eggs may be central to their food supply and/or may be an important business for them. In contrast, relatively few in the developed world have direct contact with live birds, with the result that they are highly unlikely to contract avian flu.

However, the fear is that the virus that causes avian flu might eventually transform itself into a strain that *can* be spread by casual human contact. (Other viruses have taken this route and caused global human pandemics.) Were this to occur, the increased global mobility of people would lead to a rapid spread of the disease. While there would be efforts to quarantine those who were clearly symptomatic, some would inevitably slip through and bring the disease with them to many areas throughout the world.

As of mid-2010, the feared avian flu pandemic had not occurred, and the nature of the flu appears now to be such that it may never occur. Both the number of confirmed human cases and the number of deaths from avian flu declined in 2007 in comparison to 2006. There were 115 cases in 2006, but only 86 in 2007; 79 deaths in 2006 and just 50 in 2007 (McNeil 2008: D1, D4). While the virus has not mutated into a form that can easily be contracted by humans because of its difficulty in attaching itself to receptors in the human nose, it remains lethal and widespread among birds. For example, it is rampant and seemingly impossible to control among chickens in Indonesia (where people continue to die from the disease; almost half of all the human deaths from avian flu have occurred there) (Mydans 2008: A3). As long as this is the case, there remains the possibility of mutation and perhaps a pandemic.

It may be that the reason avian flu has not mutated is that the ability to respond to such health threats globally has improved. Avian flu is most widespread in poor countries, but even there, "laboratories have become faster at flu tests. Government veterinarians now move more quickly to cull chickens. Hospitals have wards for suspect patients, and epidemiologists trace contacts and treat all with Tamiflu [an antiviral drug] – a tactic meant to encircle and snuff outbreaks before the virus can adapt itself to humans" (McNeil 2008: D4).

Some health experts argue that the threat of an avian flu pandemic never really existed: "H5 viruses have been around for 100 years and never caused a pandemic and probably never will" (quoted in McNeil 2008: D4). Others worry that the pandemic is still possible, in part because future responses will be more muted since the feared outbreak did not occur during previous alerts. In the meantime, avian flu continues to spread globally among birds (it was present in 60 countries in 2007) and it continues to mutate. Even if a human pandemic never occurs, the spread of avian flu among birds remains a global problem that must be dealt with globally. More importantly, other flu strains are likely to be the basis of a future pandemic.

SARS

An outbreak of SARS occurred in 2003 when the virus spread – largely via airline passengers – from mainland China to Hong Kong and from there to Singapore and Canada (Lee and Warner 2008). While the outbreak had only a limited effect, it demonstrated that globalization contributes to the spread of such diseases.

Ebola Virus

Ebola haemorrhagic fever is a viral disease that was first identified in Sudan and Zaire (now the Democratic Republic of the Congo) in 1976.[1] Other outbreaks of the disease have occurred in Africa in the intervening years including in southern Sudan in 2004 and in the Democratic Republic of the Congo in late 2007. The disease is highly virulent, killing between 50 percent and 90 percent of those who contract it. It is not spread by casual contact, but rather through direct contact with the blood, body fluids, and tissues of those infected with the disease. It can also occur through the handling of chimpanzees that have the disease or that have died from it. Thus far, the spread of the disease has been highly limited. This is at least in part a result of global responses to any reported outbreak. Health officials rush to the affected area and seek to contain it by ministering to the sick and by restricting contact with those outside the affected area.

Tropical Diseases in Europe

The increase in tropical diseases in Europe indicates not only the importance of borderless diseases, but also that the impact of such diseases is not restricted to the South. It is related to another global problem – global warming (see Chapter 9). One of the consequences of global warming is the increased ability of disease-bearing vectors (e.g. mosquitoes) from the hot tropical areas to survive in areas (like Europe) that are heating up as a result of global warming. According to a WHO official:

> This is the first case of an epidemic of a tropical disease in a developed, European country. … Climate change creates conditions that make it easier for this mosquito to survive and it opens the door to diseases that didn't exist here previously. This is a real issue. Now, today. It is not something a crazy environmentalist is warning about. (Quoted in Rosenthal 2007a: 21)

For example, tiger mosquitoes arrived in Italy about a decade ago from Albania in shipments of tires. Since then the mosquito has spread throughout southern Europe and even into Switzerland and France. These mosquitoes spread a tropical disease, chikungunya (a relative of dengue fever usually found in the Indian Ocean area), by drinking the blood of a person infected by the disease and then passing it on to those the mosquitoes subsequently bite. In August, 2007, there was an outbreak of the disease (about 100 people contracted it) in a small village (2,000 residents) in northern Italy; it was traced to the visit of an infected person from India. Presumably, that person was bitten by a tiger mosquito and the disease was off and running. Victims often had fevers of 104 degrees and some continued to experience symptoms (e.g. arthritis) long after they contracted the disease. The outbreak waned as the weather grew colder, but was thought likely to reemerge when the weather warmed. It seems likely that we will see more such outbreaks in the future as the mosquitoes become increasingly indigenous to a warming Europe.

CRIME

The sheer quantity of global, or cross-border (Andreas and Nadelmann 2006) crime has increased in concert with the growth of globalization. While there is, as we will see, much more to the issue of crime in the global age than this, the fact is that globalization makes more cross-border crime possible than ever before. Since there have been nation-states, and even before, there has been international crime that flowed across broad areas of the world. However, today there seems to be far more of such crime, much of it associated with the general propensity for all sorts of things, including crime, to flow more freely in the global age.

In addition, and perhaps because of the increase in global criminal flows, much more public and government attention than ever before seems to be devoted to these crimes. Attention to, as well as action against, crime flows more easily globally with the crimes themselves. This growth is largely traceable to increasing concern with drugs in the US in the late 1960s and early 1970s, as well as Western European interest in terrorism traceable to roughly the same period.

Drugs and terrorism (we also discuss terrorism separately from crime in the following section) now top the list of global concerns as far as crime is concerned, but others include "clandestine trade in sophisticated weaponry and technology, endangered species, pornographic materials, counterfeit products, guns, ivory, toxic waste, money, people [the trafficking in human beings (Farr 2005)], stolen property, and art and antiquities" (Andreas and Nadelmann 2006: 5). Especially notable is the role of globalization in changes in extant forms of crime (e.g. terrorism) and in the development of new forms of crime (cyber-crime). All of these involve flows of all sorts – drugs, money, human victims (e.g. those to be used as prostitutes), human perpetrators (e.g. terrorists), as well as the various illegal sorts of things that flow through the World Wide Web (e.g. child pornography, laundered funds, the spread of computer viruses).

These illegal flows have been aided by the decline of the nation-state and its increasing inability to stem, let alone halt, these flows. Furthermore, global criminal cartels are structures that have come into existence to better expedite illegal flows and to increase the profits that can be derived from them. In fact, a recent book, *McMafia*, attributes much of their success to increasingly sophisticated organizational methods (e.g. economies of scale, global partnerships, the opening of new markets) that are copied from leading legitimate businesses such as McDonald's (Glenny 2008). New technologies have been employed to make some criminal flows more successful (e.g. even going so far as the use of a primitive submarine to transport drugs). And then there is the Internet, the very nature of which makes a number of illegal flows much easier (e.g. pornography, Internet scams), and which is largely impervious to efforts at control by individual nation-states.

The growth in global crime has been met, of course, by "the growing importance of the international component of policing and the policing component of international relations" (Andreas and Nadelmann 2006: 6). Thus, this seems like a simple story of increases in global crime being met by increasing global policing. However, the story, as with all stories that relate to crime and efforts to control it, is far more complex than that.

Crime is always a matter of social definition or social construction (Goode and Ben-Yehuda 1994; Brownstein 1996). That is, few acts everywhere and at all times are crimes; they need to be *defined* as such by large numbers of people. Very often, that which was at one time "normal" comes to be defined as deviant. One famous example is that of cocaine which was a legal substance (small amounts of it were found in Coca-Cola – that's how the famous soda pop got its name – until 1929), but came to be defined as illegal. However, it is rarely the case that large numbers of people come to define something as deviant on their own. This is even truer of something coming to be defined as illegal, i.e. against the law, since that requires the action of government officials. In fact, for some act or product to come to be defined as both deviant and illegal, the actions of so-called "moral entrepreneurs" are almost always required. Moral entrepreneurs are individuals or groups of individuals who come to define an act as a moral outrage and lead a campaign to have it defined as deviant and to have it made illegal and therefore subject to legal enforcement (Becker 1963). Drugs are a good example of this, especially globally, since moral entrepreneurs located especially in the US have taken it upon themselves to have drugs defined as illegal and their use as deviant. They have done so even though the use of many of these drugs (e.g. marijuana) is common and accepted not only in many societies throughout the world, but also among a large portion of the American population.

This relates to the point that while the power of nation-states has generally declined in the global age, it continues to matter greatly in what comes to be *defined* as a global form of deviance and crime. In the era of globalization, it is the nation-states of Western Europe and the US that have played, by far, the central role in this; it is *their* sense of morality and *their* norms of behavior that have come to be disseminated throughout much of the world: "To an extent virtually unprecedented in world history, a few European states and the United States proved successful in proselytizing to diverse societies around the world, in shaping the moral views of substantial sectors of elite opinion outside their borders, and in imposing their norms on foreign governments" (Andreas and Nadelmann 2006: 20). While there have been a number of such efforts to define acts as deviant and illegal, they are certainly not always, and perhaps not even frequently, successful. This, of course, is reflected in the continuation, perhaps expansion, of the global drug trade in spite of great efforts by the US and other nation-states to at least slow it down.

Much of the publicity about drugs, including the ways in which they are implicated in globalization, involves cocaine and heroin. Thus, great attention is devoted to, for example, the growing of poppies in Afghanistan and drug production in Guatemala and the ways in which drugs from those areas, and many others, make their way around the world.

A relatively new global drug is methamphetamine (meth), made easily and cheaply in home-based "cooking facilities" from the main ingredient in cough medicine, pseudoephedrine. Once largely an American phenomenon, the production and use of methamphetamine is beginning to expand globally. For example, it is a growing problem in the Czech Republic and the fear is that from there it will spread throughout the European Union and many other parts of the world as well (Kulish 2007: A1, A11).

Free-trade zones are structures that expedite the flow of illegal products; they are efficient transit points (there are no tariffs and there is minimal oversight over most of these zones since goods do not officially enter the country in which the zone exists) for all sorts of illegal (and legal) products moving throughout the world. A raid on a free-trade zone in Dubai revealed the role they play in the global distribution of counterfeit drugs for a wide range of serious health problems (Bogdanich

2007: A1, A6). In this case, the fake drugs traveled from China, to Hong Kong, through Dubai, and then to Great Britain, the Bahamas, and ultimately to an Internet seller who marketed them to Americans as Canadian drugs. Such shipments are difficult to intercept and it is even more difficult to find out where the products have been manufactured.

There are several aspects of crime, especially as it relates to drugs, which help account for why global (as well as national) efforts to counter it are unsuccessful: the crimes "require limited and readily available resources," they need "no particular expertise to commit," they "are easily concealed," they are "unlikely to be reported to the authorities," and they are "those for which the consumer demand is substantial, resilient, and not readily substituted for by alternative activities or products" (Andreas and Nadelmann 2006: 22).

However, it would be wrong to judge global efforts to control drugs, as well as other illegal substances and activities, as complete failures. The fact is that while drugs continue to flow readily throughout the world for the reasons suggested above, the US has had considerable success in internationalizing its views, laws, procedures, and efforts at enforcement:

> Foreign governments have changed their own laws and enforcement methods and signed extradition, mutual legal assistance, and other law enforcement treaties demanded by US authorities. Beginning with the US prohibitionist approach to drug control during the first decades of the twentieth century, foreign governments have followed in the footsteps of the United States, adopting US-style investigative techniques, creating specialized drug enforcement agencies, stationing law enforcement representatives abroad, and enacting conspiracy statutes, asset forfeiture laws, and checks and bans on drug-related money laundering. Pressures to cooperate in US drug trafficking investigations were largely responsible for instigating changes, beginning in the 1970s, in financial secrecy laws to authorize greater assistance to US (and other foreign) law enforcement authorities. (Andreas and Nadelmann 2006: 107)

Drugs were not the first form of global crime that the US took the lead in countering and in influencing other nations in the world to work against. Its influence "was readily apparent during the first decades of the century in shaping foreign and international approaches to white slavery, during the cold war era with respect to export controls on weapons and sophisticated technology, and starting in the mid-1980s with respect to the regulation of securities markets (in particular the criminalization of insider trading)" (Andreas and Nadelmann 2006: 107).

Since 9/11, there has been a dramatic erosion of various distinctions in the world of crime (and elsewhere) that had existed for decades, if not centuries. For example, the distinction between law enforcement and intelligence operations has eroded as authorities seek to gain intelligence on potential terrorists in order to forestall further terrorist attacks and to catch or kill people defined as terrorists. Then there is the related fact that border control, especially between the US and Mexico, has increasingly become a matter of surveillance along the border, and in immigrant communities in the US, in order to better enforce the laws against illegal immigrants. In the process, many immigrants have been defined as criminals, apprehended, and then returned to Mexico. It is important to note the selectivity involved in all of this since far less attention is devoted to surveillance along the much longer border with Canada and those who do cross that border illegally are much less likely to be defined, or apprehended, as criminals.

In Europe, a similar, although not as extreme, toughening of border controls with, and surveillance of, non-EU states occurred, while within the EU, border controls and surveillance were relaxed. Border law enforcement within the EU became "more domesticated through greater homogenization of criminal justice norms and procedures and the regularization of law enforcement contacts and information exchange among member states" (Andreas and Nadelmann 2006: 186). Of great importance was the formation of Europol which allowed better and increased communication and cooperation among national police agencies.

The globalization of policing did not occur simply as a consequence of September 11th, but rather was well underway as a result of a variety of forces before the events of 9/11 occurred. However, the globalization of policing did change after 9/11. For one thing, we have witnessed an accelerating decline in the distinction between law enforcement and security (in the US, the Patriot Act [Uniting and Strengthening America by Providing Appropriate Tools Required to Intercept and Obstruct Terrorism Act], signed into law on October 26, 2001, played a key role in this by, for example, extending concern to domestic terrorism). For another, the need to deal with global issues relating to terrorism has come into conflict with the desire to keep borders open and free in order to facilitate international economic transactions.

While global crime control has improved in various ways, there are also a variety of downsides associated with these efforts. For one thing, there is great fear of threats to democracy posed by these efforts. Crime control efforts are not always as transparent as they might be and the officials involved often need to be more accountable. There is great fear of the threats to civil and human rights posed by these new policing methods and practices (e.g. laws that are more invasive, more intrusive surveillance technologies).

For another, there is the collateral damage associated with greater global law enforcement efforts by nation-states. Greater border and immigration controls have led to more daring and dangerous efforts to cross borders, leading to more deaths in the process. The global anti-drug campaign has "generated extraordinary levels of crime, violence, corruption, disease, and other ills" (Andreas and Nadelmann 2006: 251). Efforts by the US to deal with trafficking in women and children "ha[ve] been far more focused on criminalizing the traffic than helping to protect the human rights of those being trafficked" (Andreas and Nadelmann 2006: 251).

Finally, the attention and money devoted to international crime and its control have tended to distract attention, and to take money away, from efforts to deal with a wide range of fundamental issues within nation-states including the welfare of large portions of society.

TERRORISM

There is a tendency to discuss crime and terrorism as distinct phenomena, but they overlap to some degree (Shelley 2006: 42–5). In fact, we have already had some things to say about terrorism under the heading of crime. One example, of many, is involvement of the Taliban (linked to the terrorist organization, al-Qaeda) in Afghanistan in poppy growing and the opium business. More recently, the Taliban has gotten involved in the marble business in Afghanistan by demanding (extorting) flat fees and taxes from quarry owners (Zubair and Perlez 2008: A1, A8). Furthermore, both crime and terrorism are global in character and have been aided by various aspects of globalization. For example, both the operations of terrorist groups like al-Qaeda and the global distribution of opium are aided by modern means of global transportation and communication. And the global mass media fan the interest in, even hysteria about, these (and many other) problems. However, the relationship between terrorism and crime is only one of many involved in trying to get a handle on terrorism, as well as its relationship to globalization.

Objectively, terrorism can be defined as actions that cause "deaths, serious bodily injuries, and serious damage to public or private property, places, facilities, or other systems" and are aimed at intimidating citizens, governments, or international organizations (Rehman 2007: 1137). However, terrorism tends to be an idea that those in power seek to impose on those who are not in power. Thus, the US (and many other nation-states) labels al-Qaeda a terrorist organization, but resists the label itself even though it has engaged in actions ("state terrorism") that have at least some similarities with those of al-Qaeda (e.g. missile strikes from unmanned drones in Afghanistan and Pakistan that kill innocent citizens). Similarly, Israel labels Hamas and Hezbollah as terrorist organizations, but refuses the label for itself even though in the 2006 war against Hezbollah it destroyed much infrastructure (and killed many people) in Lebanon that had little or nothing to do with Hezbollah. Much the same happened in the late 2008–early 2009 Israeli incursion into the Gaza Strip in an effort to cripple Hamas.

A key distinction, alluded to above, is between stateless and state-sponsored terrorism. Both forms involve violence against non-military targets and citizens, but the former involves stateless organizations (such as al-Qaeda) while the latter is undertaken by the state (such as Israel). Both forms are increasingly global, as witnessed by al-Qaeda's 9/11 attacks on the US and US missile and bombing attacks on Iraq at the beginning of the war in 2003 that destroyed non-military targets either intentionally or because they involved collateral damage associated with the attacks on the main targets. The initial US attack was labeled "shock and awe" because it was designed to intimidate *both* the Iraqi government and its citizens. And both forms of terrorism are political in that al-Qaeda was attacking, at least in part, the American government and its policies, while the US was seeking, and achieved, "regime change" in Iraq.

Terrorism is certainly not new, but there does seem to be something different about its most recent and most important manifestations such as al-Qaeda. What appears most different about them is their global aspirations and reach. For example, a ragtag group of insurgents in Algeria made contact with al-Qaeda and engaged in what was in effect a "corporate merger" leading to an al-Qaeda affiliate, "al Qaeda in the Islamic Maghreb" (*New York Times* 2008: July 1, A1, A12). Certainly earlier terrorist organizations (e.g. Irgun and its efforts to oust the British and to foster the emergence of an independent Israel) had global aspirations and reach. For example, Jewish terrorists sought to bring their grievances to the attention of a global audience. However, while al-Qaeda achieved its status as today's paradigmatic terrorist organization through its attacks on American and Western interests in various places throughout the world, the Irgun restricted itself to actions in and around the future territory of Israel. Thus, for example, it did not launch attacks in Great Britain, but limited itself to attacks in its homeland (most famously the 1946 bombing of the King David Hotel in Jerusalem which killed and injured a number of British soldiers, officials, and citizens).

Thus, while earlier terrorist groups operated, largely because they had little choice, in and around their home territory, today's terrorist groups are much freer to launch, and much more interested in launching, attacks far from home (indeed, they may not have a "home" in a conventional sense). Furthermore, their attacks often take place in global cities (New York, Washington, London, Madrid) and are at least some of the time aimed at highly symbolic, even iconic, targets (World Trade Center, London Underground, Madrid trains) which, if they are successfully attacked, will guarantee great media attention throughout the world.

Another distinguishing characteristic of today's terrorist groups is their greatly enhanced ability to get their message across, often almost instantaneously, to a global audience. Certainly earlier terrorist groups sought to do this, but they had far fewer means at their disposal to accomplish it. They could, by their actions, garner headlines around the world (e.g. the King David Hotel bombing), but they had little or no control over the messages that were communicated to others – those messages were controlled by the international media. However, while today's terrorist groups welcome the attention of the global media, they also have more direct means of getting their message across to large numbers of people throughout the world *and* in precisely the way they want it stated and framed. Thus, al-Qaeda uses self-produced videotapes that are broadcast over major media outlets and posted on their websites to communicate directly with a global audience. The Zapatistas in Mexico are known for their use of the Internet to get their message out. Pro al-Qaeda and Zapatista bloggers also communicate their messages over the Internet. Thus, the more recent terrorist groups are distinguished by their increasingly sophisticated use of global communication channels unavailable to earlier terrorist organizations, as well as their ability to completely control the content of those messages. It is this kind of thing that leads Martin to discuss the "new terrorism" (Martin 2007: 644–61).

There are several other characteristics of the new, global age that aid today's terrorists. First, global transportation systems make it easier for individual terrorists to move around the world in order to plan and carry out terrorist acts (this was abundantly clear in the actions and activities of the terrorists both prior to, and during, the 9/11 attacks). Second, more porous national borders, and the growing inability of nations to control their borders, also make it easier for terrorists to move about relatively freely (although greater vigilance in the US and elsewhere appears to have thwarted further terrorist attacks, at least as of this writing). Third, the reactions against globalization have produced and solidified broad political alliances that are ready audiences for the ideas and actions of terrorist groups. For example, there are at least some in much of the Islamic world sympathetic to, or at least tolerant of, the ideas and actions of al-Qaeda because of global actions taken against them, real and perceived, by the West, especially the US. An even larger audience for al-Qaeda, as well as the Zapatistas, is the millions, if not billions, of people throughout the world who feel that they have been left out of, or disadvantaged by, globalization. Finally, earlier forms of terrorism, especially during the heyday of the Soviet Union and its efforts to expand globally, tended to be more narrowly ideological (e.g. socialism, communism). Today's terrorism is based on broader appeals to ethnicity and/or to a wider set of grievances against the process of globalization.

The weapons at the disposal of recent terrorist organizations are also a reflection and a part of the global age. The most obvious example is al-Qaeda's use of jetliners in the 9/11 attacks. Further, there is the rather ready global flow of weapons that can be used by terrorists. However, the great fear here is the global flow of knowledge about chemical and biological weapons, and especially about nuclear technology, and the ability of terrorist groups to make use of that knowledge. In terms of the latter, a preoccupation in the West is the development and use of a so-called "dirty" nuclear bomb by al-Qaeda. Such a bomb would not set off a large nuclear explosion, but the radiation from it would cause many deaths and could make large areas of a major city uninhabitable for many years. Given our previous discussion of the ease with which contraband passes through the world's ports, this is a real concern.

As the archetypical contemporary terrorist organization, al-Qaeda has moved in several directions that have served to make it even more global (Martin 2007: 644–61). It is believed to be organized on the basis of largely independent cells throughout the world, some of them so-called "sleeper cells" that have lain dormant and undercover for years. It can be seen as being structured as a global secret "franchise" system (versus McDonald's highly public franchise system). And, new branches of the movement seem to be being "cloned," especially at the moment as a result of American (and NATO) incursions in Iraq and Afghanistan.

Karin Knorr Cetina (2005: 215) has offered considerable insight into global terrorist organizations by considering them as examples of "complex global microstructures" with four basic characteristics. First, they are, as was mentioned in Chapter 1, and consistent with one of the major orientations of this book, *light*. By this, Knorr Cetina (2005: 215) means:

that mechanisms and structures involved suggest a reversal of the historical trend toward formal, rationalized (bureaucratic organizational) structures ... while micro-structures are on some level organized or coordinated systems, the coordinating elements involved are not the kind we associate with formal authority, complex hierarchies, rationalized procedure or deep institutional structure.

Instead they utilize methods of coordination that are more like those people use on a daily basis in face-to-face relationships. Even so, they are able to hold together systems and relationships that stretch over great geographic distances.

Second, terrorist microstructures are effective even though they do not employ the rationalized structures, especially heavy bureaucracies, we usually associate with effectiveness in the modern world. They achieve this effectiveness in several ways including augmenting and amplifying their effect by using such technologies as hijacked airplanes and the media (especially the Internet), by "outsourcing" support functions and keeping them distinct from the internal structure, and by keeping regulations to a minimum in order to maximize adaptability to large developments. They rely on both a cellular structure as well as linkages built on diaspora (in this case, the Arab diaspora; see Chapter 8).

Third, while complex global microstructures are networks through which various things, especially people, flow, there is more to them than that, including, in al-Qaeda's case, its "Islamist religious representations, its family structure and its self-reproducing mechanism" (Knorr Cetina 2005: 216). Thus, it is not just relational connectivity that holds these microstructures together; they are far richer and more textured than that.

Finally, such microstructures are not only organizationally, but also temporally, complex. The key point here is that organizations increase in complexity when they exist both spatially and temporally (Harvey 1989; Giddens 1990). That is, they not only have a spatial existence (although, by design, it is hard to pin down exactly where al-Qaeda is physically), but they have succeeded in continuing to exist over time, and the combination of the two forms of existence, spatial and temporal, gives them greater complexity. It is the global stream of developments over time stemming from al-Qaeda (e.g. terrorist attacks, threats via the media, periodic videotapes featuring Osama bin Laden, etc.) that has made it more successful than terrorist groups that are more locked into a given local or national context and have failed to maintain an existence over time. Also important in holding the widely dispersed members of al-Qaeda together from a temporal point of view is a close linkage between the situation the group faces at the moment and the past as it exists in "collective memory" (Halbwachs 1992). Al-Qaeda is also held together by a belief in a future desired state such as a successful jihad or achieving personal paradise. These perspectives and beliefs help to account for the patience and persistence of al-Qaeda and the long-term planning that must go into some of their terrorist activities.

More threatening than this unusual network of people is the transformation of al-Qaeda into more of an ideology ("Qaedaism") than a cellular organization of people. What is ominous about this, at least from the point of view of the West (and promising from the perspective of al-Qaeda), is that ideas flow around the world far more easily than people and it is nearly impossible to set up effective barriers to the flow of ideas. If large numbers of people can be converted to Qaedaism simply by the dissemination, and power, of its ideas, then it has great possibilities to expand and become an even more important global force in the future.

Of course, the fact that contemporary terrorism is much more globalized means that the efforts to respond to, and deal with, it must also be increasingly global. Hence, the US has, for example, undertaken, on its own and in conjunction with other nation-states, overt and covert steps around the world to combat terrorism. American actions in Iraq and Afghanistan are well known, but the US has also engaged in actions elsewhere such as launching air attacks in Somalia against suspected al-Qaeda hideouts and centers. This was made possible by the defeat, at least for the moment, of the Islamists in Somalia largely because of the 2006 intervention of the Christian-dominated Ethiopian army with the support and encouragement of the US. (However, the Ethiopian army has now withdrawn from Somalia and the Islamists are once again on the ascendancy.)

There have also been more multilateral efforts to cope with terrorism such as internationally binding agreements on preventing and dealing with offenses on airplanes, the hijacking of airplanes, and airport violence. There have been agreements to deal with terrorism at sea and terrorist acts committed against platforms at sea, especially oil platforms. Among the other agreements are those that deal with hostage-taking and nuclear terrorism. There have also been a number of more regional agreements on terrorism. However, there is as yet no comprehensive, universal treaty that deals with all forms and aspects of terrorism (Rehman 2007: 1139).

Both terrorism and the reactions against it raise issues of *human rights* which involve "entitlements of individuals to life, security, and well-being" (Turner 2007: 591). Clearly, by their actions, terrorists deprive people of their human rights, in some cases their lives. However, the actions against terrorism, especially the US "war on terrorism," have led to many complaints that the war is violating people's human rights in various ways, including causing their deaths (e.g. bombings in Afghanistan), the incarceration of many suspected terrorists in camps (now in the process of being closed) like those in Guantanamo Bay, Cuba, for many years without any due process, the use of torture (e.g. "waterboarding") in an effort to extract confessions from accused terrorists at the Abu Ghraib prison in Baghdad (and elsewhere) (Otterman 2007), and so on.

On the one hand it is clear that the 9/11 attacks on the World Trade Center deprived many victims and their families of their human rights and in a particularly deadly and gruesome way. While we must not lose sight of that, much of the attention in recent years has been focused on human rights abuses related to the war on terror. There is, for example, the case of an Afghan, Abdul Razzaq Hekmati, who was held in Guantanamo Bay for five years before he died in early 2008 from cancer

(Gall and Worthington 2008: A1ff.). In Afghanistan he had been regarded as a war hero for resisting the Russian invasion in the 1980s; in 1999 he had organized a jail break for three opponents of the Taliban then in power in Afghanistan. Nonetheless, he was apprehended in Afghanistan and transferred to Guantanamo Bay because he was suspected of being a Taliban commander. He did have a tribunal in 2004, but it was highly limited and deeply flawed (much of the evidence against him came from unidentified witnesses; those in Afghanistan who could have vouched for him were not called as witnesses; Hekmati was not represented by a lawyer).

More generally, there is the danger that terrorism leads nation-states to reactions that threaten their very legitimacy. For example, the US has jeopardized not only its objective in the "war on terror" (which is not a "true" war), but its overall legitimacy by, for example, "its lawless behavior at its penal colonies" (e.g. Guantanamo Bay) (Bobbitt 2008: 17). More generally, there is the danger, perhaps already the reality, that nation-states employ tactics "that are indistinguishable from those of terrorists" (Bobbitt 2008: 45). As a result, at least in part, of such behavior, the US government has weakened its ability to convince American (and, even more, global) public opinion of the justness of its cause and this, in turn, has adversely affected its ability to pursue legal objectives.

WAR

In spite of its great importance, war has not received a great deal of attention in globalization studies (Barkawi 2004: 155–70; 2007). However, it clearly deserves more attention and not only because of its great social and political importance. It is also a realm that well illustrates the basic ideas about globalization that orient this book. While it seems like a dysfunctional way to make such linkages, there is a long line of work in the social sciences that analyzes the functions of social conflict (Simmel 1908/1955; Coser 1956), including warfare.

It is increasingly difficult to find examples of warfare that are unaffected by globalization. Even the most local of wars shows the impact and effect of global processes. This can be seen in all of the types of processes we have associated with globalization. The numerous *relations* that exist among the different regions of the world mean that a war in one is likely to involve others. For example, the 1991 invasion of Kuwait by Iraq led to a coalition of armed forces led by the US that pushed the Iraqi army back across its borders and liberated Kuwait from Iraqi occupation. Many of the countries involved in the military coalition were involved in relations with Kuwait because it is a major oil-producer. The Iraqi invasion of Kuwait was seen by them as not only a threat to relations with Kuwait, but with all other oil-producing nations in the region. This, of course, is intimately related to the global *flow* of oil. The developed nations, and even almost all less developed nations, are highly dependent on a steady flow of oil. The invasion of Iraq in 1991 demonstrated once again that many nations, especially the US which is most dependent on that oil, are willing to go to war to keep the oil flowing. Flows of arms

(Chivers 2008: A5) and material, to say nothing of troops, were also necessary to conduct the war.

People are involved in various *networks* and some of those networks (e.g. among those involved in the oil business) were disrupted by the invasion of Kuwait. Furthermore, existing networks were revived and new ones created in order to mount opposition to the Iraqi invasion. Propaganda networks around the world were ramped up to create and solidify opposition to that invasion. Intelligence and military networks were also revived, or created anew, in order to make the ultimate invasion possible.

And, of course, what all of this demonstrates is that more and more social structures and social institutions are *interconnected* on a global basis. Various governments and government agencies needed to be interconnected in order to mount the invasion of Iraq. And that invasion reverberated throughout various social institutions in many of the world's nation-states. For example, it became the focal concern of the global media. Even families in many parts of the world were affected as sons and daughters, fathers and mothers went off to war.

Overall, is it possible to determine whether globalization makes war less or more likely? There are those who argue that the increasing economic bonds that accompany globalization are likely to mean a reduction in the likelihood of war (Friedman 2005; Schneider 2007: 630–43). That is, nation-states are unlikely to sacrifice valuable economic relationships by going to war with one another. On the other hand, the economic gains of war may seem so great that nations may be more likely to engage in warfare, no matter what the consequences for their relationships with other nation-states. Then there is the huge global market for, and flow of, weapons of all sorts, new and used. Such a huge market serves to make such weapons increasingly inexpensive and they can be acquired easily and quickly.

Another factor making war more likely in the age of globalization is time and space compression, both of which make it easier to engage in warfare with other countries. Militaries can be mobilized rapidly (the Israeli military is a model in this regard) and they can be moved across great distances more quickly and easily (as in the case of the coalition of military forces involved in the first war against Iraq following its invasion of Kuwait). Furthermore, new global technologies make it possible to wage wars thousands of miles away without ever leaving home. An example is the employment in Afghanistan of those drones equipped with missiles that are controlled remotely by military technicians in the US using computers and video monitors. Overall, the best we can do is to say that globalization has an ambiguous relationship with the likelihood of international warfare.

What we can say unambiguously is that in various ways globalization is changing, and will continue to change, the nature of warfare. To take one example, the decline of the nation-state and the increasing importance of state-less societies are causing the US to rethink its basic doctrines about warfare. Instead of traditional combat operations such as ground operations with major armies facing off against one another, some within the American military are arguing for the need to engage, instead, in long-lasting stability operations. In fact, that is what the US military is doing in Iraq and Afghanistan. With the increasing number of fragile, weak, or even state-less societies, the view is emerging that a major task for the military in the future will be nation-building rather than war-making (Scott Tyson 2008: A16).

Global Military Structures

Many international military organizations and alliances have been formed over the centuries, but the most important and most global of such organizations, at least until the end of the Cold War, was the North Atlantic Treaty Organization (NATO). NATO was formed in 1949 as a reaction against the growing threat of the Soviet Union and its allies (Barnhart 2007: 166–8). In response, the latter formed the Warsaw Pact in 1955. While the Warsaw Pact lasted only until 1991, NATO continues to exist. There are currently 26 nations in NATO, mostly in Western Europe, but also including Canada and the US. (NATO has been dominated by the US since its inception.) A number of former Soviet-bloc nations have joined NATO in recent years and Albania, Croatia and Macedonia have been invited to join (although there is resistance to at least some of them within NATO).

NATO was engaged in military operations in Kosovo in 1999 and since 2006 has been fighting in Afghanistan against the Taliban (and al-Qaeda). It currently has a force of about 120,000 troops in Afghanistan (by far the largest contingent is from the US; the US also has a large and growing number of additional troops there under its own command; overall, over 100,000 US troops were in Afghanistan in late 2010). Nevertheless, those troops seem bogged down in a long-term war and the Taliban seem to be growing stronger. Further, there are internal divisions within NATO with accusations that some national contingents are not fighting as aggressively as was hoped. There is also a feeling among some that various nations have not done their share in terms of contributing troops to the mission. For example, Canada has about 2,500 soldiers in Afghanistan, but it threatened to pull them out unless other NATO members sent additional troops to help in the fighting in the south of the country where they were located (Myers and Shanker 2008: A6). A US Undersecretary of State commented, "We face a crisis in Afghanistan that is extraordinarily difficult for our country and for the NATO alliance. ... For NATO it may be an existential crisis" (quoted in Myers and Shanker 2008: A6). The controversial plans to expand NATO again by bringing in more former Soviet-bloc nations are also creating problems. According to one student of NATO, the expansion is "a train that's going forward on its own momentum. ... In the meantime ... the wheels are falling off" (quoted in Myers and Shanker 2008: A6).

Technology

One of the things that makes war today increasingly likely to be global is the existence of advanced information and communications technologies (ICTs) such as computers and satellites. Of course, it is the developed countries, especially the US, that are likely to have the ability to afford, to have access to, and to use, these technologies. But, even the least developed countries are implicated in this, at least in the sense that the technologies are likely to be used against them. Thus, the US uses its satellites to keep track of developments in some of the world's least developed countries (Afghanistan, Somalia), as well as to guide the use of military technology (e.g. drones) in them.

It is important to remember that technologies do not act of their own accord. People and social organizations are needed to bring such technologies into existence, to decide how they are to be used, and then to use them in that way.

Information War

The new, advanced technologies have made possible both traditional warfare and the more recent "information war" (Tumber and Webster 2007: 396–413). This new information-technology is deeply implicated in the new advanced weaponry employed in contemporary wars. For example, the "smart missiles" employed by the US in the second Iraq war required advanced information technology so that they could be targeted to hit very minute and precise targets with a high degree of accuracy (although, these weapons, like virtually all weapons, were not immune from missing their targets and causing collateral damage). Not only do these weapons depend on advanced information technologies, but so do many other aspects of contemporary warfare such as surveillance (by satellites, airplanes, drones, and so on), as well as the "command and control" needed to run a modern military operation.

We are moving from a world dominated by *heavy* "industrial war" (e.g. that waged during WW II) to one that is best seen as dominated by *light* "information war." *Industrial war* generally involved sovereign nation-states, and the homeland deeply supported it; it was fought over territory, it involved the mobilization of a large portion of the population and led to mass casualties, it was largely symmetrical in that massed armies confronted one another, it witnessed the media harnessed in support of the war effort, and it provided the media with only a very limited view of what was taking place on the battlefield.

Information war: Information and information technology increasingly permeating warfare in developed countries.

In contrast, **information war** involves information permeating all aspects of war; it involves all sorts of new technologies (digital soldiers, drones, computer-driven weapons, etc.); it is massively asymmetrical in that only the most advanced nations, especially the US, have access to these technologies; it involves relatively small numbers of troops (many of whom are better thought of as "knowledge warriors"); it is less oriented to gaining territory; it involves only a small portion of the population; and it is likely to be a war of short duration.

Modern global warfare also increasingly involves a battle over information among and between various representatives of the media in the nation-states involved. Most generally, there is the battle among media giants to be the first to announce, and even show, an important event. For example, in the Middle East there is a rivalry between Western media giants and Arab competitors. Thus, when Saddam Hussein was hanged at the end of 2006, there was great competition to see who would be the first to announce, and show, the hanging (the Arab media companies won this one).

In addition, the combatants involved in war seek to use these media outlets to get their messages across and to further their interests. Thus, these media outlets are dominated by the "talking heads" representing the various interests involved. Increasingly, this war over the ability to influence global public opinion is a very important, even integral, part of the war itself. If public opinion in a given country turns against a particular war (as it did in the US in the case of the second war in Iraq), it is very difficult for that country to continue the war (but not impossible, as again is illustrated by the second Iraq war and America's continued involvement in spite of public opinion strongly against the war), at least for very long. Thus, the national and international competition among the media, and among the various spokespeople who appear on these media, is an integral, even often decisive, aspect of modern global warfare.

Then there is the fact that reporters from a large number of global media descend on a war zone to report on it. Thus, lots of reports are filed and many of them are in conflict with one another. These reports may reflect differences among reporters in experience and access, but they may also reflect differences in the ideological and political orientations of the specific media that they represent.

The military seeks to affect the information war in various ways. It issues news releases and holds press conferences designed to give reporters, and indirectly the global public, the information and perspective of that military and its government. The military also employs its own public relations officers to get its messages across more directly. And the military seeks to control what the reporters get to see. For example, in the war in Iraq only a select few reporters were allowed by the military to be "embedded" with the troops and therefore were the only ones who had direct knowledge of front-line battles (of course, even their view of those battles was restricted and what they saw was limited to a small number of those battles). Other reporters had to rely on the reports of those embedded in writing their own stories.

A major development from the point of view of the globalization of war (and much else) is the Internet and the coming of age of bloggers who are able to disseminate their own perspectives directly to large numbers of people throughout the world. Thus even though the global media giants are more powerful than ever, there is at the same time increased democratization of media communication, with the result that many more voices are heard, and perspectives available, to global consumers of information than ever before. Thus, early in the assault on Iraq in 2003, the so-called "Baghdad blogger" was disseminating information from the scene that was at times at odds with the views from the mass media outlets.

Similarly, the downloading of photos of the abuses of Iraqi prisoners at the Abu Ghraib prison camp led to a global uproar over the behavior of the American military. These abuses had not been reported by the major media and they probably did not have access to such information, let alone photographic evidence of it. This is another demonstration of the democratization of information dissemination in the age of the Internet. There are also now many Indymedia websites on the Internet that are systematically posting a wide range of information and perspectives on military and other matters.

Also of note here is the fact that because of the increasing sophistication of the global media, people around the globe are able to listen to and actually see war-related events in real time. Thus, they are able to form their own views on these events more directly, less shaped by the views of media representatives and spokespeople for various perspectives.

What all of the above indicates is an increasing profusion of global sources of information on war (and much else) and, as a result, it is increasingly difficult for any one nation or military to control that information. That means that the information will be carried on many fronts at the same time and that there is likely to be no single or clear winner in these media battles. While this means less ability on anyone's part to control media messages, it also means that the profusion of different messages is likely to lead to much greater ambiguity, ambivalence, and confusion in the minds of the public. This might make it more difficult for a given nation to undertake a war or carry one out for any lengthy period of time. This is complicated by a virtual "blizzard" of information that overwhelms even the most attentive students of world affairs.

Often used in this context is Joseph Nye's (2005) distinction between "soft" and "hard" war. The information war is usually seen as soft (that is, "hard" military technology is *not* employed), whereas an actual military engagement is seen as hard (involving the use of such "hard" technologies). However, because military hardware is increasingly dependent on information technology, it is more and more difficult to make such a clear distinction. Hard military war is increasingly influenced by various media (employing soft technologies) that are more important in deciding whether a war begins and even the outcome of a war.

Overall, the public are less personally involved, less personally touched, by information war than they were by industrial war. For example, far fewer fight (compare the millions of troops involved in WW II to the hundreds of thousands involved in the Iraq war) and there are fewer casualties and therefore fewer families are personally touched by war. Less directly involved and affected, the population, especially of the developed nations waging the war (often in distant lands), is much more dependent on second-hand, media-based, rather than personal (e.g. letters from loved ones at the front), information for learning about what is taking place.

Cyber-War

The increasing importance of computers and the Internet has had, as we have seen in various places in this book, many implications for globalization. One of the potentially most important and devastating is the possibility of cyber-war. Indeed, this is not just a possibility, but has already occurred, most notably in the case of Estonia in mid-2007 (Landler and Markoff 2007: A1, C7).

The "war" began when the Estonians began dismantling a statue of a WW II Russian soldier in a park in the city of Tallinn. Street protests, perhaps violent ones, were expected, but so were actions to disrupt the Internet in Estonia. The Internet is particularly important in Estonia today with people using it for many things including voting, paying their taxes, shopping, and paying for parking. The dismantling of the statue did indeed lead to what some have described as the "first war in cyberspace" as a flood of data overwhelmed the Internet in Estonia. It is believed that the flood stemmed from, or was at least instigated by, people in Russia or ethnic Russians in Estonia who were upset by this affront to them (however, there is not only no proof of this, but apparently no way to prove it, given the murkiness of sources on the Internet). Whatever the sources, computers around the world (perhaps as many as a million) were infiltrated with "bots" and became unwitting contributors ("zombies") to the assault. The Russian government denied involvement, but the war against Estonia's Internet system was probably orchestrated from somewhere and by some entity. More important from the point of view of globalization, it eventually probably emanated from virtually everywhere in the globe.

The flood of data (thousands of times the normal flow) almost shut down the Internet in Estonia and this in spite of advance preparations in anticipation of such an assault. The technique used in the attack is known as "denial of service" since it denies service to users by clogging not only servers, but also routers that direct traffic on the Web. It is the combination of the use of large amounts of data with the use of large numbers of machines that defines a denial-of-service attack and is so dangerous to the Internet. Among those most affected in Estonia were the websites of the president, prime minister, Parliament, other government agencies, the nation's largest bank, and several newspapers. Among other things, members of Parliament were without e-mail for four days and traveling businesspeople could not access their bank accounts. Estonia's defense minister saw it as a threat to national security analogous to shutting down a nation's ports. Among the devices used were masses of junk e-mail, hacking into websites, and making false postings on websites.

There are currently not only national efforts to figure out how to respond to such attacks, but also a kind of "arms race" involving China, Russia, and the US, all of which are seeking to develop more powerful "information-warfare programs." This raises the possibility of far more devastating attacks than those on Estonia, but for the moment the attacks seem less nation-based and more organized by "hacktivists" motivated by a specific cause, like the dismantling of the statue of the Russian soldier.

THE IMPACT OF NEGATIVE GLOBAL FLOWS ON INDIVIDUALS

All of the negative flows discussed above, indeed all of the analyses offered throughout virtually this entire book, deal in general and abstract terms with large-scale aspects of globalization. This is to a large degree because globalization itself is large in scale, general, and abstract (although an effort has been made throughout this book to concretize it). However, it is also the case that globalization in general, as well as the various negative flows discussed in this chapter, has a wide range of very profound effects on individuals (Lemert and Elliott 2006).

Clearly, each of the major negative flows discussed above has profoundly adverse effects on individuals: people are victimized, even killed, as a result of global crime; citizens pay the costs resulting from corruption on a global level; innocent people, like those in the Twin Towers, in the subway systems in London and Madrid, and in Bali, Indonesia are the victims, often the intended victims, of terrorists; and it is certainly the case that large numbers of innocent civilians die, and have their lives destroyed, by war.

We can also look at this in another way by thinking about the individual implications of the various insecurities iterated by the United Nations Development Report: financial volatility and economic insecurity, job and income insecurity, health insecurity, cultural insecurity, personal insecurity, environmental insecurity, and political and community insecurity. While all of these insecurities exist globally, nationally, and in other large-scale collectivities of one kind or another, they are also certainly manifest at the individual level. Individuals suffer in global economic crises; in global wars; and from fear of such things as contracting AIDS, hostile neighbors, identity theft, the effects of global warming, and being caught up in the turmoil associated with a failed or failing state.

Along these lines, one recent book (Lemert and Elliott 2006) has gone so far as to argue that globalization is toxic to individuals and their emotional lives. The authors see a variety of personal problems resulting from globalization such as hyperindividualism, privatization, and the decreasing solidity and durability of personal identity (although they recognize that globalization also brings with it the possibility of more open and flexible selves). Overall, they conclude that people are being emotionally damaged (Walker 2008) by the new "globalized individualism" and by globalization in general, at least its negative aspects.

CHAPTER SUMMARY

This chapter analyzes negative global flows and processes such as dangerous imports, cross-border crime, terrorism, and war. With globalization, such flows can move across borders with ease and at great speed. Negative globalization comprises not only flows and processes, but also structures. Negative flows also induce global counter-reactions.

Global value chains involve the importation of both products and product ingredients. The length and multiplicity of these chains leave them vulnerable to the spread of contaminants along their entire length and breadth. Further, the complexity of the chain often makes it difficult to locate the source of contamination.

The magnitude and volume of cross-border crime has increased with globalization. Correspondingly, global attention to this flow has also increased. Cross-border crime involves flows of drugs, money, victims, perpetrators, as well as illegal commodities, through physical as well as virtual (Internet-based) channels. The decline in the regulatory powers of the nation-state translates into an increasing inability to check such flows. However, the adoption of the latest technologies, as well as sophisticated organizational methods based on legitimate businesses models, is helping to improve the ability to deal with global crime.

Despite its decline, the nation-state retains the power to define global forms of deviance and crime (for instance the categorization of marijuana as illegal and harmful in the US and Europe). In the era of globalization, the nation-states of Western Europe and the US disseminated their sense of morality and norms of behavior to the rest of the world.

The growth of global crime has led to a selective tightening of border controls in the US and Europe. However, more stringent measures of global crime control have given rise to concerns about the violation of human rights as well as the threats posed to democracy. Such problems increase as the line between legal and illegal commodities becomes increasingly blurred and as global flows of both are increasingly intertwined.

The transmission of diseases across borders is not a novel phenomenon. However, it has become much more common in recent years. The spread of such diseases indicates the difficulty involved in checking the flow of disease-causing pathogens across borders. This global spread is particularly influenced by the increasing mobility of people. For instance, AIDS travels from one region to the other through human vectors. The situation calls for an appropriately global response. It is often the most vulnerable populations that bear the burden of such diseases, for instance the high incidence of AIDS cases in regions across Africa. This segment of the global population is also least likely to have access to the expensive health care required to combat such diseases. Globalization also contributes to the spread of diseases in other ways. For instance, global warming has resulted in the spread of tropical diseases to what is now a much warmer Europe.

Crime and terrorism are closely related, often through financial linkages. Terrorism is defined as actions that cause "deaths, serious bodily injuries, and serious damage to public or private property, places, facilities, or other systems" and are aimed at intimidating citizens, governments, or international organizations. There is a need to distinguish stateless terrorism (undertaken by stateless organizations such as al-Qaeda) from state-sponsored terrorism. Terrorist activities are expanding in terms of their global aspirations and reach. Terrorist groups are no longer restricted to their home territory and can strike anywhere in the world. They also have access to sophisticated technology that enables them to transmit their messages to a global audience. As a result, the counter-reaction to terrorism is also increasingly global. However, in launching such an offensive, nation-states often resort to tactics that resemble those of the terrorists they seek to combat.

Warfare is increasingly influenced by globalization. Global interconnectedness implies that a war in a region is no longer an isolated phenomenon and will involve other regions, often quite distant, directly or indirectly. In fact, this interconnectedness is interpreted by some as an indication that the incidence of war might decline with globalization. However, the economic gains of war and easy access to weapons in the global era might actually lead to an increase in warfare. Further, advanced technologies make a new form of warfare, information war, possible. This involves information permeating all aspects of war. There is also an increasing profusion of global sources of information on war, particularly through the Internet.

DISCUSSION QUESTIONS

1. Discuss the role of structures in perpetuating negative globalization.

2. What actions can be taken by nation-states to deal with dangerous imports?

3. What actions can be taken globally to deal with borderless diseases?

4. Examine the global flows of crime. What is the role of the nation-state and international agencies in dealing with such flows?

5. Discuss the concepts of "stateless terrorism" and "state-sponsored terrorism." What is the relationship between these two types of terrorism in the context of globalization?

6. Examine the impact of global media flows on warfare in the current global age.

7. Compare "heavy" industrial and "light" information war.

NOTE

1   www.who.int/csr/disease/ebola/en/.

FURTHER READING

Maj-Lis Follér and Håkan Thörn, eds. *The Politics of AIDS: Globalization, the State and Civil Society*. New York: Palgrave Macmillan, 2008.

Gina Kolata. *Flu: The Story of the Great Influenza Pandemic of 1918 and the Search for the Virus that Caused it*. New York: Touchstone, 1999.

Grace O. M. Lee and Malcolm Warner. *The Political Economy of the SARS Epidemic: The Impact on Human Resources in East Asia*. New York: Routledge, 2008.

Peter Andreas and Ethan Nadelmann. *Policing the Globe: Criminalization and Crime Control in International Relations*. Oxford: Oxford University Press, 2006.

Kathryn Farr. *Sex Trafficking: The Global Market in Women and Children*. New York: Worth, 2005.

Carolyn Nordstrom. *Global Outlaws: Crime, Money, and Power in the Contemporary World*. Berkeley: University of California Press, 2007.

Philip Bobbitt. *Terror and Consent: The Wars for the Twenty-First Century*. New York: Knopf, 2008.

Tarak Barkawi. *Globalization and War*. Lanham, MD: Rowman and Littlefield, 2007.

Carl Walker. *Depression and Globalization: The Politics of Mental Health in the 21st Century*. New York: Springer, 2008.

REFERENCES ··

Andreas, Peter, and Ethan Nadelmann. 2006. *Policing the Globe: Criminalization and Crime Control in International Relations*. Oxford: Oxford University Press.

Barkawi, Tarak. 2004. "Connection and Constitution: Locating War and Culture in Globalization Studies." *Globalizations* 1, 2.

Barnhart, Michael A. 2007. "Cold War." In Jan Aart Scholte and Roland Robertson, eds., *Encyclopedia of Globalization*. New York: MTM Publishing.

Barrionuevo, Alexei. 2007. "Globalization in Every Loaf: Ingredients Come from All Over, But Are They Safe?" *New York Times*. June 16.

Bauman, Zygmunt. 2006. *Liquid Fear*. Cambridge: Polity.

Becker, Howard. 1963. *Outsiders: Studies in the Sociology of Deviance*. New York: Free Press.

Bobbitt, Philip. 2008. *Terror and Consent: The Wars for the Twenty-First Century*. New York: Knopf.

Bogdanich, Walt. 2007. "Free Trade Zones Ease Passage of Counterfeit Drugs to US." *New York Times*. December 17.

Brownstein, Henry. 1996. *The Rise and Fall of a Violent Crime Wave: Crack Cocaine and the Construction of a Social Crime Problem*. New York: Criminal Justice Press.

Chivers, C. V. 2008. "US Position Complicates Global Effort to Curb Illicit Arms." *New York Times*. July 19.

Coser, Lewis. 1956. *The Functions of Social Conflict*. New York: Free Press.

Farr, Kathryn. 2005. *Sex Trafficking: The Global Market in Women and Children*. New York: Worth.

Follér, Maj-Lis, and Håkan Thörn, eds. 2008. *The Politics of AIDS: Globalization, the State and Civil Society*. New York: Palgrave Macmillan.

Friedman, Thomas. 2005. *The World is Flat: A Brief History of the Twenty-first Century*. New York: Farrar, Straus, Giroux.

Gall, Carlotta, and Andy Worthington. 2008. "Time Runs Out for an Afghan Held by the US." *New York Times*. February 5.

Giddens, Anthony. 1990. *The Consequences of Modernity*. Stanford, CA: Stanford University Press.

Glenny, Misha. 2008. *McMafia: A Journey Through the Criminal Underworld*. New York: Knopf.

Goode, Erich, and Nachman Ben-Yehuda. 1994. *Moral Panics*. Oxford: Blackwell.

Halbwachs, Maurice. 1992. *On Collective Memory*. Chicago: University of Chicago Press.

Harvey, David. 1989. *The Condition of Postmodernity: An Enquiry into the Origins of Cultural Change*. Oxford: Blackwell.

Knorr Cetina, Karin. 2005. "Complex Global Microstructures: The New Terrorist Societies." *Theory, Culture & Society* 22.

Kolata, Gina. 1999. *Flu: The Story of the Great Influenza Pandemic of 1918 and the Search for the Virus that Caused it*. New York: Touchstone.

Kulish, Nicholas. 2007. "Europe Fears Meth Foothold Is Expanding." *New York Times*. November 23.

Landler, Mark, and John Markoff. 2007. "After Computer Siege in Estonia, War Fears Turn to Cyberspace." *New York Times*. May 29.

Lee, Grace O. M., and Malcolm Warner. 2008. *The Political Economy of the SARS Epidemic: The Impact on Human Resources in East Asia*. New York: Routledge.

Lemert, Charles, and Anthony Elliott. 2006. *Deadly Worlds: The Emotional Costs of Globalization*. Lanham, MD: Rowman and Littlefield.

Lyons, David. 2004. "Globalizing Surveillance: Comparative and Sociological Perspectives." *International Sociology* 12, 2 (June).

Martin, Gus. 2007. "Globalization and International Terrorism." In George Ritzer, ed., *Blackwell Companion to Globalization*. Malden, MA: Blackwell.

McNeil, Donald G. 2008. "A Pandemic that Wasn't But Might Be." *New York Times*. January 22.

Mydans, Seth. 2008. "Indonesian Chickens, and People, Hard Hit by Bird Flu." *New York Times*. February 1.

Myers, Steven Lee, and Thom Shanker. 2008. "Conflicts Throw NATO Expansion, and Bush's Trans-Atlantic Legacy, into Doubt." *New York Times*. March 15.

New York Times. 2008. July 1. "A Ragtag Insurgency Gains al Qaeda Lifeline."

Nolen, Stephanie. 2006. "The African State: An AIDS Survivor." *The Globe and Mail* (Toronto). August 10.

Nye, Joseph S. 2005. *Soft Power: The Means to Success in World Politics*. New York: Public Affairs.

Ong, Paul. 2007. "Bovine Spongiform Encephalopathy." In Jan Aart Scholte and Roland Robertson, eds., *Encyclopedia of Globalization*. New York: MTM Publishing.

Otterman, Michael. 2007. *American Torture: From the Cold War to Abu Ghraib and Beyond*. Ann Arbor, MI: Pluto Press.

Patton, Cindy. 2002. *Globalizing AIDS*. Minneapolis: University of Minnesota Press.

Rehman, Javaid. 2007. "Terrorism." In Jan Aart Scholte and Roland Robertson, eds., *Encyclopedia of Globalization*. New York: MTM Publishing.

Rosenthal, Elisabeth. 2007a. "As Earth Warms up, Virus from Tropics Moves to Italy." *New York Times*. December 23.

Rosenthal, Elisabeth. 2007b. "W.H.O. Urges Effort to Fight Fast-Spreading Disease." *New York Times*. August 27.

Schneider, Gerald. 2007. "War in the Era of Globalization." In George Ritzer, ed., *Blackwell Companion to Globalization*. Malden, MA: Blackwell.

Schoenfeld, Amy. 2007. "A Multinational Loaf." *New York Times*. June 16.

Scott Tyson, Ann. 2008. "Standard Warfare May Be Eclipsed by Nation-Building." *Washington Post*. October 5.

Shelley, Louise. 2006. "The Globalization of Crime and Terrorism." *Global Issues* 1, 1 (February).

Simmel, Georg. 1908/1955. *Conflict and the Web of Group Affiliations*. New York: Free Press.

Tumber, Howard, and Frank Webster. 2007. "Globalization and Information and Communications Technologies: The Case of War." In George Ritzer, ed., *Blackwell Companion to Globalization*. Malden, MA: Blackwell.

Turner, Bryan S. 2007. "Human Rights." In Jan Aart Scholte and Roland Robertson, eds., *Encyclopedia of Globalization*. New York: MTM Publishing.

Walker, Carl. 2008. *Depression and Globalization: The Politics of Mental Health in the 21st Century*. New York: Springer.

Zubair, Pir, and Jane Perlez. 2008. "Pakistan Marble Helps Taliban Stay in Business." *New York Times*. July 14.

Inequality

Globalization: The Essentials, by George Ritzer
© 2011 John Wiley & Sons Ltd

The relationship between inequality and globalization is, needless to say, of great importance in the world today. We will discuss three aspects of this relationship in this chapter: inequality (especially economic inequality) among societies throughout the world (Sernau 2006); inequality based on race and ethnicity, and gender; as well as the ways in which inequality relates to rural–urban differences.

GLOBAL INEQUALITY

Even a casual examination of global realities makes it clear that inequalities among and between areas of the world (especially North and South) exist and are extraordinarily dramatic and disturbing. Most of those in the North are quite aware of both their absolute affluence as well as how it compares to the poverty of those in the South (there are, of course, poor people in the North; that is, there is inequality within the North). The evening newscasts showing hunger in places like Darfur, with the heart-wrenching sight of starving children with distended bellies, are a constant reminder of the differences between the two areas of the world. This is especially jarring when it is juxtaposed with TV features on overeating in the North and pictures of increasingly obese Americans or Europeans. Most of the people in the South (there are, of course, wealthy areas and certainly many well-off people in the South; there is inequality in the South, too) are also abundantly aware of both their absolute poverty as well as how much less well-off they are than those in the North.

"The Bottom Billion"

The most common way of looking at economic inequality in the world is to focus on the differences between the North and the South, core and periphery, or between the developed and less developed areas of the world. However, Paul Collier (2007, forthcoming) argues that in making that gross distinction we ignore the poorest people in the world, what he calls "the bottom billion."

The vast majority (70 percent) of the people in the bottom billion, as well as the countries in which they live, are in Africa. Among the other countries that contain large numbers of the bottom billion are Haiti, Bolivia, Laos, North Korea, and Yemen. Wherever they live, the bottom billion have incomes of only about a fifth of those in other developing countries and their situation will only grow worse unless there are dramatic changes in the near future. They also have many other serious problems such as low life expectancy (about 50 years whereas the average is 67 in other developing nations) and high infant mortality (14 percent of the children of the bottom billion die before their fifth birthday versus 4 percent in other developing countries), and they are more likely to show symptoms of malnutrition (36 percent as opposed to 20 percent in other developing countries). Perhaps of greatest importance is the fact that their situation has grown worse in recent years and they have fallen further behind those in not only the developed countries but the other less developed countries, as well.

Migration

One of the consequences of inequality is migration, usually from the South to the North. That is, those who can will generally try to move from poor areas to more affluent areas (see Chapter 8). However, the irony of this is that extreme poverty, such as that experienced by the bottom billion, makes it much more difficult for those who suffer from it to migrate to the North. They are likely to be so poor that they lack the physical strength, and even the meager resources, needed to move. They also live in countries that lack the basic infrastructure – roads, trains, ships – that would allow them to move to the North.

However, those in the bottom billion (and many others) are often forced to flee their homeland, to migrate to another country (as in the recent case of Zimbabweans fleeing their country for South Africa). Much of that migration is *not* North-to-South, but rather South-to-South, migration.

South-to-South migration: Movement of people from poorer Southern countries to somewhat better-off Southern countries.

South-to-South migration typically involves the movement from poorer Southern countries to slightly, or somewhat, better-off Southern countries. More generally, it involves movement from any less developed country to any more developed country (i.e. the countries involved need not literally be in the South) (DeParle 2007: A1, A16). South-to-South migration describes, for example, the movement from the very poor nation of Haiti (now far worse off as a result of the devastating 2010 earthquake) to the slightly more affluent country of the Dominican Republic (with which Haiti shares the island of Hispaniola). Migrants from Haiti are drawn to the Dominican Republic by the fact the average income there is six times that in Haiti ($2,850 compared to $480 – and the latter was before the earthquake). However, once they are in the Dominican Republic, Haitian migrants are almost always poorly paid compared to natives, often abused, and frequently deported back (many originally crossed the border illegally) to their home country.

Similar South-to-South migration occurs between Nicaragua and Costa Rica, Paraguay and Argentina, Nepal and India, Indonesia and Malaysia, Burkina Faso and Ivory Coast, and others. Workers who participate in this migration are involved in construction, harvesting crops, digging mines, cleaning homes, and tending fields.

The World Bank estimates that there are 74 million South-to-South migrants (there are an estimated 82 million South-to-North migrants). Of course, as with all migration, remittances (see Chapter 8) are important. While remittances are often hard to measure accurately, especially in the case of South-to-South migration, they are estimated to be somewhere in the range of $18 to $55 billion a year for those involved in that type of migration.

   With Northern countries exerting tighter control over their borders, we are likely to see more South-to-South migration in the future. Furthermore, those who move South-to-South are apt to be different from South-to-North migrants (poorer, more rural, etc.). The two forms of migration are related in the sense that, for example, those who are involved in the South-to-North migration (e.g. Dominicans who move to the US) open up jobs for those involved in the South-to-South migration (e.g. Haitians migrating to the Dominican Republic).

   There are various reasons why people move South-to-South, including push factors such as war and political crises at home, and pull factors such as the availability of work with higher pay in the destination country. Some migrate only seasonally, while others stay in their new country for long periods of time. Some illegals are welcomed, while others might be deported, perhaps on a mass basis. Some are treated well, or at least tolerated, while others are abused and perhaps even killed. One Haitian migrant in the Dominican Republic (which feels "overwhelmed by the number of Haitian migrants"), who was heading home, said: "I got desperate and went to the Dominican Republic … I'm not going back again" (quoted in DeParle 2007: A16).

E-Waste and Inequality

Another dimension of inequality in this realm involves e-waste, or electronic waste (e.g. old computers), which is laced with all sorts of hazardous and toxic materials (see also Chapter 9). In spite of the 1992 Basel Convention designed to regulate the traffic in hazardous waste and to bar its shipment from developed to less developed countries, such shipments continue to occur even though they are illegal (three countries – Haiti, Afghanistan, and the US – have yet to ratify the treaty). The reason is that developed countries much prefer to ship the hazardous material out of their domains and away from their populations. Further, it is much cheaper to have e-waste processed in less developed countries than in developed ones (in one estimate the cost is $2,500 per ton in developed countries versus as little as $3 per ton in less developed countries). The hazardous work involved in extracting useful parts and metals from old computer technology provides income for large numbers in the less developed world (Drori 2006). However, the income is very low and those who do such work are likely to become ill, at least in the long run, from exposure to dangerous elements and components. The income earned will do little to improve the economic situation in the less developed world and the negative health effects will only increase the gap between rich and poor countries, at least in terms of health.

Global Digital Divide

One of the most important contemporary consequences *and* causes of global inequality is the global digital divide. On the one hand, those in poor countries are often not able to afford – and even do not have the electricity needed to run – computers to give them Internet access. On the other hand, the lack of advanced technology, especially when it is so abundant in the North, means that the South continues to fall further behind the North economically; that global inequality is increasing.

There is great inequality in the world in terms of access to (people's ability to get their hands on the technology), and use of (once people gain access, their ability to operate the technology), the Internet, as well as, of course, computers, to say nothing of other digital technologies. Most computers are in the developed countries; the less developed countries have relatively few computers and the gap is not narrowing appreciably. As a result, the number of online users in the South is negligible. In addition, the vast majority of Internet hosts are in the North and, once again, there is little representation of such hosts in less developed countries.

The main barriers to global equality in Internet access and use are the lack of infrastructure within less developed countries and the low incomes in those areas, which make digital technologies, and therefore access to the Internet, prohibitively expensive for most in those areas. However, all of these aspects of Internet use are not only unequally distributed among nations of the world, but they are also unequally distributed within nations, even the most highly developed nations, with the poor (including immigrants from the South [Benitez 2006: 181–99]) having far less access than the middle class and the rich (Drori 2006).

Language represents another source of inequality on the Internet. The vast majority of web pages on the Internet are in English; a small number are in other languages – for example, German, Japanese, French, Spanish, and Swedish. Clearly those who do not speak any of these languages (the overwhelming majority in the South) are at a huge disadvantage on the Internet and may even find the Internet totally inaccessible because of the language barrier.

One possible solution in dealing with the global digital divide involves hardware, especially the creation and mass-production of a low-cost personal computer. A nonprofit organization, One Laptop Per Child, has created a computer for the 1.2 billion children in the developing world without one. It was originally designed to sell for about $100. However, the development of these low-cost computers ran into problems and the cost has doubled. The corporate giant Intel also has a design for such a computer, but it will be more expensive (Markoff 2007: C1, C2).

RACE AND ETHNICITY AND GENDER

Race and Ethnicity

We tend to think of race and ethnicity as being objective in the sense that they are based on such seemingly objective, phenotypic characteristics as the color of one's skin. However, the fact is that *all* racial and ethnic statuses are products of social definitions, including the social definition of seemingly objective traits. (This means that since they involve social definitions, race and ethnicity also differ – because those definitions vary – over time and from one locale to another.) This is based on one of the classic arguments in social theory: "If men [sic] define situations as real, they are real in their consequences" (Thomas and Thomas 1928: 572). This not only points to the importance of social definitions, but also to the fact that "erroneous" social definitions can and do have powerful consequences. For example, a white person defined as black, or a black person defined as white, will be profoundly affected by that definition, whatever the "objective" reality.

There is nothing intrinsic about, for example, any racial or ethnic group that makes it distinct from any other; race and ethnicity are dynamic, fluid categories that are socially defined. What *is* different about races and ethnic groups is the basis for the social definitions, but those differences do not determine whether one is considered a member of a given racial or ethnic group. Thus, it is *not* the color of her skin that makes a person black or white. Someone defined by others, or who defines herself, as black in the US might be considered, and consider herself, white in Peru. The same can be said of ethnic groups. In Great Britain, for example, whether one is considered Jewish or Italian relates, as well, to definitions of others and to self-definitions.

If both involve definitions, what serves to differentiate a race from an ethnic group? The lines are not clear because races (e.g. whites) are often considered ethnic groups (e.g. "white ethnics" [Greeley 1976: 20–36]) and ethnic groups are often considered races (Jews, most notoriously in Nazi Germany and in the effort to destroy them in the Holocaust, are frequently thought of as a race). However, the basic difference is that while a **race** is generally defined as such on the basis of some real or presumed *physical, biological, phenotypical* characteristic, an **ethnic group** is defined in that way on the basis of some *cultural* characteristic (religious beliefs and practices, what they eat, how they dress, their sexual behavior). In the American context, whites, blacks, American Indians, Asian and Pacific Islanders, and Hispanics are usually considered to be races (the main basis for the definition is physical), while Italians, Jews, Poles, and White Anglo-Saxon Protestants are considered ethnic groups (mainly on the basis of cultural characteristics).

> **Race**: Defined on the basis of real or presumed physical, biological, or phenotypical characteristics.

> **Ethnic group**: Social group defined on the basis of some cultural characteristic.

Thus, race and ethnicity are social constructions and social creations. For example, the "invention" of race as an ideological concept dates back to the Enlightenment and to the emergence of modern society (Winant 2001: 290). The concept of race has been used to refer to inherent biological differences between human groups and to justify the associated ideas of racial superiority and inferiority. In the nineteenth and early twentieth centuries, ideas about race were supplemented with "science" and allegedly fixed biological characteristics of groups were used to justify scientifically the unequal distribution of wealth, power, prestige, access to resources, and life chances.

Even though "biological" or "scientific" racism continues to exist, a new type of racism, based more on social and cultural factors, such as religion, language, and national origin, is more prevalent today. In other words, racism, as an ideological construct, was transformed, in the twentieth century as ideas of cultural superiority increasingly replaced those associated with biological superiority. Further, racism is now more a matter of *hegemony* than physical domination (e.g. by the state). That is, one race now subordinates another more on the basis of dominant ideas (especially about cultural differences) and the fact that hegemonic racist ideas come to "operate as a taken-for-granted, almost unconscious common sense" (Winant 2001: 293) in the minds of the individuals who accept them.

The emerging emphasis on culture in the understanding of race has led the concept to increasingly resemble that of "ethnicity." Since different cultural characteristics are almost always associated with racial groups and cultural discrimination is central to racial discrimination, it is increasingly difficult to differentiate between racism and ethnicism.

Racism and ethnicism serve similar functions in social discrimination; both define the Other as inherently different from, and inferior to, the dominant group in society.

> **Racism**: Belief in the inherent superiority of one racial group and the inferiority of others.

Racism is a belief in the inherent superiority of one racial group and the inferiority of others, while *ethnicism* is a belief in the inherent superiority of one ethnic group and the inferiority of others. Racial and ethnic minorities are sometimes seen as subhuman; they are denied human qualities; they are seen as destructive of not only human values, but human life. This serves to justify not only the majority status of those making the claims, and the minority status of those seen as a racial or ethnic minority, but also a variety of kinds of actions to be taken against the minority.

Racism and ethnicism are often accompanied by xenophobia which, etymologically, translates as "the fear caused by strangers."

> **Xenophobia**: Beliefs, attitudes, and prejudices that reject, exclude, and vilify groups made up of outsiders or foreigners.

Xenophobia involves the beliefs, attitudes and prejudices that reject, exclude, and vilify groups that are outsiders or foreigners to the dominant social group. Xenophobia sometimes leads to violence. Racism, ethnicism, and xenophobia are manifest in such diverse forms as murder, physical attacks, hate speech, denial of entry to stores, restaurants, clubs, and denial of access to employment.

Perhaps the most important similarity between racial and ethnic groups from the perspective of this analysis is the way in which they relate to the majority–minority issue. That is, some racial and ethnic groups tend to be minorities in many different societies around the world, while others tend to be in the majority. This is clearest in the case of the white–black distinction where whites are disproportionately in the majority and blacks are disproportionately in the minority. This is true within many societies, although not all (in most African societies blacks are the majority group). However, what is most important for our purposes is the global picture and global relationships. At the global level, whites are disproportionately in the dominant North, while blacks are primarily in the South (although this is changing with South-to-North migration). As a result, according to Winant (2004: 131): "Globalization is a re-racialization of the world. What have come to be called 'North–South" issues are also deeply racial issues. The disparities … between the (largely white and wealthy) global North and the (largely dark-skinned and poor) global South have always possessed a racial character." The key issue from the point of view of globalization is the nature of the relationship, of the flows and barriers, between predominantly white and black areas of the world and more generally between different areas dominated by different races (and ethnic groups).

Historically, most work on the issue of race and ethnicity has focused on particular nation-states and what transpires within them. This is particularly true of the US, largely because of its unique history in terms of both race and ethnicity. In terms of race it is, of course, the history of slavery and the continuing legacy of that system and its impact on black Americans. In terms of ethnicity, it is the history of massive immigration to the US, especially in the late nineteenth and early twentieth centuries. Many ethnic groups from Europe made their way to the US, but of course included here is the arrival of other racial groups, as well, especially Asians and, more recently, large numbers of Hispanics. Thus, the US was, at least until recently, a uniquely multi-racial and multi-ethnic society. This has changed as many other societies, for example those in Europe, have become much more multi-racial (largely as a result of South-to-North migration from Africa) and multi-ethnic (mostly as a result of both South-to-North [e.g. from Turkey] and North-to-North [from Eastern Europe] migration).

Of course, other societies have been in the forefront of discussions of race and ethnicity. In terms of race, South Africa was long a focus of attention (Dunbar Moodie 1975; Dunbar Moodie and Ndatshe 1994) because of its system of *apartheid*, a formal system of "separate development" for whites and blacks (the vast majority of the South African population is, and was, black) that served to perpetuate both white privilege and power and black subordination and weakness. Apartheid was formally abolished in 1991, but its history and legacy continue to be important in analyses and discussions of race in South Africa.

Brazil is another nation-state that gets much attention in discussions of race (Degler 1971/1986), largely because of the much more harmonious relationship between the races there than in the US. There is also a much more fluid definition of race in Brazil than in the US.

However, while discussions of various societies throughout the world in terms of their distinctive patterns of racial (and ethnic) relations is important, far more important from the perspective of globalization is a focus on global flows and barriers. Of special importance in this context is the global flow of *people* from various racial and ethnic groups as well as the global flow of *ideas* such as *racism*, **pluralism** (the idea that different races and ethnic groups can live together; they can coexist), or *resistance* (the idea that racial and ethnic minorities must resist discrimination and its deleterious effects).

> **Pluralism:** The idea and fact that different races and ethnic groups can live together, can coexist.

The issue of ethnicity (race) relates to a sense of who one is. It offers a sense not only of one's being, but also of the collectivities (real and imagined) to which one belongs. That is, in general, people see themselves as belonging to ethnic groups that involve others with the same or a similar identity. Identities, therefore, are at the heart of collective bonds. Because they are often so strongly felt, identities are also often at the heart of struggle among ethnic groups.

At least in the last few hundred years, if not before, ethnic (or national) identities have been closely tied to states. However, in recent years, with the increase in globalization and the corresponding decline in the nation-state, identity with the nation-state has tended to decline in importance (but global processes such as the Olympics, the World Cup, and inexpensive international phone calls, among many others, have served to reinforce such identity), although it is certainly the case that nation-state identity remains a powerful force on the global stage. It is more the case that ethnic identity and other kinds of identities – class, race, and gender, as well as age, sexual orientation, and others – have grown in importance, often because of global processes that serve to increase and to reinforce them.

The existence of so many identities on the global stage has increased the possibility of people having hybrid identities. That is, they identify not only with, say, their ethnic group, but also with their gender, race, and sexual orientation. This leads to more complex identities and to the greater likelihood of internal conflict among one's identities.

Some see globalization as a threat to ethnic identity; they see it as creating a world of homogeneous identities, or at least one where the number and variety of ethnic (and other) identities is in decline. However, others argue that globalization is not a threat to ethnic identity. For one thing, it is contended that such identities are not nearly as fragile, are far more powerful, than is often believed. For another, globalization can be seen as a force, maybe the most significant force, in the creation and proliferation of ethnic identity (Tomlinson 2000: 269–77). Ethnic identity can also be enhanced by resistance to the global pressure toward the homogenization of identity. Further, ethnic identity itself, like globalization, is seen as a very modern phenomenon. Such a position leads to the view that globalization is not opposed to ethnic identity, but that both are part of the same modern process leading to a proliferation of ethnic identities, not to a diminution in the number and variety of such identities and of the differences among them. Thus, globalization brings with it an increasingly bewildering array of ethnic (and other – class, gender, and racial identities, among many others) identities.

Ethnic identities, which might be seen as threatened by globalization, can also be seen as being enhanced and spread by that process. For example, through the development of advanced forms of communication and the media, globalization allows diasporic (see Chapter 8) groups spread throughout the world not only to retain their ethnic identity, but to develop it more strongly, perhaps even more strongly than those in the motherland. Furthermore, this more powerful sense of ethnic identity can be exported back to the home country through the same forms of global media. This is part of the broader process of deterritorialization (see Chapter 2), which in this case involves the separation of ethnic or national identity from any specific geographic territory.

Greater ethnic diversity within many nation-states has increased the possibility of ethnic conflict within their confines. Of course, such ethnic conflict is not new. Among the most notable examples have been conflicts between Turks and Armenians in Turkey, Germans (especially Nazis) and Jews in Germany, Tamils and Sinhalese in Sri Lanka, the Tutsi and Hutu in Burundi, and the conflict between various ethnic groups – Slovenes, Croatians, Serbs, Bosnians, Montenegrins, Macedonians, and Albanians – after the breakup of Yugoslavia in 1991. However, today, with more members of ethnic groups in more and more countries, there is the potential for a great increase in the number, if not the intensity, of ethnic conflicts.

Historically, efforts to "deal' with ethnic minorities have occurred within nation-states or other delimited territories. The most extreme cases involve extermination or geno-cide. **Genocide** was defined in 1948 by the United Nations Convention on the Prevention and Punishment of the Crime of Genocide as "acts committed with the intent to destroy, in whole or in part, a national, ethnic, racial, or religious group" (cited in Karstedt 2007: 1909–10; O'Brien 1968: 515–20). This was prompted by the Nazi Holocaust, committed primarily, but not exclusively, against Jews. At first, the Holocaust occurred within the confines of Germany, but it later spread to the European countries allied with, or conquered by, Germany. It was in that sense global and it would have undoubtedly become far more global had the Nazis achieved their goal of world conquest. For example, had the Nazis succeeded in conquering the US, we would have undoubtedly seen the genocide of American Jews. A later example of a more global genocide was the mass killings during the Stalin era that extended throughout the then-vast Soviet Empire. In the main, though, genocide continues to be practiced within nation-states (e.g. the murder of millions by the Khmer Rouge in Cambodia in the mid- to late 1970s).

> **Genocide**: Acts committed with the intent to destroy a national, ethnic, racial, or religious group.

However, it is important to point out that the global age brings with it at least the possibility of even more global genocide. That is, genocide could become another of the negative flows discussed in Chapter 10. In the global age, one can imagine a scenario whereby genocide that takes place in one part of the world eventually makes its way, flows, to other parts of the world. This might be a far-fetched scenario (a "Mad Max" scenario of the kind discussed in Chapter 12), but it is more likely because of globalization, because of proliferating and accelerating global flows, as well as the increased inability of nation-states to block many of these flows.

One of the processes of greatest concern in the context of ethnicity and globalization is ethnic cleansing. Ethnic cleansing can be seen as, at least in part, a specific example of another way of dealing with ethnic minorities – *expulsion*. Expulsion can take two forms (Eaton Simpson and Yinger 1985). First, it can be direct, with minority ethnic groups forcibly ejected by the majority through military and other government action. Second, such a minority group can leave "voluntarily" because it is being harassed, discriminated against, and persecuted. Of course, in the real world these two forms of expulsion occur in concert with one another. Thus, many of those involved in diasporas of one kind or another have often experienced both forms of expulsion. This is particularly true of Jews who have often moved both because they have been forcibly ejected (e.g. by the Romans from Jerusalem in the second century AD) and voluntarily (those German Jews who left before the Holocaust because of harassment or who left both Czarist Russia and the Stalinist Soviet Union for similar reasons).

Ethnic cleansing (Ahmed 1995: 1–25; Mann 1999: 18–45) is defined in terms similar to those used to define expulsion, as "various policies of forcibly removing people of another ethnic group" (Sekulic 2007: 1450–2). Of course, Nazi actions against Jews fit the definition of ethnic cleansing, but ethnic cleansing achieved more recent notoriety during the wars that were associated with the dissolution of Yugoslavia in 1991. Many of the ethnic groups that dominated various regions (e.g. Croatia) sought to create areas that were ethnically homogeneous and they did this by expelling and even killing (this is genocide rather than expulsion) members of other ethnic groups. For example, Croatians were expelled from parts of Croatia inhabited by Serbs. Bosnia, which declared independence in 1992, was composed of three major ethnic groups – Slavic Muslims (the largest single group), Serbs, and Croats. Ethnic cleansing took the form of Serbian armed forces creating ethnically homogeneous enclaves by forcibly removing the other ethnic groups, especially Muslims.

> **Ethnic cleansing**: Forcibly removing people of another ethnic group.

Gender

Turning to gender and its relationship to social definitions, we need to distinguish gender conceptually from sex. **Sex** refers to the physical differences between males and females (although, social definitions are involved here, as well). **Gender**, however, like race and ethnicity (and class for that matter), is a matter of social definition and social distinction (Bourdieu 1984). Also like race and ethnicity, gender involves more than simply making distinctions. Gender distinctions are used to organize the social world and to affect, often adversely, women. These distinctions are made even though there are great similarities between men and women and great variations exist within both (Hess and Marx Ferree 1987: 9–31). Of greatest interest from the point of view of this chapter is the way gender differences are used to advantage men and disadvantage women not only within nation-states, but also globally. Most extremely, definitions of gender employed by men often lead to acts of violence (beatings, rape, even murder) against women.

> **Sex**: Physical differences between males and females.

> **Gender**: Differences between males and females based on social definition and distinction.

Recent analyses of globalization demonstrate that gender is critical in terms of globalization's effects on human groups. Globalization reinforces preexisting gender structures, barriers, and relationships, only now on a global scale.

Mainstream perspectives on, and theories of, globalization in sociology, economics, international relations (and many other fields) often claim to be gender-neutral or gender-blind. Leaving the gendered effects of globalization aside, mainstream theories (e.g. neo-liberal theories) imply that global processes have similar effects on men and women. Women's experiences and voices, especially those in the developing world, are frequently not taken into account. However, gender is a critical aspect of globalization, especially global capitalist processes and relations.

Feminists' interest in the gendered processes of global capitalism found its way into development studies, critiques of neo-liberalism, international relations, international political economy, and transnational networking. Numerous feminist accounts of global processes have analyzed the gendered effects of globalization, which shape gendered ideologies, institutions, hierarchies, and inequality structures. Specifically highlighting the experiences of poor third-world women, these works reveal that the most devastating effects of globalization fall on women (for example, the greater risk of maternal mortality in the peripheral areas of the globe).

Gender and the economy
One of the key effects of globalization is the transformation of the nature of economic activity. From the 1970s on, production was reorganized through global production systems. To cut labor costs MNCs shifted production to low-wage economies. The effects have been significant for the labor force both in developed and developing countries. In developed countries, part-time and temporary jobs replaced manufacturing jobs. Developing countries have seen a growth in low-paying, informal, and temporary jobs as their economies have shifted from nationalized industries and public sectors to export-oriented production. Women are found disproportionately in these low-paying, part-time, and temporary jobs in both developed and less developed countries.

Within the last two decades, women's labor-force participation in paid employment has increased dramatically around the globe. Since the late 1970s and early 1980s, there has been a notable increase in women's labor-force participation rates in the Americas and Western Europe. Even though there are significant variations within and across regions, women's labor-force participation has also risen substantially in sub-Saharan Africa, North Africa, Eastern Europe, Southeast Asia, and East Asia over this period (Cagatay and Ozler 1995; Moghadam 1999: 367–88; Heintz 2006). While the progress in women's employment status is linked, at least in part, to gender equality movements, the key factor in this change appears to be the better integration of an increasing number of areas into the world economy through trade and production.

The greater involvement of women in the global paid-labor market is observable in a variety of occupations and professions in the service sector. Women are increasingly employed in public service and are more likely to work as teachers and university professors; as nurses and doctors in state hospitals; and as workers and administrators in government offices (Moghadam 1999: 367–88). Women are also concentrated in professional services such as law, banking, accounting, computing, and architecture. Women predominate in such office jobs as data entry, airline booking, credit cards, word-processing, and telecommunications (Gaio 1995; Pearson 2000: 10–18; Freeman 2001: 1007–37). There has also been a significant increase in the informal as well as the formal employment of women. Women's labor migration to work as nannies, domestics, nurses, waitresses, and sex workers (Kempadoo and Doezema 1998) constitutes a significant proportion of the international informal labor force (and of human trafficking; see below). Beyond services, women are heavily employed in agriculture, as well as in the labor-intensive manufacture of products such as garments, sportswear, and electronics.

The increasing participation of women in both the formal and informal global paid labor force has been termed the **feminization of labor** (Standing 1989: 1077–95). This refers to the rise of female labor participation in all sectors and the movement of women into jobs traditionally held by men. This global trend has occurred in both developing and developed countries. In many developed countries, educated middle-class women have made inroads in professional and managerial employment, resulting in a decline in the differences between male and female labor participation rates. The feminization of labor has also taken place in the developing world. In 74 percent of developing countries female participation in the labor force has increased, while in 66 percent male participation has decreased.

Feminization of labor: Increasing participation of women in the formal and informal global paid labor force.

The feminization of labor in the developing economies is often accompanied by the feminization of poverty and by female proletarianization. In many of those economies, women's increased participation in paid employment is caused mainly by the shift from import substitution (see Chapter 2) to export-oriented manufacturing (Joekes 1987; Standing 1989; Cagatay and Ozler 1995; Standing 1999: 583–602). Globally, more women are being drawn into labor-intensive and low-paying industries such as textiles, apparel, leather products, food processing, and electronics. For instance, women represented more than half of the workforce in electronics production in Hong Kong, Macau, Singapore, Taiwan, the Czech Republic, Malaysia, Indonesia, Puerto Rico, Slovenia, Cuba, the Philippines, Thailand, and Sri Lanka (Ferus-Comelo 2006: 43–54).

Jobs in these industries are characterized by the flexible use of labor, high turnover rates, part-time and temporary employment, and a lack of security and benefits. Women are preferred in these industries because they will typically work for lower wages and they are seen as easier for male employers and managers to supervise. They are considered not only to be more docile, but also to have greater patience and more dexterity than men in performing standardized and repetitive work (Elson and Pearson 1981: 87–107). Female employment is also characterized by poorer working conditions, more compulsory overtime with no extra pay, and more dangerous working conditions.

A great deal of attention has been focused on the relationship between globalization and the place of women in the local, regional (Bose and Acosta-Belen 1995), and global economy. Of particular importance, at least from the perspective of globalization, is the place of women in what has been called the "global assembly line in which research and management are controlled by the core and developed countries while assembly line work is relegated to semiperiphery or periphery nations that occupy less privileged positions in the global economy" (Ward 1990: 1). Clearly, women are much more likely to be employed in the latter than in the higher-level positions in the core.

Jane Collins (2003) has done an ethnography of part of this global assembly line involving the headquarters of a global apparel firm in New Jersey, a knitting mill in the southern part of Virginia, and two apparel factories in Aguascalientes in Mexico. Work in this industry is highly gendered and is dominated by females. Collins' study is of particular interest to this book, given its focus on global flows, especially its concern with the "flow of resources and power between these sites" (Collins 2003: ix). It is also of interest because wherever she looked in the world, Collins found an increasing McDonaldization (see Chapter 7) of work, especially reliance on Taylorism to measure, control, and de-skill work dominated by females. Workers, especially in Mexico, had their positions weakened vis-à-vis their employers because of sub-contracting (workers had no contact with their employers and little know-ledge of the firm) and the casualization of work. These contributed to the fact that the female Mexican workers had no way to present grievances about their work situation or to act collectively against their employer.

Export Processing Zones (EPZs) are special industrial areas, often in developing countries, designed to draw foreign companies and capital investment. EPZs offer multinational companies incentives including exemption from labor and

> **Export Processing Zone (EPZ)**: Independent area controlled by corporations and free of national control.

environmental regulations, taxes, tariffs, and quotas. EPZs are characteristically unstable as they are likely to move time and again to countries where labor is cheaper and more compliant. A wide range of products are produced in EPZs, including tennis rackets in St. Vincent (Caribbean), furniture in Mauritius, and jewelry in Thailand. However, EPZs mainly focus on the production of textiles, clothing, and electronics for the mass market. The International Labor Organization (ILO) estimates that there are 3,000 EPZs in the world with a total employment of approximately 43 million workers, most of whom are young women (as many as 90 percent in some cases) (Pearson 1992). Again, women are preferred in these production sites because they are considered more meticulous, disciplined, and compliant than men, and therefore, among other things, less likely to unionize.

It is often suggested that EPZs reduce poverty and unemployment and, as a result, facilitate the economic development of the host countries. Even if we assume that this occurs, it does not do so without serious costs. Working conditions are brutal in most EPZs, where violence and abuse are daily routines. A work day may consist of impossibly long shifts with unpaid overtime, non-payment for workers on sick leave, insufficient health and safety measures, monitored access to bathrooms, sexual harassment, physical abuse, and in some cases forced consumption of amphetamines to ensure efficiency. Working conditions are particularly hard on women, especially those who are pregnant and have infants. In most EPZs mandatory pregnancy testing is a condition for employment and for maintaining a job. In some cases gender bias intersects with age discrimination. EPZs tend to hire mostly young and single women; women over 25 years of age are usually not hired since they are seen to be more likely to bear children (Pun 1995: 18–31).

Because of the harsh working conditions and low pay, workers often burn out; the turnover rate in EPZs is very high. It is estimated to be 21 percent in the electrical and electronic firms and to be as high as 32 percent in the textile, chemical products, scientific and measuring equipment, and rubber products firms (Sivalingam 1994).

Informal employment has increased in many countries. Many formal jobs have been replaced by informal ones as lower labor and production costs have increasingly become the major organizing factor in global production. About 25 percent of the world's working population is active in the informal economy and those workers generate approximately 35 percent of global GDP (ICFTU 2004). While women's labor-force participation has increased in almost all regions, the most significant increase in female employment in developing countries has been in informal sectors of the economy (Moghadam 1999: 367–88). Two-thirds of female labor-force participation in developing countries is concentrated in the informal economy; in sub-Saharan Africa the proportion is as high as 84 percent (ICFTU 2004). Informal employment includes temporary work without fixed employers, paid employment from home, domestic work for households (Parreñas 2001), and industrial work for sub-contractors. Informal sectors are characterized by low pay and a lack of secure contracts, worker benefits, or social protection. Workers in the informal economy do not have wage agreements, employment contracts, regular working hours, and health insurance or unemployment benefits. They typically earn below the legal minimum wage and are often not paid on time.

While greater informal employment characterizes both the male and female labor force globally, women and men are concentrated in different types of informal work. Men are concentrated mainly in informal wage and agricultural employment, while women are typically concentrated in non-agricultural employment, domestic work, and unpaid work in family enterprises. Compared to men's informal employment, women's employment is much more likely to have lower hourly wages and less stability.

The trend toward flexibilization and decentralization in production has contributed significantly to the rise in informal female employment in developing countries. In order to reduce labor costs, most MNCs establish sub-contracting networks with local manufacturers employing low-paid workers, mostly women, whose employment can be terminated quickly and easily (Pyle and Ward 2003: 467). In these production networks women are more likely to work in small workshops or from home.

Traditional gender roles and ideas about femininity encourage home-based work. Gendered ideas relating to the division of labor assign reproductive work to women and productive work to men. As a result, the "real" work of women is considered care-giving and homemaking as mothers, wives, and daughters, rather than as wage earners. Since the increase in female labor participation is almost never accompanied by a decrease in their domestic workload, many women accept the lower wages and less formal working arrangements of home-based work in order to be able to continue to carry out household responsibilities.

The global economy creates jobs not only in developing economies, but also in the developed world. The advanced corporate economic centers, especially world and global cities (see below), require large amounts of low-wage labor to maintain the operation of their offices and the lifestyles of entrepreneurs, managers, and professionals associated with them. The state-of-the-art offices of MNCs' headquarters require clerical, cleaning, and repair workers, truckers to bring their software, copying paper, office furniture, and even toilet paper (Sassen 2004: 649–70). Furthermore, work such as provisioning and cleaning offices, child tending, caring for the elderly and for homes has to be done by others. The vast majority of these tasks are performed by immigrants, primarily women, from third-world countries (Acker 2004: 34).

The feminization of wage labor in the global economy has contributed to the increase in female migration. As Ehrenreich and Hochschild (2002: 2) put it, "Women are on the move as never before in history." Much of this involves women from the South moving, legally and illegally, to the North to handle women's work (as, for example, nannies [Cheever 2002: 31–8], maids [Ehrenreich 2002: 85–103], and sex workers [Brennan 2002: 154–68]) historically performed by women from the North. Nine of the largest immigrant-exporting countries are China, India, Indonesia, Myanmar, Pakistan, the Philippines, Sri Lanka, Thailand, and Bangladesh. This immigration serves to enrich the North and to enhance the already elevated lifestyle in the North. Intensifying the feminization of migration, domestic work has grown on a local and global scale and is now considered the largest labor market for women worldwide.

Since most female migration takes place in undocumented and informal ways, women laborers face the worst forms of discrimination, exploitation, and abuse. They can be held as debt hostages by the recruitment agencies for their transportation and placement fees, locked up in the houses of their employers, treated inhumanely, and sometimes even murdered. An increasing number of migrant women are victims of sexual abuse, sex-trafficking, and prostitution.

Global care chains

Arlie Hochschild (2000) argues that migration of domestic workers is part of a **global care chain**, involving a series of personal relationships between people across the globe based on the paid or unpaid work of caring. Care includes social, health, and sexual care services, and usually involves menial tasks such as cooking, cleaning, and ironing. In global care chains, women supply their own care labor to the employer while consuming

> **Global care chains**: Series of personal relationships between people across the globe based on the paid or unpaid work of caring.

other women's care labor, both paid and unpaid. Migrant domestic workers often rely on female relatives, neighbors, and daughters as well as paid domestic workers for the care of their children. For instance, while a mother works as a nanny in a developed country, her young children may be cared for by an older daughter or by a nanny who migrated from some even less developed country. On one end of the chain is a woman in the North pursuing professional employment and finding herself unable to fulfill her duties within the family. On the other is a domestic worker's oldest daughter taking over her mother's familial duties.

Referred to not only as the *global care chain*, but also the *international transfer of caretaking, global nanny chain*, and *racial division of reproductive labor*, the transfer of reproductive labor from women in advanced economies to those in developing economies points to a paradoxical situation in women's empowerment through participation in the labor force. While women in the North are able to undertake careers, they tend to pass their household duties and reproductive labor on to low-wage immigrant workers. Rather than pushing for a redistribution of household responsibilities among family members, women as employers maintain the gender division of labor by transferring the most devalued work to disadvantaged women. As a result, the worth of reproductive labor (and of women) declines even further (Parreñas 2001). In this sense, women's labor-force participation does not necessarily result in a change in traditional gender roles, but rather in the greater exploitation of immigrant women by middle- and upper-class women.

The provision of reproductive labor by migrant domestic workers is not new. It has been obtained by class-privileged women for centuries. However, the flow of reproductive labor has increased due to globalization and the growth of the global economy. There is a substantial and increasing demand for migrant domestic workers in the North and the bulk of the supply comes from the South.

Trafficking in the sex industry
The increased global flow of people creates a greater opportunity for traffickers to transport women for the purposes of sexual exploitation. Trafficking in women for sex work has far more deleterious consequences for women than trafficking for domestic work not only because the former is far more demeaning, but also because victims are exposed to health risks – sexually transmitted diseases, HIV/AIDS, drug addiction – and a wide variety of other life-threatening situations.

The sex industry has become increasingly important to global capitalism. Bars, dance clubs, massage parlors, the pornography industry, international hotel chains, airline companies, and the tourist industry create and help to meet the demand for sex labor around the globe. Each year, an estimated four million people, mostly women and girls (and children more generally [O'Connell Davidson 2005]; more than one million of them), are trafficked throughout the world and enter the global sex industry (Altman 1996: 77–94; 2001), earning traffickers an estimated $6 billion a year (Hughes 1999). Over the last few decades, most of the countries of the South and many of the countries of the ex-Soviet Union and Eastern Europe have experienced an unparalleled growth in prostitution. Many of these prostitutes find their way to the developed world.

The flow of people in the global sex industry not only moves from the third world to the first world, but also in reverse. The growth of sexual tourism over the last 30 years demonstrates the role of sex work in the global market economy. Thailand alone receives approximately five million sex tourists from the US, Western Europe, Australia, and Japan, bringing in about $26.2 billion every year (Bales 1999). In sex-tourist destinations, poverty leads women to participate in the industry. Inexpensive travel opportunities have permitted more, less well-off, sex tourists to circle the globe in search of sex (Brennan 2004).

The great expansion of communication technologies in the global age has opened up further avenues for sex labor on a global scale. The Internet has become the key site for promoting global trafficking and sexual exploitation of women (and children). "Customers" can find a sex worker almost anywhere in the world instantly, read reviews about the individual sex workers posted on websites, exchange information on where to find prostitutes and the prices for sex workers, etc. Websites for commercial prostitution tours from North America and Europe to Southeast Asia and the Caribbean offer package tours, quote prices, and advertise the sex workers and their services to the men of the North. Racism, sexism, and global inequality intersect in the global sex industry.

Mail-order brides

Another aspect of global trafficking in women involves mail-order brides. The mail-order bride business has become a multimillion-dollar global industry thanks, especially, to the Internet. In March 1999, the United States Immigration and Naturalization Service reported that there were over 200 mail-order bride agencies operating in the US. Between roughly 4,000 and 6,000 women are brought to the US each year by "mail-order-bride" agencies. Women who are trafficked through mail-order-bride agencies are mostly from the Philippines, Laos, Burma, Vietnam, Thailand, and the former Soviet Union. This is a segmented market much like any other. For example, Thai women are often promoted as sex workers, while Filipina women are advertised as helpers and wives. The common characteristic of all women trafficked in the mail-order-bride industry is that they are "pleasers not competitors. They are feminine, NOT feminist" (http://www.latineuro.com/agency.html).

Responding to and resisting global minority status: the case of women

The International Women's Movement has a long history traceable back to the late 1800s (Rupp 1997), and its greatest triumphs have related to the increasingly global acquisition of the rights of suffrage (Ramirez, Soysal, and Shanahan 1997: 735–45). However, it has grown dramatically in recent years both because of problems created for women by globalization and because of the increased ability to create a global women's movement. Key events were the United Nations International Women's Year in 1975, and four world conferences – Mexico City (1975), Copenhagen

(1980), Nairobi (1985), and Beijing (1995) (Alter Chen 1995: 477–94). (Snyder [2006: 24–50] sees the UN as an "unlikely godmother" of the women's movement.) Personal networks throughout the globe emerged from these meetings and the Internet has greatly increased the ability of women to interact and to mobilize on a global basis.

A variety of specific issues were the focus of the UN meetings as well as the larger global movement that developed, including human rights (Yuval-Davis 2006: 275–95), economic concerns, health-care issues, and violence against women. Later, concern came to focus on the adverse effects of global capitalism (e.g. increased global trafficking in women), the lack of a voice in global civil society, the growth of antifeminist fundamentalist movements (e.g. the Taliban), and the HIV/AIDS epidemic. More positively, the global women's movement has come to focus on issues of global justice for women and other minorities. It has come to have a strong impact on the UN and has helped to create strong linkages between the UN, national governments, and NGOs (George 2007: 1257–60).

Women throughout the world have not only been involved in the global women's movement, but they have responded at local and regional levels to a variety of problems caused by globalization (for many examples, see Naples and Desai [2002a]). They interact and organize across borders and at transnational and global levels to deal with common problems caused by globalization. They also localize global political activities undertaken by the women's movement, global human rights groups, etc., and they organize against global activities (e.g. militarism) and use global organizations (such as the UN and INGOs) to help in local and regional activities (Naples and Desai 2002b: 34–41). While these and other global linkages are important, it is also the case that many of the activities undertaken by women have been primarily or exclusively local in nature (Basu 1995). Nevertheless, many of these actions have had a profound effect globally. Even with all the local variations, Marx Ferree and Tripp (2006: viii) argue that feminism still needs to be seen as "a truly global phenomenon."

RURAL–URBAN AND INEQUALITY

We turn now to the third major topic in this chapter – the rural–urban relationship, with particular attention to how it relates to global inequality. As we will see, there are important linkages between the two issues, but there is also much more to the relationship between rural and urban, especially as it relates to globalization.

Rural

In conceiving of the rural from the point of view of globalization, we are generally thinking of agricultural areas in the South. While it is true that there are agricultural areas in the North (e.g. the American Midwest), they are comparatively inconsequential (although not economically) in relation to the size and local importance of agricultural areas in the South. That being said, it is the case that agricultural areas in the North are, as we will see, profoundly implicated in, and affected by, globalization, although that impact is in many ways more negative than positive.

The South encompasses about four billion people and has been seen as being in the "vortex of globalization." This is not the first time the South has played a central role in global relations, especially global agriculture. For example, the British outsourced agricultural production to the South (e.g. to India) during the height of their empire. However, contemporary globalization has profoundly affected and altered North–South relationships in agriculture and much else.

Among these transformations are the new "relations of agricultural production" (McMichael 2007: 216–38). The crucial development here is the rise of global agribusiness, dominated by the North in general, and the US in particular. Also of great importance is the factory farm, with the same points of origin. Both global agribusiness and the factory farm involve new relations of agricultural production (e.g. between global corporations and local farms) compared to relations that existed in and between local, more traditional farms.

Most generally, these new relations of agricultural production have come to be defined by the "law of comparative advantage." In practice, this has come to mean that the South produces what are for it non-traditional products (e.g. flowers, fruit, vegetables, shrimp), for which it comes to have a comparative advantage, and it exports those products to the North. This means that Southern countries are producing and consuming less of their own traditional products (e.g. corn in Mexico), including those that have been the staples of their diet. Instead, they are increasingly coming to consume cheap (sometimes, but often not, cheaper) industrialized food imports from the North (the latter are subject to both great fluctuations in availability, depending on the global market for such products, and even greater price fluctuations). These imports not only serve to replace traditional staples, but also to displace large numbers of local farmers who are either forced off the farm or into different types of farming.

The US, its agricultural model, and its emphasis on commercial mono-crops and capital-energy-intensive agriculture are often accorded responsibility (and the blame) for most of these changes. The US model has transformed the rural landscape not only in the South, but throughout much of the world. Indeed, post-WW II Europe was one of the early targets of this transformation through the Marshall Plan. Later, agribusiness disseminated this model throughout the world. It was also fostered by the "green revolution" (a post-WW II revolution in agriculture brought about by research, new technologies, new farming methods, and the like) which, among other things, led to the decline of traditional mixed crops and their replacement by capital-intensive hybrids of wheat, corn, and rice.

Also involved in this is the development and exportation of US-style consumption patterns, in this case of food. This has led to global convergence on a diet that includes a narrowing base of staple grains; increased consumption of animal protein, edible oils, and salt and sugar; and a decline in dietary fibre. Such a diet has contributed, among other things, to a rise in such diseases as diabetes as well as to the global epidemic of obesity (Hashemian and Yach 2007: 516–38). In fact, in recent years obesity has come to be as common throughout the world as malnutrition (about 1.3 million people are afflicted with each). Even in places like Crete, renowned for its healthy "Mediterranean diet," the expansion of American-style fast food has led to greater obesity and other health problems, even, and most disturbingly, among children (Rosenthal 2008: A1, A12).

Another US-based development (although the UK is also a huge player in this) – the supermarket revolution – has also played a key role here. It has obviously centralized food processing and retailing, but it has also exerted increasing control over farmers, ranchers, and so on. (The same could be said about the fast-food chain revolution [Schlosser 2005; Ritzer 2008].) However, these farmers and ranchers rarely have binding contracts, are rewarded only if they meet centrally defined quality standards, and have tended to face declining prices for their products because virtually all of the power in this relationship rests with the great supermarket chains. The creation of both public and private standards for things like food quality and packaging is central not only to increasing global inequality (the North tends to set the standards that the South must follow), but also to homogenization of both food production (e.g. industrial agriculture, factory farms) and food consumption (less grain, more animal protein).

Overall, the South is enveloped by new relations of production which, among other things, mean the displacement of local farmers, the transformation of many who remain from being producers of local staples to producers of non-traditional exports for which there is a global demand (e.g. flowers, more exotic fruits and vegetables), involvement in global specialized commodity chains, and so on.

These changes in the South have not eliminated poverty and hunger, but have led to a change from poverty/hunger amidst scarcity to poverty/hunger amidst abundance. Neo-liberal philosophies and policies (see Chapter 2), including free trade, serve to advantage the North and its enormous agribusinesses (and supermarkets). In the meantime, rural economies everywhere are in depression and crisis with low prices, declining public supports, rural exodus, increases in rural suicides, and so on. The rural South has been forced to open its farm sectors to the global market (while the North retains huge farm subsidies and trade barriers). The removal of subsidies and barriers, and increasing openness to the global market, has led to declining prices and less income for Southern farmers. De-agrarianization and de-peasantization have been accompanied by the rise of rural industrialization, beginning with Export Processing Zones.

Mexico's 1965 Border Industrial Program was a key development, leading to the creation of a series of *maquiladoras* (see Chapter 4) designed to compete with the rising economies of East Asia. This sparked the revolutionary movement of low-wage factories and manufacturing jobs from the North to the South. By the early twenty-first century there were 70 million *maquila* jobs in existence, but most who work in those settings take home only about a third of a living wage. As a result, they are forced to supplement their incomes in various ways and, thereby, in a sense, subsidize the factories and their work. But the *maquilas*, themselves, are now being undercut by the increasing importance of low-wage Chinese, and more recently Vietnamese, manufacturing (even the Chinese are now sending work to Vietnam), making even those settings increasingly tenuous in the "race to the bottom" (see Chapter 4).

Urban

The world has always been predominantly rural, but some time between 2000 and 2010 a "watershed in human history" occurred as for "the first time the urban population of the earth" outnumbered the rural (Davis 2007: 1). However, cities have been central to both scholarly and popular discourse on globalization from the beginning of interest in it as a topic and a phenomenon (Timberlake and Ma 2007: 254–71). Cities were seen as "cosmopolitan" (Beck 2007: 162–76), and therefore inherently global, because they encompassed a range of cultures, ethnicities, languages, and consumer products. Cities also exerted a powerful influence (cultural, political, and economic) over surrounding areas. The many city-based organizations were also linked, through elaborate networks, to organizations in other cities throughout the home country and the world. The system of national and global cities was hierarchical, with substantial flows of people, information, and objects moving both up and down the hierarchy.

The most important of the world's cities are **global cities** (Sassen 1991), with only New York, London, and Tokyo usually included in that elite category. It is no coincidence that the world's most important stock exchanges are located in those cities. More generally, those cities tend to be chosen by many organizations as sites for key offices through which they exert great control over the world's political economy and, in the process, accrue great riches to themselves and the denizens of those cities.

> **Global cities**: Key cities in the global, especially capitalist, economy.

The idea of a global, or a world, city has a long history, but it has exploded as a topic of interest in the study of globalization since the publication of Saskia Sassen's *The Global City: New York, London, and Tokyo* (1991). She, and many others, have continued to work on the topic in the intervening years and to advance our thinking on global cities (Marcuse and van Kempen 2000; Abrahamson 2004; Brenner and Keil 2006; King 2007: 496–500; Paquin 2007: 1953–6; Timberlake and Ma 2007: 254–71). Sassen clearly embeds her notion of global cities in the process of globalization and focuses on economic, especially capitalistic, globalization. In this context, she privileges the three cities mentioned above on the basis of their place in the new world economy. Specifically, they are the key locations for leading industries and marketplaces, the centers of the production and creation of innovative, cutting-edge financial services, the homes of new financial, legal, and accountancy products, and the settings from which businesses and organizations exercise global command and control.

To Sassen, and others, a key point is that global cities are central nodes in a new international division of labor. Of great importance are the linkages among and between these global cities and the flows among and between them. In many ways the global cities have more in common with one another than with the smaller cities and the hinterlands within their own country. They are also more integrated into the global economy than those hinterlands.

However, others have a much more expansive sense of what constitutes such cities and recognize that the number of such cities is likely to grow in the future. Many have come to prefer the far broader notion of "world cities" to the highly limited, and limiting, notion of global cities (Alderson and Beckfield 2004: 811–51; Beckfield and Alderson 2006: 895–904).

The categorization of cities in this way clearly conveys a sense of hierarchization, and therefore inequality (see below), among them (Beaverstock et al. 2002: 111–32). However, as Friedman (1986, 1994) notes, there are other important inequalities to take into consideration. For one thing, as one descends his list of cities, and the countries in which they exist, we encounter more and more deprived, marginal, even subsistence economies in which people in general fare far worse than those in the world cities at the top of the list. For another, there are many other cities, even large cities, in the world that do not make any "top ten" lists and their economies are likely to be in even worse shape. Furthermore, even the global cities are likely to have internal inequalities, with the well-to-do living in elite areas of the cities, while the poor are likely to live in inner-city ghettos (more the America pattern) or in suburban squatter housing (more the European and Latin American pattern). The key cities are much more tied into the world economy than the hinterlands, with the result that those who live in the latter are more likely to be isolated from that economy and therefore less likely to be well-off than those who reside in the cities.

Why are global/world cities still important in a supposedly flat world of computer-enhanced telecommunications (Friedman 2005)? Since everyone can, at least theoretically, have access to this system from anywhere, the world's great cities should cease to be so important. However, contradicting the flat world thesis once again, these cities remain important. The cities are, in effect, "hills," if not "mountains," that are yet another factor giving the lie to the idea of a flat world. In fact, beyond their continued centrality in the global economy, these cities tend to be the centers for the various aspects of the telecommunications industry, as well as the places where the most important innovations take place.

Increasingly, global/world cities can be seen, following Castells (2000), as key nodes in a variety of networks and flows. In fact, leaders in those cities compete to make their city a central node in one or more flows and networks. For example, one type of flow is that of people, especially airline passengers. Cities compete with each other to become hubs for airlines, that is central nodes where many flights connect and through which many passengers flow. It is relatively easy to quantify the number of passengers passing through such nodes and thereby to determine whether a city has been successful in becoming a central node, at least in this particular flow (Choi,

Barnett, and Bum-Soo 2006: 81–99). This means, of course, that locales (e.g. airport hubs) remain important, even in a world increasingly dominated by networks and flows (Yeoh 2006: 150–2).

Some have argued that the global, or world, city network is of such great importance that it can be equated with globalization (Timberlake and Ma 2007: 254–71). While it is clear that cities, especially global/world cities, are important in globalization, this is clearly a bit of hyperbole, especially given the many different aspects of globalization discussed throughout this book.

A major empirical study of the world-city system demonstrated that there is a fairly strong hierarchy among world cities and a small number of them have a monopoly on power and prestige (Alderson and Beckfield 2004: 811–51). At the top in this study were the cities most often identified as world cities – New York, London, and Tokyo. However, this research indicated that Tokyo may be more powerful than is usually thought and Paris may need to be considered as being in the first rank of world cities. There is also a strong relationship between the power and the prestige of a world city; that is, cities with power also tend to rank high in prestige. World cities tend to be differentiated between "core" and "peripheral" cities, with the former being far more central to the global system. There is also a strong relationship between the position of world cities and the nation-states in which they exist in terms of the degree to which both exist in the core or in the periphery of the world system.

Cities: the main locus of global problems
While global or world cities are generally rich, powerful, prestigious, and the main beneficiaries of globalization (for example, the income and other benefits derived from being at the heart of global financial flows), it is also the case that cities, including the global or world cities, are especially hard hit by a wide range of global problems. Among other things, it is the world's cities that have been the targets of major terrorist attacks; the destination for large numbers of immigrants, many of them illegal, who are impoverished and in need of public assistance; the settings where large numbers of those affected by global health problems are likely to end up in search of medical help, and so on. Thus, according to Bauman (2003: 101), "*cities have become dumping grounds for globally forgotten problems.*"

In spite of their global nature and source, dealing with these problems becomes a local city problem; it is a political problem for the city. This represents a huge difficulty for city officials who often lack the economic resources to even begin to deal with many of these problems. Furthermore, since the sources are global, whatever city officials seek to do is doomed to failure. Thus, for example, the Mayor of London is helpless in dealing with the roots of terrorism in the tribal territories of Pakistan, the global epidemic of HIV/AIDS, or the air pollution being generated in nearby cities on the Continent. To quote Bauman (2003: 102) again: "*Local politics – and particularly urban politics – has become hopelessly overloaded.*" While all large cities face great, perhaps overwhelming, problems, it is the large and impoverished cities in the South that are the most affected by such problems.

CHAPTER SUMMARY

This chapter analyzes inequality among societies, as it relates to race, ethnicity, and gender, as well as some of the ways in which it is manifest in rural and urban areas.

One major form of inequality relates to economics. In this context, Paul Collier focuses on the poorest billion people, nearly 70 percent of whom reside in Africa. There also exists a significant global digital divide, with the poor lacking access not only to computers and the Internet, but also to basic infrastructure such as electricity. This contributes to a widening economic divide between the North and the South. Language represents another barrier for the poor in the South, since 80 percent of the content on the Internet is in English. The world's poor are also forced to handle a large proportion of the world's highly dangerous e-waste.

A major consequence of inequality is an increase in migration, especially South-to-North and South-to-South migration. This movement may be the result of push factors such as wars and other political crises, as well as pull factors such as better work and pay. South-to-South migration is likely to increase in the face of stricter controls over migration to the North. South-to-South migrants are generally poorer and more rural as compared to the South-to-North migrants.

All majority and minority statuses involve social definitions. As a result these statuses tend to differ, with variations in social definition from one locale to another and over time. For instance, there is nothing intrinsically distinctive about any racial or ethnic group that distinguishes it from others – these are fluid categories that are socially defined.

While some argue that globalization poses a threat to ethnic identities, they may in fact be reinforced by resistance to global pressures toward homogenization of identity. Indeed, globalization and the creation of ethnicity may be seen as part of the same modern process. Greater ethnic diversity within nation-states has increased the possibility of ethnic conflict within their confines. Various methods may be adopted to "deal" with ethnic minorities in nation-states or other delimited areas. The most extreme involve genocide.

Racial minorities are sometimes seen as subhuman and destructive of not only human values but human life. Globalization has aggravated race relations in many developed countries. As a result of massive international migration, most developed industrial societies have become increasingly diverse in terms of racial (and ethnic) composition. This rapid influx can lead to racism and xenophobia.

Globalization reinforces gender structures, barriers, and relationships. A key aspect of globalization has been the transformation of the nature of economic activity. Women are found disproportionately in low-paying, part-time, and temporary jobs in both developed and less developed countries. The increasing participation of women in both the formal and informal paid labor force has been termed the feminization of labor. In developing economies, this may be accompanied by the feminization of poverty as well as female proletarianization. It is also accompanied by an increase in female migration. A large part of this migration takes place in illegal and informal ways, leaving female laborers vulnerable to discrimination, exploitation, and abuse.

The chapter also explores the rural–urban differentiation and its relationship to globalization. Globalization has deeply altered North–South relations in agriculture. For instance, the relations of agricultural production have been altered due to the rise of global agribusiness and factory farms. In this scenario, the South produces non-traditional products for export, and becomes increasingly dependent on industrialized food exports from the North. Consequently, this leads to a replacement of the staple diet as well as the displacement of local farmers. As commercial agriculture replaces local provisioning, the relations of social production are also altered. Rural economies are exposed to low prices and mass migration.

Sassen uses the concept of global cities to describe the three urban centers of New York, London, and Tokyo as economic centers that exert control over the world's political economy. World cities are categorized as such based on the global reach of organizations found in them. Not only are there inequalities between these cities, there also exist inequalities within each city. Alternatively, following Castells, these cities can be seen as important nodes in a variety of global networks.

Although cities are major beneficiaries of globalization, they are also the most severely affected by global problems. Therefore the city faces peculiar political problems, wherein it is often fruitlessly seeking to deal locally with global problems.

DISCUSSION QUESTIONS

1. Examine the trend toward inequality within nations in the context of globalization.

2. Examine the impact of global flows on ethnicity and nationality.

3. Analyze the impact of global flows and structures on gendered social relations, particularly in the global South.

4. Examine the impact of global flows on race relations.

5. Can the success of the women's movement be a model for other minority groups seeking to combat the negative effects of globalization?

6. Examine the gap between rural and urban areas across the globe. How is that gap affected by global flows?

7. Discuss the impact of global flows on the agricultural sector.

FURTHER READING ···

Scott Sernau. *Worlds Apart: Social Inequalities in a Global Economy*, 2nd edn. Thousand Oaks, CA: Pine Forge Press, 2006.

Paul Collier. *The Bottom Billion: Why the Poorest Countries Are Failing and What Can Be Done About It*. New York: Oxford University Press, 2007.

Gili S. Drori. *Global E-Litism: Digital Technology, Social Inequality, and Transnationality*. New York: Worth, 2006.

Howard Winant. *The World is a Ghetto: Race and Democracy Since World War II*. New York: Basic Books, 2001.

Howard Winant. *The New Politics of Race: Globalism, Difference, Justice*. Minneapolis: University of Minnesota Press, 2004.

Paul Gilroy. *The Black Atlantic: Modernity and Double Consciousness*. Cambridge, MA: Harvard University Press, 1993.

Carl Degler. *Neither Black Nor White: Slavery and Race Relations in Brazil and the United States*. Madison: University of Wisconsin, 1971/1986.

Jane L. Collins. *Threads: Gender, Labor, and Power in the Global Apparel Industry*. Chicago: University of Chicago Press, 2003.

Rachel Salazar Parreñas. *Servants of Globalization: Women, Migration and Domestic Work*. Stanford, CA: Stanford University Press, 2001.

Barbara Ehrenreich and Arlie Hochschild, eds. *Global Woman: Nannies, Maids and Sex Workers in the New Economy*. New York: Henry Holt, 2002.

Kevin Bales. *Disposable People: New Slavery in the Economy*. Berkeley, CA: University of California Press, 1999.

Leila J. Rupp. *Worlds of Women: The Making of an International Women's Movement*. Princeton: Princeton University Press, 1997.

Nancy A. Naples and Manisha Desai, eds. *Women's Activism and Globalization: Linking Local Struggles and Transnational Politics*. New York: Routledge, 2002.

Mike Davis. *Planet of the Slums*. London: Verso, 2007.

Saskia Sassen. *The Global City: New York, London, and Tokyo*. Princeton: Princeton University Press, 1991.

REFERENCES ···

Abrahamson, Mark. 2004. *Global Cities*. New York: Oxford University Press.

Acker, Joan. 2004. "Gender, Capitalism and Globalization." *Critical Sociology* 30, 1.

Ahmed, Akbar S. 1995. "'Ethnic Cleansing': A Metaphor for Our Time?" *Ethnic and Racial Studies* 18.

Alderson, Arthur S., and Jason Beckfield. 2004. "Power and Position in the World City System." *American Journal of Sociology* 109, 4 (January).

Alter Chen, Martha. 1995. "Engendering World Conference: The International Women's Movement and the United Nations." *Third World Quarterly* 16, 3.

Altman, Dennis. 1996. "Rupture or Continuity? The Internationalization of Gay Identities." *Social Text* 48.

Altman, Dennis. 2001. *Global Sex*. Chicago: University of Chicago Press.

Bales, Kevin. 1999. *Disposable People: New Slavery in the Economy*. Berkeley, CA: University of California Press.

Basu, Amrita, ed. 1995. *The Challenge of Local Feminisms: Women's Movements in Global Perspective*. Boulder, CO: Westview.

Bauman, Zygmunt. 2003. *Liquid Love*. Cambridge: Polity.

Beaverstock, J. V., M. A. Doel, P. J. Hubbard, and P. J. Taylor. 2002. "Attending to the World: Competition, Cooperation and Connectivity in the World City Network." *Global Networks* 2, 2.

Beck, Ulrich. 2007. "Cosmopolitanism: A Critical Theory for the Twenty-First Century." In George Ritzer, ed., *Blackwell Companion to Globalization*. Malden, MA: Blackwell.

Beckfield, Jason, and Arthur S. Alderson. 2006. "Whither the Parallel Paths? The Future of Scholarship on the World City System." *American Journal of Sociology* 112, 3.

Benitez, Jose Luis. 2006. "Transnational Dimensions of the Digital Divide among Salvadoran Immigrants in the Washington DC Metropolitan Area." *Global Networks* 6, 2.

Bose, Christine E., and Edna Acosta-Belen, eds. 1995. *Women in the Latin American Development Process*. Philadelphia: Temple University Press.

Bourdieu, Pierre. 1984. *Distinction: A Social Critique of the Judgment of Taste*. Cambridge, MA: Harvard University Press.

Brennan, Denise. 2002. "Selling Sex for Visas: Sex Tourism as a Stepping-Stone to International Migration." In Barbara Ehrenreich and Arlie Hochschild, eds., *Global Woman: Nannies, Maids and Sex Workers in the New Economy*. New York: Henry Holt.

Brennan, Denise. 2004. *What's Love Got to Do with it?: Transnational Desires and Sex Tourism in the Dominican Republic*. Durham, NC: Duke University Press.

Brenner, Neil, and Roger Keil, eds. 2006. *The Global Cities Reader*. New York: Routledge.

Cagatay, Nilufer, and Sule Ozler. 1995. "Feminization of the Labor Force: The Effect of Long Term Development and Structural Adjustment." *World Development* 23, 11.

Castells, Manuel. 2000. *The Rise of the Network Society*. New edn. Malden, MA: Blackwell.

Cheever, Susan. 2002. "The Nanny Dilemma." In Barbara Ehrenreich and Arlie Hochschild, eds., *Global Woman: Nannies, Maids and Sex Workers in the New Economy*. New York: Henry Holt.

Choi, Junho H., George A. Barnett, and Chon Bum-Soo. 2006. "Comparing World City Networks: A Network Analysis of Internet Backbone and Air Transport Intercity Linkages." *Global Networks* 6, 1.

Collier, Paul. 2007. *The Bottom Billion: Why the Poorest Countries Are Failing and What Can Be Done About It*. New York: Oxford University Press.

Collier, Paul. forthcoming. "Bottom Billion." In George Ritzer, ed., *Blackwell Encyclopedia of Sociology Online*. Oxford: Wiley-Blackwell.

Collins, Jane L. 2003. *Threads: Gender, Labor, and Power in the Global Apparel Industry*. Chicago: University of Chicago Press.

Davis, Mike. 2007. *Planet of Slums*. London: Verso.

Degler, Carl. 1971/1986. *Neither Black Nor White: Slavery and Race Relations in Brazil and the United States*. Madison: University of Wisconsin.

DeParle, Jason. 2007. "A Global Trek to Poor Nations, from Poorer Ones." *New York Times*. December 27.

Drori, Gili S. 2006. *Global E-Litism: Digital Technology, Social Inequality, and Transnationality*. New York: Worth.

Dunbar Moodie, T. 1975. *The Rise of Afrikanerdom: Power, Apartheid, and the Afrikaner Civil Religion*. Berkeley, CA: University of California Press.

Dunbar Moodie, T., and Vivienne Ndatshe. 1994. *Going for Gold: Men, Mines and Migration*. Berkeley, CA: University of California Press.

Eaton Simpson, George, and J. Milton Yinger. 1985. *Racial and Cultural Minorities: An Analysis of Prejudice and Discrimination*, 5th edn. New York: Plenum.

Ehrenreich, Barbara. 2002. "Maid to Order." In Barbara Ehrenreich and Arlie Hochschild, eds., *Global Woman: Nannies, Maids and Sex Workers in the New Economy*. New York: Henry Holt.

Ehrenreich, Barbara, and Arlie Hochschild. 2002. "Introduction." In Barbara Ehrenreich and Arlie Hochschild, eds., *Global Woman: Nannies, Maids and Sex Workers in the New Economy*. New York: Henry Holt.

Elson, Diane, and Ruth Pearson. 1981. "Nimble Fingers Make Cheap Workers: An Analysis of Women's Employment in Third World Export Manufacturing." *Feminist Review* 7.

Ferus-Comelo, Anibel. 2006. "Double Jeopardy: Gender Migration in Electronics Manufacturing." In Ted Smith, David A. Sonnefield, and David Naguib, eds., *Challenging the Chip*. Philadelphia: Temple University Press.

Freeman, Carla. 2001. "Is Local: Global as Feminine: Masculine? Rethinking the Gender of Globalization." *Signs: Journal of Women in Culture and Society* 26, 4.

Friedman, Jonathan. 1986. "The World City Hypothesis." *Development and Change* 17.

Friedman, Jonathan. 1994. *Culture Identity and Global Processes*. London: Sage.

Friedman, Thomas. 2005. *The World is Flat: A Brief History of the Twenty-First Century*. New York: Farrar, Straus, Giroux.

Gaio, Fatima Janine. 1995. "Women in Software Programming: The Experience in Brazil." In Swasti Mitter and Sheila Rowbotham, eds., *Women Encounter Technology*. London: Routledge.

George, Kimberly. 2007. "Women's Movements." In Jan Aart Scholte and Roland Robertson, eds., *Encyclopedia of Globalization*. New York: MTM Publishing.

Greeley, Andrew. 1976. "The Ethnic Miracle." *The Public Interest* 45.

Hashemian, Farnoosh, and Derek Yach. 2007. "Public Health in a Globalizing World: Challenges and Opportunities." In George Ritzer, ed., *The Blackwell Companion to Globalization*. Malden, MA: Blackwell.

Heintz, James. 2006. "Globalization, Economic Policy and Employment: Poverty and Gender Implications." Employment Strategy Unit, International Labor Organization. www.ilo.org/public/english/employment/strat/download/esp2006-3.pdf

Hess, Beth B., and Myra Marx Ferree. 1987. "Introduction." In Beth B. Hess and Myra Marx Ferree, eds., *Analyzing Gender: A Handbook of Social Research*. Beverly Hills, CA: Sage.

Hochschild, Arlie. 2000. "Global Care Chains and Emotional Surplus Value." In W. Hutton and Anthony Giddens, eds., *On the Edge: Living with Global Capitalism*. London: Jonathan Cape.

Hughes, Donna M. 1999. *Pimps and Predators on the Internet: Globalizing the Sexual Exploitation of Women and Children*. Kingston, RI: Coalition Against Trafficking in Women. www.uri.edu/artsci/wms/hughes/pprep.pdf.

ICFTU – International Confederation of Free Trade Unions. 2004. "The Informal Economy: Women on the Frontline." Trade Union World Briefing, No. 2, March 2. Available at www.ilo.org/public/english/region/ampro/cinterfor/temas/informal/doc/wom_flin.pdf.

Joekes, Susan P. 1987. *Women in the World Economy: An INSTRAW Study*. New York: Oxford University Press.

Karstedt, Susanne. 2007. "Genocide." In George Ritzer, ed., *The Blackwell Encyclopedia of Sociology*. Malden, MA: Blackwell.

Kempadoo, Kamala, and Jo Doezema, eds. 1998. *Global Sex Workers: Rights, Resistance, and Redefinition*. London: Routledge.

King, Anthony D. 2007. "Global Cities." In Jan Aart Scholte and Roland Robertson, eds., *Encyclopedia of Sociology*. New York: Routledge.

Mann, Michael. 1999. "The Dark Side of Democracy: The Modern Tradition of Ethnic and Political Cleansing." *New Left Review* 235.

Marcuse, Peter, and Ronald van Kempen, eds. 2000. *Globalizing Cities: A New Spatial Order?* Malden, MA: Blackwell.

Markoff, John. 2007. "At Davos, the Squabble Resumes on How to Wire the Third World." *New York Times.* January 29.

Marx Ferree, Myra, and Aili Mari Tripp. 2006. "Preface." In Myra Marx Ferree and Aili Mari Tripp, eds., *Global Feminism: Transnational Women's Activism, Organizing, and Human Rights.* New York: New York University Press.

McMichael, Philip. 2007. "Globalization and the Agrarian World." In George Ritzer, ed., *Blackwell Companion to Globalization.* Malden, MA: Blackwell.

Moghadam, Valentine. 1999. "Gender and Globalization: Female Labor and Women's Mobilization." *Journal of World-Systems Research* 5, 2.

Naples, Nancy A., and Manisha Desai, eds. 2002a. *Women's Activism and Globalization: Linking Local Struggles and Transnational Politics.* New York: Routledge.

Naples, Nancy A., and Manisha Desai. 2002b. "Women's Local and Transnational Responses: An Introduction to the Volume." In Nancy A. Naples and Manisha Desai, eds., *Women's Activism and Globalization: Linking Local Struggles and Transnational Politics.* New York: Routledge.

O'Brien, William. 1968. "International Crimes." In David Sills, ed., *International Encyclopedia of the Social Sciences.* New York: Macmillan.

O'Connell Davidson, Julia. 2005. *Children in the Global Sex Trade.* Cambridge: Polity.

Paquin, Jamie. 2007. "Global/World Cities." In George Ritzer, ed., *Blackwell Encyclopedia of Sociology.* Malden, MA: Blackwell.

Parreñas, Rhacel S. 2001. *Servants of Globalization: Women, Migration, and Domestic Work.* Stanford, CA: Stanford University Press.

Pearson, Ruth. 1992. "Gender Issues in Industrialisation." In T. Hewitt, J. Johnson, and D. Wield, eds., *Industrialisation and Development.* Oxford: Oxford University Press.

Pearson, Ruth. 2000. "Moving the Goalposts: Gender and Globalization in the Twenty-First Century." *Gender and Development* 8, 1.

Pun, Nagi. 1995. "Theoretical Discussions on the Impact of Industrial Restructuring in Asia." In *Silk and Steel: Asian Women Workers Confront Challenges of Industrial Restructuring.* Hong Kong: CAW.

Pyle, Jean L., and Kathryn B. Ward. 2003. "Recasting Our Understanding of Gender and Work During Global Restructuring." *International Sociology* 18.

Ramirez, Francisco O., Yasemin Soysal, and Suzanne Shanahan. 1997. "The Changing Logic of Political Citizenship: Cross-National Acquisition of Women's Suffrage Rights, 1890–1990." *American Sociological Review* 62.

Ritzer, George. 2008. *The McDonaldization of Society*, 5th edn. Thousand Oaks, CA: Pine Forge Press.

Rosenthal, Elisabeth. 2008. "Fast Food Hits Mediterranean; Diet Succumbs." *New York Times.* September 24.

Rupp, Leila J. 1997. *Worlds of Women: The Making of an International Women's Movement.* Princeton: Princeton University Press.

Sassen, Saskia. 1991. *The Global City: New York, London, and Tokyo.* Princeton: Princeton University Press.

Sassen, Saskia. 2004. "Local Actors in Global Politics." *Current Sociology* 52, 4.

Schlosser, Eric. 2005. *Fast Food Nation.* New York: Harper Perennial.

Sekulic, Dusko. 2007. "Ethnic Cleansing." In George Ritzer, ed., *The Blackwell Encyclopedia of Sociology.* Malden, MA: Blackwell.

Sernau, Scott. 2006. *Worlds Apart: Social Inequalities in a Global Economy*, 2nd edn. Thousand Oaks, CA: Pine Forge Press.

Sivalingam, G. 1994. *The Economic and Social Impact of Export Processing Zones: The Case of Malaysia*. Geneva: International Labor Organization.

Snyder, Margaret. 2006. "Unlikely Godmother: The UN and the Global Women's Movement." In Myra Marx Ferree and Aili Mari Tripp, eds., *Global Feminism: Transnational Women's Activism, Organizing, and Human Rights*. New York: New York University Press.

Standing, Guy. 1989. "Global Feminization through Flexible Labor." *World Development* 17.

Standing, Guy. 1999. "Global Feminization through Flexible Labor: A Theme Revisited." *World Development* 27, 3.

Thomas, W. I., and Dorothy Thomas. 1928. *The Child in America: Behavior Problems and Programs*. New York: Knopf.

Timberlake, Michael, and Xiulian Ma. 2007. "Cities and Globalization." In George Ritzer, ed., *Blackwell Companion to Globalization*. Malden, MA: Blackwell.

Tomlinson, John. 2000. "Globalization and Cultural Identity." In David Held and Anthony McGrew, eds., *The Global Transformations Reader*. Cambridge: Polity.

Ward, Kathryn. 1990. "Introduction and Overview." In Kathryn Ward, ed., *Women Workers and Global Restructuring*. Ithaca, NY: ILR Press.

Winant, Howard. 2001. *The World is a Ghetto: Race and Democracy Since World War II*. New York: Basic Books.

Winant, Howard. 2004. *The New Politics of Race: Globalism, Difference, Justice*. Minneapolis: University of Minnesota Press.

Yeoh, Brenda S. A. 2006. "Mobility and the City." *Theory, Culture & Society* 23, 2–3.

Yuval-Davis, Nira. 2006. "Human/Women's Rights and Feminist Transversal Politics." In Myra Marx Ferree and Aili Mari Tripp, eds., *Global Feminism: Transnational Women's Activism, Organizing, and Human Rights*. New York: New York University Press.

Dealing with, Resisting, and the Future of, Globalization

Globalization: The Essentials, by George Ritzer
© 2011 John Wiley & Sons Ltd

The reader should find several things jarring about the title of this final chapter. First, there appears to be a lot going on, seemingly too much, in one chapter. In addition, the first part of the title of this chapter seems to imply that there is a broad consensus that globalization is problematic and, as such, needs to be dealt with and/or resisted. While there are many throughout the world who *do* see globalization in this way, many others are quite content with it, and there are even some who extol its virtues. Thus, the title and focus of this chapter should *not* be interpreted to mean that there is universal consensus that globalization is problematic.

Another prefatory remark is needed. As we have seen throughout this book, and pointed out on several occasions, there is no one globalization, there are many globalization*s*. Thus, there is no single phenomenon, no single globalization, to be dealt with; to be resisted. Almost everyone would want to deal with or resist the globalization of crime, but most would be quite happy to see further globalization of the distribution of pharmaceuticals, for example, the "cocktail" needed to treat AIDS. Within the economy, there are huge differences in the way people respond to great concentrations of wealth in comparison to the ever-escalating ability to distribute goods and services globally. The former may need to be dealt with or resisted, but most would want to see the latter encouraged further. Thus, as we discuss various coping mechanisms in this chapter, we need to keep in mind which globalization, or which aspect of it, is being dealt with and/or resisted.

The same point applies to the third topic of this chapter – the future of globalization – there is *no* single future for globalization. Because there are many globalization*s*, there are many futures. While we will need to make do with a few generalizations about the future of globalization and of a few of the globalization*s*, the reader should also keep this in mind.

DEALING WITH GLOBALIZATION

Given limited space, this section will only cover dealing with the economy, the polity, and health care.

Dealing with the Global Economy

From the perspective of that which needs to be responded to, no issue gets more attention, undoubtedly mainly because of the profound economic inequality in the world, than the economy. This is especially true today as many around the world attempt to deal with the profound economic disruptions caused by the Great Recession. We examine three broad ways of responding to/resisting economic globalization.

Protectionism

Trade exists, of course, within nations (among individuals, companies, and so on) but it is of particular interest here because it occurs globally, and at an accelerating rate in the era of globalization. There has been a general consensus that the free flow of global trade benefits the nations engaged in it. Yet trade, especially free trade, has its critics and there are those who seek to restrict trade through barriers – protectionism – of one sort or another (Mann and Pluck 2007: 1159–66).

Protectionism, or more specifically trade protectionism, is "a policy of systematic government intervention in foreign trade with the objective of encouraging domestic production. This encouragement involves giving preferential treatment to domestic producers and discriminating against foreign competitors" (McAleese 2007: 1169–74). There are various ways to protect and encourage domestic production including tariffs and quotas on foreign imports. Domestic production can be helped more directly through export subsidies (widely used in American agriculture) and more indirectly by such policies as tax relief to producers. Protectionism has existed since the mercantilist era (1500–1800), as well as the early days of the Industrial Revolution, and has been practiced by almost every nation (Chorev 2007). It reached something of a peak following the onset of the Depression in 1929. However, following the end of WW II, and as a result of GATT (1947), and later the founding of the European Economic Union (1958), the tide began to shift away from trade protectionism and toward trade liberalization (Tan 2007: 735–9). This led the way toward the great expansion of foreign trade and investment.

> **Protectionism**: Government intervention in order to encourage domestic production.

A broad consensus emerged that protectionism did not work, but nonetheless it continued to be practiced by many nations and in various economic sectors. Trade protection continued to coexist – *very* uncomfortably – with trade liberalization. In spite of its rhetoric of trade liberalization, the United States, among others, was often accused of practicing protectionism (especially in agriculture). And, the US, in turn, often accused many other nations, most notably China and Japan, of continuing to engage in protectionism.

Many reasons have been put forth in defense of a protectionist policy, some as early as the pioneering work of Adam Smith (1953). Smith argued that it was legitimate to protect a nation's important defense industries, to impose a tax on foreign imports, to retaliate against a country imposing a tax on a given nation's exports, and to use protectionism to ease the transition to a more liberal trading position. Other reasons that have emerged to legitimate protectionism include assisting in the birth of new industries (as the EU did in the case of Airbus), protecting such new industries as they develop, as well as more generally protecting new economies. In spite of these and other rationales, there was, given the ascendancy of neo-liberal economics, a decline in both the belief in, and the practice of, trade protectionism (at least until very recently). Nevertheless, various forms of protectionism remained in place and have been resurrected in various parts of the world, especially in the

South, from time to time when the adverse effects of the global neo-liberal economy took center stage.

Trade protectionism declined because of a perception that its negative effects outweighed the benefits. First, those industries that receive protection tend, over time, to grow increasingly inefficient. They seem to require the competition brought about by free trade to hone their operations. It clearly is not in a nation's interest to support inefficient industries, at least in the long run. Second, protectionism not only discourages imports, but also exports because the tariffs on imported components raise the cost of production to industries in the nation engaging in protectionism. This leads to increases in prices and tends to make a protectionist nation's exports less competitive, especially compared to those of nations without the kinds of trade barriers that tend to raise costs. Third, the protected industries have little interest in, and motivation for, innovation; their protected position makes innovation unnecessary. Fourth, protectionism tends to lead, especially in developing nations (but not, historically, in the US), to a focus on manufacturing with the result that agriculture is adversely affected, or at least not similarly advantaged. Such countries are highly dependent on their agriculture for subsistence and its decline can have disastrous consequences for the population as a whole.

Interestingly, those nations that have restricted imports (engaged in protectionism) tended to suffer more from protectionism than those countries (the "victims" of protectionism) that were impeded from exporting to those nations. Thus, the US, for example, would gain more from eliminating its protective agricultural policies than would those nations that would then be freer to export their products to the US.

While trade liberalization became dominant, especially in the hegemonic neo-liberal perspective, there continued to be pressures toward protectionism. On the one hand, developed nations often wanted trade protection because of fear that inexpensive imports from less developed countries would destroy indigenous industries. On the other hand, less developed countries often complained about continuing trade barriers in developed nations and about pressures on them (but *not* developed countries) by the IMF and the World Bank to liberalize – and rapidly – much of their economy. Furthermore, less developed countries often felt that as a result of trade liberalization they were engaged with other less developed nations in a "race to the bottom" (see Chapter 4) in which they competed with one another to produce more at lower cost for the developed world. Instead, of their standard of living improving as a result of trade liberalization, they frequently found that it was at best stable and more likely in decline.

In spite of these, and other, issues, the trend for many years after the end of WW II was certainly in the direction of trade liberalization. However, there were critics who argued that trade liberalization really didn't offer the benefits it was supposed to and that it disproportionately helped the developed rather than the less developed nations. Some, especially in the South, saw trade liberalization as part of neo-liberal economics designed to help the richer nations at their expense. In spite of such arguments and views, there were few in those days anywhere in the world who would have argued for a resurrection of full-scale trade barriers.

There are a large number of factors that explain periodically renewed calls for increased protectionism (Reuveny and Thompson 2001: 229–48) – for example, shocks to the economic system, a long-term shift from one system to another (from agrarian to industrial), the preferences of voters and the politicians they elect, the use of protection to further a nation's foreign policy objectives and the interests of one's allies, the absence of a free-trade ideology and the persistence of an ideology favoring protectionism, reciprocity because of protectionism practiced by another nation, and so on. These and other factors continued to foster protectionism, but they were subordinated, at least at the time, to the global triumph (not without deep and continuing resistance) of neo-liberalism and trade liberalization. Nonetheless, resentment toward trade liberalization, as well as the ways in which it seemed to benefit the rich nations and disadvantage the poor, continued to stimulate efforts at protectionism, especially in less developed nations. For their part, the rich nations generally wished to retain their positions and were often hostile to the advantages (e.g. lower wages) industries in less developed nations had over their own industries. Thus, there were pressures in *both* developed and less developed nations to retain, or re-impose, trade barriers even in a global economy increasingly characterized by trade liberalization.

The onset of the Great Recession led to a widespread questioning of the neo-liberal model of free and unregulated trade. As in the Great Depression, there was a resurgence of interest in protectionism as a way of warding off the worst effects of the recession. Thus, as mentioned previously, President Barack Obama's 2009 stimulus plan involved a "buy American" provision. That is, public works and building projects that used funds derived from the plan were to use goods and materials, including iron and steel, made in the US. Similar positions were being taken elsewhere in the world. How far various nations move in the direction of greater protectionism depends to a large degree on how long the recession lasts and how deep it gets. Whatever happens, the increased use of protectionism fits with the general orientation of this book because protectionism is being used as a *barrier* in an attempt to ward off the worst effects of the *negative flows* associated with a deep global recession.

Fair trade

Taken to its logical extreme, trade protectionism implies a rejection of the global economy, especially in its neo-liberal form. However, there are less extreme ways of dealing with inequities in the global economy and one of them is "*fair trade*" (Nicholls and Opal 2005; Stiglitz and Charlton 2005; Raynolds, Murray, and Wilkinson 2007; Zaccaï 2007; Stehr 2008), which stands in opposition to the "free trade" that is at the heart of neo-liberalism.

Fair trade is defined by the International Fair Trade Association as a "concern for the social, economic and environmental well-being of marginalized small producers" (Downie 2007: C1–C5). In contrast to the purely utilitarian

> **Fair trade:** Concern for the social, economic, and environmental well-being of marginalized small producers.

orientation of neo-liberalism, fair trade is oriented toward a more *moral* and *equitable* global economic system. It is concerned with:

- creating direct relationships between producers, usually in the South, and consumers, ordinarily in the North;
- "establishing more just prices"; price should not be set simply by the "free" market, but by what is just as far as producers, and the social and ecological environment in which they live and work, are concerned; price is not to be set by the "market" but negotiated openly, transparently, and equally by producers and those who seek to acquire what they produce; each should seek to understand and accommodate the other's needs;
- protecting producers, especially farmers, from dramatic swings in prices for their products;
- providing work for those, especially in the South, who are economically disadvantaged;
- protecting workers' rights, including the right to unionize;
- providing work that is safe and not exploitative of women and children;
- engaging in environmentally sound practices; in sustainable production;
- being sure that that which is produced is healthy to consume;
- educating consumers and encouraging them to put pressure on producers to engage in fair trade practices.

While other parts of the developed world, especially Europe, have been great supporters of fair trade for some time, there are signs that interest in fair trade is finally growing in the US, as well. For example, in 2004 only 12 percent of Americans said they were aware of fair trade, but by 2006, 27 percent had become conscious of it. In terms of its share of, for example, the American coffee market, in 2006 fair trade coffee was 3.3 percent of the total (it was a fraction of 1 percent in 2000). In terms of specialty coffee sales in the US, fair trade rose from less than 1 percent in 2000 to over 7 percent in 2006. Chains such as Starbucks and Dunkin' Donuts are buying more fair trade coffee and warehouse chains like Sam's Club are stocking their shelves with more of it. Worldwide it is estimated that $2.2 billion dollars was spent on certified fair trade products in 2006, up 42 percent from the preceding year.

Fair trade coffee serves to benefit approximately 7 million people in the developing world, including Brazilian coffee growers who get at least $1.29 per pound of coffee beans compared to the current market price of $1.25. In order to qualify for the fair trade designation, a farmer must follow many rules on pesticide use, farming techniques, recycling, etc. While Brazilian farmers who meet fair trade standards get higher pay and a better standard of living, some coffee growers in other parts of the world do not gain nearly as much. For example, some Ethiopian farmers (as well as some from Columbia and Guatemala) grow the highest-quality beans, but they receive little more for these beans than the growers of lower-grade Brazilian coffee. However, these high-quality beans become gourmet brands in Starbucks and other outlets and sell at a premium. In other words, Starbucks makes a higher profit on such coffee, but Ethiopian (and other) coffee farmers see little or none of it. It is estimated that a coffee farmer receives barely one cent from a $5.00 cup of specialty coffee sold at Starbucks (Chanda 2007: 92).

Fair trade is the popular term for the more formal idea of "alternative trade schemes" (McMichael 2007: 32–5). Such schemes have a long history going back to WW II. They were built on the base of the sending of aid by England's Oxfam to areas in Europe overrun by the Nazis. Faith-based organizations emerged out of this to import handicrafts from Eastern Europe, and later from less developed areas, to be sold directly to consumers in non-profit (e.g. church-based) shops. In the 1970s organizations like Traidcraft emerged. Traidcraft used "mail order and other social networking devices to connect producers in lesser-developed countries directly with conscientious consumers in the developed world" (Carducci forthcoming). Interest in such schemes has expanded dramatically since the 1980s and 1990s with the growth of, and reactions against, neo-liberal economic globalization.

There are several global organizations involved in the fair trade movement including the International Fair Trade Association (IFAT), the Rainforest Alliance, as well as the Fairtrade Labeling Organization (FLO), formed in 1997 on the base of three organizations that had been involved in the European market.

> The FLO's goal is to educate consumers to use their purchasing power as a weapon against the abuses of the corporate system. The certification of fair trade practices, via a guaranteed superior (world) price, includes demands for representative associations of producers or workers to monitor labor conditions, protect worker rights, prohibit child and forced labor, promote safe and healthy working conditions, and sustain communities and environments. (McMichael 2007: 34)

Thus, for example, a Chilean farmer involved in growing bananas acquired FLO registration by "eliminating herbicide use, reducing chemical fertilizers, building democratic union procedures, raising wages, and establishing a fund, or 'social premium,' set-aside for community projects such as housing improvement, electrification, and environmental monitoring" (McMichael 2007: 34).

Many products have become the focus of fair trade interest and concern, including coffee (Linton, Chiayuan, and Shaw 2004: 223–46; Jaffee 2007; Bacon et al. 2008: 259–64; Lewis and Runsten 2008: 275–90) and bananas (mentioned above) (within, within (Moberg 2008: 291–304), tea (Dolan 2008: 305–18), and chocolate.

However, there are limits to, and problems with, fair trade: there are questions as to whether a fair trade system can really supply a mass global market (e.g. for coffee); it is difficult to see how fair trade can be used in the far more globally significant area of mass-manufactured products; and while fair trade has made inroads among "enlightened" consumers in the developed world, it may be harder to get producers (and consumers) in the less developed world, given far more pressing problems, to buy into it.

Helping the "bottom billion"

The most common way of looking at economic inequality in the world (indeed the way we introduced the issue in this chapter) is to focus on the differences between the North and the South, core and periphery, or between the developed and less developed areas of the world. However, Paul Collier (2007) argues that in making that gross distinction we ignore the poorest people in the world, what he calls "the bottom billion." It is clear that if any population needs economic assistance, if any global economic problem needs to be dealt with, it is this one. There are several areas in which things can be done to improve the situation facing the bottom billion in the global age.

The first is aid. While much of the world discussion focuses on economic aid, Collier tends to discount its importance. In the 2005 G8 summit at Gleneagles, Scotland, seven of the G8 nations (Russia refused to be involved) agreed to double their aid to Africa by 2010. However, there is cause to be dubious about these nations achieving this goal. Data from 2006 indicated that aid to Africa had increased only marginally (Germany), decreased (France, by 1 percent), and in one case decreased dramatically (Italy, by 30 percent) (Dugger 2007: A8). Japan and Britain were on target to meet the goal and the US seemed to be moving in that direction.

In any case, Collier is not optimistic about aid – even if it is doubled – for a variety of reasons, including the fact that:

- while some aid will help, the effect tends to diminish as aid increases;
- the bureaucracies involved do not function well and tend to interfere with one another;
- aid money tends to flow into dysfunctional areas such as the military;
- it can stimulate civil wars by making the control of the government more valuable;
- it has little effect on the lack of natural resources;
- it has failed to improve transportation links;
- it has rarely alleviated the problem of bad governance.

In spite of all this, it is possible that aid could help, but only in concert with other actions from the developed countries, especially the G8.

Military intervention can be useful in restoring order, maintaining peace after a conflict ends, and preventing later military coups. While external military intervention can be helpful, the militaries in the world's poorest countries often make matters worse. For example, once in power through a coup, the military can demand (extort) huge sums of money.

Also of use are changes in laws and charters. Changes are needed in the laws of developed countries in order to better prevent their companies and banks from engaging in exploitative and corrupt practices (e.g. bribes) that adversely affect the bottom billion. International norms, standards, and codes which were largely developed in and for the developed countries need to be adapted and modified (e.g. emphasizing greater transparency) to fit the needs of the bottom billion.

The marginalization of less developed nations can be reversed through trade policy. One course of action is the reduction and elimination of trade barriers (see above) in both developed countries (in part at least through unreciprocated barrier reduction within the WTO) and those that contain most of the bottom billion. The latter would need at least temporary trade protection until they were more competitive economically.

It is interesting to note that Collier is *not* a big fan of fair trade. He sees it as a kind of "charity" to, for example, coffee growers in less developed countries. He sees it as even less beneficial than straight aid because higher fair trade prices tend to keep people involved in what they have always done – that is, in this case, producing coffee. The problem is a lack of diversification for the least developed countries, and fair trade serves to reinforce a single-minded focus on producing that which has served to lock such countries into poverty.

Dealing with Political Globalization

As was the case with economic issues, there is a near-endless array of things that can be done to deal with global political problems. Space constraints will limit us to the issues of accountability and transparency, as well as special attention to Transparency International (TI).

Accountability

In a world of increasingly global organizations, especially in this case political organizations, the issue of accountability (or lack thereof) is increasingly important (Germain 2004: 217–42). On the one hand, all political organizations, including the nation-state, need to be held more accountable for their actions. On the other hand, the decline of the nation-state has freed various organizations (including political organizations) from the constraints of being embedded in it. With the nation-state of declining importance, or out of the picture, the issue arises of to whom or to what such organizations are to be held accountable politically (and in many other ways). Furthermore, there is the more practical problem of whether there is any way that political organizations can be held accountable. One route to ensuring accountability is to have enhanced surveillance over such organizations in order to be sure they operate not only in accord with their own rules and regulations, but also international norms about how such organizations should behave. Another route involves having more organizations and individuals involved in what these political organizations do and involved in a greater dialogue and reciprocity with those who have a stake – the stakeholders – in political organizations.

Transparency

Organizations of all types, including, and perhaps especially, political organizations (including nation-states), are generally inclined to secrecy on many matters and this means that much of what they do is *not* transparent. Contemporary examples include the lack of transparency by Iran in terms of its nuclear weapons program, as well as by the US and Israel (which has never publicly revealed that it has a nuclear weapons program that has produced a number of nuclear weapons) over whether they have plans to attack Iran should it be shown to be getting close to obtaining nuclear weapons.

While much political secrecy remains, and this is also the case for many other types of organizations, one recent book on the topic concludes that transparency is growing. However, at the same time, it argues that transparency "is still surrounded by an ocean of opacity" (Holzner and Holzner 2006: 336). Implied here is a historical and ongoing dialectic between transparency and secrecy (the deliberate withholding of information), as well as opacity (an absence of information). However, there is also a grand narrative offered describing a long-term increase in transparency. Three cases are compared – the United States, the European Union (with particular attention to the very different examples of Sweden and Greece), and Japan. Health care and the business world are two of the major contexts in which the dialectic is examined. Overall, while there are important differences, there is a general trend over time in the direction of greater transparency.

Some of the most interesting discussions deal with case studies – such as the Holocaust, World War II crimes, the Tuskegee syphilis study, and so on – which tend to show the deleterious effects of government secrecy. They also show the movement over time toward more open acknowledgment and discussion of these cases, as well as the ways in which they, and innumerable other heinous crimes, were greatly aided by the secrecy and opacity that surrounded them.

A variety of developments have aided in increased transparency, including transnational justice systems and movements, international tribunals, civil society, and more specifically Transparency International.

Transparency International (TI)

Transparency International is an INGO founded in 1993 by Peter Eigen, who had become frustrated with his work at the World Bank. He felt he had been forbidden from addressing the issue of corruption in many nations throughout the world because it would adversely affect the image of the World Bank. As a result, at least in part, of this, Eigen left the World Bank and created TI, headquartered in Berlin, which now has about 100 national chapters. It focuses on combating corruption, especially by pushing for greater transparency (Florini 2007: 1201–4). Along these lines in 1995 TI created the Corruption Perceptions Index (CPI). It is based on, and brings together, a number of studies of the perceptions of experts on corruption in their countries. Countries obtain scores ranging from zero (extreme corruption) to ten (no corruption). Later TI created the Bribe Payers Index in order to get at the propensity of companies from developed countries to bribe public officials in emerging market economies such as Brazil, Mexico, and Russia. Australia and Sweden were the least prone to such bribery, the US ranked in the middle (this contradicts the argument that the US is a paragon of virtue as far as corruption is concerned), and Russia was the most bribe-prone nation. The idea behind the publication of such indices is that greater public transparency about the breadth and depth of bribery and other forms of corruption will lead to increased concern about them, and that, in turn, will lead to efforts to reduce them and their deleterious effects.

TI has been involved in other activities as well. It publishes *National Integrity Systems: The TI Source Book* (translated into many languages), offering local activists practical strategies for dealing with corruption and for developing greater transparency. It was also instrumental in negotiating an agreement among global banks to combat money laundering, providing small sums of money to those fighting corruption in less developed countries, as well as efforts to combat corruption and bribes that lead to environmental destruction (e.g. through deforestation). Overall, TI seeks a world free of corruption and with far greater transparency. However, there are various barriers to the latter, with a notable one being the global concern over terrorism which is leading to greater secrecy and opacity, and these, in turn, tend to feed greater corruption.

RESISTING GLOBALIZATION

Globalization, or rather globalizations, has/have created enemies and generated resistance for innumerable reasons. One broad view on this is that resistance has arisen because, for much of the world, globalization has not delivered on its promises (Cohen 2006). It has served to raise the expectations of many, but not afforded them the wherewithal even to begin to fulfill those expectations. Billions throughout the world, especially the "bottom billion," continue to lack the infrastructure – schools, roads, telephone lines – needed to start to move toward fulfilling those expectations. Worse, they often lack the bare necessities needed to survive – food, water, shelter, safety, and so on.

In addition, Daniel Cohen argues that the less developed world has, in effect, been disenfranchised. In those cases where parts of that world have been able to obtain Northern innovations – telephone, television, Internet – they often find themselves feeling as if these technologies have been imposed on them; that they have no role in the creation of these technologies. A more just world would be one in which people from every part of the globe contribute to these developments as well as to human destiny in general.

Thus, globalization produces critics, opponents, and "enemies" and it is they who are most likely to resist globalization. Cohen, for example, identifies two broad enemies of globalization. The first is the enemies of Westernization (he identifies the "mullahs" of the world with this position and therefore with Huntington's thinking on the war of civilizations; see Chapter 7). The second is those who are opposed to capitalism and who see much of globalization as motivated by, and advancing, capitalism (this is in tune with the kind of global class struggle discussed by Marx and various Marxists). To Cohen, both sets of enemies are unified in the view that a world that they do not want (Western or capitalistic) is being imposed on them.

Cohen's argument is a useful beginning, but it is limited in several ways. Most importantly, he makes the mistake of reducing globalization to economic and geo-political globalization; as we know, there are many globalizations. The latter leads us to the realization that there are also many other types of enemies of other kinds of globalization (e.g. Slow Food's opposition to global fast food), and they engage in a wide range of actions designed to resist them. Restricting our sense of globalization limits much else about our understanding of this process, including the myriad forms taken by resistance to it.

While globalization is seemingly omnipresent, resistance to it has grown dramatically in recent years and in some cases (e.g. the World Social Forum) it, too, has become globalized. A wide variety of specific aspects of globalization have become the focus of resistance movements. These include the exploitation of indigenous labor by MNCs, the adverse effect on the environment of actions taken in the developed world (e.g. global warming), the threats posed by global culture to indigenous culture, and so on (Kahn and Kellner 2007: 662–74).

Resistance, like globalization itself, must be seen as being highly complex, contradictory, and ambiguous, ranging from the radically progressive (the positions taken by the World Social Forum and its participants) to the reactionary and conservative (including frontier-style self-determination, isolationism, fundamentalism, neo-fascism, and ultra-nationalism). In addition to making immediate gains, the resistance movement could constitute the beginning of a global civil society, of a new public sphere, that might uphold such progressive values as autonomy, democracy, peace, ecological sustainability, and social justice. While the forces that resist globalization have tended to portray globalization in a negative light (as, for example, being top-down, neo-liberal capitalism, imperialism, and terror war; involving the McDonaldization of the planet, creating disequilibrating social changes, and so on), they are themselves products of globalization that often survive by using such globe-straddling technologies as the Internet.

There is some debate over what to call the groups that resist globalization. Historically, they have been seen as constituting the anti-globalization movement, but as we saw above and previously, the problem with that label is that the resistance groups themselves are often global in scope and their orientations and actions make them very much a part of globalization. For another thing, the movement is not, as we have seen, opposed to all aspects of globalization; to all globalizations. It is opposed to *some* varieties of globalization (e.g. neo-liberal economic globalization) and not to others (e.g. the global spread of human rights in the political realm).

As a result, it is better to think of these resistance movements as part of globalization from below (or alter-globalization), and as such they stand in opposition to globalization from above. The latter would include the globalizing efforts of neo-liberal economic systems, of MNCs, of aggressively expanding nation-states, of large and proselytizing religions, of McWorld, and the like. These efforts involve globalization from above since they emanate from powerful entities and are imposed on those with less or little power (they involve grobalization; see Chapter 7).

The heart of the resistance to globalization lies in individuals, groups, and organizations that we associate with globalization from below. It arises among those who are, or feel they are, wronged or oppressed by globalization from above (e.g. the

Zapatistas [Gilman-Opalsky 2008] in Chiapas, Mexico), or among organizations supported more by those who come from the same social classes as those involved in globalization from above (e.g. the members of an INGO like the Rainforest Alliance or Greenpeace), but which seek to represent the interests of those who are adversely affected by it. Their actions often translate into opposition to neo-liberal globalization, or the "Washington consensus." They also involve opposition to globalization, especially economic globalization, stemming from the West in general, and the US in particular. And there is opposition to the main IGOs involved in globalization – the World Bank, the IMF, the WTO – as well as more regional efforts such as NAFTA. More positively, the movement seeks a more democratic process of globalization; one that actively involves those from "below." It also seeks greater justice in globalization – a fairer and more just process of globalization; it is the global justice movement (Brooks 2008).

While the above emphasizes globally active groups and organizations, globalization from below also occurs at various other levels (Mittelman 2004: 24). Individuals can take an array of actions that serve to resist the aspects of globalization that they oppose. Examples include José Bové and his actions in France against the expansion of McDonald's, individuals refusing to buy global products (e.g. Coca-Cola), refusing to buy coffee in global chains of coffee shops (e.g. Starbucks), or refusing to shop in Wal-Mart because its ruthless commitment to low prices often translates into low-wage work in the South (the latter is one of the "high costs of low price"). There are also small, more locally active, grassroots groups that oppose globalization, or at least some aspects of it. These may develop into the kind of globally active groups and organizations discussed above, but they can also remain wholly local phenomena (see below).

As mentioned above, while we often associate globalization from below with the left, there are less visible, more right-wing elements involved in this movement. First, there are groups (e.g. the Scottish National Party) that represent a kind of "frontier" mentality, emphasizing self-determination, and which, as a result, oppose global efforts to limit their freedom or to impinge on their territory. Second, there are other groups (e.g. the America First Party) that can be thought of as isolationists, which seek to protect the borders of their nation and to limit its (and their) involvement in global processes. Third, there are religious fundamentalists (e.g. the Taliban in Afghanistan) who seek a return to (at least their vision of) a pure version of their religion, and resist global processes that they think are a threat to that purity. And there is an array of other groups and organizations that would fit into this category, including those with ultra-nationalist and neo-fascist orientations.

Today, globalization from below includes many individuals, groups, social movements (Jackie Smith 2008), and issues from every part of the world. Many have ties to one another, but they are generally very weak ties (although "weak ties" can be quite strong and very useful [Granovetter 1973: 1360–80]), and overall they form a very loose system. It is a highly fluid system and it is continually changing its style, messages, and constituencies.

Of great and growing importance today is the technopolitics of global resistance, especially use of the Internet. These are new terrains for political struggle and places where new voices can be heard. Use of these technologies tends to be highly democratic and generally decommodified. They create domains where campaigns can be waged against global corporations. Wholly or primarily web-based forms of resistance include McSpotlight, the Clean Clothes Campaign, the campaign waged in 2004 that led to the ousting of a pro-Iraq war regime in Spain, and the paradigmatic globalization-from-below activities in Seattle in 1999 which led to the formation of the Independent Media Center and later Indymedia.com. Mention should also be made in this context of the "hacktivists" who can create, and have created, havoc on the Internet and perhaps one day will cause a "digital Pearl Harbor."

There are several theories that relate to this resistance, many of which have been covered at one or more points in this book. They include Karl Polanyi's ideas on countermovements; Antonio Gramsci's thinking on hegemony/counter-hegemony; and Michael Hardt and Antonio Negri's thinking on empire/multitude. While they are all of use in thinking about resistance, they have all been found wanting as complete explanations of this resistance for one reason or another. There are those who see the need for more complex and critical theories of global resistance. Furthermore, such theories need to avoid the extremes of "globophobia" (Kahn and Kellner 2007: 662–74).

Local Resistance

The actions of local groups or communities face severe limitations in terms of their chances of having an impact on globalization from above. Their major problem is that while they are largely local in nature, the problems they are confronting (e.g. global warming) are often global in scope and have their sources perhaps half-way around the world. There is little or no way in which such groups, acting alone and in isolation, can have much of an impact on such global issues (although alliances among a number of them would fare better [Saguier 2007: 251–65]).

One example of resistance undertaken by a small, local community (Hall and Fenelon 2008: 1–11) involves the Amungme and Kamoro peoples of Papua, Indonesia, and their resistance to the world's largest gold and copper mine, Freeport McMoRan Copper & Gold (Abrash 2001: 38–44). Before Freeport arrived in 1967, the two peoples had been involved in a subsistence economy based on agriculture, fishing, hunting, and the use of products derived from the forest. Freeport displaced many of these people and forced them to resettle elsewhere. The company seized and despoiled their land and resources. There is also evidence of torture, rape, disappearance, and even murder. Adding to the disruptions caused by the company itself, thousands of migrants found their way there in search of the jobs created in and around the mine and they brought with them different customs and ways of life. Freeport, and all the developments in and around it, disrupted what the locals considered a harmonious relationship among people, the environment, and their ancestral spirits. The Amungme consider at least part of the area being mined to be sacred.

Local protests began soon after the arrival of Freeport in 1967. Among the mecha-nisms employed by the locals were the positioning of Amungme "taboo sticks" around a Freeport base camp, public demonstrations, sit-ins, and attempts at open dialogue with the company. Some modest concessions were made (e.g. Freeport agreed to construct schools and clinics), but the fundamental problems remained. In 1996 the Amungme brought two civil suits against Freeport in US federal and state courts. They have also appealed to, among others, the US government, the Indonesian government, and even directly to the shareholders of the company. There have been additional concessions by the company over time (e.g. job training, scholarships, land payments, and support for local businesses). Overall, however, these changes brought about by local resistance have not, at least until now, led to fundamental changes in activities undertaken by Freeport that are destructive to the local community. In the main, the most important players in this – the company and the government of Indonesia (as well as the US government) – have been largely unresponsive to local needs and interests.

A Social Movement?

Donatella della Porta, along with several colleagues, studied two specific Italian protests against globalization (della Porta et al. 2006). One involved protests against the G8 meeting in Genoa in July 2001, and the other involved protests during the European Social Forum in Florence in November 2002. The study examined the characteristics of the protesters, the networks of the organizations involved and their activities, and the relationship between those involved in the protests and their larger environment.

The key issue addressed in this study is whether the various groups involved in protests, and more generally in globalization from below, are sufficiently organized and integrated to be considered a global social movement (Jackie Smith 2008). A social movement has the following characteristics: "networks of groups and activ-ists, with an emerging identity, involved in conflictual issues, using mainly uncon-ventional forms of participation" (della Porta et al. 2006: 234). The authors conclude, contrary to the views of most observers, that the groups *do* constitute a social move-ment. A loose network of formal and informal organizations and groups has been sustained over time. This allows the authors to conclude that these disparate groups and organizations do form a global, or at least a transnational, movement in opposi-tion to globalization from above. Two facts are crucial to this conclusion. First, there are frequent overlaps among individuals and organizations in various anti-globalization campaigns. Second, the interactions among the individuals and groups have intensified over time. Thus, the authors conclude: "the results of our research seem to indicate that a movement on global justice is truly in the making" (della Porta et al. 2006: 233).

They also conclude that these are not only social movements, but they are also global in nature. First, large numbers of those involved *identify* themselves with a movement that is critical of the process of globalization, define themselves as global citizens, know about global developments, and express a sense of solidarity with the deprived in the world, especially in the South. Second, they engage in unconventional *action* (e.g. street protests), and such action is increasingly aimed at global targets. Third, they have developed a global *organizational structure*, especially via the Internet. Fourth, their *definition of the conflict* is that it is global in scope.

The heart of these movements is *protest* and it is based on three logics. First, protest has at least the potential to cause *material damage* and merely this threat, let alone whatever damage may actually be caused, has great symbolic value. Second, protests require great *numbers* of people to participate. When the numbers are there, this demonstrates not only the strength of, but also the extent of the danger posed by, these movements to those in power. Finally, there is the logic of *witnessing* in that those involved engage in acts – e.g. civil disobedience – that constitute potential risks to them – they are putting their bodies, even their lives, on the line.

These social movements involve flexible organizational forms and are involved in networks linked to a number of other networks. This looseness leads to the use of another term associated with globalization from below, *movement of movements*, which has come to be employed by a number of observers and analysts. Of course, perhaps the best term applied to all of this, one we have used on several occasions throughout this book, is alter-globalization. It reflects, once again, the fact that many of these groups are themselves global in nature and that they are not opposed to globalization per se, but rather the way it (e.g. neo-liberalism) is practiced today.

More Formal Social Movements

Those who resist globalization often use globally similar "philosophical, bureaucratic, and technological defenses" (Niezen 2004: 170). As a result, "over the long term they homogenize societies even further through globally similar struggles for recognition and self-determination. Both the ills and the remedies of modernity are rapidly becoming part of every cultural community. The cumulative effect of such global transformations has already been a reduction of possibilities for the expression of collective character" (Niezen 2004: 170). The paradox here is that those who resist globalization may use techniques that serve to make them increasingly integral to that process. While this is less likely to be the case with highly local and informal social movements, it is much more likely with formal social movements, including those involved in globalization from below.

World Social Forum and Cyberactivism

The existence of the Internet has given those opposed to globalization in general, or some specific aspect of it, a powerful tool to mount their opposition on a regional and even a global basis. Indeed the origins of the anti-globalization movement at the WTO meetings in Seattle in late November 1999, as well as ensuing protests in Washington, DC (April 2000), Prague (September 2000), Genoa (July 2001), and others, were based on cyberactivism. Further, the formation of the World Social Forum (WSF) (Fisher and Ponniah 2003; Sen et al. 2004) and its first meeting in January, 2001, in Porto Alegre, Brazil, were also largely the result of such activism. Later, and much larger, meetings of the WSF in Porto Alegre and Mumbai (January 2004) were even more dependent on cyberactivities.

The WSF was formed in 2001 as a reaction against the World Economic Forum, but it had other roots, as well, such as the 1999 protests against the WTO in Seattle. A key overall focus was the lack of democracy in global economic and political affairs. It was born of the idea that more needed to be done about this problem, and others, than protests. That is, there was a need for more positive and concrete proposals to deal with such issues (especially greater democracy [Jackie Smith 2008]) as well as a forum in which they could be generated. Its slogan has been "Another World Is Possible" (Teivainen 2007: 1302–4). That is, there must be, and there is, an alternative to the neo-liberalism (Peter Smith 2008: 13–33) that dominates the world economically and politically. While the slogan is powerful, as yet the WSF has not gone much beyond it to produce actions that actually help make that world a reality.

The initial meeting of the WSF in Porto Alegre, Brazil (Byrd 2005: 151–63), drew about 5,000 participants, and the number of participants grew to 100,000 at the 2004 meetings in Mumbai, India, and in 2005 in Porto Alegre. In 2006 the meeting was decentralized and held on three continents, and many local, national, and regional meetings have developed.

The WSF is, by design, not a political movement or an actor, but merely an arena in which like-minded people can exchange ideas on global issues. The very diversity of those involved in the WSF makes the development of concrete political proposals, let alone actions, difficult. The WSF continues to struggle with this issue and its identity and role in globalization.

The WSF was formed initially and in large part on the basis of cyberactivism. The WSF is a huge social network and it should come as no surprise that cyberactivism (as well as the WSF) is based on the "cultural logic of networking" including: the creation of horizontal ties and connections among diverse and autonomous elements; the free and open communication of information among and between those elements; coordination among the elements that is decentralized and involves directly democratic decision-making; and networking that is self-directed (Juris 2005: 189–208).

A more specific case of the power of cyberactivism involves a series of events following the 1997 Asian financial crisis, specifically in Indonesia where anger over the crisis was aimed at ethnic Chinese (Ong 2003: 82–100). By May 1998, Chinese stores in Indonesia had been looted and burned and Chinese residents had been attacked and women raped. Vigilante groups were reported to have hunted Chinese, killed them, and paraded about with the victims' heads on the ends of spikes. The police were reported to have looked on. There has been a long history of anti-Chinese feeling in Indonesia, and the government, as well as the international community, has been seen by Chinese in Indonesia and around the world as having done little or nothing to help the victims of anti-Chinese violence.

Beginning in August 1998, rallies against the violence against Chinese residents in Indonesia were held in many cities in the US, as well as in Canada, Australia, and Asia. These protests were made possible and coordinated through the creation of a website – Global Huaren (Global Chinese People) – and the formation of the World Huaren Federation.

There are something like 50 million people with Chinese ancestry in the Chinese diaspora and they are scattered throughout well over 100 countries in the world. And a large number of them are users of computers with access to the Internet. Their great numbers and their high level of computer literacy make them an ideal group to form a cyberpublic such as that involved in Global Huaren.

What Global Huaren did was, in effect, to create a global Chinese public where one did not exist before. Further, Global Huaren became an interesting global watchdog for Chinese interests. It was a disembedded organization, that is, it was not embedded in any particular geographic location; it existed solely on the Internet; it was a "virtual organization." Another way of saying this is that it was a *placeless* organization. That is, it existed in no single place; it had no headquarters. We are likely to see more such global organizations as access to the Internet continues to proliferate.

While one cannot quarrel with the objectives of Global Huaren, it should be noted that the Internet can easily be used to create, with only a few keystrokes, a global movement with nefarious objectives. Further, even if the objectives are high-minded, the information that is disseminated can be confusing and it can have a series of unanticipated consequences.

Resistance to globalization, or to some aspect of it (as in the case of ethnic Chinese being blamed for the economic crisis in Indonesia), can be largely or totally virtual, or it can take quite material forms, for example as in riots and in individual pronouncements and actions.

Is the Resistance to Globalization Significant?

While resistance globally is generally strong and diverse, such resistance is to a large extent dismissed by the supporters of globalization and believers in its continued, if not inevitable, expansion. For example, in dismissing the opposition to globalization, de la Dehesa (2006: 182) offers two "empirical truths":

> The first is that those minorities, who are adversely affected by a phenomenon, or those who choose to protest, generally have the loudest voice, while those who benefit tend to remain silent. The second is that it is mainly the best-organized groups – those that exert most pressure on decision-makers – that lead the debate. This often leaves less organized but majority groups out of the picture.

In other words, the opponents of globalization are dismissed as being a small number of well-organized loudmouths while the supporters represent a less well-organized "silent majority." Readers might keep this critique in mind as they think about this chapter and review in their minds the various forms of coping, opposition, and resistance to globalization discussed previously.

Of course, it remains to be seen what the effect of the Great Recession will be on resistance to globalization. It seems clear, however, that if the recession grows deeper and extends over a long period of time, it will spur much greater resistance to globalization.

THE FUTURES OF GLOBALIZATION

We close this book with a brief discussion of the future of globalization (Zedillo 2007), although as the heading makes clear, we are talking about a complex scenario that involves multiple futures for multiple globalizations (Turner 2007: 675–92). To put it another way, since there is no single globalization, there can be no single future for it. But just as in the preceding sections of this chapter we have only been able to discuss a few of the methods of dealing with and resisting globalization, we can only touch on a few aspects of the future of globalization, or a few of the futures of a few globalizations. It would simply be impossible to offer an overview of the future of economic, political, educational, religious, sport, urban–rural, and demographic, to mention just a few, globalizations. Complicating matters is the fact that each of these broad areas encompasses a number of more specific globalizations. For example under the heading of the economy, we could discuss the future of neo-liberal economies, MNCs, the labor movement, consumption, and the economies of China, India, the US, EU, and on and on.

It is also worth noting that while the social sciences are pretty good at analyzing the past and even the present, their prognostications about the future are notoriously weak. The history of social thought is littered with wrong-headed (Marx on the collapse of capitalism, at least so far) and sometimes downright ridiculous (Auguste Comte on the coming of a new positivistic religion of which he would be supreme pontiff) predictions for the future. Given this history, the book will offer no bold predictions about the futures of globalizations, but rather will be content with some ruminations about, and some sketchy scenarios on, them.

Seemingly the most obvious conclusion to be drawn from all that has gone before in this book, and all that has happened globally in at least the late twentieth and early twenty-first centuries, is that both globalization in general, and at least most globalizations, will continue and most likely grow and expand. This prediction seems safest within the economy which has globalized faster and farther than any other aspect of the social world.

However, various experts on the economy are not prepared to guarantee its future globalization. Jeffry Frieden points strongly to the fact that the previous epoch of economic globalization died with the outbreak of WW I. He is quite aware that globalization, especially economic globalization, did reemerge and grow enormously in the last half of the twentieth century and into the early years of the twenty-first century. And while this new phase of globalization has been extraordinarily powerful, Frieden does not believe that its future is necessarily assured (Frieden 2006: 470–2). The major impediments, in his view, are political in nature and are likely to come from two sources. On the one hand, supporters of globalization and its markets want to gain greater control over it and its vagaries and difficulties through better forms of global governance. On the other hand, critics of globalization see the need for greater accountability (see above) through the creation of various political institutions that can exercise greater control over those markets. Both of these involve external oversight, if not control, over the global economy, and, at least from a neo-liberal perspective, such external direction could spell the death knell for an economy which, from that perspective, operates best when it is left to its own devices.

However, the major threat to globalization appears to stem from the economy itself. As long as the state of the global economy is good, globalization is likely to thrive. However, economic catastrophes have in the past threatened and, in the case of the Great Depression, all but destroyed globalization. That threat is clearly with us again as the current great global financial, credit, banking, and economic crisis rages. If the future of economic globalization is not assured, then it seems even more likely that one cannot unequivocally forecast continued growth and expansion of globalization more generally.

A grim, but slightly more optimistic, economic scenario is offered by Immanuel Wallerstein (2005: 1263–78), noted for the creation of world-system theory, who looks at the future of the global economy in terms of three related issues.

First, can every part of the world in the not-too-distant future achieve the standard of living (as well as similar cultural and political institutions) of the most economically advanced and progressive nations in the world (e.g. Denmark)? That is, will we see economic and social equality in the future? Wallerstein responds in the negative. For one thing, he argues that the history of the world has always involved increases rather than decreases in inequality. For another, if a few countries and their industries can no longer monopolize productive activity, "the *raison d'être* of a capitalist world-economy will be undermined" (Wallerstein 2005: 1268). The assumption is that capitalism cannot and will not permit its basic reason for being, and the inequality that underlies it, to be threatened.

Second, can the currently highly unequal world persist pretty much as it is? Wallerstein says no for two basic reasons. First, the ability of capitalism to accumulate capital is declining and this is weakening the political structures that are based on such accumulation. This is related to the second point and that is that the weakened states will increasingly be unable to control the rise of the "dangerous classes." Already, Wallerstein sees "spreading anarchy" in the twenty-first century.

Third, what alternatives present themselves? Wallerstein foresees the likelihood of the collapse of the current world-system (that does seem more likely in the midst of the Great Recession), but what will replace it cannot be discerned with any great precision, although the possibility of the development of less developed countries is more likely than ever before. Wallerstein sees more hope in social movements (e.g. those associated with the World Social Forum) than with the actions of nation-states. He sees these movements as best advised to push decommodification. Such a process runs counter to the objectives of neo-liberalism and it can provide the base for an alternative political system.

Given the fact that Wallerstein is a Marxist, he can't help but offer some hope for the future in a decommodified economy that would be the basis for a different political system. However, since commodities lie at the base of the modern economy, it is not at all clear what kind of an economy a decommodified economy would be and, whatever it is, whether it has any chance of success.

A "Mad Max" Scenario

At the most extreme, one observer foresees a global future that he calls a "Mad Max" scenario (Turner 2007: 675–92). This refers to a movie that dealt with an apocalyptic vision of the future with people thrown back into primitive and extremely violent ways of life. In fact, it could be argued that we are already beginning to see anticipations of this on the streets of cities in Iraq, Afghanistan, Pakistan, Somalia, and so on. It could be that it is states without governments, non-states, such as Somalia, that offer the most extreme examples of the Mad Max scenario, where such a world is closest to, if not already, a reality.

The Mad Max scenario is made more likely, for larger portions of the global population, by a variety of ongoing trends:

- ever-accelerating crises in the capitalist economy;
- dramatically rising oil prices (while they have dropped recently, they seem sure to rise again soon, given limitations on supply) will contribute, among things, to higher prices of food, food shortages (already a "silent Tsunami" affecting perhaps 100 million people [Sullivan 2008: A1, A13]), and riots, because of the increased cost of producing and transporting food of all sorts;
- increasingly short supplies of oil will not only lead to higher prices, but battles and perhaps outright warfare over the declining number of functioning oil wells, oil reserves, and, perhaps, oil-producing countries;
- population growth in less developed areas will lead to pitched battles over food that is available only in limited quantities;
- declining supplies of fresh water will lead to similar battles between the "water haves" and the water "have-nots";
- rising sea water will displace large numbers of people from islands and coastal areas, with those from the latter moving inland where they will come into conflict with residents unwilling to give up, or even share, their territory;
- nuclear exchanges that could lead to larger nuclear wars and possibly "nuclear winter." Among the most likely nuclear combatants today are Israel and Iran, India and Pakistan;

- the collapse of a nuclear power (Pakistan would seem most likely) could lead to a series of events through which nuclear weapons would fall into the hands of rogues, or terrorists;
- even the explosion in a major Northern city of a "dirty bomb" packed in a suitcase would devastate that city, primarily through the creation of high levels of radiation that would linger for a long period of time making at least part of the city uninhabitable;
- the detonation of such a suitcase bomb would lead to retaliation, likely involving nuclear weapons, against the presumed perpetrators.

There is no end to such bleak, Mad Max scenarios; there are undoubtedly many more that are not listed and have yet to be imagined. Any one of them, let alone some combination of them, has the potential to put an end to this era of globalization (if the Great Recession does not do it first) in the same way that previous cataclysms – WW I and the Great Depression – ended an earlier global age.

CHAPTER SUMMARY

Globalization is not a single phenomenon, rather there are many globalizations. While some need to be resisted, others are welcome and should be encouraged. There are bound to be multiple futures for multiple globalizations.

There are three approaches to global economic resistance. Trade protectionism involves systematic government intervention in foreign trade through, for example, tariffs and non-tariff barriers, in order to encourage domestic producers and deter their foreign competitors. Although there exists a widespread consensus regarding its inefficiency, protectionism is still popular since it shields the domestic economy from systemic shocks.

"Fair trade" is a different approach to economic globalization, which emerged as a counter to neo-liberal "free trade" principles. Fair trade aims at a more moral and equitable global economic system in which, for instance, price is not set by the market; instead it is negotiated transparently by both producers and consumers. While it is popular among consumers in the North, it has met only limited acceptance among producers. Its ability to supply a mass market and its applicability to manufactured products are also doubted.

The third form of resistance to economic globalization relates to helping the "bottom billion." Increasing aid is only one of the many measures that are required. International norms and standards can be adapted to the needs of the bottom billion. The reduction of trade barriers would also reduce the economic marginalization of these people and their nations.

Increased accountability and transparency are key issues in dealing with political globalization. All political organizations, at different levels, should be more accountable for their actions; they are now surrounded by an "ocean of opacity." Increased transparency has been aided by various mechanisms such as transnational justice systems, international tribunals, civil society, and Transparency International.

Like globalization itself, resistance to globalization is multiple, complex, contradictory, and ambiguous. This movement also holds the potential of emerging as the new public sphere, which might uphold progressive values such as autonomy, democracy, peace, ecological sustainability, and social justice. These forces of resistance are themselves products of globalization and can be seen as "globalization from below." The impetus for such a movement comes from individuals, groups, and organizations which are, or perceive themselves to be, oppressed by globalization from above (neo-liberal economic systems, aggressively expanding nations and corporations). They seek a more democratic process of globalization. However, globalization from below also involves less visible, more right-wing elements, such as the America First Party and the Taliban.

The World Social Forum (WSF) is centered on addressing the lack of democracy in economic and political affairs. However, the diversity of elements involved in the WSF hinders the development of concrete political proposals. A significant influence on the WSF has been that of cyberactivism, which is based on the "cultural logic of networking." As well as "virtual movements" such as Global Huaren, positive resistance can take more material forms (e.g., riots).

Since there is no single globalization, the future is also multi-dimensional. Some foresee the continuing expansion of globalization both in general as well as in more specific globalizations. Others have a far more pessimistic vision of "Mad Max" scenarios that could well end the current era of globalization.

DISCUSSION QUESTIONS

1. Discuss the contradictory and ambiguous nature of the resistance to globalization.

2. Examine the three approaches to global economic resistance.

3. Examine the concepts of accountability and transparency with respect to political globalization.

4. What is *your ideal vision* of the future of globalization?

5. In contrast to your ideal vision, what do you think is the *most likely future* of globalization?

FURTHER READING ···

A. Nicholls and C. Opal. *Fair Trade: Market-Driven Ethical Consumption*. London: Sage, 2005.

L. Raynolds, D. Murray, and J. Wilkinson. *Fair Trade: The Challenges of Transforming Globalization*. New York: Routledge, 2007.

N. Stehr. *Moral Markets: How Knowledge and Affluence Change Consumers and Products*. Boulder, CO: Paradigm, 2008.

J. E. Stiglitz and A. Charlton. *Fair Trade for All: How Trade Can Promote Development*. Oxford: Oxford University Press, 2007.

E. Zaccaï, ed. *Sustainable Consumption, Ecology, and Fair Trade*. London: Routledge, 2007.

Daniel Jaffee. *Brewing Justice: Fair Trade Coffee, Sustainability and Survival*. Berkeley, CA: University of California Press, 2007.

Burkart Holzner and Leslie Holzner. *Transparency in Global Change: The Vanguard of the Open Society*. Pittsburgh: University of Pittsburgh Press, 2006.

Daniel Cohen. *Globalization and Its Enemies*. Cambridge, MA: MIT Press, 2006.

Donatella della Porta, Massimiliano Andretta, Lorenzo Mosca, and Herbert Reiter. *Globalization from Below: Transnational Activists and Protest Networks*. Minneapolis: University of Minnesota Press, 2006.

Jackie Smith, et al. *Global Democracy and the World Social Forums*. Boulder, CO: Paradigm, 2008.

Bryan Turner. "The Futures of Globalization." In George Ritzer, ed., *Blackwell Companion to Globalization*. Malden, MA: Blackwell, 2007.

REFERENCES

Abrash, Abigail. 2001. "The Amungae, Kamoro and Freeport: How Indigenous Papuans Have Resisted the World's Largest Gold and Copper Mine." *Cultural Survival Quarterly* 25, 1.

Bacon, Christopher M., Ernesto Mendez, Maria E. Flores Gomez, Douglas Stuart, and Sandro R. Diaz Flores. 2008. "Are Sustainable Coffee Certifications Enough to Secure Farmer Livelihoods? The Millennium Development Goals and Nicaragua's Fair Trade Cooperatives." *Globalizations* 5, 2.

Brooks, Thom, ed. 2008. *The Global Justice Reader*. Malden, MA: Blackwell

Byrd, Scott. 2005. "The Porto Alegre Consensus: Theorizing the Forum Movement." *Globalizations* 2, 1.

Carducci, Vince. forthcoming. "Fair Trade." In George Ritzer, ed., *Blackwell Encyclopedia of Sociology Online*. Oxford: Wiley-Blackwell.

Chanda, Nayan. 2007. *Bound Together: How Traders, Preachers, Adventurers, and Warriors Shaped Globalization*. New Haven: Yale University Press.

Chorev, Nitsan. 2007. *Remaking U.S. Trade Policy: From Protectionism to Globalization*. Ithaca, NY: Cornell University Press.

Cohen, Daniel. 2006. *Globalization and Its Enemies*. Cambridge, MA: MIT Press.

Collier, Paul. 2007. *The Bottom Billion: Why the Poorest Countries Are Failing and What Can Be Done About It*. New York: Oxford University Press.

de la Dehesa, Guillermo. 2006. *Winners and Losers in Globalization*. Malden, MA: Blackwell.

della Porta, Donatella, Massimiliano Andretta, Lorenzo Mosca, and Herbert Reiter. 2006. *Globalization from Below: Transnational Activists and Protest Networks*. Minneapolis: University of Minnesota Press.

Dolan, Catherine. 2008. "In the Mists of Development: Fairtrade in Kenyan Tea Fields." *Globalizations* 5, 2.

Downie, Andrew. 2007. "Fair Trade in Bloom." *New York Times*. October 2.

Dugger, Celia W. 2007. "Rock Star Still Hasn't Found the African Aid He's Looking For." *New York Times*. May 15.

Fisher, William F., and Thomas Ponniah. 2003. *Another World Is Possible: Popular Alternatives to Globalization at the World Social Forum*. London: Zed Books.

Florini, Ann. 2007. "Transparency." In Jan Aart Scholte and Roland Robertson, eds., *Encyclopedia of Globalization*. New York: MTM Publishing.

Frieden, Jeffry A. 2006. *Global Capitalism: Its Fall and Rise in the Twentieth Century*. New York: W. W. Norton & Co.

Germain, Randall D. 2004. "Globalising Accountability within the International Organisation of Credit: Financial Governance and the Public Sphere." *Global Society* 18, 3 (July).

Gilman-Opalsky, Richard. 2008. *Unbounded Publics: Transgressive Public Spheres, Zapatismo, and Political Theory*. Lanham, MD: Lexington Books.

Granovetter, Mark. 1973. "The Strength of Weak Ties." *American Journal of Sociology* 78.

Hall, Thomas D., and James V. Fenelon. 2008. "Indigenous Movements and Globalization: What Is Different? What Is the Same?" *Globalizations* 5, 1.

Holzner, Burkart, and Leslie Holzner. 2006. *Transparency in Global Change: The Vanguard of the Open Society*. Pittsburgh: University of Pittsburgh Press.

Jaffee, Daniel. 2007. *Brewing Justice: Fair Trade Coffee, Sustainability and Survival*. Berkeley, CA: University of California Press.

Juris, Jeffrey. 2005. "The New Digital Media and Activist Networking within Anti-Corporate Globalization Movements." *Annals* 597 (January).

Kahn, Richard, and Douglas Kellner. 2007. "Resisting Globalization." In George Ritzer, ed., *The Blackwell Companion to Globalization*. Malden, MA: Blackwell.

Lewis, Jessa, and David Runsten. 2008. "Is Fair Trade-Organic Coffee Sustainable in the Face of Migration? Evidence from an Oaxacan Community." *Globalizations* 5, 2.

Linton, April, Cindy Chiayuan, and Kelly Ann Shaw. 2004. "A Taste of Trade Justice: Marketing Global Social Responsibility via Fair Trade Coffee." *Globalizations* 1, 2.

Mann, Catherine L., and Katharine Pluck. 2007. "Trade." In Jan Aart Scholte and Roland Robertson, eds., *Encyclopedia of Globalization*. New York: MTM Publishing.

McAleese, Dermot. 2007. "Trade Protectionism." In Jan Aart Scholte and Roland Robertson, eds., *Encyclopedia of Globalization*. New York: MTM Publishing.

McMichael, Philip. 2007. "Alternative Trade Schemes." In Jan Aart Scholte and Roland Robertson, eds., *Encyclopedia of Globalization*. New York: MTM Publishing.

Mittelman, James H. 2004. "Globalization Debates: Bringing in Microencounters." *Globalizations* 1, 1 (September).

Moseley, William G. 2008. "Fair Trade Wine: South Africa's Post-Apartheid Vineyards and the Global Economy." *Globalizations* 5, 2.

Nicholls, A., and C. Opal. 2005. *Fair Trade: Market-Driven Ethical Consumption*. London: Sage.

Niezen, Ronald. 2004. *A World Beyond Difference: Cultural Identity in the Age of Globalization*. Malden, MA: Blackwell.

Ong, Aihwa. 2003. "Cyberpublics and Diaspora Politics among Transnational Chinese." *Interventions* 5, 1.

Raynolds, L., D. Murray, and J. Wilkinson. 2007. *Fair Trade: The Challenges of Transforming Globalization*. New York: Routledge.

Reuveny, Rafael, and William R. Thompson. 2001. "Explaining Protectionism. 17 Perspectives and One Common Denominator." *Global Society* 15, 3.

Saguier, Marcelo I. 2007. "The Hemispheric Social Alliance and the Free Trade Area of the Americas Process: The Challenges and Opportunities of Transnational Coalitions Against Neo-liberalism." *Globalizations* 4, 2.

Sen, Jai, Anita Anand, Arturo Escobar, and Peter Waterman, eds. 2004. *World Social Forum: Challenging Empires*. New Delhi: Viveka Foundation.

Smith, Adam. 1953. *The Wealth of Nations*. Chicago: Henry Regnery.

Smith, Jackie. 2008. *Social Movements for Global Democracy*. Baltimore: Johns Hopkins University Press.

Smith, Peter. 2008. "Going Global: The Transnational Politics of the Dalit Movement." *Globalizations* 5, 1.

Stehr, N. 2008. *Moral Markets: How Knowledge and Affluence Change Consumers and Products.* Boulder, CO: Paradigm.

Stiglitz, Joseph E., and Andrew Charlton. 2005. *Fair Trade for All: How Trade Can Promote Development.* Oxford: Oxford University Press.

Sullivan, Kevin. 2008. "Food Crisis Is Depicted as 'Silent Tsunami.'" *Washington Post.* April 28.

Tan, Celine. 2007. "Liberalization." In Jan Aart Scholte and Roland Robertson, eds., *Encyclopedia of Globalization.* New York: MTM Publishing.

Teivainen, Teivo. 2007. "World Social Forum." In Jan Aart Scholte and Roland Robertson, eds., *Encyclopedia of Globalization.* New York: MTM Publishing.

Turner, Bryan. 2007. "The Futures of Globalization." In George Ritzer, ed., *Blackwell Companion to Globalization.* Malden, MA: Blackwell.

Wallerstein, Immanuel. 2005. "After Developmentalism and Globalization, What?" *Social Forces* 83, 3.

Zaccaï, E., ed. 2007. *Sustainable Consumption, Ecology, and Fair Trade.* London: Routledge.

Zedillo, Ernesto, ed. 2007. *The Future of Globalization: Explorations in Light of Recent Turbulence.* New York: Routledge.

GLOSSARY

Americanization is the import by non-Americans of products, images, technologies, practices, and behavior that are closely associated with America/Americans.

Asylum seekers are refugees who seek to remain in the country to which they flee.

Autarky is the turn inward of a nation-state in order to create as much economic self-sufficiency as possible.

Civil society is the process through which individuals negotiate, argue, struggle against, or agree with each other and with the centers of political and economic authority.

Colonialism entails the creation by the colonial power of an administrative apparatus in the country (or geographic area) that has been colonized in order to run its internal affairs, including its settlements.

Creolization involves a combination of languages and cultures that were previously unintelligible to one another.

Cultural convergence is when cultures are subject to many of the same global flows and tend to grow more alike.

Cultural differentialism involves barriers that prevent flows that serve to make cultures more alike; cultures tend to remain stubbornly different from one another.

Cultural hybridization is the mixing of cultures and the integration of the global and the local leading to unique combinations.

Cultural imperialism indicates that one or more cultures impose themselves, more or less consciously, on other cultures thereby destroying local culture, in whole, or in part.

Dependency theory is a body of work critical of the development project. It emphasizes that the development project contributed not to the development of the nation-states of the South, but more to a decline in their independence and to an increase in their dependence on the countries of the North, especially the US. Underdevelopment is not an aberrant condition, or one caused by the less developed nations themselves, but it is built into the development project itself (as well as into global capitalism).

Deregulation is the commitment by nation-states to limit or eliminate restraints on the free market and free trade.

Deterritorialization is the declining significance of the geographic location in which culture exists.

Development is a "project" that was primarily concerned with the economic development of specific nation-states, usually those that were not regarded as sufficiently developed economically.

Diaspora is the large-scale dispersal, dislocation, and deterritorialization of a population.

Double movement is the coexistence of the expansion of the laissez-faire market and the reaction against it.

Globalization: The Essentials, by George Ritzer
© 2011 John Wiley & Sons Ltd

Ecological modernization theory argues that the economic and technological development favored by neo-liberal economists can go hand-in-hand with a decline in the negative effects on the environment that are the focal concerns of environmentalists.

Economic globalization is the most well-known form of globalization and refers to growing economic linkages at the global level.

Empire involves global dominance without a nation-state at its center; decentered global dominance.

Ethnic cleansing involves various policies oriented to forcibly removing people of another ethnic group.

Ethnic group is a social group defined on the basis of some cultural characteristic(s).

Ethnoscapes involve the actual movement, as well as fantasies about moving, of mobile groups and individuals (tourists, refugees, guest workers).

Export Processing Zones (EPZs) are independent areas controlled by corporations and free of national control; an EPZ is denationalized.

Fair trade is defined as a concern for the social, economic, and environmental well-being of marginalized small producers.

Feminization of labor involves the increasing participation of women in both the formal and informal global paid labor force.

Financescapes involve the processes by which huge sums of money move through nation-states and around the world at great speed through commodity speculations, currency markets, and national stock exchanges.

Flows involve the movement of people, things, information, and places due, in part, to the increasing porosity of global barriers.

Foreign direct investment (FDI) is investment by a firm in one nation-state in a firm in another nation-state with the intention of gaining control over it.

Free market – a free market is one which is allowed to operate free of any impediments, especially those imposed by the nation-state and other political entities.

Gender refers to differences between males and females that are based on social definition and distinction.

Genocide is defined as acts committed with the intent to destroy, in whole or in part, a national, ethnic, racial, or religious group.

Global care chains involve a series of personal relationships between people across the globe based on the paid or unpaid work of caring.

Global cities are the key cities in the global, especially capitalist, economy.

Global civil society is a global, non-governmental, pluralistic form of society composed of interlinked social processes and oriented to civility.

Globality is the omnipresence of the process of globalization.

Globalization is a transplanetary process or set of processes involving increasing liquidity and growing multi-directional flows of people, objects, places, and information as well as the structures they encounter and create that are barriers to, or expedite, those flows.

Glocalization is the interpenetration of the global and the local resulting in unique outcomes in different geographic areas.

Globalization from above is a process that is created and disseminated by largescale forces (such as the nation-state and the MNC), especially those associated with the North, and imposed on the South (especially their nation-states and businesses).

Globalization from below takes the form of individual actors, and groups of actors, opposing and acting to oppose globalization in both developed and less developed countries.

Greenfield investment involves the building of totally new corporate facilities in another country.

Grobalization is the imperialistic ambitions of nation-states, corporations, organizations, and the like and their desire, indeed need, to impose themselves on various geographic areas throughout the world.

Hybridization involves a process in which external flows interact with internal flows producing a unique cultural hybrid that combines elements of the two.

Hyperconsumption involves buying more than one can afford.

Hyperdebt involves owing more than one will be able to pay back.

Ideoscapes involve flows of images that are primarily political in nature, produced either by nation-states in line with their ideology, or as counter-ideologies produced by movements that seek to contest those in power.

Imperialism involves methods employed by one nation-state to gain control (sometimes through territorial conquest) of another country (or geographic area) and then to exercise control, especially political, economic, and territorial, over that country (or geographic area), and perhaps many other countries.

Import-substitution is a development strategy whereby countries (usually in the global South) were "encouraged" to develop their own industries instead of focusing on producing for export and relying on imports from other countries (especially the North).

Industrial upgrading involves processes through which economic actors – nations, firms and even workers – move from low-value to relatively high-value activities in global production networks.

Information war reflects the fact that information and information technology are increasingly permeating all aspects of warfare perpetrated by developed countries.

Intergovernmental Organizations (IGOs) are organizations such as the UN that are international in scope.

International non-governmental organizations (INGOs) are international not-for-profit organizations that perform public functions but are not established or run by nation-states.

Isomorphism is the idea that a series of global models in a variety of different domains – politics, business, education, family, religion, and so on – have led to a great uniformity throughout the world.

Labor migrant – a labour migrant is one who is driven to search for work outside his/her home country by "push" factors such as lack of work or low pay in his/her homeland as well as "pull" factors such as jobs and higher pay available elsewhere.

Leapfrogging involves developing nations bypassing earlier technologies, enabling those nations to adopt more advanced technologies.

Limited government involves the idea that no government or government agency can do things as well as the market. This renders a government less able, or unable, to intervene in the market.

Liquidity is the increasing ease of movement, the mobility, of people, things, information, and places in the global age.

McDonaldization is the process by which the principles of the fast food restaurant are coming to dominate more and more sectors of American society, as well as the rest of the world.

Mediascapes involve both the electronic capability to produce and transmit information around the world as well as the images of the world that these media create and disseminate.

Metaphors involve the use of one term to better help us understand another term.

Migrants are populations on the move; both vagabonds and tourists, but especially vagabonds.

Multinational corporation (MNC) – an MNC is a corporation that operates in more than two countries.

Nation – a nation is a social group that is linked through common descent, culture, language, or territorial contiguity.

Nation-state – a nation-state integrates sub-groups that define themselves as a nation with the organizational structure that constitutes the state.

National identity is a fluid and dynamic form of collective identity, founded upon a community's subjective belief that the members of the community share a set of characteristics that make them different from other groups.

Nationalism is a doctrine and (or) political movement that seek to make the nation the basis of a political structure, especially a state.

Neo-liberalism is the theory (as well as an ideology) that involves a combination of the liberal commitment to individual liberty with neoclassical economics devoted to the free market and opposed to state intervention in that market. Entrepreneurs are to be liberated, markets and trade are to be free, states are to be supportive of this and to keep interventions to a minimum, and there are to be strong property rights.

Non-people are those who occupy positions that lead them to be devoid of distinctive content (al least in those positions); for example, employees associated with non-places, such as telemarketers (who may be virtually anywhere in the world) who interact with all customers in much the same way, relying heavily on scripts.

Non-places are settings that are largely devoid of distinctive content.

Non-services are services that are largely devoid of distinctive content such as those provided by ATMs (the services provided are identical; the customer does all the work involved in obtaining the services) as opposed to those offered by human bank tellers.

Non-things are objects that are largely devoid of distinctive content such as chain-store products and credit cards (there is little to distinguish one credit card from the billions of others, all of which work in exactly the same way for all who use them anywhere in the world).

Nothing involves (largely) empty social forms; forms largely devoid of distinctive content.

Offshore outsourcing involves the transfer of work to companies in other countries in exchange for money.

Outsourcing involves the transfer of activities once performed by an entity to a business (or businesses) in exchange for money.

Pluralism is the idea and fact that different races and ethnic groups can live together; they can coexist.

Portfolio investment is the purchase of equities in companies in other countries for financial gain, not control.

Post-colonialism relates to various developments that take place in a former colony after the colonizing power departs.

Prosumers are those who simultaneously produce what they consume.

Protectionism is government intervention in order to encourage domestic production.

Race is defined on the basis of real or presumed physical, biological, or phenotypical characteristics.

Race to the bottom is the phenomenon whereby countries are involved in a downward spiral of competitiveness as a result of undercutting prices, lowering wages, making working conditions poorer, lengthening hours of work, and increasing pressure on and demands of workers.

Racism is the belief in the inherent superiority of one racial group and the inferiority of others.

Refugees are those who are forced to leave their homeland, or who leave involuntarily, because they fear for their safety.

Remittances are monetary transactions by which successful migrants send money back to their country of origin for the care and support of various family members.

Sex refers to the physical differences between males and females.

Solidity refers to the fact that people, things, information, and places "harden" over time and therefore have limited mobility.

Something involves (largely) full social forms; forms rich in distinctive content.

South-to-South migration is the movement of people from poorer Southern countries to slightly, or somewhat, better-off Southern countries.

Sovereign wealth funds are funds controlled by nation-states (not corporations or individual investors) and that often invest in other countries.

State – a state is an organizational structure with relatively autonomous office-holders outside other socio-economic hierarchies, with its own rules and resources increasingly coming from taxes rather than from feudal, personal, or religious obligations.

Structural adjustment involves the conditions of economic "restructuring" that are imposed by organizations such as the World Bank and the IMF on borrowing nations. Receiving nations are expected, among other things, to put into place tight monetary and fiscal policies, to liberalize financial markets and trade, to privatize, and to deregulate.

Sustainable development involves economic and environmental changes that meet the needs of the present, especially of the world's poor, without jeopardizing the needs of the future.

Technoscapes are the fluid, global configurations of high and low, mechanical and informational technology and the wide range of material that now moves freely and quickly around the globe and across borders.

Tourists are people who move about the world because they *want to* (and because they are "light").

Trade-Related Aspects of Intellectual Property Rights (TRIPS) is an agreement negotiated through the WTO to protect the interests of those individuals, organizations, and states that create ideas.

Trade-Related Investment Measures (TRIMs) is a WTO agreement on a range of operating or performance measures that host-country governments impose on foreign firms to keep them from having a distorting effect on trade in goods and services.

Transnationalism involves processes that interconnect individuals and social groups across specific geo-political borders.

Transnationality is the rise of new communities and formation of new social identities and relations that cannot be defined through the traditional reference point of nation-states.

Vagabonds are people who, if they are able to move at all, are likely to be doing so because they are forced to (e.g. forced to migrate to escape poverty [and to find work], by war, because of discrimination).

World culture involves the spread of global models leading to global convergence.

World system theory envisions a world divided mainly between the *core* and the *periphery* with the nation-states associated with the latter being dependent on, and exploited by, the core nation-states.

Xenophobia involves the beliefs, attitudes, and prejudices that reject, exclude, and vilify groups that are outsiders or foreigners to the dominant social group.

INDEX
